Catholic Theological Ethics in the World Church

Catholic Theological Ethics in the World Church

The Plenary Papers from the First Cross-cultural Conference on Catholic Theological Ethics

JAMES F. KEENAN, S.J., EDITOR

continuum

NEW YORK • LONDON

2007
The Continuum International Publishing Group Inc
80 Maiden Lane, New York, New York 10038

The Continuum International Publishing Group Ltd
The Tower Building, 11 York Road, London SE1 7NX

Continuum is a member of Green Press Initiative, a nonprofit program dedicated to supporting publishers in their efforts to reduce their use of fiber obtained from endangered forests. For more information, go to www.greenpressinitiative.org.
Printed in the United States of America

Library of Congress Cataloging-in-Publication Data

Catholic theological ethics in the world church : the plenary papers from the
  first cross-cultural conference on Catholic theological ethics / James F. Keenan,
  editor.
      p. cm.
    Includes bibliographical references and index.
    ISBN-13: 978-0-8264-2765-6 (hardcover : alk. paper)
    ISBN-10: 0-8264-2765-0 (hardcover : alk. paper)
    ISBN-13: 978-0-8264-2766-3 (pbk. : alk. paper)
    ISBN-10: 0-8264-2766-9 (pbk. : alk. paper)
    1. Christian ethics—Catholic authors—Congresses. I. Keenan, James F.
  II. Title.

BJ1249.C193 2007
241'.042—dc22

                                    2007008785

DEDICATED

TO

STICHTING PORTICUS

WITH GRATITUDE

Contents

James F. Keenan, S.J.

Introduction

The Conference at Padua

One summer while teaching at the Gregorian University in Rome, I invited my colleague from Boston College, Steve Pope, who was in town, to dinner with three other moral theologians from the Roman universities. It was a wonderful evening, and there, I began thinking, what if we moralists held an international meeting where we could have simple, face-to-face conversations. It had never been done before.

Later, I was approached by the staff of a European Catholic foundation who asked if I would be willing to host a seminar of eight international scholars in moral theology. The seminar would meet annually for four years, and at the end of it, we would publish a text on themes from our field: the conscience, moral decision making, the magisterium, etc. I responded, "Could you fund, instead, an international planning committee for four years to plan an international conference for two hundred moral theologians?" They agreed to host the first planning meeting. They would decide from there whether they would fund more meetings, which eventually they did.

Our first challenge was to set up an international planning committee. I began to work with the foundation's personnel, particularly, Hans Wennink and Peter Merkx. Together we put together the committee.

The first person invited was from the Catholic University of Leuven, Paul Schotsman. Over the years, Paul was an advisor to the foundation and a trusted counselor. From the United States, I wanted another ethicist and immediately lighted on Margaret Farley from Yale University. We also needed at least another European, and one each from India, East Asia, Africa, and Latin America.

After a period of four months, we formed an international planning committee: Soosai Arokiasamy (India), Bénézet Bujo (Congo), Margaret Farley (United States), Linda Hogan (Ireland), José Roque Junges (Brazil), José Rojas (Philippines), and Paul Schotsman (Belgium).

Paul suggested that we have our first meeting in Leuven in November 2003. Our first evening was, naturally, a meal. The leading moralists of India, Congo, and Brazil were there with such international scholars as Farley and

Schotsman. Again we learned that the act of meeting one another was itself the agenda. We convened the next morning and spoke about . . . visas. Three in our group were not able to secure the Schengen visas from their country's Belgian embassies. Each decided to apply to the Italian embassies to get the same visa and succeeded. If we were going to host a major international conference, we would have to meet in a country from which our participants could secure visas.

To be truly international, we would have to underwrite the transportation and housing for scholars from the developing world. This would mean substantive fund-raising. Sensitive to the difficulty of securing visas for developing-world participants, we recognized the impossibility of hosting it in the United States. We also realized that inevitably, for reasons of costs and travel, Europe would be the best setting. For instance, if we were to meet in Latin America those from Africa or Asia, in all probability, would be routed through yet another continent, Europe or North America, to get to the south. Holding it in Europe meant again finding a hospitable country for securing visas, and Italy naturally emerged.

Where would we meet in Italy? We quickly decided on Padua: a medieval city, with one of the world's oldest and most respected universities as well as a center of religious pilgrimage. This city where Giotto painted, Anthony lived and preached, Galileo lectured, Harvey discovered the circulatory system, and Elena Piscopia became the first woman to earn a doctorate (1678) would be perfect for contemporary moral theologians.

Schotsman made another key recommendation: if we were to meet in Padua, I would have to meet with a priest, Don Renzo Pegoraro, a bioethicist who was the director of the Fondazione Lanza. Pegoraro would become the key link to hosting a conference for moral theologians in Padua.

What would be the nature of the conference? The conference would have to be a place where we could learn how to share ideas and meet one another. To do this we needed to determine who would come and how we would organize the meeting.

At first we thought exclusively of fundamental moral theologians. In some countries, especially in Europe and Africa, there has been a strong tendency to differentiate moral theologians from social ethicists. But in North America, Latin America, and Asia, the boundary between the two is fairly fluid. We found a more inclusive description for our identity: theological ethicist would cover both groups.

Would we invite others? We decided that the nature of being an ethicist is to have as an interlocutor many other professionals, in medicine, philosophy, law, public health, etc. We realized we needed to meet exclusively as Catholic theological ethicists. Would we invite those from other Christian denominations or other religions? Again, we decided that many of us had ecumenical opportunities for meeting, but nothing as uniquely Roman Catholic.

How would we fortify the conference as a meeting? We made an early decision: to help one another into a listening mode at the meeting, we would host plenary sessions in the form of "continental panels." There would be five panels (African, Asian, Latin American, European, and North American): each would have three panelists answering the same questions: what are our moral challenges; how are we responding; and what hope do we have for the future? This would serve as a way of "introducing" those from the different continents to learn about the discourse elsewhere. Furthermore, we became concerned that participants might discriminate with the panels and so we decided they would be presented in alphabetical order: Africa, Asia, Europe, Lain America, North America.

By the end of our first full day of planning, we knew what we were about. And so we closed by agreeing on two matters. First, we settled on the title for the conference: "Catholic Theological Ethics in the World Church: The First Cross-cultural Conference on Catholic Theological Ethics." Then, we articulated the mission statement:

> Since moral theology is so diffuse today, since many Catholic theological ethicists are caught up in their own specific cultures, and since their interlocutors tend to be in other disciplines, there is the need for an international exchange of ideas among Catholic theological ethicists. Catholic theological ethicists recognize the need: to appreciate the challenge of pluralism; to dialogue from and beyond local culture; and to interconnect within a world church not dominated solely by a northern paradigm.
>
> In response to these recognized needs, Catholic theological ethicists will meet to refresh their memories, reclaim their heritage, and reinterpret their sources.
>
> Therefore, Catholic theological ethicists will pursue in this conference a way of proceeding that reflects their local cultures and engages in cross-cultural conversations motivated by mercy and care.

We turned our attention to another meeting that evening. With Paul Schotsman's help, we built into our programming that we would meet on Saturday evening with theological ethicists from local universities to see what they thought of our deliberations. We invited the ethics faculty from Leuven (among whom were Joseph Selling, Roger Burggraeve, Johann De Tavernier, Johan Verstraeten), from Tilburg (Jan Jans and Veerle Draulans), from Utrecht (Frans Vosman) and others.

The regional ethicists proposed that we add another component to the conference: to cover specific themes particularly relevant to the nature of theological ethics. Later we adjourned and had a dinner and again found the actual meeting of theologians key for the charism of our organization.

On Sunday morning the planning committee met. This was an important gathering because in meeting our colleagues from the previous evening, we had become an organization. It was no longer my proposal; it was ours. We were meeting now, convinced of our vision.

In light of the previous evening's discussion, we proposed another set of plenary sessions: rather than continental panels, these would be intercontinental ones: three major panelists, from different continents, on four key themes: conscience and the magisterium; the theological method; globalization; and religious pluralism. We also decided on a date for the conference, July 8–11, 2006.

We had a mission, a title, an international planning committee, a location, nine plenary sessions, and above all, a vision. Three years before Padua we were well under way.

In June 2004, I went to Padua to meet Don Renzo Pegoraro. Though I had visited Padua several times in the past, Renzo quickly oriented me to the city: the medieval district, the duomo, the two basilicas, the university, and, of course, the restaurants. For a conference center, he suggested the Antonianum, a one-hundred-year-old Jesuit college, which had an enormous corridor, six rooms that could hold several hundred people, a chapel, and a five-hundred-seat theater, with its own gardens and fountains adjacent to the botanical garden. The Antonianum adjoined a much more modern Jesuit youth center, with several breakout rooms, more gardens, and a beautiful chapel. Together, the two facilities would offer a setting for convivial meeting and discourse.

At the university, Renzo showed me the Great Hall where Galileo lectured for eighteen years. We would have opening night of the conference in that room. For hotels, there were plenty for those paying their own way, but for those we were covering we found two: one would hold benefactors, plenary speakers, and the planning committee; the other could host those funded from Africa, Asia, and Latin America. They were a minute apart from each other. Finally, Renzo and I met Padua's Archbishop Antonio Mattiazzo, who welcomed us and the conference.

After meeting Renzo, I then took on a project that many, many people helped me with, though I would have to do this work alone: to raise money for the conference. As the conference's expectations grew, so did our need for money.

A year later, the planning committee met in Padua. For the opening session, we wanted scholars outside of theological ethics to answer the question, "How Can Theological Ethicists Respond to the World's Needs?" We chose three international scholars from Europe in the field of human rights, bioethics, and business ethics to address us as a plenary session in the Galileo hall. We then began work on two lists. First, we needed thirty international speakers for our (now) ten plenary panels. Second, we needed to think of those from Africa, Asia, Latin America, and Eastern Europe who would be invited to the conference. We also realized as we made our lists that we would need simultaneous translators for each of the plenary sessions. English, Italian, French, and Spanish became the working languages.

At this 2005 meeting in Padua, we asked Renzo to bring the local Italian theological ethicists to meet with us. We would meet bilingually and the meeting went well. Because the scholars from northern Europe had suggested the intercontinental panels, the Italians suggested we build into the program two or three conversations about how we were proceeding and a final session addressing "where we would go from Padua." Our meeting with them concluded with a dinner and a conversation. The next day, Renzo announced that the Italian association of theological ethicists would hold their biannual meeting before and after our meeting in Padua. We would have at least fifty Italian moralists. At that point we realized we would be more than the anticipated two hundred.

We made one other decision. We wanted applied-ethics sessions on environment, war, health issues, sexuality and gender, and globalization. We coupled this aspect of the program with the realization that those coming from the industrialized world could receive a subsidy from their school if they were presenting a paper. We would have three periods of concurrent sessions in ten breakout rooms, each room hosting three speakers, thereby giving us ninety slots. We concluded the 2005 meeting articulating a call for papers.

Surprisingly, 125 proposals were sent in. We realized interest in our organization was growing faster than we expected. From here other stories can be told: finding an Italian travel agency to manage the tickets of all our subsidized participants; inviting different Vatican and Italian cardinals; helping over 125 people get visas; raising more funds; finding translators; designing programs; etc.

On July 8, the planning committee, Renzo, Archbishop Mattiazzo, and I welcomed 400 theological ethicists from 63 countries, with 175 of these having had their transportation and housing covered. Sitting in the university's Great Hall we could hear Galileo inviting us to rethink our place in the universe, in the church, and in the academy. Thus, we began a four-day conversation with one another.

What Did We Achieve?

First, as Archbishop Mattiazzo told us, it is one thing to read or cite colleagues; it is another to meet and discuss with them. Here we had the opportunity to ask our colleagues questions, to see what they were like as persons, and to tell them how our own work was proceeding. It was not simply a sharing of ideas; it was a meeting of persons.

Second, we discovered a lot in common, above all, that "we shared the same vocation," a comment frequently uttered. This extraordinary lesson prompted a strong intellectual and affective solidarity among us all. It also gave us a renewed sense of the good we bring to the church.

This solidarity played out across generations and gender. On the closing

night we sang happy birthday to Florence's Enrico Chiavacci, who turned
eighty. The other senior moralists of our lifetime were there: Klaus Demmer,
Marciano Vidal, Giuseppe Angelini, Kevin Kelly, Karl-Wilhelm Merks, Roger
Burggraeve, Paul Valadier, Enda McDonagh, Antonio Autiero, Charles Curran, Marcio Fabri dos Anjos, Soosai Arokiasamy, John Mary Waliggo, Brian
Johnstone, and Bishop Kevin Dowling. These seniors were bookended by
the more than fifty graduate students who attended, twelve of whom were
among the one hundred and fifty participants delivering papers.

In a field that only twenty-five years ago was practically completely clergy,
women were strongly in evidence. From the industrialized world there were
Lisa Cahill, Margaret Farley, Jean Porter, Marie-Jo Thiel, Cathy Kaveny,
Chris Gudorf, Barbara Andolsen, Carolyn Sharp, Patricia Beattie Jung,
Frances Baker, Linda Hogan, Veerle Draulans, Cecilia Borgna, Maureen
Junker-Kenny, Marianne Heimbach-Steins, Haruko Okano, Julie Clague,
Theodora Rossi, and Frances Baker. From the south there were Pushpa
Joseph, Maria Oca, Agnes Brazal, Teresia Hinga, Philomena Maura, Tina
Astorga, Ylan Tran, and Bernadette Mbuy-Beya, among others.

Third, with so much goodwill and respect toward one another, we were
able to challenge one another. When three senior ethicists concluded their
remarks on the African continental panel, three African women ethicists took
them to task for not mentioning anything about living in profoundly
patriarchal settings. When a French scholar spoke of the primacy of the
conscience, an Italian responded speaking about the competency of the
magisterium. The most significant exchange came when, after the North
American panel spoke at length about the military aggressiveness of the United
States, several others asked, Were scholars from the States doing enough in
light of the impact such policies were having on their own countries?

Fourth, appreciating the need to meet and dialogue spawned the
formation of other groups. The Africans formed their first pan-African
Association of Theological Ethicists, and the Asians explored similar
possibilities. Women theologians established a list serve, after sixty of them
shared a dinner together. That same evening, fifty doctoral students held their
own dinner while fifty-five Jesuit ethicists gathered as well. Meeting was
defining us.

Fifth, above all the need to continue the dialogue emerged. At the closing
session we announced that Continuum International Press agreed to publish
the thirty plenary presentations and that Orbis would publish thirty of the
applied ethics papers (forthcoming). We pledged to meet again in four years,
to establish a committee to work toward implementing organizational
structures for our solidarity, and, to develop a monthly newsletter (appearing
monthly on our Web site, www.catholicethics.com) to keep in touch with
one another.

It was a wonderful first meeting. I believe these papers convey that.

Part I

How Can Theological Ethicists Respond to the World's Needs?

I. How Can Theological Ethicists Respond to the World's Needs?

Antonio Papisca (Italy)
The Needs of the World and the Signs of the Times: The Challenge of Human Rights

Adela Cortina (Spain)
Challenges of Economic Activity in a Global World

Henk ten Have (France)
Universal Declaration on Bioethics and Human Rights

"We have entered the era of an authentically universal law, *ius novum universale*, which has initiated a process of 'human-centric cross-fertilization.' The era of the *plenitudo iuris* has truly begun." So Antonio Papisca announces at the opening of the First International Cross-cultural Conference of Catholic Theological Ethicists. These words capture the promise that ethicists have before them with the challenges that accompany them. Toward that end, Papisca maps them out:

> The paradigm of human rights entails an *agenda*. In other words, we must translate rights into operative programs, public policies, and specific actions. The sacred principles of the old law between states—*pacta sunt servanda* and *consuetudo servanda est*—are not immune to this pressure to look to the telos, which finds expression here in the primacy of the "new" principle *humana dignitas servanda est* (that human dignity must be served).

Based on human dignity, Papisca covers a variety of topics that ethicists must promote in the service of human dignity: universal citizenship, the recourse to force, a world economy, the outlawing of war, the recourse to international law, the promotion of the care of children, and the need to promote within religions a sense of due process and of mutual respect among believers.

Adela Cortina begins with an assumption that we find throughout this book, especially in the essays that deal with globalization. She writes, "Ever since Max Weber formulated his principle of scientific Neutrality (*Wertfrei-*

9

heit), the social sciences, including economics, have often considered themselves neutral. In many schools of economics it is described as a 'strict science,' without moral evaluations. And yet no human activity is immune to moral evaluations; all are implicitly or explicitly infused with one set of values or another." For Cortina, "A good economy helps to create a good society; it is an ethical economy." She claims, therefore, "A moral theology that thinks about the economy will see itself, then, as a *critical hermeneutic of economic activity*." From here she elaborates ten issues that need to be examined, at the heart of which we find her exposé on the three dominant models of corporative life: the economist, with its crude Weberian assumptions; the institutional, which appropriates a social contract only among the elites; and a stakeholders' model that weighs the variety of influences that corporate life has on humanity. Clearly, Cortina moves toward the last model. She concludes on consumerism, noting that "according to Adam Smith, consumption is the end [goal] of the economy. Nevertheless it has become the engine."

Henk ten Have tells the story of "UNESCO's attempt to examine the possibility of developing a universal instrument on bioethics." There the feasibility study drafted by the International Bioethics Committee "concluded that it was possible to find common ground in divergent bioethical positions by focusing on basic principles. . . . The study also stressed the necessity to develop a universal instrument because scientific practices are now developing rapidly and extending beyond national borders. Developed and developing countries should therefore achieve broad consistency in regulations and policies." In short, "The global character of contemporary science and technology and the increasing number of research teams coming from different countries imply the need for a global approach to bioethics." He concludes, "The Declaration, although a non-binding legal instrument, is therefore the first international document in bioethics adopted by all governments." In a globalized world, setting international standards and making their applications work in each nation is the task of today's ethicist. The narrative is evidence of the possibility of realizing that task.

Antonio Papisca

The Needs of the World and the Signs of the Times

The Challenge of Human Rights

1. In the present historical period, which is marked by large-scale processes of structural transformation—a complex global interdependence, unbalanced globalization, the transnationalization both of solidarity and of profit, etc.—the world needs a positive peace, in the sense indicated by article 28 of the Universal Declaration of Human Rights: a just economy, respect for legal systems, the mobilization of educational resources in the pursuit of the common good, and the diffusion of the culture of *global (good) governance* guided by the principle of co-responsibility.

Above all, the world needs a new generation of political leaders of high quality who have human rights in their heads and in their hearts. We all know the maxim *nolite iudicare,* but I must confess that I sometimes wonder whether there is anyone among the participants at today's intergovernmental "summits" who could credibly say: "The 'poor means' are closely linked to the primacy of the spirit. . . . They are the certain signs of the presence of the Spirit in the history of humanity. It seems that many of our contemporaries are moved to manifest a special understanding of this scale of values: to mention only some non-Catholics, it suffices to recall Mahatma Gandhi, Dag Hammarskjöld, and Pastor Martin Luther King" (John Paul II, first discourse to the Diplomatic Corps, January 1979). This great pope explicitly included himself in this group of leaders of high quality; and he was genuinely entitled to do so, since his wish was to reinvigorate political life by the power of his own example.

The grave dangers of the present hour include infinite war, permanent political destabilization in many regions of the world, the praxis of falsehood and cynicism, the insolent violation of the rule of law, homicidal and suicidal terrorism, the impudent practice of torture, indifference and even contempt vis-à-vis the poor, the destruction of the natural environment, and the employment of dehumanizing biotechnologies.

Nevertheless, in the course of the 1940s, and in particular between 1945 and 1948, enlightened and far-seeing leaders introduced a powerful factor of positive discontinuity into the millennial history of humanity. The obvious metaphor here is the sowing of the "universals," or (if one prefers) the discovery and actualization of important talents in history. I refer here above all to the Charter of the United Nations and to the Universal Declaration of Human Rights, and to the statutes of the specialized agencies of the United Nations, especially UNESCO. For the first time in the history of international relations, principles of universal ethics were formally accepted by international law, thus calling into question the logic intrinsic to the system of regulations of the Peace of Westphalia (1648), that is, the absolute sovereignty of states. The Universal Declaration proclaims that "recognition of the inherent dignity and of the equal and inalienable rights of all members of the human family is the foundation of freedom, justice and peace in the world." Thus, the value of human dignity is made the foundation of the world order and of every other regulation. This is further explained by article 28 of the Universal Declaration: "Everyone is entitled to a social and international order in which the rights and freedoms set forth in this Declaration can be fully realized." This means that peace is a human right, no longer an exclusive prerogative of states. We must recall that the old international law governing relations between states, which had its origin in the Peace of Westphalia, regarded peace and war on the same level—as the *ius ad pacem* and the *ius ad bellum*—as the very heart of the sovereignty of states.

A number of legal conventions have followed the Charter and the Declaration, supplementing these with a body of principles and norms that form the source of the universal system of human rights and of those regional systems (European, Inter-American, African) which, in close coordination with the universal system, have the task of inculturating and developing the international standards. Thanks to the adoption by the Council of the League of Arab States of the Arab Charter of Human Rights at Tunis 2004, the first steps have been taken toward an Arab system of human rights.

We have entered the era of an authentically universal law, *ius novum universale*, which has initiated a process of "human-centric cross-fertilization." The era of the *plenitudo iuris* has truly begun. This leads to a strong pressure on legal systems and on institutions to find their orientation in the *telos*. The challenge of the *telos*, that is, of the need to specify what must be down to pursue universal values, reveals very clearly the necessarily instrumental nature of states and of systems of government. Jacques Maritain's book *L'homme et l'état* has lost none of its relevance in this regard.

The paradigm of human rights entails an *agenda*. In other words, we must translate rights into operative programs, public policies, and specific actions. The sacred principles of the old law between states—*pacta sunt servanda* and *consuetudo servanda est*—are not immune to this pressure to look to the *telos,* which finds expression here in the primacy of the "new" principle *humana dignitas servanda est (that human dignity must be served).* This in turn entails the following question: What objectives lead us to respect written agreements and the customary rules?

We can indeed speak of a dynamic *spill-over* from the international law of the rights of the person. The culture, or better the "knowledge," of human rights is an axio-practical knowledge that is consolidated precisely in virtue of its international juridical acknowledgment. In other words, the moral paradigm that has been adopted by the new *ius positum* is a veritable hard core of this interdisciplinary and transcultural knowledge. It represents a providential aid in the work of education and teaching, with regard both to contents and to legitimation. The great strategies or visions about positive peace are seasoned with the human dimension: security is now called *human security,* and development *human development.* The varied and lively nongovernmental organizations and the transnational movements that promote solidarity are encouraged to express themselves and to act in a way that goes beyond the boundaries of individual states. This global civil society is concerned about the effectiveness of the new universal law, and denounces the ambiguities, the instrumentalizations, and the mystifications that many governments make of this law.

The great religions too, beginning with Christianity in its various confessional articulations, are paying increasing attention to the phenomenon of the international laws that enshrine human rights. In the Catholic Church, the popes have elaborated a systematic magisterium on this subject. The encyclical *Pacem in Terris* of John XXIII counts the Universal Declaration of 1948 and the United Nations among the "signs of the times." Paul VI spoke of a diaconal ministry of human rights. John Paul II offered both an academic and a pastoral exegesis of human rights, and a passionate personal testimony: this great pope was truly one of those *"human rights defenders"* envisaged by the Declaration of the United Nations in March 1999 on the right and the responsibility of individuals, groups, and societal organs to promote and protect the universally recognized basic liberties and human rights.

2. We may wonder about the source of this compelling force of the paradigm of human rights; and an initial answer is that the compelling force is intrinsic to the nature of this paradigm which has been placed at the heart of international law. Antonio Rosmini said that "the person is substantial law." Article 1 of the Universal Declaration explicitly adopts this metajuridical affirmation: "All human beings are born free and equal in *dignity and rights."* Since the fundamental rights belong to the ontology of the person, the increasingly frequent usage of the expression "human rights" is justified, for the "right" becomes "human" precisely in response to the vital

needs of the person in his or her integrity (soul and body, spirit and matter). This is why the fundamental laws, which bear the names civil, political, economic, and social, must be protected—that is, granted in practice—according to the principle of their interdependence and indivisibility. Thanks to this consubstantiality between the person and the rights, the *ius positum* of human rights can be infringed, but never destroyed. It possesses an intrinsic power of resistance to even the most serious violations, and it does not lose its legal validity. Here, we are in the field of the *ius cogens*.

Since the basis of the international law of human rights is the value of human dignity, it is a right to life and a right that serves life. This makes it a right to peace and a right that serves peace. In this context, life cannot be understood in terms of patrimonialist approaches, nor simply in terms of criminal law. If one kills, or relativizes life, one calls into question the *raison d'être* of the entire edifice of the universal law. The death penalty and war are radically incompatible with a law that has abolished the *ius necis ac vitae* and the *ius ad bellum* of states and of every other institution. The needs of justice and security do not justify the homicidal goals of the death penalty and of war: there are "alternative paths" to these. Abortion, euthanasia, human cloning, and the destruction of the natural environment are on the same level of lawlessness.

The international law of human rights has adopted and broadened the basic *raison d'être* of the state. In other words, it complements the principle *ne civis ad arma veniat* by means of the further principle *ne populi nec nationes nec civitates ad arma veniant*. The supreme authority with regard to the use of force belongs to the United Nations, which can employ soldiers to impose justice and to safeguard life: these are police operations, not wars.

This is the law of universal inclusion: *ad omnes includendos*. The French Declaration of 1789 was that "of the human person *and citizen*," but the Universal Declaration is simply that "of the human person," or more precisely, of human rights.

The concept of citizenship has changed and has become plural. Thanks to the essential fact of being a bearer of fundamental rights that are recognized by international law, each human being has universal citizenship as the "original statute" of his person. The citizenships recorded in the registries, the national citizenships *ad alios excludendos* which are antecedent historically and juridically to universal citizenship, must be brought into harmony with this citizenship *ad omnes includendos*.

It follows that the principle of reciprocity is completely alien to the egalitarian, nondiscriminatory, inclusive logic of the paradigm of human rights.

It is important to emphasize that the international law of human rights is a "reproductive" law in the sense that it fertilizes legal systems in a way that at first sight seems paradoxical: for it is the law itself that makes it legitimate to bypass existing law in order to make this law better; the law has need of institutions (to "guarantee" and protect it), but it bypasses these institutions in virtue of the fact that the person is an original legal subject with an individual and societal responsibility. And this responsibility is now visible on the international level too, where international penal law can call people to account. We may well say that this universal law is *par excellence* the law *de lege ac institutione semper perficiendis.*

One final point: it is the law that promotes the encounter between the civilization of law and the civilization of love by acting with the authority of the *ius positum* as a "transporter of ethics" in the fields of politics and economics.

3. Quod barbari non fecerunt, fecerunt Barberini. (What the barbarians didn't do, the Barberinis did). Sadly, some governments today are mounting an attack on the edifice that has been constructed systematically from the mid-twentieth century onward. This tendency is both irresponsible and hostile to history. In the ongoing process of globalization, we need to share the responsibilities of government, and there has been an exponential growth in the movements and the organizations of global civil society. Providentially, we have a law that is *bonum et iustum,* multilateral institutions, and processes of regional integration; at the same time, however, we have immensely powerful political leaders who pursue a world strategy that runs absolutely contrary to the strategy inherent in the principles of the "new" international law.

The moral, legal, and political imperative is to react to the inroads of barbarity (*bellum omnium contra omnes,* "preventive war," terrorism, unilateralism, a situation of unrestrained competition, torture, pollution, dehumanizing biotechnologies), above all by promoting the exercise of the reproductive function of the internationalized paradigm of human rights, which provides the orientation to the proper *telos.*

If this truly civilizing task is to be carried out, we must perceive and deeply understand the signs of the times; we see that providence continues to be patient, but for how long . . . ? The first step is an empirical observation that is also a challenge: the new universal law, which was born of ethics, is returning today like a boomerang to the sphere of ethics. We could say that when ethics returns home, it is enriched by the extra value of a law that is positive and, hence, so to speak, "confirmative." The task of an authentically universal ethics is now to ensure its own further progress and, at the same time, to promote the *ius positum,* which finds its inspiration in the universal ethics. On the operative level, this means enforcing the "universals"—the talents available in the course of history—by formulating principles and rules on the lines of UNESCO's approach, aiming at action from the local microlevel to the macrolevel of international institutions and policies.

Let me mention a few axio-political "provocations":

- Universal citizenship: the primacy of the *ius naturae humanae* over the *ius soli* and the *ius sanguinis* must be enforced.

- The processes of multiculturalization must be supervised. The paradigm of human rights is a "transcultural code" for developing the intercultural dialogue, but what is the goal of such a dialogue? The answer is: the rights of citizenship and shared responsibilities in the inclusive city.

- The praxis of democracy: the crisis of democracy is not only a crisis of substance, but also a spatial and methodological crisis. What is the point of the "power of the people"? What kind of democracy do we need? The response from the perspective of human rights can only be the following: we need "entire" democracy, founded on human, civil, political, economic, social, and cultural rights. The big decisions are increasingly taken on a level above and beyond the "domestic jurisdictions," and transparency is often lacking. We must therefore broaden the space for the exercise of democracy—by means of the democratization of the international institutions, not by the forcible export of democracy. The spread of a democracy based on human rights must be achieved by the force of example, and the appropriate forum here is the "common home" of the international institutions. The institutionalization of intergovernmental "summits" (e.g., the G8) slows down the progress of democracy. The representative and participatory democratization of the United Nations and of the other multilateral institutions is urgent and necessary in order to strengthen action "on the ground."

- World economy: it is necessary to enforce the principles of social justice, and thus to regulate economic, financial, and media activity by appealing to law and to the deontology of economic and social human rights, especially to the principle of the interdependence and indivisibility of these rights. This principle attempts to translate into the *ius positum* the ontology of the integral quality of the human person.

- The idea of the state: the crisis of governance of states is not generated only by the incapacity or corruption of the decision makers and the political elites. This is a structural crisis of the traditional state as a form, that is, the sovereign armed nation with its own borders. We must resist the suicidal choices of nationalism, unilateralism, the crises to which the regional systems of integration are deliberately subjected, as well as the boycott of the system of the United Nations, of the supranational machinery of human rights, and of the development of international penal law.

- International justice: Three factors have opened up a large horizon here: the development of international penal law, with the principles of the universality of penal justice and of international personal penal responsibility; the development of the praxis of "truth and reconciliation"; and the promotion of the international court of penal justice by thousands of nongovernmental organizations.

- Recourse to force for the solution to conflicts: both war and the use of force on the part of states are forbidden (with the exception of self-defense in response to the armed aggression of one state against another). Security needs are met by putting in place a system of collective security in keeping with the Charter of the United Nations. States have a legal obligation to make this system work. The one remaining superpower and other powers tend to ignore this obligation and to re-establish and exercise in a unilateral fashion (or by means of ad hoc coalitions) the *ius ad bellum*. In other words, they replace the system of the United Nations by the old system of armed national sovereignties, each of which is *superiorem non recognoscens*. The most recent report of the secretary general on the reform of the United Nations (*In Larger Freedom*, March 2005) seems to lend support to this trend of withdrawal, since it imprudently envisages four types of threat to security and peace: "imminent," "non-imminent or latent," "aggression in course," and "massive violations" of human rights. The states would be entitled in law to respond to each threat with military intervention—and in keeping with the different types of menace, this intevention would be respectively "preemptive," "preventive," "subsequent," or "protective." In this perspective of "the nightmare of the easy war," the role of the United Nations would be wholly marginalized by the *fait accompli* of individual states. This extension of the possibility for states to employ military force is absolutely illegal, because it reverses the logic of the Charter of the United Nations and opens the door de facto to "preventive war." We should pay close attention to the ambiguities of the newly fashionable principle of the "responsibility to protect." No one dares to call this into question, but we should note how "urgency" is used as a trap—for this is a mystifying instrumentalization of the moral appeal. In order to avoid the danger of a return to barbarity, we must explain the "alternative paths to war." John Paul II insisted strongly on this point, saying that peace is a duty because it is a possibility. This duty, both moral and legal, is reinforced by the fact that the possibility is real. We may sum up these alternative paths as follows: getting the system of collective security of the United Nations to function; strengthening and democratizing the UN and its system of specialized agencies; promoting regional integration projects, etc. Alternative paths include cooperation in favor of human development and of international penal justice; the reduction of armies and their conversion into international police forces under the supranational authority of the United Nations and of other international organizations linked to the UN; and the use of these forces for nonhomicidal goals, that is, for the protection of the life of the civilian populations, for separating the parties in a conflict, for the pursuit of criminals, etc. It is along these paths that the *animus iustitiae et pacis* replaces the *animus bellandi* (which is synonymous with the *animus destruendi*).

- *Bellum iustum:* the time has come to bury this concept, *inter alia,* by taking literally the Latin text of the encyclical *Pacem in terris: alienum est a ratione bellum* ("war is foreign to reason"). The historical fact of the existence of a new international law, of the United Nations, and of other important international organizations means that it is no longer acceptable from an ethical point of view to justify war—not even a war of defense. Today, the double obligation (legal and moral) incumbent upon states and upon all persons is to make the world system of international organization work. Just as we hope that the death penalty will be "buried," so we hope to see the "burial" of the entire philosophical and teleological tradition of arguing in favor of the *bellum iustum.* May we hope for an explicit apostolic exhortation on this topic one day soon, a papal text that speaks of war as a "structure of sin"?

- Interreligious dialogue: the paradigm of human rights is a precious instrument in this dialogue, since it offers each religious group the possibility of confronting the same "universal," namely, human dignity. This is, of course, a process that requires humility and a sensitivity to history. This work of purification through contact with the "universal" permits religious leaders of goodwill to discover more easily the elements that unite, and to choose these in preference to those elements that divide. The religions would be fully entitled to point out to states the objective limits of the secular dimension, that is, the *Universal Declaration of Human Rights,* which specifies that all persons enjoy all the human rights. This would be a very significant contribution to domestic and international peace. Its initial impact would be to neutralize those who dream longingly of the "clash of civilizations" and ethnic or religious wars.

- For the Catholic Church, the international legal recognition of human rights offers numerous opportunities and challenges, including the democratization of its own structure of governance, the promotion of the status of women, etc. In particular, it is possible to get rid of one insidious secular aspect, that is, the analogy with the sovereignty of states which is adduced in support of the international juridical personality enjoyed by the Holy See (or even by the "sovereign" pontiff). It would be easy today to reconstruct this juridical personality on the basis of the human rights of the *christifideles,* in particular their right to religious liberty. As a Catholic Christian, I have the right not only to believe and to pray in private and in public, but also to practice my faith in, through, and with the organized institution of my faith. The church is a transnational entity whose independence must be preserved for the sake of my right to religious liberty, quite apart from a long tradition of international relations. In other words, it is on the basis of the fundamental rights of the members of the "people of God" that the international juridical personality belongs to the church as a whole—institution, government, faithful—and not solely to one or other organ of the church. From the perspective of positive law, providence offers hermeneutical instruments in the course of history to purify the church from ambiguous and dangerous analogies to states—analogies that are ultimately useless.

• The best interest of children: this is proclaimed by article 3 of the 1989 International Convention on the Rights of Children. We must consider this principle not only from the "corporative" or "political" point of view of the situation of children but as a general principle of international law, on the same level as the principles of the universality, interdependence, and indivisibility of rights and of the outlawing of torture, slavery, war, and the death penalty. The dignity and the infinity of the human person shine out in children.

4. Prophecy and realism: the "reality" of the *ius positum* of human rights, since it is a path leading to greater perfection, actualizes once again the prophetic tension found in religious milieux. Above all, we must put pressure on the new universal law in order to develop its specific potential. We must help this law in its work of fertilizing the human city.

In the mission to secure peace and human rights, spirituality is a fundamental resource. It supplies the strength necessary to exercise the difficult virtues of free giving, service, sharing responsibilities, due caution (e.g., in problems concerning interreligious dialogue, the environment, biotechnologies, etc.), and discernment—in short, it puts our feet on the path of the beatitudes, especially of the blessing pronounced on the poor in spirit, those who dare to act in *spes contra spem,* who are not afraid of being laughed at by those who have power in this world, and who have the courage to denounce the fact that at the present point in history, there are many merchants in the temple.[1]

Adela Cortina

Challenges of Economic Activity in a Global World

1. State of the Question: The Failure of the Economy[1]

According to reports from the World Bank and the United Nations Development Project, approximately one-fourth of human beings are living below the international poverty line; a third of all deaths (some 18 million people) are from poverty-related causes; 790 million people do not have adequate nutrition; more than 880 million lack basic health care; access to potable water is not even considered a human right; differences in quality of life among the different regions have increased; unemployment is growing, and employment is becoming more precarious.[2]

And yet we know there are more than sufficient means to cover the basic needs of all human beings; we know that the process of globalization can be beneficial to all, if it is guided by principles of justice.

Already there are realities leading to a different orientation in that process: the Global Compact for corporations proposed by United Nations Secretary General Kofi Annan in 1999; the discourse of social responsibility exemplified (among other projects) by the Green Book *"Fomentar un Marco Europeo para la Responsabilidad Social de las Empresas,"* sponsored by the Commission of the European Union in 2001, in the Multi-stakeholder Forum proposed by the European Parliament in 2004, and in the European Alliance for Corporate Social Responsibility, proposed in 2006; the promotion of microloans in poor countries, thanks to initiatives such as that of Muhammad Yunus; the growing acceptance of "ethical banking" in the developed countries; the growing awareness of fair trade and responsible consumption; the proposal by specialists such as Joseph Stiglitz to democratize the international economic institutions; the proposals of economic solidarity and an economy of gratuitousness.

Indeed some authoritative voices, such as that of the 1998 Nobel laureate in economics, Amartya Sen, remind us that the goal of the economy is not simply growth but the creation of a good society;[3] that an authentic economy is an ethical economy. For that reason it might have been more appropriate to award the 2006 Nobel Prize in Economics to Muhammad Yunus than to give him the somewhat-tattered Nobel Peace Prize. A good economy helps to create a good society; it is an ethical economy.

Civic ethics, which increasingly means *transnational ethics*, is expressed in universal and international declarations defending human rights and the equality of basic capacities, while *Christian ethics* focuses on the sacred value of human beings and on care for nature. Both of these ethics stand in brutal contrast to the data we have on people's quality of life and on the plunder of nature. We must recognize that *our achievements have not lived up to our declarations.*

Does not all this express the *failure of the economy* as a human activity, involving corporations, politicians, and citizens? Should not the economy be oriented by goals that give it social meaning and legitimacy, like any other activity involving human participation? So then *the first great challenge* is to *transform the economy from within.* It is to reconstruct the economy, situating it at its proper level as a human activity, and strengthening the activities that are already moving in that direction.

Naturally, theological ethicists cannot resolve the economic problems. But they can help to rethink the economy from within, working with experts and with those affected by it, trying to understand with them the goals of economic activity and the orientations that would lead it to become an ethical economy, that is, one capable of achieving its proper tasks.

2. Moral Theology as a Critical Hermeneutic

A moral theology that thinks about the economy will see itself, then, as a *critical hermeneutic of economic activity.* That is, as a hermeneutic that aims to uncover the conflictive ethical core issues of economic activity and to find solutions that lend themselves to the service of people (beginning with the most helpless) and that assume responsibility for nature. By this method, moral theology will take on a structure appropriate to one of the applied ethical systems, in this case an ethic of the economy and the corporation.

Thus in my view, an economic ethic becomes, like any other applied ethic, a critical hermeneutic of human activity; as such it is concerned with at least two levels.

In the first place it is the ethic of a social *activity.* Such an activity can perhaps best be understood in terms of the neo-Aristotelian concept of a "practice," as proposed by Alasdair MacIntyre: a cooperative social activity that derives its social meaning and legitimacy from pursuing goods within itself, and demands the development of certain virtues on the part of those who participate in it.[4] This is what we might call the *agathological* moment, which refers to the goods to be pursued.

But in the second place, the fact that this activity must occur at the post-conventional level in the development of moral consciousness, the level that has been reached by institutions in the developed countries, requires an effort to achieve its internal goods within the deontological framework of post-conventional ethical principles. This is what we might call the *deontological moment*. In this sense teleology and deontology are not opposed to each other, but it is the special dignity or value of one type of beings (the deonto-logical moment) that gives meaning to the question of the consequences of decisions taken for the good of those beings (the *agathological* moment).[5]

To understand moral theology with respect to the economy as a "critical hermeneutic of economic activity" requires an effort to understand the econ-omy of the early twenty-first century *from within*, and to identify the ethical core issues within it, supporting those interpretations which would orient it to the service of people, especially of the least privileged, which is the appro-priate perspective for a Christian theology and a modern ethic.

In this task we must remember that although the process of globalization has clearly given primacy to neoliberal economics, there is not in fact one "economy" but multiple "economies," in different contexts and concrete sit-uations; we are not looking for single solutions but seeking to understand the concrete situations and to find solutions in dialogue with those affected by them.

3. Ethical Core Issues in Debate

The economy is an activity in which people are involved and which is based on institutions. At its heart are issues in debate that have an ethical charac-ter, because they affect people's lives and the sustainability of nature.

These problems do not belong only at the level of specialized discussion; choosing one position or another places economic activity at the service of some causes or others. In this essay I shall point out some of these issues, which are truly central to people's lives and the sustainability of nature, and which pose challenges for economic activity in a global world. This obvi-ously is not intended as an exhaustive list.

Human Freedom or Determinism?

Some of the prevailing positions (Hayek's evolutionism, historical material-ism) tend to interpret the economy as a fatal mechanism, thus exempting the economic and political agents from responsibility. But if there are no respon-sibilities, then there is no place for social justice; inequality in the distribu-tion of wealth cannot be considered unjust.

Other positions in contrast, mine among them, understand economic activity as an act of freedom. The invisible hand of the market rests in very visible hands: in the decisions and actions of corporations and politicians, and also of citizens. On that view the economy is not neutral.

Neutral Science or Value-Laden Knowledge?

Ever since Max Weber formulated his Principle of Scientific Neutrality (*Wertfreiheit*), the social sciences, including economics, have often considered themselves neutral. In many schools of economics it is described as a "strict science," without moral evaluations. And yet no human activity is immune to moral evaluations; all are implicitly or explicitly infused with one set of values or another.

In the case of economics it may be the values of economic efficiency, competitiveness, economic growth, and a high rate of consumption; or it may be those focused on reducing inequalities, satisfying basic needs, developing people's basic capacities, strengthening self-esteem, promoting freedom.

It is necessary to identify the values infused in economic processes and decide which ones to strengthen if the economy is to achieve the goals that give it social meaning and legitimacy.

The Goals of the Economy

The prevailing positions interpret the goals of the economy as economic growth and the satisfaction of the choices made by those with the resources to choose. In this view, growth may require great sacrifices by the present generations in developing countries, but—they say—in the long run those sacrifices will benefit society as a whole.

Other positions, however, understand economic growth and the gross domestic product as means to the end which gives authentic social meaning and legitimacy to the economy: the satisfaction of people's needs, beginning with basic needs; the development of their capacities, which enables them to live the kind of life that they have reason to value; in short, the creation of a good society. Certainly political power must play a part through public policies, and it is not surprising that countries such as Norway head the list of developed peoples precisely because they also have appropriate social policies. But because the goal of the economy is also to create a good society, it is not enough to pay attention to the macroeconomic parameters. We must also be concerned with something simple but often forgotten in economic calculations: the well-being of the people.

Development on an Economicist Model, or Human Development?

After World War II it was taken for granted that development means promoting economic growth through such means as the liberalization, modernization, and privatization of the economy, without considering the people affected by those decisions in different countries. But after twenty-five years the situation of the developing countries had not improved much, and in today's globalized world the *inequalities* between elites and nonelites have increased. Is the consensus of Washington the only possible economic model for development?

Clearly it is not the only possible model. In this sense, there is helpful guidance in Sen's distinction between two concepts, which he respectively calls BLAST (blood, sweat, and tears) and GALA (getting by, with a little assistance).[6] BLAST sees development as a cruel process, while GALA sees it as a process of cooperation, in the sense that those who participate in the market are interdependent; the public services can also promote cooperation among individuals. In practice these two concepts may take different forms, and some of their characteristics may be seen in very different plans and projects. GALA recognizes the interdependence between quality of life and economic productivity and understands that social development may promote overall growth if it is accompanied by favorable policies. It understands that *human capital* is indispensable even for the generation of *physical capital*; that a country needs human capital, human resources, in order to develop.

Economic Model and Ways of Life

Also, is the economicist model a model of the good life that should be universalized? Models of the good life cannot be imposed; on this point we must distinguish between *the just* and *the good*, between the demands of justice that a society must satisfy and invitations to the good life that people must accept. Thus the question is: what can be socially required?[7]

We cannot socially require the universalization of a model of the good life, nor is it morally admissible to do so; for that reason it is also *unjust* to universalize the economicist model. What can be socially required is the fulfillment of certain *demands of justice*, that is, the requirement of creating certain minimal conditions in all peoples, which permit each person to choose his or her own way of living the good life.

In identifying those conditions, the most relevant thinkers mention utility (the satisfaction of one's preference), primary goods (Rawls), the satisfaction of basic human needs (Streeten, Galtung, Gasper); the protection of human rights (Pogge), the development of basic skills (Sen, Nussbaum,

Crocker, De Martino, the UN Development Program).[8] Denis Goulet offers a reply that in my view embraces the best of those listed above: the inherent goods of development consist of offering more and better ways to sustain the life of a society's members; creating better conditions for the development of self-esteem; freeing men and women from oppressive servitude and enabling them to carry out the life plans they choose in a society that does not distinguish among life plans as long as they meet certain minimal standards of justice.[9]

Indeed, economic models do make different ways of life possible; therefore what can be required is to create the basic conditions of justice, in dialogue with those who are affected in different contexts, without destroying their different living communities.[10] According to the Principle of the Ethics of Discourse, all human beings who possess communicative competence are valid interlocutors and should be included in the dialogue on issues affecting them. The economy cannot be treated as a "knowledge of domination," in which the expert manages the other subjects as if they were objects, but rather as a "knowledge of understanding." The expert aims for mutual understanding with others who are also subjects, to understand their needs and aspirations, and proposes to cooperate with them, enabling them to carry out their life plans. For this purpose it is necessary to initiate dialogues, respecting each participant's cultural baggage and their "living cultural communities."

Now, to carry out these dialogues we must distinguish between "external protection" and "internal restrictions." That is, we must not permit the elites in each community to oppress internally the individuals that comprise it, under the pretext of protecting their culture from external interference and aggression.[11]

Corporate Models

Although each context requires measures tailored to its own needs, we can think in terms of three corporate models or types that are prevalent today:[12]

(1) *The economicist model*, in which the goal of the corporation is to maximize the benefit to stockholders at any cost. Based on individualistic methodology, it assumes that all rational individuals tend to maximize success in their moves, and corporate organizations in turn tend to maximize the benefit to their investors or leaders.[13]

The economicist model, however, does not exist in reality but in what the social contract classics call a "state of nature," prior to the birth of the "state of law"; the former is a state without law, in which the choices of the strongest prevail. But even a demonic people, a people comprised of beings without moral sensitivity, "as long as they possess intelligence," will choose a state of law.[14] Any intelligent corporation will prefer a legal order to a war without quarter.

(2) *The institutional model*, in which the corporation is seen as the outcome of a pact agreed upon by those who invest labor, money, services, and patronage in it, and to whom the corporation thereby assumes obligations. The institutional model takes the place of the so-called economicist model; differing choices are resolved by means of agreements, norms, and exchange contracts that must be fulfilled, and self-interest is subjected to the rules governing the exchange, production, and distribution of goods and services.[15]

(3) *The stakeholder model*, which considers the interests of those affected and understands the corporation as the outcome of a moral contract among them.[16] This is the model supported in the discourse on Corporate Social Responsibility, which is gaining wide acceptance at the local and global level.

Corporate Social Responsibility is *not simply disinterested philanthropy*, but rather an effort to design the activities of the corporation in such a way that it considers the interests of the people it affects and can show positive change in measurable ways. The concept of *benefit* is broadened to include economic, social, and environmental effects, and *beneficiary* includes everyone affected by the corporation's activities. In my view, social responsibility must become a *management tool*, a *matter of prudence,* and a *requirement of justice.*

As a management tool, it must become part of the "hard core" of the corporation, its basic management, rather than a form of charity that coexists with low wages, poor product quality, low job stability, even exploitation and violation of basic rights. Whatever belongs to the hard core of the corporation affects its *ethos*, its *character*; it is not a sudden acquisition but must *transform the character of the corporation from within.*

As a matter of prudence, in Corporate Social Responsibility the people affected become "accomplices" in a venture that seeks the common good, in a time when the rapid pace of change makes it wiser to have friends than adversaries, accomplices than enemies.

But that is not all, because the radical part is to be found at the root. Indeed social responsibility must be *rooted in the character of the organization*, generating the necessary habits for acting with excellence, in the conviction that it is appropriate to do so by practicing—among other things—the virtue of prudence. This protects Corporate Social Responsibility from being reduced to a *cosmetic or bureaucratic change.*

Justice is another essential aspect of ethics. At the beginning of the third millennium, justice requires consideration of the *stakeholders*, those affected by the corporation's activity; they are *of interest both for corporate survival and in their own right.*

It is just to consider all those affected by corporate activity when decisions are made, not only because it is obviously in the company's interest to do so, as even a "city of demons" can understand; but also because they are of interest in their own right, as a "city of persons" with intelligence and moral sensitivity understand. Thus, there is a *moral obligation* to all those affected, which a just organization must not evade.[17]

Certainly the dispute continues even when laws of social responsibility are enacted, but at least one thing is clear: with or without laws, *character and justice* form the ethical humus in the corporate soil, which gives meaning to a sense of social responsibility that resolves not to be reduced to cosmetic and bureaucratic change.

Social Citizenship: Labor and Unemployment

The canonical concept of citizenship (T. H. Marshall's social citizenship)[18] includes a first and a second generation of rights. Among these, the right to work is the means by which most people are able to obtain an income and become an integral part of society. Yet there is massive unemployment, especially in the least developed countries, and employment is precarious at the world level.

Is it a necessity of the economy to maintain a reserve of unemployed workers and an unstable work situation, or is it rather a necessity of the economy to create a stable work force which allows people to build their lives, thus making social citizenship universal?[19]

Certainly people have a basic need for skills or abilities that will generate sufficient freedom to live the kind of life that makes them happy, and work is one of these. Therefore whatever changes are made in the social structure, a political community fails to meet the minimum standards of justice if it does not work to guarantee its citizens the right to work. We should add that one condition of legitimacy for any institution is its purpose of doing justice, and that in a global context, we must always speak of a human right in cosmopolitan terms.

Consumption: End or Engine of the Economy?

According to Adam Smith, consumption is the end of the economy. Nevertheless, it has become the engine, especially the almost compulsive consumption of the one-fifth of humanity that possesses acquisitive power. This presents at least two types of problem: first, the distribution of consumer goods is radically unjust, and second, mass production requires massive consumption, which leads producers to try to create an ethos of consumption. We may wonder, therefore, whether consumption-based models of life are truly free and productive of happiness.

Does not the unjust distribution of consumer goods, within each country and at the global level, require a Global Compact regarding consumption? Do we not need to develop "consumer citizenship"?[20]

The Ethical Principles of the Economy and the Aporoi

At least two ethical principles seem to govern economic activity: the principle of possessive individualism ("all people are owners of their own faculties and of the product of their faculties, and do not owe anything to society for them"),[21] and the principle of Matthew ("to those who have, more will be given . . . from those who have nothing, even what they have will be taken away"). These principles necessarily create excluded people: the poor, the *aporoi*. Those who have nothing are marginalized in a world characterized not only by "xenophobia" but by "aporophobia."

Nevertheless, both modern ethics and Christian ethics ought to defend the recognition of the equal dignity of persons, take sides with the most vulnerable, and assume responsibility for nature. This does not permit any exclusions from economic life.

Possessive Individualism or the Sociality of Goods?

The principle of possessive individualism is false, because it is so abstract, and in reality all people are what they are in relation to others.[22] It follows that their possessions are owed in part to society, especially in a globalized world. The goods of the earth are social goods, and should therefore be distributed globally.

From this in turn follows the need to promote a system of global governance; to promote activities such as microloans, ethical banking, fair trade, responsible consumption, projects of economic solidarity, and a basic income for all citizens; to abolish rich-country protectionism; and to transform intergovernmental political-economic institutions like the World Bank, the International Monetary Fund, and the World Trade Organization, increasing their transparency, changing the mechanisms by which their representatives are elected, and replacing the use of universal formulas with procedures that consider specific contexts and allow the participation of those affected when economic policies are carried out.[23]

Finally, not all the goods of the earth are subject to the market; there is a creative economy of [freely given] gifts which opens up, in the face of unrestricted trade, the wide path of gratuitousness.[24] Christian ethics is entirely at home in taking that path.

Henk ten Have

Universal Declaration on Bioethics and Human Rights

Introduction

When the United Nations Educational, Scientific and Cultural Organization (UNESCO) was established sixty years ago, its constitution declared that peace must be founded on the intellectual and moral solidarity of humanity. Julian Huxley, the first director-general, pointed out that in order to make science contribute to peace, security, and human welfare, it was necessary to relate the applications of science to a scale of values. Guiding the development of science for the benefit of humanity therefore implied "the quest for a restatement of morality . . . in harmony with modern knowledge."[1]

Since its foundation, UNESCO has been concerned with moral issues in relation to science. From the 1970s onward, the emergence of the life sciences, in particular, has led to international examination of bioethical questions. This global focus on bioethics was institutionalized in 1993 with the establishment of the International Bioethics Committee (IBC) with a work program and budget for international activities. The program was expanded in 1998 with the foundation by UNESCO of the World Commission on the Ethics of Scientific Knowledge and Technology (COMEST), which is addressing other areas of applied ethics such as environmental ethics, science ethics, and technology ethics. Since 2002, UNESCO has been coordinating the activities of international bodies in the area of bioethics through the Inter-Agency Committee on Bioethics of the United Nations (with, among others, FAO, OECD, and WHO). In the same year, the 191 Member States decided that ethics should be one of the five priorities of the organization. This concern with ethics, and in particular the need to orientate the development of science and technology within a framework of values and moral principles, has, of course, for a long time also been the concern of theological ethicists all over the world. But the important difference nowadays is that it is on the agenda of the international community and a matter of intergovernmental political consultations and negotiations.

29

Standard Setting

One major objective of the work in ethics in UNESCO has been the development of international normative standards. This is particularly important since many Member States have only a limited infrastructure in bioethics. They lack expertise, educational programs, bioethics committees, legal frameworks, and public debate. Technological progress, new knowledge and its applications, new diagnostics, preventive and therapeutic interventions have significantly changed medicine and the life sciences as well as the context of health care, giving rise to bioethical dilemmas both in highly developed and less developed countries. Bioethics also is no longer the exclusive concern of scientists, medical professionals, or policy makers. It concerns all people. Disease, disability, death, and suffering are human experiences that sooner or later affect everybody. This is all the more true from an international perspective. Because of globalization, not only scientific and technological advances spread around the globe but also bioethical dilemmas. As the example of cloning demonstrates, when a new technology has been developed in one country, it can be applied elsewhere, even if some countries want to ban its use. On the other hand, bioethical issues may arise because of inequality and injustice. If an effective medication for diseases such as HIV/AIDS, malaria, and tuberculosis is available in some countries, it is morally problematic when patients die in other countries because of a lack of resources. It is not acceptable that research institutes and pharmaceutical companies carry out clinical trials in developing countries without applying the same standards of informed consent and risk assessment as in developed countries. The global character of contemporary science and technology and the increasing number of research teams coming from different countries imply the need for a global approach to bioethics. Such a global approach assumes that all persons, whoever and whereever they are, should benefit from the advances of science and technology. This is precisely what UNESCO aims to promote.

International Bioethics

In the past, UNESCO has adopted two declarations in the field of bioethics: the *Universal Declaration on the Human Genome and Human Rights* (1997) and the *International Declaration on Human Genetic Data* (2003). The scope of standard setting was expanded significantly with the mandate given by the Member States to develop a universal declaration on bioethics. The previous declarations had focused on the specialized area of genetics and genomics. When the new mandate was given, all topics relevant to bioethics were placed on the table for negotiation.

In October 2001, the General Conference, supported by the Round Table of Ministers of Science, invited the director-general of UNESCO to examine the possibility of developing a universal instrument on bioethics. The feasibility study drafted by the IBC concluded that it was possible to find common ground in divergent bioethical positions by focusing on basic principles.[2] Some of these principles had already been identified in previous declarations. The study also stressed the necessity to develop a universal instrument because scientific practices are now developing rapidly and extending beyond national borders. Developed and developing countries should therefore achieve broad consistency in regulations and policies.

In October 2003, the General Conference provided a mandate to submit a draft declaration in two years. In the meeting, the president of France (Mr. J. Chirac) made a vigorous plea for a universal normative framework, preferably a convention, to guide the progress of the life sciences and to protect the integrity and dignity of human beings. The subsequent process of drafting, entrusted to the IBC, taking into account the short time frame, the variety of ethical cultures and traditions, and the controversial nature of many bioethical issues, had various stages.

First, to explore ideas about the scope and the structure, all Member States were consulted early in 2005, as well as intergovernmental organizations (e.g., FAO, WIPO, Council of Europe), NGOs (e.g., WMA, HUGO), National Bioethics Committees (e.g., from Japan, Korea, New Zealand, Mexico, Republic of Congo), and international bioethics societies. Questions debated at this stage included whether the focus should be on human beings or broader; which fundamental bioethical principles could be identified; and whether specific areas of application of the principles should be explored.

During the second stage of drafting the text later in 2005, the IBC extensively consulted many stakeholders. The UN Inter-Agency Committee on Bioethics discussed drafts during two of its meetings. Consultations with regional experts took place in Buenos Aires and Moscow. National consultations were held in the Netherlands, Iran, Lithuania, Turkey, Korea, Mexico, Indonesia, and Portugal. In August 2004, the IBC organized a public hearing in Paris, with representatives of religious and spiritual perspectives. It was interesting that almost all representatives agreed on the basic principles proposed. Finally, the draft text was subjected to a written consultation with all Member States between October and December 2004.

The third stage was the political negotiation. Dealing with bioethics in an intergovernmental organization such as UNESCO implies a linkage between science and politics. Any normative instrument needs to reflect the scientific and ethical state of the art. But in the end it is submitted for approval to the Member States, which then decide if they want to adopt it. The draft text developed by independent scientific experts of the IBC was necessarily subjected to political negotiations among the governmental experts who represented the governments of Member States. The result is that the cogency of the final text, in some respects, may be diminished in order to create maximum adherence by all of the governments involved. In order to facilitate the opportunities for compromise, the work of the independent IBC was connected at an early stage with that of governmental experts. Several amendments to the IBC text were made by the governmental experts, but in general the main body of the text has met with consensus. Finally, on October 19, 2005, the 33rd General Conference of UNESCO, meeting in Paris, unanimously adopted the Universal Declaration on Bioethics and Human Rights.[3]

The Contents of the New Declaration

One of the contentious issues in the elaboration was the scope of bioethics. At least three views were advanced. These were that bioethics has to do with (1) medicine and health care; (2) the social context, such as access to health; and (3) the environment. In different parts of the world, different conceptions, definitions, and histories of bioethics are evident.

The scope of the adopted text of the declaration is an obvious compromise among these views. It addresses "ethical issues related to medicine, life sciences and associated technologies as applied to human beings, taking into account their social, legal and environmental dimensions" (Art. 1a).

The aims of the declaration are multiple. The most important aim, however, is to provide "a universal framework of principles and procedures to guide States in the formulation of their legislation, policies or other instruments in the field of bioethics" (Art. 2i). One characteristic of present-day bioethics is that it is not merely an academic discipline; it is also an area of public debate and policy making. This is why the declaration primarily addresses States. But at the same time, since the bioethical principles identified are founded on human rights and fundamental freedoms, every individual is involved in bioethics. The declaration, therefore, also aims "to guide the actions of individuals, groups, communities, institutions and corporations, public and private" (Art. 2).

The heart of the declaration is to be found in the fifteen principles that are listed. The principles determine the different obligations and responsibilities of the moral subject ("moral agent") in relation to different categories of moral objects ("moral patients"). The principles are arranged according to a gradual widening of the range of moral objects: the individual human being itself (human dignity; benefit and harm; autonomy), other human beings (consent; privacy; equality), human communities (respect for cultural diversity), humankind as a whole (solidarity; social responsibility; sharing of benefits), and all living beings and their environment (protecting future generations and protection of the environment, the biosphere, and biodiversity).

Some of the principles are already widely accepted (e.g., autonomy; consent). Others have been endorsed in previous declarations (e.g., sharing of benefits). What is innovative in the set of principles in the new declaration is the balance struck between individualist and communitarian moral perspectives. The declaration recognizes the principle of autonomy (Art. 5) as well as the principle of solidarity (Art. 13). It emphasizes the principle of social responsibility and health (Art. 14), which aims at reorienting bioethical decision making toward issues urgent to many countries (such as access to quality health care and essential medicines, especially for women and children, adequate nutrition and water, reduction of poverty and illiteracy, improvement of living conditions, and the environment). Finally, the declaration anchors the bioethical principles firmly in the rules governing human dignity, human rights, and fundamental freedoms.

The section on the application of the principles (Arts. 18 to 21) is also innovative because it provides the spirit in which the principles ought to be applied. It calls for professionalism, honesty, integrity, and transparency in the decision-making process; the setting up of ethics committees; appropriate assessment and management of risk; and ethical transnational practices that help in avoiding exploitation of countries that do not have an ethical infrastructure.

Implications and Impact

Bioethical problems commonly arise because conflicts exist between several competing ethical principles. Sometimes it is not obvious which principle is to prevail. Accordingly, a careful balancing of principles is usually required. The new declaration states principles that may occasionally seem inconsistent. Ethical decision making in practice, however, frequently requires rational argumentation and the weighing of the principles at stake. In order to advance decision making, the principles are to be understood as complementary and interrelated (Art. 26).

It is significant that all 191 Member States of UNESCO were able to agree on the relevant bioethical principles. The declaration, although a nonbinding legal instrument, is therefore the first international document in bioethics adopted by all governments. Other very influential documents have been adopted by nongovernmental organizations (e.g., the Declaration of Helsinki). Generally, however, these do not create the same commitment on the part of governments. It is significant that the UNESCO declaration has already been cited as a relevant international text in the recent judgment of the European Court of Human Rights in the case of *Evans v. the United Kingdom*.[4] The new declaration is furthermore the beginning rather than the end of a process of internationalization of bioethics. Special attention therefore needs to be given to the application of the principles and the dissemination and the promotion of the declaration. Member States that have not already done so will be encouraged to establish bioethics committees; to promote informed pluralistic public debate; to foster bioethics education and training; and to take appropriate legal measures to facilitate transnational research. It is also here that theological ethicists can take a new starting point for their contributions. Regardless of all plurality of values and diversity of views on life and death, happiness and suffering, at least there is agreement on the fundamental principles. The challenge now is to "translate" these shared moral values into various practices so that, indeed, all human beings everywhere can benefit from the advances of science and technology within a framework of respect for human rights and fundamental freedoms.

Part II

Moral Theology on the Five Continents

Each author answers these questions regarding their continent:

- *What are our moral challenges?*
- *How are we responding?*
- *What hope do we have for the future?*

Africa

Mawuto R. Afan, O.P. (Ivory Coast)
The Main "Building Sites" of Ethics in West Africa

Laurenti Magesa (Tanzania)
Locating the Church among the Wretched of the Earth

Sébastien Muyengo Mulombe (Congo)
Authenticity and Credibility: Moral Challenges after the African Synod

Mawuto Roger Afan was the first speaker and he set the themes that his colleagues echo: the identity crisis in Africa, the postcolonial moves to democracy, and the reconstruction of Africa itself. Afan helps us to see immediately the urgency of doing theological ethics in Africa. With African nations experiencing great instability, the ethicist is called to understand Africa better, to see that its affirmation of the community is not a negation of the individual, and to retrieve from the African tradition a rootedness that could stabilize both personal and social upheaval.

Laurenti Magesa was unable to attend the conference. In his stead, John Mary Waliggo read Magesa's paper. Here Magesa reflects on the identity crisis and names it as the effect of the horrendous suffering in Africa brought on both by the slave trade and the simultaneous colonial rape of the continent's rich resources. But he also raises other challenges, those resulting from gender inequities, elitism, political and economic corruption, and the long-standing compromise of the environment. He turns to the two movements of liberation theology, which includes feminist and womanist contributions, and inculturation theology. He admonishes theologians to recognize that these are complementary theologies and that no true African theological ethicist can afford to overlook either of these significant theological claims. He concludes by urging theologians to locate themselves more immediately with "the wretched of the earth" and to find more constructive ways of encouraging Africa's hierarchy to promote, rather than inhibit, the type of theological discourse Africa needs, one that is relevant and action oriented for God's people.

Sébastien Muyengo Mulombe reflects on the African Synod that was held in 1994 and reflects on the apostolic exhortation *Ecclesia in Africa* in order to describe contemporary Africa. Reflecting on the Parable of the Good Samaritan and seeing Africa as the "wretched" man robbed and wounded in that parable, the inevitable question becomes, who will be Africa's Good Samaritan. The answer becomes the preacher whose words and deeds are recognized by their credibility and authenticity, the two main challenges that Muyengo puts to today's theological ethicist. He concludes by calling for a theological ethics that at one end of the spectrum recognizes and articulates properly the genesis of Africa's situation and, at the other end, proffers a strategic course of action leading to Africa's proper reconstruction.

Mawuto R. Afan, O.P.

The Main "Building Sites" of Ethics in West Africa

Contemporary ethical reflection in Africa deals with complex problems, each of which involves cross-disciplinary work by thinkers of different religious confessions: this makes their investigations an ecumenical "workplace." The questions they pose are neither totally new nor mere repetitions of the tradition. They reactivate in a new context challenges that are more or less ancient. The anthropological twist that these questions have taken in the context of globalization obliges us to situate our fundamental ethical reflections in an interdisciplinary framework.

My intention in this essay is not to present an exhaustive list of contemporary ethical challenges. Such a task is clearly impossible, when we consider the balkanization of Africa and the consequent exponential growth of research and publications in the various geographical and linguistic areas. However, in an epoch marked by globalization, this pluralism in ethics offers us a positive opportunity. I shall attempt to sketch the focal points of ethical investigation, for these are the locus of discernment where ethical propositions are elaborated in a dialogue with the questions that preoccupy Africans today.

I. Ethical Challenges in Africa

Crisis of Identity

African countries envisaged an independence that would be economic, political, and cultural—an independence in keeping with their access to national sovereignty. Theoretically, it is accepted that each country determines independently and in a *sovereign* manner its own external actions and chooses its bilateral relationships. The ideology underlying independence said that a country could lead a self-sufficient life without needing to import goods and services.

After independence was proclaimed, despite the spirit of nationalism that

39

found such an enthusiastic audience at that time, the African countries opened up in a genuine, and sometimes a systematic manner, to the external market. The unease caused today by the presence of foreigners in African countries is due not only to the conviction that this presence makes a significant contribution to the unemployment in the country where these foreigners are living but also because this presence offends the feeling of pride and the national identity of the country.

Cultural independence denotes the collective awareness in one specific region of an identity that is specific to one community and allows it to express a positive feeling of welcome and tolerance vis-à-vis other communities—or, in negative terms, a feeling of rejection, fear, or even contempt. In other words, if cultural independence is to be effective, it is essential that the inhabitants of a country feel that they exist with a specific identity of their own.[1]

When we speak of the specific culture of a country in the context of the African countries—where the borders do not follow logical or obvious criteria (whether geographical, sociological, linguistic, or cultural)—we must note that this factor can divide the population of a country, instead of functioning as an element that binds them together. It is also possible *de facto* that this factor may unite the borders and populations of one country with those of neighboring countries.

In the former case, the *language,* considered as the central element of a culture, is a striking example. The constitution of the African states presupposed linguistic divisions that have never been overcome. To lay claim to one's own identity by excluding and scorning others may increase the difficulties in the relationships between neighboring populations. Ultimately, such provocations may even lead to confrontations and civil wars.

A second example can illustrate this problem: the rights that are linked to one's place of birth. A number of people are excluded from political life in the country in which they live because they were not born in the national territory. In view of the fact that the creation of our territories is later than the date of the *birth* of the persons in question, we must acknowledge that the criterion of *birth* does not suffice to provide a positive definition of national identity in Africa.

The Reconstruction of Africa

According to the Congolese theologian Kä Mana, "The problems entailed by reconstruction amount to a crucial battle which must be won, if we are to organize successfully the emergence from colonialism to a new society; how are we to exist and to act in an awareness of the permanent 'production' of ourselves and of the invention of the future, thanks to the creative power of the ethical imagination and of the rational spirit?"[2] The task of reconstruction entails the further task of awakening in every African the concern for her or his own existence, the appreciation of values, of creativity, of the exuberance of the body, and concern for a rational coherence in the organization of life in common.

In the process of the reconstruction of Africa, we must insist above all on respect for life in its essence, and therefore prohibit anything that leads to the shedding of human blood. This leads us to reflect anew on the transcendent character of the human person, since the person is the bearer of life. And this is why we must condemn all inhuman conduct that offends the dignity of the human person.[3] Rather, we must consider the human person anew: what constitutes his integrity and makes him a subject in relation to ourselves? What is it that makes him another, a unique being?[4]

The obvious objection here is that the integrity of the person is not flouted in Africa today as it was in the periods of slavery and colonization. But whatever accusations we may make against foreigners in the past, today it is Africans who massacre other Africans in an unprecedented demonstration of barbarity. Support for human life, therefore, means combating barbarity, whatever forms this may take, and building up ramparts against the powers of death which disfigure life.

The Democratic Process

The lack of finances has made those in power incapable of responding to societal demands and satisfying their networks of clients. The people no longer look on the state as the legitimate guarantor of the common good and they refuse to obey official directives. The international institutions that supported the existing governments against attacks by opposition groups were finally obliged to accept that the major obstacle on the path to development was the apparatus of government itself.

The 1989 Report of the World Bank noted that the long list of problems of development in African countries indicated a crisis of power: in view of the almost total breakdown of the apparatus of the state, restructuring for development is possible only if it is backed up by a realistic political strategy that emphasizes democratic freedom, the service of the common good by means of basic social services, and a large-scale diffusion of information. A climate of dialogue is necessary in order to explain to the people their political choices, their conditions, and the contribution they could make to society as a whole.

A number of donor organizations and governments have already demanded a "political dialogue" between the African governments and their people: this is a first step toward a position that links economic adaptation to democratization.

It is a simple fact that a political regime—as in Nigeria—which practices an inequitable distribution of its income cannot experience genuine economic growth. A policy that envisages a relatively equitable distribution of income and a consensus about the allocation of public expenses can however make a significant contribution to improved results in economic growth.

II. Ethical Approaches to the Challenges

An Ethical Approach to the Identity Crisis

One of the reasons for the failure of development projects in Africa is the lack of awareness of the communal dimension of the person.[5] African ethics is based on the holistic conception of the person, which presupposes a reflection on the promotion of the values related to life in common, as well as respect for the rights of each individual. As a framework within which people live, the community is made up of persons who are gathered together under an authority in order to live in peace and justice.

This, however, is not a communalist conception of community.[6] According to the Ivorian H. Memel-Fotê, the category of communalism has often been employed as a designation of the precolonial society in Africa before Christianity and Islam.[7] But a communalism of this kind was never practiced in the traditional African communities.[8] The fact that traditional praxis was far removed from communalism preserved the communities from a conception of the individual as totally free and completely devoid of responsibility, a conception that also posits an antithesis between the individual and the community.

We must think of the relationship between the person and his or her community in such a way that the promotion of the one does not entail the breakdown of the other. Those Western authors who seem to be rediscovering the ethical dimension of the community today are thereby drawing close to the traditional African concept. According to Charles Taylor's analysis, it is impossible for the human person to be a moral agent, and hence dedicated to the realization of human goodness, outside a community of language and of mutual discourse about good and evil, about justice and injustice.[9] And in fact, if it is true to say that the identity of an African cannot have any other foundation than the mutual dependence of the person and the community, it follows that the African is not considered as an individual but as a person who belongs to a family and a community.

An Ethical Approach to the Reconstruction of Africa

Most of the contributions to the ethics of the reconstruction of Africa have recourse to values borrowed from Christianity. This is also the strategy of the All Africa Conference of Churches (*Conférence des Eglises de Toute l'Afrique, CETA*), which has made the concept of reconstruction a paradigm for a new theology.[10]

The most systematic formulation of the problems involved in the ethics of the reconstruction of Africa, by Kä Mana, is profoundly influenced by Christianity. On the basis of the gospel, this author seeks to construct a body of requirements, practical norms, and existential structures for the political, economic, social, and cultural reconstruction of the African continent. Committing himself to the ethical perspective, Kä Mana seeks to "promote an ethical thinking centered on the idea of reconstruction. This concept is understood in the light of the Word of God, on the basis of the existential principles which the Bible shows us when we examine how the fundamental human crises were tackled in the course of Israel's history, and above all in the Gospel itself, which is a pivotal moment in the formation of the conscience of humanity."[11]

In a context of pluralism—which may perhaps not extend to ethics, but certainly exists in the religious sphere—it is scarcely necessary to emphasize that this quasi-exclusive option in favor of Christian values cannot simply be taken for granted when we plan to take action in the specific context of Africa. This is no doubt why Kä Mana finds it necessary to justify his choice: "We have turned to Christianity, the Christian faith, and the biblical revelation because they forge a global vision of reality, with a meaning that can be converted into a practical force in African societies, into an ethics of change in the perspective of the human dimension."[12] The ethics of the reconstruction of Africa is thus an ethics based on Christian moral values. It cannot be denied that Christianity, with the power of the gospel and with its own specific social and human values, has a legitimate role to play in the reconstruction of Africa.

Nevertheless, theories about the reconstruction of Africa, although based on Christian values, share one weakness: they do not sufficiently insist on the contribution that African tradition can make to this work of reconstruction. If recourse to Christian values nonetheless remains valid, this is because the reconstruction of Africa, envisaged in all its dimensions, is not merely an economic and political problem. It is essentially a religious problem, where the meaning and goal of human life are at stake. It must offer the possibility of leading a different and a better life. One can and must appeal to Christian values, although one should never forget that faith can become *intégriste,* that is, linked to a Western culture that belongs to the past and has lost its relevance, a culture detached from the concrete reality of Africa and incapable of helping Africans to make a response to their present-day needs.

The Ethical Requirements of African Democracy

Traditionally, the community possessed a political and religious structure that inculcated appropriate ideas and behavior in the young African, thus preparing him to confront the challenges of life. Thus, by means of the rite of initiation, the young man was integrated with his whole being into his culture. This initiation encompassed four essential functions.[13]

First, the young man is made aware of his responsibility: the period of initiation is marked by the break with static rigidity, with all the traditional frameworks that prevented the individual from taking initiatives of his own. The initiation is a recognition of the authority of the Ancients; at the same time, it supplies the basic boldness that the young man will need in order to transgress arbitrary limits. During the initiation, the person is submitted to a number of physical and moral tests. The young man is given a measure of liberty to take a responsible decision, since the solutions to the various difficult situations are not all laid down in advance.

Second, the initiation is more than a socialization. It shows the young man something: it helps him to get to know himself (the laws of the body), to join his group fully (the laws of the family), and to enter the cosmos (the laws of the village and of nature). In this way, the initiate becomes aware of the personal and communal dimensions of liberty and of responsibility.

Third, there is a function of projection. The fact that the secondary meanings of each symbol are relatively undefined leaves space for a personal reflection in which the unconscious tendencies of the young man can take on objective form. The initiate is led to perceive and understand the reality that lies beyond the words, the proverbs, and the stories. At the same time, since the human person and the world are a mystery, he must be sensitive to the secret: he is taught the secret as the beginning and the end of all other social values. This mastery of the word (and of oneself), which is the primary object of the initiation, is marked by silence.

Fourth, there is an educative function. The symbolic elements of the environment in which the initiation takes place are organized in a ritual, constituting both a spectacle and an action that influence the unconscious part of the personality. The initiatory framework creates in each initiate an attitude that favors the serene exchange of ideas and the development of habits that do him good. In the sacred enclosures, the Ancients teach the young men the history of the clans and of the foundation of the villages, the secrets of life, the hierarchy of the spirits and their principal functions. The initiates memorize lengthy texts in a secret language, and it is their task to declaim these texts from the top of the terraces on commemorative occasions, until other initiates, designated in the next initiation session, take over this charge.

One may, of course, ask what the value of the initiation is; but regardless of the way in which we might wish to evaluate it, it undoubtedly offers the young man the impression of certainty and a confirmation of his own self. A whole series of subsequent actions seem to be linked back to this foundational moment of responsible societal action.

III. Perspectives for the Future

A Crisis of Identity and Solidarity

When we take up the subject of solidarity[14] in Africa, we need to look at the concrete ways whereby Africans can move on from the legendary African solidarity to a solidarity that goes beyond the borders of the group to which one belongs, and crosses over national frontiers.[15]

The African discovers his own self in a direct relation to the members of his family, his village, and the group to which he belongs. These relationships are the object of a personal knowledge based on the notion of belonging; and they are felt to be connected with a spontaneous moral responsibility.

However, life in a more complex modern community adds other relationships constituted by psychological, cultural, social, political, and economic networks, mechanisms, and structures that can condition human conduct antecedently to any knowledge on the part of the acting subject.

In the traditional communities, there are fraternal societies that look after the sick and the widows; these services appear to be motivated directly by the obligations that the community has vis-à-vis its members. On the material and financial level, people organize themselves in such a way that they can offer economic advantages to every minority and disadvantaged social group. This solidarity is practiced between persons in the same group who know one another, but the bond of solidarity can also be broadened to include people who are more or less distant. The pact of blood[16] symbolizes this brotherhood, reciprocity, and mutual devotion which can lead two people of different origins to unite and to go even to the point of laying down their lives for each other. Once it is made, the pact of blood goes beyond the restricted circle of the two contracting parties and extends to their respective groups, which are thereby united in solidarity.[17]

The practical consequence of the pact of blood in societal life is that each contracting party becomes a guest in relation to the other. The basis of this hospitality is not membership in the same group, but the alliance that has been negotiated between different groups.

African solidarity is not meritorious per se, and it can be employed in support of behavior that runs contrary to true solidarity. But when it is explained and practiced intelligently, it widens out to become the source of a new life. The interaction that African solidarity brings about, and the rectification of external actions that oblige one to have contact with persons of very different characters, opinions, and social conditions, can help promote open relationships. In the same way, the specific orders given by those in positions of responsibility and the laws that they lay down for society, as well as all their duties of solidarity with regard to the sufferings, the tasks, and the joys of the members of one and the same group, have a formative impact. African sol-idarity could thus make an important contribution to the realization of the democratic project in Africa, which invites everyone to emerge from the straitjacket of his or her own identity.

What Shape Will the Reconstruction of Africa Take?

The ethical problems posed by the reconstruction of Africa today are linked to Christian morality but are not at all identical with it. If we take ethics to mean "aiming at the good life with and for other people in just institu-tions,"[18] it is certain that this was not unknown to the African tradition. Although no ethical treatises were written, the very varied forms of discourse and behavior that go back to those nonprofessional philosophers to whom we give the generic name of "sages" take account of this ethical concern. This rich experience that the African tradition possesses should be taken up anew in the framework of an ethics for the reconstruction of Africa.

By means of its wisdom, the African tradition transmits meaning and sketches a truth about that which is experienced in time, by using the past to put questions to the present. This memory is drawn on through legends, stories, proverbs, and myths. The tradition, understood as a rootedness that is ancient and has lasted from time immemorial, weaves a reality that is superior to change. The African sage is above all a man who possesses the word and who finds in this ability to speak and communicate the source and the guarantee of his social, political, and moral virtues.[19] It is not sur-prising that respect for the word is a prominent recommendation of African wisdom.

It follows that the distinction between the wisdom of the Ancients and ethics could be somewhat artificial in the specific area of human action. Although reflection in the African tradition has above all a pedagogical aspect, the ethical component is far from absent. The discovery of the sapi-ential thinking of the Ancients—or, more precisely, academic research into this subject today—shows its ethical relevance. The proposals of the Ancients are concerned with ethical questions because they seek knowledge in its authentic form and spirit: in other words, recourse to the word of the Ancients is regarded as the best means to practice ethics and to help the human person to develop his own humanity. The ethics propounded by African wisdom is neither secular nor religious; it is both at once, since it is generated by the African anthropology, which considers the human person as the happy unity of secular and sacred.[20]

The specific character of African wisdom is its systematic exploration of the means by which human qualities can be exercised in the life of the com-munity, and the possibility which it gives to the person to affirm her or his own self. This establishes the link between the personal and the collective dimensions of the formation process, which takes diverse forms depending on the various angles from which we consider human life in society.

National Identities and the Future of Democracy

The idea of a national identity based on culture may perhaps not be hollow, but it is certainly confused. At the same time, if we want democracy to function, it is difficult to avoid talking of "national identity." We must pay attention, however, to the exclusive tendency, when identity is involved; in order to avoid this risk, it is good to promote and activate regional and sub-regional groupings.

Democracy presupposes the existence of a nation, which is the fusion of all the various elements in one indivisible ensemble and is manifested by means of nationalistic behavior—in the positive sense of this word. Nationalism is essentially a political principle that affirms that there must be congruence between political and national unity.[21] It is necessary that those in power should belong to the same nation as the people whom they represent, for if this is not the case, the people will feel oppressed and badly represented. This democratic principle must coexist today with the type of unified society, uniform in its internal life and strengthened by the bond of a common language and place of birth.[22] Before the advent of modern democracy, it was unimportant whether a ruler was a foreigner to the nation; but in the democratic era, nationalist feeling leads people to call some persons "foreigners"—a hostile term. At the same time, the advent of democracy has brought us into a society where no one is defined in law in terms of where he "belongs." The democratic program bears within itself the seeds of rivalries and civil wars, given that it presupposes not only equality but also the freedom of groups and of persons to govern themselves.

It follows that the affirmation of national identity is both the precondition and the expression of democracy. This same affirmation is the reference point and the source of the conflicts that are born of democracy. The paradox of democracy lies in this ambivalence of the idea of national identity.

National identity risks dealing democracy a fatal blow, if we use it as a Trojan horse when we fight for our cultural independence. We can be tempted to try to protect ourselves by going to war against whatever threatens the purity of our culture. We may perhaps emerge with a provisional victory—provisional, because gained by violence. The cycle of violence is a truly vicious circle, not only from the viewpoint of the one defeated (who never definitively admits defeat and nurtures vengeance in his heart), but also from the viewpoint of the victor, who ought to know that no one has a monopoly on violence. There is a fundamental rule here, which must never be forgotten: in every victory gained by violence and humiliation, there is always an element of defeat. We are summoned to work toward a *modus vivendi,* not in order that our society may be free of conflicts but in order to create conditions that allow us to negotiate our conflicts.

Africa is destroyed, and more and more Africans are becoming aware of the necessity to reconstruct it. This concern is shared by the official churches and by the so-called independent churches. Unfortunately, the visions of the independent churches sometimes remain inadequate to cope with the reality of life in Africa. Their reflections remain mere dreams, because they lack all critical distance, as well as a base in rationality that could free these dreams from sterile repetition.[23] Some of the "reconstructionist" theories that are elaborated in the official churches are marked by a rejection of "foreign" doctrines and a return to absolutist positions on questions of morality. Contemporary African thought sometimes drinks from these springs in an eclectic manner, fusing them with both ancestral customs and customs identified by the historians, wherever these seem to have a permanent value. All these thinkers contribute to the construction of a body of commonplaces which constitutes the repertoire on which the theoreticians of the reconstruction of Africa constantly draw.

My hypothesis is that the unique and specific situation of Africa compels the ethics inspired by Christianity to engage in a dialogue with the wisdom of the African tradition. This could lead to an ethics that is better adapted, because more incarnate, linking concern for reconstruction to the requirements for life in society while refusing to submit to a paradigm that considers only the material means for the reconstruction of Africa. If there is one criticism that can be made of the Christian thinkers who reflect on the ethics of the reconstruction of Africa, it is that they are so intent on achieving Christian ethical orthodoxy that they are no longer fully conscious of the specificity of the African context. We must, therefore, maintain both the principle of recourse to Christian ethics and the necessity of an approach that pays heed to the foundations of African ethics.[24]

Laurenti Magesa

Locating the Church among the Wretched of the Earth

To the essence of ethics or practical morality there belongs a deeply pragmatic aspect. Theoretical abstractions and analyses, as in moral philosophy, become relevant to ethics only if they shed light on the behavior of human beings toward one's person, one another, or the universe in general. They are pertinent if they inspire personal or social sentiments and attitudes that inform or cause such behavior. Seen in this light, ethics or morality is fundamentally a question of relationships marked by love, justice, reconciliation, and peace. In short, discussion about ethics involves how persons and societies relate to one another and to the order of creation, positively or negatively.

But relationships are shaped by many factors. Chief among them are religion and culture. These are always to some degree a mixture of each other.[1] Thus they influence each other. To talk about religion or culture, or religion and culture, however, is to talk about historical reality, since religion and culture are always both a source and a consequence of humans living in and interpreting their existence in the world, their history.[2] And, of course, history remains an abstraction, inconceivable even, without the processes that make up politics and economics—the processes, that is, that constitute human social organization and physical survival. These are essential aspects of human civilizations, of ethics and morality. It means, therefore, that to talk about religion or culture, or religion and culture, is also at the same time to some extent or other, to talk about politics and economics, even if indirectly.

Looking at this intricate relationship among religion, culture, politics, and economics in terms of Africa's modern and contemporary history, three major elements have been isolated that inform the sentiments and attitudes in the African people in relationship to self, the other, society, and the universe. These are poverty, ignorance, and disease. Beyond attitudes, these elements also *condition* to a large extent the African person's behavior. I do not mean by the expression, of course, that they totally control the African. To assert this would be rather deterministic and simplistic, untrue for any human being's moral responsibility. However, it is certainly accurate to say that they fundamentally *influence* her or his ethical orientation. Any discussion seeking to shed light on and understand the ethical issues facing Africa today and to some extent in the near future must therefore keep these elements in mind.

I. Ethical Challenges

Among the major ethical challenges facing the African continent today, in terms of the ethical principle of human relationships and care for the earth, the most significant and all embracing are perhaps the issues of identity, dignity, the environment, gender relations, social elitism, corruption, and bad governance. Let me briefly elaborate on each of them.

Identity

A significant part of the history of Africa and its peoples is slavery and colonialism. There has never been a tragedy in human history to rival these experiences in cruelty and destructiveness of human dignity and identity. In a very fundamental way, they have formed the concrete perception of the African peoples all over the continent in their own and other people's eyes as really "nonpeople," whose life and civilization are not of much significance, if indeed any at all, for humanity. We can refer to this only as a process of "negation." It was at bottom a denial of the humanity of the African people and consequently of their civilization.[3]

To understand the ethical import of these phenomena in the continent of Africa, their impact on the African population on the psychological, economic, and social levels cannot be relegated to the past. If there is hunger, mismanagement of human and material resources, civil strife, and war in Africa today, the source of it can be traced back directly or indirectly to these experiences. On the material economic scene, the poverty of Africa, a continent incredibly rich in material resources, is a direct result of the exploitation of imperialism and colonialism, both of which continue to devastate the continent and its peoples under the name of globalization.[4]

African self-doubt is perhaps the most embracing factor in African "anthropological poverty," the kind of poverty that is not merely material but affects the personality itself. It has enormous ethical consequences, one of which is the psychological situation that instinctively obstructs initiative in many areas of personal and social development. It occurs as a result of the fact that African self-appreciation as fully human, with as many God-given intellectual and spiritual gifts as those of any other people, has been severely diminished, or in some cases almost destroyed. For this reason, these gifts are rarely put to use by Africans for the benefit of the continent as a whole. In the cases when they are used by some, they are resented and blocked by others. All of this contributes to the challenge of African identity.

Dignity

The link between identity and dignity is straightforward. Lack of identity robs the African continent and its peoples of their dignity, because the situation it creates renders it very difficult to fight poverty, ignorance, and disease. International structures of trade are weighted against Africa. As is well known, if Africa is an economic basket-case today, it is not because it lacks resources, but because its natural wealth is expropriated from it for the benefit of others. There is no fair trade; instead, the so-called aid that is often offered puts Africa in a state of indignity on account of the conditions attached to it by such organizations as the World Bank and the International Monetary Fund. Plans conceived and hatched elsewhere without Africa's participation are often imposed on the continent. This cannot bring about development in the sense of holistic human growth.[5]

The injustice inherent in international structures of trade, aid, politics, and social relations works to promote ignorance and disease in Africa. For instance, the fact that the human immunodeficiency virus (HIV) causes the acquired immune deficiency syndrome (AIDS) is clear. It is equally clear that the virus is transmitted and the deficiency of immunity is "acquired." The question is how and in what circumstances this happens. It is narrow-minded to rule out poverty and ignorance as elements that contribute to creating the environment that, as statistics show, helps HIV to spread quickly in Africa more than anywhere else.[6]

Care for the Earth

There were spiritual traditions in place in African religion that guarded against the destruction of the environment, but with the coming of colonialism and Christianity these were ridiculed and dismissed. In their place were brought the philosophy and spiritual tradition of "man as the master of the universe," called upon by divine mandate to "subdue the earth." This spiritual tradition, expressed most radically in the ideology of capitalism, has unleashed disaster on the African world. Forests are disappearing through indiscriminate logging; deserts are expanding yearly at an unprecedented rate through unwise commercial farming; lakes are drying up by mismanagement of feeder river sources; the air is being polluted through uncontrolled and careless mining of different ores and drilling of oil, and so on. The profit motive is put ahead of environmental well-being. It is the nature of the capitalist ideology and practice.

In African traditional religious consciousness the environment is not mere matter; it is suffused with energy or power. This energy connects persons with other persons, with their communities, and with the whole universe, including people who have preceded us in death and offspring not yet born. To ridicule this tradition as "animism" is to throw away values that could save the earth.[7]

Misuse of the universe through unnecessary exploitation indicates one's attitude toward others, whether it is ethical or not. The question is: what kind of world are we bequeathing to new generations?

Gender Relations

Increasingly, African women are pointing out shortcomings in African cultures and social structures with regard to gender relations.[8] With practically unanimous voice they are saying the biases inherent in these cultures against women must be acknowledged by society as a whole and addressed. Questions about the education of girls, their forced marriage at a young age, sexual harassment and violence against women, laws about women's inheritance of property, and women's participation in political and religious leadership are all important ethical issues of immediate consequence.

All of this does not concern women alone. It means that men must change their mentality and attitudes toward women in African societies. It means also that social structures must be examined anew and, where appropriate, changed to be in line with the requirements of the human rights and dignity of women. The continent as a whole cannot acquire and enjoy dignity if more than half of its population is denied it internally by structures of oppression and discrimination.

Elitism, Corruption, and Bad Governance

Through colonial education, the colonial system colluded with the African elite, usually living and working in the urban areas, to discriminate against the workers in the same urban areas, but especially the farmers in the rural areas. Even up to the present time, many Africans who have had school education tend to see themselves as superior men and women, and often disregard the views and opinions of people who have had no chance of going to school, which is a sizeable percentage of the African population. This is wrong and an abuse of the leadership positions that, because of their education, they usually hold in society.[9]

Far from being simply a psychological aberration, elitism in Africa is a source of corruption and bad governance. Both are attitudes that are individualistic and selfish. They lack social conscience because they indicate a lack of concern for the general welfare of the population. Megacorruption by highly placed people in government deprives society of resources that could be used for education and health, for example. But a particularly heinous type of corruption in Africa is when the poor have to pay bribes for essential services in the hospital or in the courts. And since they usually cannot afford to, they have to do without them at the cost of untold suffering and often loss of life or means of sustenance.

The arrogance that elitist attitudes breed inhibits in Africa the process of democratization because of the above reasons: mindless love for power unrelated to service. It breeds not only corruption but also tendencies of lack of dialogue, a recipe for dictatorial use of authority and power. Although with the fall of some well-known notorious dictators such as Idi Amin, Mobutu Sese Seko, and Jean-Bedel Bokasa and the establishment of multiparty politics democratic consciousness is emerging in Africa, much work still needs to be done in that area.

II. Approaches by African Theologians:
Strengths and Weaknesses

What Is Being Done?

In various ways African theologians are confronting these challenges by showing through creative action the image of the Creator in the African person. They are working to recapture Africa's own particular cultural and religious—and even political and economic—identity. To speak about the blurred or obliterated identity of Africa is to speak about Africa's concrete experience of slavery, colonialism, social degradation, and economic exploitation. Ethical questions in themselves, these have become deeply even more so considering the fact that they have affected negatively the self-perception of the African people, as well as other people's perception of African humanity and value as human beings.

African theologians are also engaged in the struggle for liberty. The struggle for identity is jeopardized where there is no concomitant struggle for liberty which is born of justice. Liberty and justice bring about peace, and peace is the commodity that is in short supply in the African continent in general. Some of the most horrific human tragedies toward the end of the last century and the beginning of this century have taken place in Africa. The genocide in Rwanda in 1994 is one of them, but there have been other pogroms in Liberia, Sierra Leone, Northern Uganda, and Sudan, to mention only a few. Some of these are of long-standing duration and are still going on as the first decade of the new century comes to an end. Somalia has not enjoyed a stable government for almost a generation, and one can only hope that Burundi and the Democratic Republic of the Congo will soon enjoy permanent peace.

All of these create ethical situations, especially when the lack of stability in Africa leaves the continent wide open to all kinds of unscrupulous elements: from illegal sale of arms to mercenaries causing grief for money or sport; from fraudulent corporations whose activities destroy the environment to fake religious groups whose hidden agenda is spiritual and economic exploitation; from organizations that exploit Africa's vulnerability—such as the HIV/AIDS situation—for their own economic benefit to the much vaunted, but for Africa in general essentially oppressive, movement referred to as globalization. African moral theologians are addressing these issues as well.

Theological Approaches

In tackling these situations, African theologians have followed two main approaches: the *liberation* and *inculturation* orientations. The former orientation has usually addressed mainly the socio-economic and political aspect of the African situation, within which the feminist/womanist liberation movement has concerned itself with the question of gender oppression. The latter—the inculturation orientation—has dealt largely with the socio-religious dimension.

African liberation theologians[10] have pointed out in their writings the connection between the Good News of Jesus Christ and political freedom and economic well-being, pointing as validation to Jesus' own description of his mission, for example in the Gospel according to Luke (4:18–19) and that according to Matthew (25:31–46). But they have also relied heavily on the message of the prophets of the Hebrew Scriptures, the Old Testament, as well as the writings of the early fathers of the church, from whom Catholic social teaching since the end of the nineteenth century has largely been derived. Because of the elitism, bad governance, and corruption we have discussed above, the advocacy by African liberation theologians for justice has not been readily acceptable by those in power, especially after the end of colonialism. Liberation theologians have often been accused by their governments of meddling in politics, and some have had to pay with their lives for their convictions. The Ugandan bishop Janani Luwum is an example, but there are other less known instances. Even much more painful has been the fact that many more have been silenced by their own churches in collusion with government authorities.

The inculturation theologians have not been spared a kind of "martyr-dom" from their own churches. Advocating for the dignity of African cultures as a worthy vehicle for the revelation of the divine in Africa and African religious identity, they have sometimes suffered censure from church authorities. Inculturation in Africa, with the exception of the African Initiated Churches, has not made any significant headway because of this, to the detriment of truly enrooting the Christian faith in the continent.[11]

Strengths and Weaknesses

Both liberation and inculturation theologians in Africa have made important contributions in the general awareness of Christians both in Africa and abroad of the role of Africa in world Christianity. Also, they have tried to make the Christian churches conscious of the role of the Christian faith in the integral liberation of Africa. If the gap between faith and action has narrowed in Christian peoples' understanding of their faith in many places in Africa, it is certainly partly due to the work of African theologians.

It must be said, however, that far too many theologians of liberation and inculturation have not realized sufficiently that their respective theological orientations and approaches are only two sides of the same coin. Inculturation is an aspect of the total liberation of the continent, and liberation cannot be comprehensive without inculturation. It has been a failure in coordination, but it is slowly being overcome. Also, African theologians have perhaps been too "academic," by which I mean that they have not integrated themselves enough into the lives of the people. In this way, they have perhaps unwittingly perpetuated the elitist attitude they should have resisted with their words and actions.

Through integration at the grassroots level, theologians would have become better voices for the voiceless and better representatives of the "wretched of the earth," to borrow Franz Fanon's expression. They would have become more credible advocates for the sufferings of the excluded humanity. In theological terms, they would have been engaged in the ministry of prophecy so well represented by the prophets of the Hebrew Scriptures. Looking at reality from a Christian perspective, if there is one comprehensive need in African society today, it is the need for prophecy in its double role of denunciation and affirmation: denouncing the evils we have enumerated above and affirming any and all efforts that seek to affirm the dignity and humanity of the African person. But these are in short supply among African theologians. If they are teachers, they need to do so by example in the circumstances of contemporary Africa.

It is vitally important that theologians also sometimes speak and act in concert, as a community, especially in matters that touch society fundamentally. We are not here advocating robbing the individual theologian of her/his personal voice; we are simply cautioning against too much individualism and personal cultism, which can happen in theological academia in many parts of the world. The strength of community is still recognized and valued in Africa, and it should not be disregarded by theologians. Instead, it should be put to use for the sake of building God's reign already here and now.

III. Recommendations

The situation I have outlined in Africa challenges theologians in two major ways. One is to influence minds, especially church leaders, to look at the African predicament as an ethical issue and devise ways to address this issue in the process of ongoing catechesis. It is a challenge of Christian imagination. The other is practical: to engage directly in the process of change themselves. The latter is possible in Africa through theologians engaging in the activities of small Christian communities as pastors, spiritual directors, and chaplains. What are the prospects for each of these approaches?

Although it has made some impact in some academic institutions in Africa, it cannot be said that African theology addressing the challenges we have mentioned facing the continent has had much influence on church leaders in Africa. The seminaries are the problem in the case of priests. Sadly, social analysis is hardly part of the theological curricula. Philosophy, not anthropology and sociology, is still overly emphasized as a prerequisite for theology. As a result, the practical side of theology does not get enough attention. As far as the hierarchy is concerned, little time is devoted to theological updating, so that many bishops do not get to hear or understand what African theologians are saying about issues.

Most African theologians genuinely interested in Africa's ethical challenges are working in institutions of higher learning, in Africa or overseas. As I mentioned earlier, very few are engaged at the grassroots level with the people. This means that little new theological thought gets to this level where it is needed most. So the prospects of tackling the issues in a practical and broad-based way are not yet very bright, from my point of view. This is not to say that some changes are not happening, but they are coming all too little, too slowly. The pace of change in the world today would indicate a different commitment: the need for greater, more decisive, and rapid advances in thinking and action. But this needs some restructuring of vision in the Church. This is also taking too long in coming. One reason is that there is still too much control of theological imagination and thought by church authorities, so that many African theologians can be called "court theologians." What is needed in the theological community is the freedom of the mind to serve God's reign by their thought and life.

Sébastien Muyengo Mulombe

Authenticity and Credibility

Moral Challenges after the African Synod

By a happy chance, this academic meeting is taking place on the tenth anniversary of the African Synod. Coinciding with the movement to see the establishment of democracy, many of our bishops, having been chairs of national episcopal conferences, participated in the synod, which became a tremendous source of hope for the continent.[1] Since then, however, despite some places that warrant hope, Africa has plunged more deeply day by day into crisis and desolation.[2]

I am grateful to the organizers of this symposium for offering me the opportunity for reflection. I shall revisit the synod in order to underline the ethical challenges that *Ecclesia in Africa* offered us a decade ago and that have lost none of their relevance today.

My essay has two parts. My starting point is a survey of the situation of the continent—a situation of urgency, just as the apostolic exhortation described it ten years ago. I shall then highlight some of the major challenges with which this situation confronts us. I conclude with a note of hope for the continent, indicating the resources and methods on which moral theology can draw in its response to the challenges I have outlined.

1. A Man by the Wayside

At the heart of the apostolic exhortation *Ecclesia in Africa*, we find a question that cannot leave any preacher of the gospel indifferent: How can the Christian message be the "Good News" in Africa? The document takes up this theme by showing how the continent is saturated with bad news—a terrible distress in almost every country, poor administration of the scarce resources that are available, political instability, and societal disorientation, etc. These result in famine, wars, and despair (cf. EIA 40).

Africa is then compared to the man who went down from Jerusalem to Jericho and fell into the hands of robbers who stripped him, inflicted blows on him, and then went off, leaving him half-dead (Luke 10:30–37). This man is the image of those innumerable African men and women, children and young people today, who are stretched out (so to speak) by the wayside, sick, wounded, powerless, marginalized, and abandoned (see EIA 41a). In the last decades, Africa has been the scene of fratricidal wars which decimate the population and destroy their natural and cultural riches. In addition to causes external to Africa, this painful phenomenon has also internal causes, such as "tribalism . . . and the thirst for power taken to extremes by totalitarian regimes which trample with impunity on the rights and dignity of the person. Peoples crushed and reduced to silence suffer as innocent and resigned victims all these situations of injustice" (EIA 117a).

In a world controlled by the rich and powerful nations, Africa has in practice become an unimportant appendage, often forgotten, and neglected by everyone (EIA 40). Where are we to look for the Good Samaritan who will deliver the wounded man from this impasse, so that he can regain his ability to react properly and rediscover the resources that nourish his humanity (EIA 41b)? In the perspective of the new evangelization, this is an immense challenge to the preachers of the Good News. John Paul II asks: "How could one proclaim Christ on that immense continent while forgetting that it is one of the world's poorest regions? How could one fail to take into account the anguished history of a land where many nations are still in the grip of famine, war, racial and tribal tensions, political instability and the violation of human rights?" (EIA 51).

2. That the Wretched Man May Not Die of His Wounds

The apostolic exhortation *Ecclesia in Africa* cites a number of challenges, including the new evangelization, the construction of a church which is the authentic family of God, the taking of our lives into our own hands, and the need for solidarity, justice, peace, and development. Bearing in mind the internal and external causes of the ills that afflict us, we can divide these challenges into two overarching categories.

The Challenge of Credibility

This challenge is generated by the internal causes of our distress in Africa. The testimony of our own lives is in fact an essential requirement, if our preaching is to be effective (see EIA 21c) and if society is to be genuinely transformed and become morally healthy. The challenge that is addressed to us as the church is expressed in three question: "Do you really believe what you are proclaiming? Do you live what you believe? Do you really preach what you live?" (EIA 21).

This question has a profound ethical relevance both to the preaching of the Gospel and to the words spoken by the elite of society (which includes moral theologians). A question like this gives us a criterion to evaluate our credibility with regard to the many development plans that have been drawn up to extricate our countries from distress and poverty; with regard to the forums for dialogue which have been set up in many of our countries in order to leave the wars behind and to build up a society where peace reigns; and with regard to pastoral options for the construction of the church as the family of God, which is our primary concern today. The same criterion can be applied to many other options that have been chosen in our local churches, where the fruit is not always visible.

Church as family, solidarity, sharing . . . is this an "option," a "pastoral project," or just one more slogan to add to the many to which we have become accustomed in the tropics? What *is* a "church as family" when some have everything they need for life while the majority stagnate in misery? What is a "church as family" when a person is not accepted for the simple reason that he comes from somewhere else? What is a "church as family" when unity, brotherhood, and peace are compromised by intolerance, suspicion, a lack of confidence in one another, the inability to forgive, or the spirit of revenge?

The family has always been a major theme of Christian theology, and I suspect that it was the idyllic picture of the African family that inspired the synod fathers to choose this project. We must believe in this project; we must believe that it can indeed be realized. But a number of conditions must first be met, not least the profound evangelization that entails a conversion of hearts and a purification of customs and behavior. This is the ethical dimension of the problem. When we note the reasons that lead to wars in Africa, the egoism that impoverishes us, or the favoritism and tribalism that still influence our relationships—even within the church—the danger is that the project of "church as family" may remain a pious wish, without any impact on the life of our communities.

Two examples can illustrate this problem.

First, before the genocide in 1994, Rwanda had the reputation of being 60 percent Christian. How is it possible that these people who lived and prayed together on their mountains came to commit the "sin of Cain," this tremendous scandal that we call genocide?

Second, my own country, Congo, is one of those African countries that have benefited from a large-scale Christian educational infrastructure. How is it possible that this elite, formed under the fire of the gospel, does not always succeed in bearing witness to what it has received, in order to transform the popular mentality and thus promote the common good, lasting peace, the unity of the peoples, etc.?

The crisis that we are experiencing in many of our countries can be seen to be a crisis of *morality*. More and more, a situation ethics is plunging society into what Pope John Paul II used to call "the structure of evil or of sin," that is, a situation in which people lose all motivation to seek what is good, true, beautiful, or just. This makes it a moral duty to work for the purification of our entire environment. We must help Christians and other citizens of goodwill to be what scripture calls "the remnant of Yahweh," that is, those who in a crisis refuse to resort to tricks or easy ways out; they stand firm and do not allow themselves to be swept away by the waves of history. Where everything is collapsing, there must be some people who put up a resistance, for otherwise there is no hope for the rebirth of a new society through a new generation and a new culture—the culture of the good, the beautiful, the true, and the just. This is what it means to be a Christian: in a situation of crisis (and especially of moral crisis), one should not be afraid or ashamed to swim against the current. One should not be afraid or ashamed to proclaim one's membership in the church, or to appeal to the gospel. And one must take care that the implications of what one says never contradict one's faith and one's convictions.[3]

The Challenge of Authenticity

When he visited Malawi in 1989, Pope John Paul II issued to the African people what we might call the challenge of authenticity, which consists in rejecting a way of life that does not correspond to the best elements in our traditions and in our Christian faith: "Many people in Africa look beyond Africa for the so-called 'freedom of the modern way of life.' Today I urge you to look inside yourselves. Look to the riches of your own traditions, look to the faith which we are celebrating in this assembly. Here you will find genuine freedom—here you will find Christ who will lead you to the truth" (quoted in EIA 48).

In the so-called age of globalization, which we in Africa see as a form of westernization, we can identify three areas in which this challenge must be faced. First of all, we have the ethical dimension of life itself, the family, sexuality, and marriage. Confronted with the materialism and utilitarianism which the Western world imposes on us, African morality proposes a morality of gift. We are determined to preserve this, since it is essential for the survival of our own people and of humanity as a whole. For if Africa has something great, beautiful, and noble to contribute to the world, something it shares in common with the Christian understanding of life, it is surely this truth: namely, that life is the gift par excellence that we receive from the Creator, the gift of nature, of the human species, of the family, of our relatives, of other people. A gift is something that one receives gratuitously; there is no price to be paid. This is why it is so costly. What counts is not its material value but what it symbolizes. This is the meaning that Africans attach to life and to everything that contributes to life: love, sex, family ties, the family, the body, relationships, etc. From this standpoint, there is no need to draw up an elaborate casuistry with regard to urgent problems such as contraception, abortion, euthanasia, the prolongation of life by medical means, etc. In Africa, when a new life is conceived, we wait for it. When it is born, we welcome it. When it declines, we support it. And when it finally departs, we accompany it.[4]

Obviously, the second major area where we face the challenge of authenticity is the field where globalization is particularly pronounced, namely, the media. Underdevelopment condemns us to be mere passive recipients, although this is in fact a concert in which all are invited to give *and* to receive. Here too, the challenge of authenticity entails the moral requirement of preparing our people to be able to resist all kinds of trickery—for otherwise it will lose the wealth of our own traditions and of our faith when it opens up to the processes of globalization.

In the sphere of social ethics, our task is to develop systems genuinely adapted to our reality and to our aspirations, when we consider the frequent failures of our economic plans, which have gotten mired down again and again since our countries achieved their independence; or when we consider the failure of the democratic plans, which have collapsed in the face of civil wars, etc. Have we now stopped dreaming of a specifically African path of development? Is an African-style democracy really unthinkable? Are we condemned forever to keep on borrowing the paths taken by others?

Finally, there is the famous question of the African languages. How can we carry out useful work, bring about change, influence the mentality of a people, take charge in the political arena or in the fields of economics or even anthropology when we are condemned to reflect, to think, to learn, and to transmit information, science, knowledge, and, above all, ethical values in a language that is not our own? An example will make this point clear: ten African scholars are speaking at this conference. They come from five different countries, namely, the Democratic Republic of Congo, Kenya, Tanzania, Rwanda, and Uganda. They speak the same language, Swahili. But they are divided by French and English. What applies to all theology applies to moral theology as well: the best way to assimilate the Christian customs, values, and mysteries, in order to transmit them and communicate them in the best manner possible, is in one's own language.

Conclusion

One of my compatriots has written a book with a suggestive and provocative title: "Is Africa going to die?"[5] No, "Africa is not destined for death, but for life!" (EIA 57a). Africa will not die, because it has abundant vitality and energy; it has a tremendous dynamism. If this were not so, it would have already disappeared from the world scene, together with all the agonies it has known in the course of its history. The secret of its survival lies primarily in the faith and hope of its people. Africans are sustained by an unwritten philosophy based on the enjoyment of life, and they believe in the future. No matter what difficulties they may face—hunger, war, natural disasters, etc.— they know how to create mechanisms of self-defense.

It follows that one of the major tasks of moral theology in Africa consists in stimulating the intellectual elite to make the most of these energies, this dynamism, this faith and hope which dwell in the hearts of our people, in order to transform its shame—and the challenge which this shame contains—into an opportunity to eradicate once and for all the virus and pandemic of underdevelopment, and the lack of democracy, peace, justice, etc.

This requires a genetic-praxiological methodology: in other words, it is not enough to observe and criticize the facts of the situation. Rather, we must go deeper, to the genesis of the phenomena, in order to analyze their causes and work efficiently in the struggle to transform society and to change people's behavior and mentalities, drawing on the participation of the individuals and groups concerned in this process. This requires us to popularize the discussions of the ethicists, so that society as a whole may learn what is at stake. Ethical debate fulfills its function only when the individuals or groups who are its primary concern can make the discussion their own in a dialogue with the elite about their existential situation. In our countries, true ethics must be an ethics of liberation which seeks both to awaken the consciousness and sense of responsibility in the elite and to educate and instruct the masses.

If we are to hope for a transformation of society and a change of mentality and behavior, we must look to the people "on the ground," to those on the bottom rung of society, who are the primary and secondary agents of the basic education that children receive. We must look to the pastoral workers who care for children, young people, families, etc. And we must look to the workers in social communications and other members of nongovernmental organizations who have a cultural and educational task, since it is they who are inventing new means of permanent contact with the masses.[6]

Asia

Thomas Hong-Soon Han (Korea)
*Moral Challenges and the Church in Asia Today, with a
Specific Consideration of Korea*

Agnes M. Brazal (Philippines)
*Globalization and Catholic Theological Ethics:
A Southeast Asian Perspective*

Clement Campos, C.Ss.R. (India)
*Doing Christian Ethics in India's World of Cultural
Complexity and Social Inequality*

Thomas Hong-Soon Han covers four topics in his essay. First, he offers
a stunning overview of the challenges facing Asia today. He names
three of them: violations of the right to life, which includes abortion, particularly those done for sex selection; violations of the right to religious freedom; and corruption. Then, he turns to the steps that theological ethicists
take today to first make the connections through the concept of human dignity between prolife church teachings and social ethics. Here we discover the
deep religious impulse behind these teachings, which in turn promote interreligious dialogue. Third, he turns to South Korea and to their church programs through which bishops, theological ethicists, and lay leaders
cooperatively generate concrete strategies for bettering life in that region. He
concludes with a note of hope in which theological reflection, leading to
greater interreligious dialogue, in turn promotes politically a greater respect
for life and human dignity.

Agnes M. Brazal looks at her native country, the Philippines, and neighboring Indonesia to raise up the challenges facing Southeast Asian theological ethicists. In fairly specific terms, Brazal describes how globalization at
once causes yet brings together issues of poverty and migration which inter-
face with issues such as religious fundamentalism and the unjust treatment
of women. In response, theological ethicists propose more integrated models that appropriate insights from local communities and feminist claims.
Other directions include attempts to critically re-examine existing religious
and cultural traditions, proposals to opt for the poor "other," and an Asian

appropriation of human rights claims. Her essay conveys the urgency with which her colleagues work.

Clement Campos takes the context of his India as rife with cultural complexity and social inequality and examines a host of the major issues his nation faces: globalization, environment, access to health care (in a land with great health care resources available), discrimination based on gender caste, and religion, violence, and the failure to recognize human rights. In each instance, he highlights the work of contemporary Indian theological ethicists responding to these needs, but he concludes with outstanding challenges facing today's ethicists: to move both beyond the confines of a seminary setting so as to become involved in political debate on issues of urgent social concern and beyond the search for pastoral solutions so as to offer ethical solutions to the dilemmas that confront individuals; to dialogue with other religions and cultures and the poor so as to participate in humanity's search for the truth by which we all live; and finally to develop a moral theology that is contextualized, truly Indian, authentically human and socially liberative.

Thomas Hong-Soon Han

Moral Challenges and the Church in Asia Today, with a Specific Consideration of Korea

I. Challenges

The Asian continent is home to nearly two-thirds of the world's population with their different cultures, religions, social structures, and political systems. It is a continent of sheer contrasts. While there has been enormous economic and technological progress, there still exist situations of extreme poverty and injustice. Most of the developing countries in Asia are evaluated as least democratic in terms of public sector corruption, respect for human and political rights, and freedom of speech. In fact, in *World Democracy Table*, published by World Audit in October 2005, we find North Korea in 82nd position among 150 states, China in 128th, Vietnam in 138th, and last (in the list) and least democratic is Myanmar (149th).[1]

Violation of the Right to Life

One of the more serious moral issues facing Asia today is the violation of the right to life of the unborn child. In most cases, it has been committed in pursuit of a better material life. According to an estimate, of approximately 46 million abortions annually performed worldwide, 59 percent, that is, 27 million abortions, are carried out in Asia, of which 10 million (37 percent) are illegal.[2] Illegal abortion is associated with unsafe abortion, which is apt to end up in maternal death. In fact, it is estimated that maternal deaths because of unsafe abortions numbered 34,000 in Asia in 2000, accounting for 50 percent of the world total.[3] It can be said that unsafe abortion is a cause and effect of poverty and is also intimately linked to gender inequality.

With the advent of prenatal diagnosis to determine the gender of the fetus, abortion has been focused on the female baby because of a preference for boys over girls that many male-dominated societies have. In fact,

65

sex-selective abortion has become common in areas such as East and South Asia, especially China, India, and Korea. It is evidenced by rising sex ratios at birth, which means that gender discrimination is increasingly extended before birth. "This is high-tech sexism."[4] Victims of gender discrimination both before and after birth, the so-called missing women, number more than 100 million according to an estimate based on the benchmark gender ratio of women to men (1.05).[5] In China alone abortions number 50 million, because of its one-child policy.[6] Thus, abortion, an abominable crime committed against the defenseless human person, is linked with gender discrimination as well.

Asian people live in countries where abortion is legal if pregnancy endangers a woman's life, and three-fourths of the countries in Asia permit abortions to protect a woman's physical and mental health. Abortion is legal virtually for every plausible reason in China, India, Japan, South Korea, North Korea, Cambodia, Mongolia, Singapore, and Vietnam.[7] Regardless of the legal status, however, abortions are performed at any cost. Abortion, "a new Holocaust,"[8] continues to be one of the great modern tragedies. Abortion laws that exist in many countries are clearly in conflict with God's law and the law of nature.

Another form of the violation of the right to life is human embryonic stem-cell research, which destroys the embryo that should be regarded as a human person entitled to all the rights of any human being. When a South Korean scientist Dr. Hwang had claimed in May 2005 to have extracted stem cells from cloned human embryos for the first time in the world, he was immediately considered as a national hero in South Korea. Some observers called this research result a breakthrough, hailing it even as worthy of a Nobel Prize. But it is clear that this kind of research is equivalent to abortion. Although it turned out later that he had falsified scientific data, not a few people still take the side of Dr. Hwang.

Violation of the Right to Religious Freedom

Another serious moral issue facing Asia today is that the vast majority of the people in Asia are not allowed the right to freedom of conscience and religious freedom. In fact, in some countries freedom of religion is severely restricted and religious fundamentalism poses many problems for religious minorities, especially for Christians, while in others, Christians are persecuted outrightly. Many of them are increasingly threatened with their basic security. Not a day passes that the media does not carry reports of such cases happening in Asia.[9]

The evidence is the ongoing religious persecution in China, North Korea, and persecution in various parts of Hindu and Islamic states. The Chinese government insists on state-managed religion: those Christians who refuse to comply are subjected to restrictions, including intimidation, harassment, and detention. In North Korea genuine religious freedom does not exist. In India so-called proselytism is forbidden in several internal states: the murder of Christians and the destruction of churches by mobs are not uncommon. Basic security is threatened. Conversion out of Islam, viewed as apostasy, is either forbidden or regarded as a criminal offense under most state Islamic laws. In Malaysia, "apostates" may be fined, detained, and imprisoned. In Pakistan, Christians constitute a separate electoral college and are subject to the blasphemy law. An affront to the Qur'an, Muhammad, or Islam, however trivial, can place any Christian before a court and exposes all Christians to the danger of public vengeance. In Bangladesh, the situation is somewhat similar.

During the first six years of the twenty-first century, twenty-seven persons (priests, religious, and lay persons),[10] not to mention many more possible "unknown soldiers of God's great cause,"[11] were killed in Asia while engaged in missionary work. Seventeen of them were killed in India, and the rest were killed in Pakistan, Indonesia, Siberia, and the Philippines.

Corruption

A no less serious moral issue facing Asia today is widespread corruption. In many countries corruption is a way of life. For example, "corruption in China has now reached epidemic proportions and few escape the squeeze."[12] The situation is somewhat similar in India.[13] Corruption, an inevitable consequence of the "structures of sin,"[14] has affected different spheres of life, such as political life, the business environment, personal life, and family life. Even in the education sector corruption is present in many countries and is widespread in some countries of South and Southeast Asia.[15] Either on the demand or on the supply side, bribery is a fact of public life. While on the supply side a bribe is offered to avoid problems with the authorities, on the demand side this bribe is tacitly requested or bureaucratic processes are deliberately slowed to solicit grease money.

Anything can be faked, not to mention the top-brand products, ranging from liquor and medicine to TV sets and computers. The largest market in the world of fake products is in Shanghai, China. Fraudulent diplomas and certificates are sold.[16] Counterfeit currencies, sham statistics, often confected by cadres to hide shameful deeds and embarrassing incidents, are not uncommon. Even scientific research results are fabricated, as evidenced in the recent case of Dr. Hwang Woo-Suk in Korea that scandalized the world of science and all the people of goodwill on earth.

According to the World Bank's World Business Environment Survey conducted during 1998–2000, the percentage of firms that offered bribery payments appears to be highest in Asia (except in developed Asia) among the world's regions: 65 percent in South Asia, 62 percent in developing East Asia, whereas 52 percent in Africa, 33 percent in Central and Eastern Europe, and 28 percent in Latin America and the Caribbean.[17]

In terms of the Corruption Perceptions Index score, which ranges between 10 (highly clean) and 0 (highly corrupted), compiled by Transparency International (TI) for the year 2005 for 159 countries, most of the Asian countries ranked rather "highly corrupted" with the score ranging between 3.8 and 1.7. For example, China ranked 78th with the score 3.2, India 88th with the score 2.9.[18]

In the twelve Asian countries surveyed by Gallup International for TI in 2005,[19] political parties, parliament/legislature, police, and tax revenue are considered the most corrupt institutions. More than 50 percent of citizens from the Philippines, Taiwan, Indonesia, India, South Korea, and Thailand perceive that corruption affects political life to a larger extent. As political life is closely related with the business environment, more than 50 percent of citizens from the Philippines, South Korea, and Taiwan feel that business has been adversely affected by corrupted practices.

II. Responses

Basic Arguments

In the face of such moral challenges, theological ethicists in Asia have made various efforts, first of all, to fight against the "culture of death." They argue that "the common outcry, which is justly made on behalf of human rights . . . is false and illusory if the right to life, the most basic and fundamental right and the condition for all other personal rights, is not defended with maximum determination."[20] For them, these efforts represent their desire "to safeguard the moral conditions for an authentic human ecology."[21]

They stand up against the ethical relativism that justifies the violation of fundamental human rights in the name of democracy. Truth cannot be determined by a parliamentary or social majority. "Democracy cannot be idolized to the point of making it a substitute for morality or a panacea for immorality. . . . Its 'moral' value is not automatic but depends on conformity to the moral law to which it, like every other form of human behavior, must be subject. . . . The value of democracy stands or falls with the values which it embodies and promotes."[22]

Emphasis is laid on the respect for the dignity of the person, which implies the defense and promotion of human rights. The dignity of the person should be respected in every phase of development from conception until natural death. "The inviolability of the person which is a reflection of the absolute inviolability of God, finds its primary and fundamental expression in the inviolability of human life."[23]

All offences against life itself, such as abortion and euthanasia; all offences against human dignity, such as subhuman living conditions, the selling of women and children, degrading working conditions where men are treated as mere tools for profit rather than free and responsible persons; all these and the like are certainly criminal: they poison human society, and they do more harm to those who practice them than to those who suffer from the injury. Moreover, they are a supreme dishonor to the Creator.[24]

Respect for the dignity of the human person demands the recognition of the religious dimension of the individual, whose relation to God is "a constitutive element of the very 'being' and 'existence' of an individual."[25] "Religious freedom, an essential requirement of the dignity of every person, is a cornerstone of the structure of human rights, and for this reason an irreplaceable factor in the good of individuals and of the whole of society, as well as of the personal fulfillment of each individual. It follows that the freedom of individuals and of communities to profess and practice their religion is an essential element for peaceful human coexistence. . . . The civil and social right to religious freedom, inasmuch as it touches the most intimate sphere of the spirit, is a point of reference for the other fundamental rights and in some way becomes a measure of them."[26]

Corruption debases and debilitates the human person and society, thereby deteriorating the human ecology. Cause and effect of the corruption are structures of sin, which are characterized by an all-consuming desire for profit and the thirst for power.[27] The profusion of fraudulence and chicanery is a millstone around the neck of political modernization. Corruption undermines also the moral foundation of market economy, which presupposes a basic level of honesty and trustworthiness. Apart from its negative moral aspect, recent empirical evidence attests that corruption lowers economic growth.[28] Thus, various forms of corruption contribute to poverty.

Promoting Interreligious Dialogue and Cooperation

These arguments are clearly in line with traditional Asian values that give priority to respect for life, humanity, and righteousness in relationships of human beings in society. In fact, Confucianism emphasizes that "life" originates from the interaction between heaven and earth, and it considers *ren* (humanity or humaneness), which means "loving human beings,"[29] as the supreme virtue. Buddhism states that all things are inextricably interconnected and mutually interpenetrated on the basis of the principle of dependent origination and advocates not only respect for human life but also respect for all forms of life, insisting on the precept of *ahimsa* (noninjury, or nonviolence). Thus, Christianity and these Asian religions share many elements in common in their moral precepts. For example, all of them share the ethics of reciprocity. That is to say, the so-called Christian Golden Rule, "Treat others as you would like them to treat you,"[30] finds its equivalent, albeit expressed in a negative way, in Confucianism ("What you do not wish for yourself, do not impose on others"[31]), and in Buddhism ("Treat not others in ways that yourself would find hurtful"[32]). Such a fact can thus serve as a valid basis for Christianity to engage in dialogue and cooperation with these religions for the sake of the common good of all people.

Channels for Ethicists' Activities

In addressing these moral challenges, the Catholic theological ethicists have played an important role: announcing the gospel of life in their respective local situations while denouncing the injustices and violations of human rights; imparting the church's social teachings, while applying these to their local situations.

These activities are carried out through their research and lecture at the university and institute, through their efficient utilization of mass media, and through their active participation in various activities undertaken by organizations such as the Office of Human Development of the Federation of the Asian Bishops' Conferences, local bishops' conferences, various national and diocesan committees, including justice and peace committees, various religious congregations and their associations, and various lay associations and movements. In these activities, they have also sought to engage in dialogue and cooperation with the people of other churches and religions. In fact, these activities have served as an effective channel for interreligious as well as ecumenical dialogue and cooperation.

Emphasis has been placed on the formation and inspiration of the people, with a view to realizing a social reform. Social reform in any valuable sense must include reform of institutions as well as of the spiritual attitude of the individual. Institutions and individuals interact with one another. There is urgent need for conversion of individuals to reform the social structures, which in turn should be reformed to induce them to live a more human life.

Social formation has been given to seminarians and priests, religious, and the laity. Special attention needs to be paid to social formation of the laity. It is their task to animate temporal realities with Christian commitment, by which they show that they are witnesses and agents of the culture of life, justice, and peace. There is urgent need for social formation of lay leaders, who are supposed to take part in the decision-making process of government, businesses, trade unions, and other private and public organizations.

III. Experiences in Korea

Various Episcopal Committees

The Committee for Justice and Peace, the Committee for Family Pastoral, and the Bioethics Committee of the Bishops' Conference, and their counterparts at the diocesan level are major channels for Catholic theological ethicists to carry out their proper role in addressing the above-mentioned moral challenges. In fact, the ethicists' role has been pivotal in the activities of these episcopal committees, in the discernment and decision making, and in the formation programs. For example, they have contributed both to the annual publication of messages for the Human Rights Sunday, the Day for Life, and the Week for Sanctification of the Family, which have been celebrated every year in the church in Korea, and to the publication of occasional papers of these committees.[33] These documents have served as a valid instrument for the conscientization of the people toward their responsibility for life, their responsibility to respect human rights, and their responsibility to combat corruption. They have also served as a useful means to insist that human rights, especially religious freedom, be allowed in North Korea.

In addition to these documents, another instrument that deserves mention is the annual message prepared by the Catholic Lay Apostolate Council of Korea to celebrate the Sunday for the Laity. This message has been used as the basic text for the homily delivered by a lay person on this Sunday.

School of the Social Doctrine

Since 1995, the School of the Social Doctrine has been run by the Archdiocese of Seoul, Korea. This school offers three levels of courses, each consisting of two-hour sessions per week for ten weeks, every Monday evening. The first level consists in the study of the social encyclicals and *Gaudium et Spes*; the second level consists in systematic study of the fundamental principles of social doctrine; the third level consists in the practical application to the concrete cases in the various fields. So far, about 1,300 religious and lay faithful participated in the first level; about 600 in the second level; about 300 in the third level.

Committee for Life

While Dr. Hwang's embryonic stem-cell research result was hailed as a "revolution" in May 2005 and gained massive financial support from the government, the bishops in Korea publicly criticized it, pointing out that it is definitely anti-life. They stated: "Even though it is cloned, an embryo is a human life and therefore it is against the dignity of the person to conduct experiments on or to manipulate the human embryo."[34]

Later the Seoul Archdiocese established the Committee for Life October 2005. The purpose of this committee is to promote adult stem-cell research as the alternative to embryonic stem-cell research and spread the gospel of life. This committee will raise the "Fund for the Mystery of Life" of 10 billion *won* (about US$ 10 million) in order to support research into the use of adult stem cells, instead of embryonic stem cells, to treat several serious diseases. All the faithful of the diocese will join in the contribution of 100 *won* (about 10 cents) a day to this fund, which will serve as a kind of matching fund to induce contributions from non-Catholic sources as well. To encourage such research, this committee will also award an annual "Mystery of Life Prize" to the one who has performed brilliant achievements in adult stem-cell research, starting this year. The award will be 300 million *won* (about US$ 300,000).

Reform-oriented Action

Formation must lead to action, which is needed to reform society. For example, the church in Korea conducted an anti-abortion signature campaign and an anti–death penalty signature campaign in close cooperation with the people of other churches and religions. The Catholic Lay Apostolate Council of Korea, for its part, in addition to actively joining in these campaigns, has conducted its own campaigns in society, such as the *mea culpa* campaign and the "act properly" campaign. These campaigns are intended to convince all people, Catholics and non-Catholics alike, of the need to change their own mentality, behavior, mode of existence in order to realize social reform.

International Solidarity

Since most of the social matters have a worldwide dimension in this era of globalization, action for social reform requires the participation of all people of goodwill on the globe. Some matters require especially solidarity of the international community. The above-mentioned organizations have pursued international alliances as well, either on the Asian level or on the global level.

IV. Hopes for the Future

Since Catholics are a tiny minority in Asia, one may legitimately ask: Could we effectively address those moral challenges? Could we realize social reform? In reply to this query, there are solid reasons to feel that we may be optimistic. Some may be prejudiced against our ideas in view of their source, but those ideas, if only properly presented, must carry a considerable appeal on the basis of their intrinsic value. Moreover, many Catholics have given heroic witness to the gospel even in a life of suffering and martyrdom. "The Church's social message will gain credibility more immediately from the witness of actions than as a result of its internal logic and consistency."[35] We are profoundly grateful for this example and this gift. They are indeed hope for Asia.

We must join in action organizations or establish them, if necessary, and work together with all people of goodwill, regardless of their religious adherence. True Christians seek to be positive. They never confine their concern to denunciation of the world's evils. They seek to be positive and active. Confronted with evils, they look for causes and solutions, not merely occasions to criticize. If they find some obstacles in the way to reform, they are not discouraged, but explore other ways. They expect failures, and yet keep trying, while "[being] constant in joyfully accepted trials and praying with trust to obtain from God the gift of wisdom, thanks to which we succeed in understanding that the true values of life are not in transitory riches."[36]

Agnes M. Brazal

Globalization and Catholic Theological Ethics

A Southeast Asian Perspective

In representing Asia, I will try to highlight the Southeast Asian context and responses of those doing theological ethics, particularly in the Philippines and Indonesia.

The overarching experience in relation to which one can adequately discuss any moral challenge today is the phenomenon of globalization. Because the term has become so loaded with meaning, I find it necessary to clarify that I am using it to refer to the intensification in the speed with which information, service, capital, and goods are now exchanged across national borders. As primarily a cultural phenomenon, made possible by developments in instantaneous global communication and mass transportation,[1] globalization is not a monolithic process but an ambivalent one bringing in its wake some new challenges as well as new dimensions to traditional moral problems.

I. Moral Challenges

Poverty/Ecological Destruction/Migration

With the fall of most communist-ruled states, the phenomenon of economic globalization today takes the form of global capitalism. While this neoliberal market economy has led to progress in some societies—the Asian tigers, such as Hong Kong, South Korea, Taiwan, and Singapore, and the cubs, such as Thailand and Malaysia—other Asian nations continue to experience large-scale poverty. Ecological destruction (e.g., deforestation of Southeast Asia) has resulted from this widespread poverty and the capitalist system of economic development.

The widening gap between Asian societies has also led to massive internal and external migration in the economically underdeveloped sectors.

According to a 2004 report of the International Labor Organization (ILO), 22.1 million or one-fourth of the 86 million economically active migrants worldwide are in Asia. Most of labor migration in Asia occurs within and is necessary to maintain the competitiveness of the tiger and cub economies. In Southeast Asia (as well as East Asia), migration has increased seven times between 1980 and 2000.[2] Almost half of those migrating into Malaysia and Thailand are illegal. Migration poses a moral challenge as migrant workers are mainly deployed in 3D (dirty, dangerous, difficult) jobs and are often victims of various forms of discrimination (racism/ethnocentrism, unfair labor practices, sexual harassment, etc.).

Ethnic Polarization/Religious Extremism

While religious-cultural diversity has traditionally characterized Asia, globalization processes (e.g., weakening of nation-states) have fueled the rise of local nationalist movements. There are ongoing Muslim secessionist struggles in the Philippines, Indonesia, and Thailand, and communal flare-ups have erupted against the ethnic Chinese in Indonesia, especially from 1995 to 2000. The Islamic resurgence in Malaysia in the seventies and eighties, together with discrimination in favor of the largely Muslim Malays, has led to increased ethnic polarization and gradual erosion of non-Muslims' religious rights.[3]

While Catholic fundamentalism is strong in the Philippines, Islamic religious extremism is on the rise as well in the region. In recent years, there has developed the unfortunate tendency toward religious segregation as Muslims were instructed not to mix with Christians or express Christmas greetings, thereby pushing back the level of intercultural dialogue in Indonesia[4] and some parts of the southern Philippines.

Fundamentalism is problematic because, in its intolerance of ambiguity, it fosters unconsciously or consciously violence toward the "other" or the one who is "different."

Gender Stereotyping/Violence against Women

The problem of gender stereotyping/violence against women, buttressed by religious anthropologies, has regrettably remained with us in the twenty-first century and has assumed new forms within the global context. Asian women now constitute the "fastest growing category of international migrant workers" (also referred to as the feminization of migration). This is partly due to the need for foreign domestic workers in East and Southeast Asia (Singapore, Thailand, and Malaysia), to allow local women to work in the paid labor market.[5] Thus, while migration has equalized work opportunities and mobility for women and men, it is questionable to what extent this is really promoting gender equality since women migrants are concentrated in specific jobs (domestic work, care giving, and sexual entertainment), which are not only unprotected sectors but also simply extensions of the gender division of labor at home.

Capitalist commodification of life also reinforces the traditional notion that women are the property of men and perpetuates violence against women in the form of wife battering, sex selection of children through abortion and infanticide (India and China), and sex trafficking. Sexual violence continues to be used as a tool in ethnic warfare as in the gang raping and sexual harassment of hundreds of Chinese women in the Indonesian 1998 communal flare-up. Common too among various types of religious extremism is the insistence on preserving patriarchal family values and the traditional roles of women in particular. The implementation of Islamic *Shariah* in Aceh requiring women to wear the veil has increased sexual harassment, with some men forcibly cutting the hair of those without a veil.[6]

II. Catholic Theological Ethicists' Responses

As interlinked within the economic and cultural processes of globalization, the above moral challenges demand holistic and integrated approaches to their solutions.

A More Multidimensional Analysis of Globalization

The phenomenon of increasing poverty in some countries on the one hand and the rise of Asian tiger economies on the other have challenged Southeast Asian theological ethicists to go beyond dependency theories which had been the traditional dialogue partner of liberation theologies/ethics. Dependency theory posits that dependency and development cannot co-exist. The progress of the Asian tigers proved this supposition wrong.

Dominador Bombongan explores globalization theories (Wallerstein, Anthony Giddens, Roland Robertson) that help provide a more holistic analysis of our changing economic and political conditions.[7] Without trivializing the system of unequal function and exchange between core, semi-periphery, and periphery within the capitalist world system (Wallerstein), a number of Southeast Asian theological ethicists[8] have appropriated more the multidimensional approach of the sociologist Anthony Giddens. Giddens posits that while the earlier phases of globalization were characterized by a one-way imperialism, the current phase (late modernity) is a two-way process that involves three basic factors—the global, the local, and the personal. This is made possible by the transformation of time-space interactions in late modernity, making possible "action at a distance." This means that due to the development of instantaneous global communication and mass transportation, a far-away event can have immediate impact on one's locale, and the community response can shape as well the further unfolding of that event. Daily activities are influenced by events happening on the other side of the world and likewise, what we do on the local level can have global consequences

Giddens's ten-point agenda for a postcapitalist order includes, among others, encouraging social movements and drawing from indigenous resources, sustaining family ties while undermining patriarchy, as well as critically welcoming the assistance of businesses, states, and international agencies that are sensitive to local sentiments and protective of the environment.[9]

The ethicist Eduard Kimman, who resided in Indonesia for ten years, seems to follow this same line as he emphasizes the moral responsibility of corporations and the need for the church to develop a moral sense among those working in the private sector. Likewise, he underlines that economic development should not mean the abandonment of traditional values and religion.[10]

While affirming the need to confront global capitalism which causes economic polarization, Southeast Asian theological ethicists recognize that other types of struggles (against gender, racial, religious discrimination, etc.) are no less vital. Percy Bacani, for instance, underlines the importance of the feminist values of mutuality and partnership in all relations (in contrast to sheer complementarity) as "an alternative and corrective to the excluding and marginalizing character of globalization today."[11] Within a similar multidimensional approach, Aloysius Cartagenas directs his critique not only to external factors that produce poverty, such as the structural adjustment program imposed by the IMF-WB, but, in the context of widespread corruption in the country, he also focuses on the importance of inculcating a sense for the common good among Filipinos and for understanding citizenship as an expression of discipleship and a path to holiness. Basic ecclesial communities, he posits, should function as "democratic communities that search for and envision the common good" and must serve as forums where the voices of the marginalized can be heard.[12]

Renewing the Support of Asian Religious-Cultural Traditions

The globalization theorist Roland Robertson noted the importance of symbolic responses to and interpretation of globalization in shaping its trajectory.[13] The Catholic social tradition and the Scriptures, in particular, have been a central source for moral theologians of ethical norms and "images" necessary for what Fausto Gomez calls "good globalization/localization,"[14] or what Romeo Intengan refers to as a "socially responsible market economy."[15] Gomez reappropriates the teaching of St. Thomas on justice, property, and the poor in today's context and argues that "'superfluous goods' belong in justice to the poor."[16] He likewise rereads the Eucharist in relation to global justice,[17] while Dionisio Miranda draws on the food images and feeding stories in Scripture to critically evaluate transgenic food being hailed by agribusiness transnational corporations as a solution to world hunger resulting from poverty.[18]

Option for the Poor "Other"/Suffering Victims as Moral Criterion

Since the 1970s, Asian bishops have identified the option for the poor as a basic principle of mission in Asia.[19] Underlining the fact that the experience of poverty in Asia interweaves with cultural and religious identities and any attempt to eradicate poverty must take seriously Asia's religiousness, Carlos Ronquillo proposes a broadening of the "option for the poor" to an "option for the poor other." The "other" includes the "oppressed, the 'non-person,' the 'non-christian,' the 'uncultured,' the women and children."[20] Whereas, traditionally, the subject of moral responsibility is the autonomous, conscious, rational, and free person, in this heteronomous perspective, which appropriates as well insights from the philosopher Emmanuel Levinas and the ethicist Enrique Dussel, the breakthrough comes not primarily from within but from the outside, that is, via meeting with the "other." This option for the poor "other," Ronquillo emphasizes, involves a triple dialogue with the poor, the living cultures, and the religions of Asia.[21]

Drawing on the resources of Indonesian culture, J. B. Banawiratma situates the importance of giving priority to the victims, the oppressed, particularly women, within the holistic Javanese worldview, which values participation and feeling for the whole. Banawiratma critiques the traditional Javanese focus on harmony within a hierarchical collective order. He builds, however, on its liberating strands such as the practice of *musyawarah* (communal consultation and consensus) and its feel for the cosmic order. Within this worldview, sensitivity to the demands of feminists will lead, according to him, to the betterment not only of women but also of men and the community as a whole.[22]

Banawiratma likewise critically appropriates the Indonesian *Pancisala* philosophy, influential in ancient Hindu kingdoms in Sumatra and Java, for a development ethics that strives to reduce all forms of suffering. *Pancisala* philosophy consists of the following five principles: belief in one Supreme God, humanism, national unity, Indonesian-style democracy, and social justice.[23]

While not explicitly referring to the "option for the poor other," Cristina Astorga pleads for freeing poor couples from burdening further their conscience when they opt to use artificial methods of birth regulation in their desire to provide a decent life to their children. She argues that the distinction between natural and artificial approaches to family planning should not be taken as ethically decisive.[24]

Human/Cultural Rights of the Other

The challenge of migration/ethnic conflicts/religious extremism brings to the fore as well the need to address the question of human/cultural rights, most especially of minorities. It is worth noting that Asia is the only major region in the world without its own version of a human rights instrument.[25]

Roland Tuazon explores the uneasy relationship between human rights viewed as an expression of the individualistic Western mentality and the more communitarian values of (Asian) religions, for instance. He underlines the need to recognize that both human rights and religious values are rooted in divergent philosophical foundations (e.g., the religious ethos vs. secular perspective, the community vs. the individual). Following Alasdair MacIntyre, on the one hand, he argues that any ethical rationality (including human rights discourse) is based in a particular tradition. Appropriating Martha Nussbaum, on the other hand, he stresses that religions must be open as well to the critique of other particular traditions of rationality. The human rights discourse can thus challenge religious traditions from its particular standpoint and vice-versa, they can mutually enrich each other. Tuazon further posits that a global ethics based on a "necessary minimum" of common values, criteria, and basic attitudes remains viable, when this is understood as a "historical and revisable guide for the ongoing conversations between religions or particular traditions of rationality."[26] This implies a need to strengthen efforts at interreligious dialogues.

Banawiratma, on the other hand, underlines that human rights are "universal demands and are not merely the product of Western liberal thinking."[27] Human rights should not be viewed as a priori demands but as emerging from a history of suffering, which leads to the formulation of "do-not" imperatives. The Indian economist Amartya Sen also argues that in antiquity, one finds anticipatory components of human rights (such as freedom and tolerance as individual entitlement) not only in Western but also in Asian religions. Speaking against those Westerners who argue that the human rights discourse is a peculiarly Western contribution, Sen points out that they "often give ammunition to the non-Western critics of human rights. The advocacy of an allegedly 'alien' idea in non-Western societies can indeed look like cultural imperialism sponsored by the West."[28]

Presupposing the globalization of human rights discourse and noting the fact that Asian countries eventually reaffirmed the declaration of human rights in the Vienna conference, Graziano Battistella focuses on the specific issue of the rights of migrants. He situates his discussion of the universal and Asian churches' teaching on the protection of the rights of migrants in the ecclesiological view of migrants as "icon of the Church"—"the Other who calls us into communion within diversity."[29] This image goes beyond the simple view of the migrant as "needy" and underscores that their presence can enrich host societies as well.

In my latest article, I explore the largely underdeveloped notion of cultural right in the context of migration.[30] It appropriates Pierre Bourdieu's concept of cultural practice as shaped by both *habitus* (cultural unconscious) and fields of power to highlight cultural right as the right to self-expression, development, and identity, of an individual-in-social relation. In a critical dialogue with Will Kymlicka, a liberal theorist of multiculturalism, I examine as well the possibility of speaking of group-specific cultural rights for immigrants (e.g., in the context of Malaysia, the right to equal allocation of grounds for religious worship). It proposes the Trinitarian model characterized by relationality, equality in diversity, and creativity/fecundity as theological basis for cultural rights. The Trinity is conceived here as a communion of diverse *kapwa* in equal and mutual relations. *Kapwa* is the Philippine category for "other" but unlike the English term, the stress here is on the "shared inner self" with both the "one-of-us" and the "not-one-of-us," the "similar" and the "different." *Pakikipagkapwa*, a Philippine virtue, refers to treating the "*kapwa*" equally and justly.[31]

Institutional Support of Catholic Theological Ethicists

Aside from Asia-wide groups such as the Federation of Asian Bishops' Conferences and its offices (e.g., Office for Human Development) and the Ecclesia of Women in Asia (an association of Catholic women theologians), there are local organizations and offices that encourage Southeast Asian theological ethicists, together with those in other fields of theological specialization, to reflect and respond creatively to contemporary moral challenges (e.g., Center for Research and Training of Contextual Theology in Indonesia, DAKATEO-Catholic Theological Association of the Philippines, Center for Contextual Theology and Ethics at the University of St. Thomas, Scalabrini Migration Center, etc.). A number of theological institutions also integrate exposure to poor communities, women, indigenous groups, other religions and offer courses on socio-cultural-gender analysis as a necessary pretheological preparation for the teaching of a more contextualized and relevant moral theology.[32]

Personal Hopes for the Continent

In an editorial, one sociologist lamented that our generation of Philippine martial law babies—who grew up during the twenty-year, U.S.-supported dictatorial regime of Ferdinand Marcos, fought, got arrested, and went through two people-power revolutions—is, in a certain sense, already a lost generation . . . with the better future still absent from the horizon. Most have reached middle age, and many have already died, but we have yet to see the fruits of our struggles and sacrifices. But, in another light—with hope as our last word—we can continue to dream for the future of our children and the continent: daily "bread" to eat for everyone, clean air, fresh water, sound sleep, and freedom to express and develop one's self and one's identity in intercultural and cosmic harmony with "others."

Toward such a globalization without marginalization, ecclesial conversion is an imperative: "anyone who ventures to speak to people about justice must first be just in their eyes."[33] In one very concrete area, I hope that in the coming years there will be more women theological ethicists based on our continent, especially in East and South Asia. Let us heed the call in the final statement of the third Asian Bishops' Institute for Lay Apostolate on Women: "more opportunities need to be provided for women to study and teach theology in theological schools and seminaries."[34]

Clement Campos, C.Ss.R.

Doing Christian Ethics in India's World of Cultural Complexity and Social Inequality

In this presentation I shall speak about the situation of moral theology with specific reference to India. The reason why I limit myself to one part of South Asia is that India is a subcontinent in itself with a population well over a billion. It is also in a sense most representative of the Asian continent. Over three decades ago, the Federation of Asian Bishops' Conferences stated that evangelization in Asia called for a threefold dialogue: dialogue with Asia's religions, dialogue with local cultures, and dialogue with the poor.[1] These are the three elements that dominate the Asian landscape: religious plurality, cultural diversity, and dehumanizing poverty; and they apply most forcefully to the Indian subcontinent and may be called its defining characteristics.

India indeed presents a bewildering mixture. It is the birthplace of some of the great religions of the world. While it is predominantly Hindu, it is good to remember that "India is the third largest Muslim country in the world; 80 percent of the world's Zoroastrians live in India; and the population of Christians and Sikhs exceeds the total population of many nation states in the world."[2] An indication of the cultural diversity is the staggering fact that there are twenty-two officially recognized languages in the country.[3] Rich in religion and culture, highly advanced in science and technology, India is also a country with massive poverty, large-scale illiteracy, and a dehumanizing caste system. In this context, the challenge facing theological ethicists is to create a theology that is at once liberative and yet rooted in the pluriform cultural and religious traditions of the land.

What is offered here is a panoramic view of the issues of major concern that are being addressed by Indian theological ethicists.

Globalization

One of the major concerns in India is globalization. Globalization has promised much in terms of potential benefits for all and has been enthusiastically received by the elite and the media with a flood of goods, increased connectivity, and the tantalizing prospect of a better lifestyle. The reality is that these benefits have reached only a small minority. Poverty has increased and life has become far more insecure. A few statistics should suffice to indicate this. In the period immediately after the economic reforms were introduced in India, the real per capita consumption in rural India, which stood at Rupees 164.00 per month in 1991, went down to Rupees 153.00 in 1998. The percentage of people below the poverty line during the decade of reform has gone up from 35.1 percent in 1993–94 to 43 percent in 1998.[4] To put faces on these figures, I cite just one example. In recent years thousands of farmers across the country have committed suicide. According to *Navdanya*, a Research Foundation,

> In 1997 India experienced its first bout of farmers' suicides and since then over 25,000 farmers have taken their own lives. The crisis has stemmed from a number of hardships which have led to the irreversible indebtedness of small and marginal farmers from even the most historically productive regions of the country. India's agriculture has turned into a negative economy due largely to three main factors: rising costs of cultivation, plummeting prices of farm commodities, and lack of credit availability for small farmers. Most of these factors can be attributed to corporate globalization and unjust free trade policies implemented by the World Trade Organization.[5]

Privatization, the aggressive front of globalization, often comes into conflict with the goals of social justice and the common good. Apart from the economic fallout, there has also been a negative impact on local cultures and a devastating assault on the environment. Theological ethicists by and large have taken an extremely critical stand against globalization. They have based their position on a critique of capitalism and the market economy, which is in reality a new form of economic imperialism, together with the principles that are part of the social teaching of the church:

(a) Every person is sacred and must be treated with dignity and equality;

(b) the criterion to evaluate economic systems and decisions is whether it protects or undermines the rights and dignity of individuals;

(c) all people have a right to participate in the economic life of society as equals;

(d) society has a special obligation to care for the marginalized;
(e) the objective of economic institutions is the common good, not vested interests;
(f) there can be no common good without justice.[6]

Environment

As everywhere else in the world, there is a major ecological crisis brewing in India.[7] How does a theologian respond? The approach of the Indian theologians[8] is to draw from the wisdom of the indigenous peoples who through their myths and rituals, their respect for mother earth and their simple lifestyle have fostered conservation and a symbiotic relationship with nature. There is much to learn also from the ancient religions and their scriptures, which reveal a mystical perception of the earth as the home in which one experiences the life-giving power of the Divine. Reverence for and protection of the earth is seen as a logical ethical response. This complements Christian theology based on the biblical insights of creation and care for the earth.

There is a reaction, however, against the use of the model of stewardship. This model, while an improvement on the domination model, can go hand in hand with oppressive structures without necessarily changing them. It still retains anthropocentric and instrumental connotations, ignores the dimension of the intrinsic worth of creation, and so does not go far enough in integrating the concerns of ecological balance and social justice.

An environmental ethic for India calls for a denunciation of the forces that conspire to despoil the earth, the support of campaigns to preserve life-sustaining water, air, and land, the preservation of biodiversity together with a critique of the consumerist culture and lifestyle, and the fostering of an eco-spirituality. What Indian eco-ethics also stresses is the need to repair the rape of nature by rendering justice to the victims of such exploitation.[9] The first victims are always the poor. They have a claim in justice to the earth's resources for the fulfillment of basic needs of decent human living besides the right of all to a healthy and livable habitat.

For example, in the state of Kerala, the Hindustan Coca-Cola Beverage Pvt. Ltd Company obtained permission from the government to obtain forty acres of land located in the vicinity of a main irrigation canal, a couple of reservoirs, and a major river. They have sunk sixty-five bore wells and, according to the report of the company, they consume 600,000 liters of water a day for production purposes. This has created water scarcity for the poor tribal people nearby. The carcinogenic waste contamination of available water within a radius of two kilometers has reached a critical level, destroying the livelihood support systems of the local communities. In a high-court judgment on a petition filed by the local people against the company, the judge held that the ground water belonged to the people and the government had no right to allow a private party to extract such a huge quantity of ground water, which was "a property held by it in trust." The core principle of public law is that the state is a trustee of all natural resources, and it has a legal duty to protect them. These scarce resources are meant for public use and cannot be converted into private ownership.[10] Here is a clear case of how one of the most basic necessities of life now becomes a commodity for trade and profit. This act of privatization removes the government from a basic area of social concern where the very existence of the poor is threatened. One sees here why environmental ethics must be linked to the common good, not in the sense of the good of merely the local community or the human community but in the broader and more inclusive sense of a biosphere sustained by God's loving energy.

Bioethics

There has been a great deal of writing in the field of bioethics. Several dissertations have been published in India dealing with individual issues in areas as diverse as the quality of life, organ transplants, the human genome, and population control, but in approach these efforts only reflect the concerns of the rest of the world and use traditional arguments. Let me address two issues: justice in health care and HIV/AIDS.

"Health indices in India have seen substantial improvements in recent decades but quality and affordable health care services continue to elude the poor. Making equitable and affordable medical care accessible to rural and urban poor remains a challenge."[11] The irony in India is that it has the most sophisticated means of treatment and state of the art medical facilities, but millions die of preventable diseases, with no access to primary health care. An example of how the poor are affected is the availability of drugs. Globalization with its new patenting laws, the monopolistic practices of pharmaceutical companies, and the increasing privatization of health care places an enormous burden on the poor, who cannot have access to life-saving drugs. The nexus between the medical profession and the pharmaceutical companies and the irrational prescription of drugs and diagnostic tests represents the worst side of privatization.[12]

Therefore, one of the issues of vital interest to India is the question of justice in health care and the just allocation of resources. The approach is based on an appeal to human rights. There is a fundamental right to health care, a right founded on the dignity of the human person. This right implies that access to health care must be provided for all people, regardless of economic, social, or legal status with special attention given to the health needs of the poor. What is required is a comprehensive health care that focuses not so much on the cure of acute diseases and extending of life by means of sophisticated technologies but rather gives priority to preventive medicine and to the promotion of positive health. This is done by eliminating the environmental and social causes of disease and by changing unhealthy lifestyles as well as educating people in a way that enables them to take responsibility for their own health. Priority should be given to the problems of the most powerless, poorly informed, and least able to pay.

India today probably has the highest number of people with AIDS. According to surveys by the National AIDS Control Organization in 2005, the estimated number of adults (age group of 15 to 49) living with AIDS is 5.206 million.[13] Strangely, there have not been too many articles dealing with this issue. In a slight variation of the ABC approach, theological ethicists have helped the Health Commission of the Catholic Bishops Conference of India to formulate an approach that speaks of abstinence, being faithful, and containing the infection together with a drive to educate people and provide care for people with AIDS. There has, however, been a reluctance to speak on the issues of condoms (even in the context of marriage) and to be involved with agencies that have a different approach from that of the church.

Discrimination

Among the victims of discrimination two groups especially should be mentioned: women and *Dalits* (the oppressed victims of caste discrimination). After looking at these, I turn to discrimination on the basis of religion.

Gender discrimination and the denial of rights to women are widespread in India. An alarming sign is the selective abortion of the girl child and the falling birthrate of women. There are also, unfortunately, repeated incidents of dowry deaths, domestic violence, rapes, and the denial of equal rights to women in the matter of education. Theological ethicists have not sufficiently addressed these issues and the voices are mostly those of women activists and feminist theologians.

The moral response to discrimination on the basis of caste is in the first place one of protest. Protest is not only a revolt against unjust structures but also an effort to indicate the absence of a public conscience. Protest is a tool in the hands of the powerless, the first step in the praxis of liberation. The moral content of protest is to affirm the moral worth and the dignity of the individual human person. This protest involves, on the part of the victims, a rejection of the worldview of the oppressor and of the oppressor's value system, as well as a noncompliance with their own victimization. A final step is empowering the victims to become moral agents of their own destinies. This is one example of an ethics of liberation.[14]

Finally, while the great Indian religions were noted for their profound

Scriptures, their spiritual and contemplative traditions, and their spirit of tolerance, today the atmosphere is vitiated by a militant religious fundamentalism that wishes to leave no room for religious pluralism or religious freedom. Several states have imposed laws that make it difficult for conversion from one religion to another, what Pope Benedict referred to as "the reprehensible attempt to legislate clearly discriminatory restrictions on the fundamental right of religious freedom"[15] The theological response has been on the basis of human rights and the freedom to follow one's conscience. An added dimension is the recovery of the prophetic tradition of religion to counter the temptation to use religion as a tool of alienation and legitimization of unjust structures and practices.

Violence and Terrorism

In this land of *ahimsa* acts of violence and terrorism are a daily occurrence. Some of these are for political rights (as in Kashmir) and others for social justice and land reform (e.g., Peoples' War Groups) and still others are inspired by religious fundamentalism (e.g., the riots in Gujarat). Theologians dealing with these issues point out that while these random acts of violence on innocent victims are to be condemned, one must not lose sight of the fact that often there is a form of violence imposed by the political authorities or structures by the denial of fundamental rights and justice to various social groups. This is one reason why writing on sin focuses on social sin and sinful structures and stresses the need for a broader concept of reconciliation.[16]

Often too the response to terrorism involves acts of counterterrorism and draconian laws curtailing people's rights and liberties. There is thus a vicious spiral of violence. One must not forget that at the root of terrorism are real grievances: denial of rights, injustice suffered, poverty, frustrated aspirations, and the exploitation of people who feel there is no other way out than violence.[17] These need to be recognized and addressed first and only then can dialogue and nonviolent means lead to peaceful resolutions. Gandhi has shown the way.[18]

Human Rights

In an unjustly divided country like India, violation of the human rights of the powerless and the marginalized is structurally easy. An ethical approach, based on the dignity of the human person, that is merely individualistic is inadequate because it can be exploited to the advantage of the elite or the dominant class. Another approach is required.

Strangely, as Felix Wilfred points out, in recent times some Asian countries wish to distance themselves from the common standard of human rights adopted by the United Nations in 1948. They do so on the alleged difference of Asian values. China and Singapore are cases in point. There is no denying the fact of cultural differences derived from various worldviews, histories, traditions, and cultures. This should only lead to a new intercultural discourse on human values and the rights in which they are enshrined.

Wilfred argues that the modern understanding of human rights was based on the theory of natural law and an appeal to reason. An Asian approach would be more spiritual in the sense of a movement away from the world of the self toward the world of the other. It is a movement provoked by the *dukha* or the suffering of the other. Even Gandhi underlined the importance of *ahimsa*—not inflicting suffering on others (which could be translated as a nonviolation of human rights). What is implied here is a different anthropology, one from the perspective of the victims. In this anthropology "human beings are defined not simply in terms of reason; human beings are compassionate beings. In this anthropological perspective, human rights are expressions of the compassion for the sufferings of the poor. Human suffering and compassion offer the anthropological and spiritual key to interpret human rights as the rights of the poor."[19]

The approach of Indian ethicists to human rights, seen from the perspective of the victims, is therefore also social and communitarian, with a preferential option for the rights of the powerless. The claim to human rights of the powerless and the marginalized is also necessarily a struggle for liberation. It is not a struggle for rights within an existing structure, or even for reforms under it, but for radical societal change.[20]

Marriage and Sexuality

As is to be expected, there are several books and articles published in the area of marriage and sexuality. While there have been some attempts to study marriage from an Indian perspective,[21] by and large the literature deals with these issues from a Western theological point of view.[22]

A problem of growing pastoral concern in India is the number of marriages with disparity of cult. This is inevitable given the fact that Christians are a tiny minority in the country and find themselves intermingling with others in educational institutions, workplaces, and housing colonies. While issues are raised about the sacramentality of such marriages[23]—traditionally not considered strictly sacramental—some theologians wonder whether there could not be a more positive attitude toward such unions. Their reasons are based on the positive statements about other faiths in the documents of Vatican II, especially *Lumen Gentium* and *Nostrae Aetate*, the divine origins of human love, and the ecumenical possibilities that they open up as prophetic signs indicating to the world that it is possible for people of different faiths to live together in peace.[24]

Fundamental Morals

This area of theology presents a real challenge. Some years ago a leading Indian theologian bemoaned the fact that in most seminaries in India the basic text used is K. H. Peschke's *Christian Ethics*, which is a modern manual written by a European.[25] This is not a criticism of the author but an indicator of the lack of a genuine Indian approach to moral theology. While many theological ethicists have done their doctoral research on Indian religious scriptures and on Indian thinkers or dealt with issues pertinent to India, there has not been any sustained attempt to develop a contextualized moral theology. The challenge is to try to weave the various strands of wisdom from these religions and little traditions together with the insights of Christian theology into a comprehensive moral discourse.

There have been some exploratory articles. These have, however, been chiefly concerned with a moral theology from the perspective of the poor, the "nonpersons" in history. The poor present a point of entry to engage in dialogue in a pluralistic society. The criterion by which to evaluate any ethical paradigm is whether or not this morality is concerned primarily with the liberation and transformation of every person in society beginning with the last and the least.[26]

Pluralism also presents a challenge to create a theological ethics that is universally comprehensible especially if one is to participate in public debate on ethical issues. The most common approach is to resort to the natural law or to appeal to the *humanum* in its relational and responsible dimensions or to seek common ground in dialogue on the basis of shared human values and universal human rights. Dialogue is vital. We have much to learn, for example, from the teachings of Jainism and Buddhism about inward purity in ethical action and the ways of peaceful coexistence with all people and indeed with all creation. As Vatican II advised us, we must be "joined to other people in the search for truth and for the right solution to so many moral problems. . . . "[27]

Association of Moral Theologians

An Association of Moral Theologians of India was formed in 1988. Its aim was (a) to be a forum for moral theologians to meet and discuss current moral issues; (b) to promote Christian ethical reflection in the sociocultural context of India; (c) to foster publication of books or monographs useful to students of theology and to the church in India at large. Unfortunately, while meetings take place regularly and current issues are discussed, very little is published. This is a major failure of theological ethicists in India. As a result, little is being contributed to moral education in the public forum whether it be on a major issue such as India going nuclear or bribery and corruption, which is endemic to Indian society in the political and economic spheres.

Hopes for the Future

I live in the hope that India, which once showed the world a nonviolent way of achieving political freedom, will find a nonviolent way of achieving peace within the country, based on justice for all with room for a diversity of religions and cultures. To achieve this end, the only way forward in a pluralistic and unjustly divided situation, is through dialogue and reconciliation. My hope is

- that moral theologians will contribute to this process by moving beyond the confines of a seminary setting and becoming involved in political debate on issues of urgent social concern;
- that they will not confine themselves to the task, important though it is, of finding pastoral solutions to ethical dilemmas that confront individuals;
- that through dialogue with other religions and cultures and the poor, they may participate in humanity's search for the truth by which we live; and
- that because of their involvement in the struggles of the people there may emerge a moral theology that is contextualized, truly Indian, authentically human, and socially liberative.

Europe

Marciano Vidal, C.Ss.R. (Spain)
*Theological Ethics in Europe (Especially Southern Europe):
Past, Present and Future*

Marianne Heimbach-Steins (Germany)
*Political-Ethical Challenges in Europe: A Christian Socio-
Ethical Perspective*

Piotr Mazurkiewicz (Poland)
On Stem Cells and Homophobia

The European panel provided very diverse viewpoints. After describing what Philippe Delhaye called the "thirty-year war" between those wanting to maintain a neoscholastic casuistry and those who did not, Marciano Vidal turns to the challenges on the horizon for Europe. These are, basically fundamental, conceptual ones that need to be better resolved so as to respond to urgent problems. Two of these, adequately grasping the notions of secularity and laicity (what he calls "the constitutive dimension of the political organization of social relationships at the highest level"), would allow Catholicism a better way of expressing its moral vision in the twenty-first century not only for the sake of the European community, but also for its own benefit. Similarly, two other challenges, religious pluralism as well as the on-going, emerging self-understanding of the European community, when adequately met, will shape the expression of the Catholic ethical vision for both society and the church.

These urgent conceptual challenges for theological ethics inevitably confront the reality of Europe today. Marianne Heimbach-Steins provides an extraordinarily dense read of a European society shaped by deep social disparities and unequal chances of participation and personal development. At the outset, she signals two social phenomena: a deeply rooted insecurity on both individual and collective levels caused by political change, growing economic pressure, and social disparities, and an increasing cultural and religious plurality that forces different identities to meet and interact within one and the same society. This combination of insecurity and pluralism leads to the fundamental challenge to create a fundamental ethical consensus within these pluralist societies. This challenge requires, then, forms of discourse that could eventually attain to such a consensus. She sees this challenge as specific to today's theological ethicists so that they may engage fellow Christians, including the Orthodox, in a sustained ecumenical critical ethical discourse.

If Vidal and Heimbach-Steins are calling for discourse, then Piotr Mazurkiewicz wants to provoke at least the question as to whether Catholics who adhere to particular magisterial teachings will be able to participate in that discourse. Mazurkiewicz is explicitly provocative as he looks at three recent policies that emerged from the Euopean Parliment on matters dealing with homosexuality and stem-cell research. His contention is that obedient Catholics are de facto excluded from a much needed debate. Moreover, he sees this exclusion as a sign of a self-rejection of Europe's own moral tradition. He closes, musing with the Spanish bishops, that many theologians themeslves are being compromised by the very forces that are silencing their more adherent lay Catholics.

Marciano Vidal, C.Ss.R.

Theological Ethics in Europe (Especially Southern Europe)

Past, Present, and Future

The subject of this presentation is the recent past, the present situation, and the foreseeable prospects of Catholic moral-theological reflection in Europe, especially in Southern Europe (France, Italy, Portugal and Spain). I shall focus primarily on basic and general issues within the wide field of what today is called theological ethics.

1. The Recent Past

In the second half of the twentieth century, there was a decisive change within Catholic moral theology that marked the end of one era and the beginning of another. On the one hand, moral-theological reflection, like the moral life of the believers, was breaking away from the *casuistic model* that characterized life and theology since the Council of Trent. On the other, a convergence of factors encouraged the development of a *new moral-theological model* for thinking about and then living out the ethical dimensions of Christian faith.

No impartial observer can fail to recognize that now, forty years after the Second Vatican Council, moral-theological reflection in Europe has shown a notable improvement. Moral theology, freed from the theological corpus as an autonomous discipline in the late sixteenth century, has been radically transformed. We owe this to the moral theologians of the whole church, but especially to those who have been working in Europe.

As a discipline, theological ethics has ceased to be a manual of resolutions for cases of conscience for the practice of the sacrament of penance and has recovered the epistemological status that pertains to theological knowledge. Thus it has returned to its biblical roots, its theological sources, and its own way of seeking Christian moral truth.

At the same time it has remained in fruitful dialogue with the culture of

our time. In particular it has been concerned with recovering the valid elements of Modernity: the critical character of reason and the inalienable value
of the human subject. It has also been sensitive to the more recent variations
of what we call Postmodernity.

In this sense, the ecclesial event of Vatican II marked the end of casuistic
or post-Tridentine morality and the beginning of a new paradigm. This
change was felt as a "victory" by some and as a "defeat" by others, in what
Philippe Delhaye has called a "thirty-year war" between the supporters of
moral casuistry and those who sought to introduce a new and nourishing
element into Catholic moral theology.[1]

The achievement of these two goals—the recovery of theological identity
and dialogue with present-day culture—has not been easy. There have been
internal tensions and external pressures.

In the fundamental moral tracts, the historian Louis Vereecke points out
the following issues of noteworthy importance and interest: the debate over
the specificity of Christian morality, the confrontation between the models of
autonomous morality and an ethic of faith, the debate over norms of moral
life, and the question of intervention by the Magisterium in natural law.[2]

I believe all these debates are interrelated. Together they can be analyzed
from the perspective of one question in particular. That is the debate between
the models or paradigms of "theonomous autonomy" and "the ethics of
faith." Here we find one of the interpretive keys to the different positions,
which oppose one another within the field of present-day Catholic moral
theology.[3]

Theological ethics, like the lived morality of Christians, moves within the
horizon of faith. The Christological confession of Jesus, the acceptance of
God's presence in history, the living-out of the Spirit in the community of
believers, the certainty of eschatological hope: these are the reference points
and bases of support for Christian moral commitment. But, how should we
interpret the role of faith in the world of moral values?

To simplify the differing positions, we can detect two ways of understanding and explaining the influence of faith on the ethics of Christians. For
one group, faith is the "source" of a specific ethic, which must be understood and lived as a specifically faith-based ethic. For another group, faith
is the "context" or frame of reference for an ethic that must be at the same
time an ethic of autonomous reason. The first position, by highlighting the
role of faith, understands Christian morality as an *ethic of faith* (Bernhard
Stöckle, Heinz Schürmann, Josef Ratzinger, Hans Urs von Balthasar, Karl
Hilpert, Joachim Piegsa).[4] The second position, with more emphasis on the
substantive aspect of morality, understands Christian ethics as an ethic of
theonomic autonomy (Alfons Auer, Franz Böckle, Josef Fuchs, Dietmar
Mieth, Bruno Schüller).[5]

Some great theologians might have preferred a stronger emphasis on *Christonomy* rather than a radicalized confrontation among "autonomy," "heteronomy," and "theonomy." For Yves Congar, the "theonomy of the living God" is simply the normativity reflected in Christ, that is, Christonomy.[6] Von Balthasar contends that "the Christian imperative goes beyond the problem of autonomy and heteronomy" and is concretely expressed in the reality of Christonomy.[7] Despite this Christological option, another great theologian, Walter Kasper, holds that the situation of Christianity in present-day culture must be understood with the categories of autonomy and theonomy.[8]

Despite the tensions and problems that have surrounded theological-moral reflection in Europe in the decades since Vatican II, we can affirm, nevertheless, that the postconciliar balance is clearly positive. In the literature,[9] I think we can speak of an authentic *re-grounding* of the theological-moral discipline. Vincente Gómez Mier reached this conclusion after a detailed and original study on the change of "disciplinary matrix" in the manuals of morality published after Vatican II.[10]

2. Present-day Resources

Still, the present stage of moral-theological reflection in Europe is not very hopeful, especially with regard to the academic teaching of theological ethics. The number of students is dropping, and so therefore is the number specifically dedicated to the study of theological ethics. There are also fewer efforts to produce moral-theological literature. This is especially true for France and Spain.

Today, moral-theological reflection in Europe still has sufficient resources. Here I shall mention those of a structural nature.

- There are *academic centers* specifically focused on teaching and research in the field of theological ethics. Tied in with these centers are staff, libraries, reviews, and other publications. Worthy of special note are the Academia Alfonsiana in Rome, on the model of a Roman Atheneum, and the Instituto Superior de Ciencias Morales in Madrid.[11] There are also institutes in fields of applied morality. Particularly excellent are the Centers of Bioethics in Southern Europe, and the Institutes of Social Ethics in the German-speaking world.
- There are *reviews* dedicated exclusively to moral-theological themes. Worth mentioning are the three reviews of Catholic moral theology: *Rivista di Teologia Morale*, a publication of the association of Italian moral theologians;[12] *Moralia*, from the Instituto Superior de Ciencias

Morales;[13] and, *Le Supplément: Revue d'Ethique et de Théologie Morale*, a publication of the association of French-speaking moralists.[14] Also, *Studies in Christian Ethics, Zeitschrift für christliche Sozialwissenschaften, Ethica,* and *Studia Moralia.*

- There are *collections of studies* which publish, with a certain regularity, works dedicated to moral themes. Worth noting are the collection of the University of Münster (with two series) and the collection of the University of Fribourg in Switzerland. Also the collections of the publishing houses of Dehoniane (Bologna) and Citadella (Assisi) in Italy, and Cerf in France.
- In Europe there are *associations of moralists.* The German-speaking ones formed the interconfessional Societas Ethica, in 1964. In the Anglo-Saxon world there is a Society for the Study of Christian Ethics. The Italians are especially active (ATISM), both at the national level since 1966 and in regional groups.[15] The French-speaking moralists formed ATEM in 1966. The Spanish and Portuguese moralists are less associative.

3. Challenges for the Future

The challenges that lie ahead for moral-theological reflection are many and varied. It is enough to consider the problems of applied morality: bioethics, sexual ethics, the ethics of marriage, social ethics (economic, political, cultural), etc. I shall mention only the challenges of a general nature. I divide them into four groups of challenges: secular culture, lay society, religious pluralism, and Europe as a unit within the world community.

European societies, even those of long Catholic tradition, are going through a time of decisive change. Culturally, the societies are increasingly secular. Politically, they are organized as lay societies. Neither secularity nor laicity is contrary to Christian faith; indeed, in many aspects they are rooted in Christianity. But working out these two conditions in concrete ways has proven difficult for Christian ethics.

The understanding and living-out of Christian morality must take place today within the demands of secularity.[16] By the secularity of morality I mean, first, the just autonomy of human beings as it was expressed at Vatican II (*Gaudium et Spes* 36); second, the need to introduce into moral-theological discourse the "mediation of reason" or critical analysis vis-à-vis our humanity.

Secularity is incorporated in Christian morality when that morality is lived and expressed in a tone of "theonomous autonomy" (or better, "Christonomy"), and when the moral-theological discourse is consistent with the epistemology proposed by Vatican II: analyzing moral issues "in the light of the Gospel and human experience" (*Gaudium et Spes* 46).

To have public meaning in European societies, a theological ethic must hold together these preconditions:

- The relationship between morality and the whole of Christian faith. Christianity is not a form of morality; Christian faith offers a horizon of meaning within which to think about and live one's commitment in the world, which must be discerned through "socio-anthropological mediations."
- The specifically Christian content of concrete moral concepts. Edward Schillebeeckx was referring to that concrete content, rather than to the horizon of faith and the basic intentionality of the believer, when he said years ago that "a Christian ethic does not exist." That is the orientation of many theologians today.[17]
- Secularity—with its roots in both autonomy and the mediation of reason—is as yet an uncompleted task in Catholic morality. In this sense I agree with those who hold that Catholic moral theology has not yet dealt with the critique of "modernity," and that for this reason there is a "moral conflict" in today's church; this despite the fact that the conflict was resolved earlier in the fields of biblical hermeneutics (in the early twentieth century) and dogmatic theology (in the mid-twentieth century), precisely because in those areas theology had incorporated the valid aspects of modernity.[18]

With the challenge of "autonomy" still unresolved, a new one is appearing on the human horizon: that of *laicity*. I am not referring to the ways in which the lay character of the society is managed politically, neither in the extreme forms of "laicism" (as in France) and of "civil religion" (as in the United States), or in the intermediate way of "aconfessionalism" (as in Spain). I am thinking of "laicity" as a constitutive dimension of the political organization of social relationships at the highest level (the state).

Laicity in this sense has been explicitly affirmed by the Catholic ecclesiastical magisterium. Vatican II stated, "the political community and the Church are independent of one another, each autonomous in its own sphere. Nevertheless both, in different ways, are at the service of the personal and social vocation of the people themselves" (*Gaudium et Spes* 76). John Paul II, rather surprisingly, conceded that "the lay principle is part of the social doctrine of the Church."[19] Benedict XVI in turn has accepted the existence of a "healthy laicity."[20]

These theoretical affirmations are not yet fully verified in the presentation of the content of Christian morality in society. This is sometimes because Christians are "mute" in the face of the difficulty of presenting, and especially receiving, the discourses that might follow. And sometimes because the proposals do not maintain the coherence of laicity:

- By not respecting the plurality of ethical options within the society, or by monopolizing the meaning of "civil ethics," which by definition is not identified with the moral cosmic vision of any religious or ideological universe.
- By intervening in the juridical sphere without respecting the just autonomy of politics, when neither sphere (juridical or political) necessarily coincides with ecclesial positions or even with the full content of "natural law."
- By not explicitly stating—and worse, not subjecting to scientific criticism—the "anthropological mediation" on which the Christian cosmic vision bases some of its affirmations (for example, on the morality of new forms of affective relationships).
- Not knowing how to live in a "plural, democratic and lay normality," but rather resorting to positions of either "martyrdom" or "crusade."

The challenge of *laicity* is closely related to the challenge of *secularity*. In my view the failure to consider them, or the insistence on a false solution, is the underlying cause of the malaise of present-day Catholicism.

The *laicity* of the modern State requires us to think and act out the public function of theological ethics on the basis of new presuppositions that emerge from the answer to the two following questions:

- The relationship between Christian values and laws. What is the meaning of laws? What is the relative priority of the juridical and the moral order? What kind of moral coherence should we expect of Christians when they carry out public functions?
- The pluralism of options. A lay state must by necessity manage a pluralism of options. To what extent can we offer publicly valid guidance based on theological ethics?

An answer to the challenges of secularity and laicity requires Christian ethics to reinterpret its role as "theological" ethics. If, on the one hand, moral-theological thought must retain its "theological" identity, on the other, it must also function publicly with forms of "de-theologization."[21]

Europe has lived through many centuries of religious confrontation: first with the external religious enemy, especially Islam; second, with the heretics of its own religion. The crusades, the religious wars, and the persecution of heretics have been important components of European history. We all know the implications this has had for the lived morality and the expressed ethics of European Christians.

Europe has attained such a high degree of social tolerance and respect for the freedom of personal conscience that it seems as if any danger of religiously or ideologically based social conflict has been eliminated. But that is not the case. The tension of religious and cultural pluralism has returned to Europe, due to many other factors, including immigration. Europe is already, and will be even more in the not-so-distant future, a pluricultural and pluri-religious society.

This demands of theological ethics a special effort to manage the situation of religious (and cultural) pluralism with the least possible risk and the greatest benefits. That will require:

- Dialogue between Christian ethics and other religious ethics in order to (1) neutralize the violent mechanisms inherent in religions; (2) establish a common front in favor of the basic values that shape human life. There is room here for proposals, like that of Hans Küng, on the ethical convergence of the great religions.[22]
- Specifically, on the basis of genuine religious experience and valid theological reflection, we must unmask the false religious justification of any form of violence. John Paul II said it brilliantly: "The name of the one God must increasingly be, as it already is in itself, a name of peace and an imperative for peace."[23]

Finally, amid the normal difficulties, Europe is developing an increasing awareness of its role as a unified human space. This awareness holds important advantages for our common moral-theological task, but it also raises new ethical questions. I shall mention two of them: one looking inward on the Christian tradition, the other with regard to relations between Europe and the rest of the world.

Within the tradition itself: moral-theological reflection must ask about the so-called Christian roots of Europe. We must ask, without confessionalizing European society, are there "values" whose native soil has been the Christian "humus"? To what extent must Christianity retain its influence in order to maintain and develop those "values"?

Toward the human community: Europe has important responsibilities, and ethical-theological reflection must collaborate in the discernment and formulation of these responsibilities. I am thinking especially about the defense of an "inclusive" ethos in the face of the exclusive tendencies now appearing in this world of unsolidarity. In the Judeo-Christian tradition there are many "narratives," "symbols," and "prophetic announcements" that seek to guide humanity toward a praxis of inclusion vis-à-vis the other—the foreigner, the sinner, even the enemy. Europe must bring this tradition into its present-day life.[24]

I shall end with the words with which Leo Tindemans greeted the King of Spain, Juan Carlos I, upon receiving the Carlomagno prize in Aquisgrán,

May 20, 1982: "Europe is more than a continent. It is above all a concept of life based on humanistic and Christian principles, oriented to the search for justice and freedom, both of these in the service of the common good and of human dignity." This would be a good working agenda for theological ethics in Europe, today and in the future.

Marianne Heimbach-Steins

Political-Ethical Challenges in Europe

A Christian Socio-Ethical Perspective

Since it is impossible to point out the whole variety of major moral challenges in Europe in one short paper, I would like to identify some crucial issues from the point of view of political ethics.[1] This necessarily means dropping other issues that are definitely no less interesting and urgent, such as the huge field of biomedical challenges.[2]

Since 1989/90 Europe has been facing remarkable challenges. At least two major societal trends that mark serious ethical challenges in European political contexts have come out of both the European integration processes and the dynamics of globalization:

1. a deeply rooted insecurity on the individual and the collective level caused by *political change, growing economic pressure,* and *social disparities;*
2. an *increasing cultural and religious plurality* which forces different identities to meet and interact within one and the same society.[3]

Both aspects have a strong socio-ethical impact and require answers in various fields of action such as law, (social) politics, education, and religious and interreligious activities. Both point to the double responsibility of Europe as a political entity, and of European Christianity as part of the world church. On the one hand, the social, political, and economic dynamics within European societies cause certain problems of social cohesion and peace; on the other hand, Europeans have to take responsibility within the global dynamics of power, social disparities, and unequal chances of development.

1. Growing Social Disparities and Insecurity

We are facing growing social disparities within national societies as well as on the continental level and in a worldwide dimension. This leads to questions of justice.

1.1 Social Insecurity, Inequality, and the Problem of Justice

In Germany and other European societies that have developed as welfare states with a high level of social support and security, we recently have had to observe a certain anxiety over *social insecurity*. An important reason for this is the still normative predominance of labor serving as a major means of gaining life support and social participation for the vast majority of the population. This is in contrast to the precariousness of employment with which a considerable number of people are confronted.[4] Finding oneself excluded from the labor market does not only cause economic problems; the longer it lasts the more it means social exclusion. The vicious circle of unemployment, poverty, and social exclusion threatens especially people who are not well educated, such as members of minorities with a migration background. The whole issue has serious implications in terms of gender inequality, as far as women's access to labor and education, just wages, social insecurity, etc. are concerned.[5] More and more education is turning out to be a key issue regarding the access to social, economic, political, and cultural participation.

The ethical impact may be best expressed in terms of *justice*—justice as a question of the just distribution of goods, chances, and responsibilities, but also as access to and participation in societal decision making and political action. It is not a coincidence that recently an intensified ethical debate on the aspect of justice as participation has come up, which, of course, is related to the aspect of distribution.[6] A genealogy of references can be drafted from impulses of liberation theology on the one hand and John Rawls's *Theory of Justice* (first published in 1971) on the other. Since then there has been a constantly developing debate in the fields of practical philosophy and Christian social ethics (both Roman Catholic and Protestant) about the understanding of social justice. There are some landmarks in the magisterial teaching on both the universal and the local level, too. One very important text in this discussion is, of course, the U.S. bishops' letter *Economic Justice for All* (1986), which is often referred to in European local churches' major texts, such as the document *For a Future Founded on Solidarity and Justice. A Statement on the Economic and Social Situation in Germany* by the German Bishops' Conference and the Council of the Protestant Church in Germany (1997).[7]

To set up a link between ethical theory and the more practical level of law making and political decision making, the problem can also be expressed in terms of *human rights*. The complex relationship between both types, individual rights and freedoms, and social, economic, and cultural rights, has been and should, in my opinion, remain a prominent topic of further ethical research. This is because neither group can serve as a normative basis for an integral human development on its own—both are necessary counterparts.

Catholic theological ethicists are challenged to make a specific contribution to this issue, starting with the outlines of a Christian anthropology and the basic normative orientations of Christian social ethics and the social teaching of the church. In this context the Catholic reception of human rights as it was drafted by Pope John XXIII in the encyclical *Pacem in Terris* (1963) is worth reexamination.[8]

1.2 Worldwide Social Disparities and the Needs of Future Generations

European welfare-state systems are facing constantly growing pressures, partly due to the demographic change within rapidly aging societies in at least some European countries. At the same time the world population as a whole is still rapidly growing and so are the social disparities between those countries that are participating in the globalized economic interactions and technical development and those more or less excluded from these interactions.[9] The need to restore the welfare systems in a sustainable way, connected with the need for sustainable development in a more general understanding (i.e., the treatment of the natural resources, energy, and climate politics), therefore marks another complex dimension of justice which is becoming more and more crucial: the tension between *intragenerational social justice* in a worldwide dimension and *intergenerational justice* toward those who will follow us on earth and need us to care for a sustainable treatment of the physical preconditions of further life support.[10] Reflecting on this challenge properly requires a global perspective that, on the one hand, takes into account the extreme tension between *haves* and *have-nots* as a challenge of justice and a threat to peace worldwide. In Europe coherent asylum and migration politics are required that pay attention not only to economic interests but to the needs of global solidarity as well.[11] Attention must be paid to the ecological dimension as a challenge to capitalist economics and a consumption-oriented way of life.[12]

Indeed, this is a major ethical challenge not only for the population of industrialized countries in general but also for Christian ethics and the related value priorities. For decades we have known quite well that the Northern and Western economies with their huge needs for energy and natural resources cannot be globalized. As long as around 20 percent of the world population require around 80 percent of the natural resources, goods, and capital, we have a scandalous problem of distributive as well as participatory or contributive injustice. Besides the economic and political challenges marked by these facts, they at the same time challenge our ideas of the *quality of life*, of what a good life is like, and to what ends we submit ourselves to a certain "capitalist" way of life. For Europe to become a union not only in terms of economic interactions but also as a political and cultural entity that faces up to its global responsibilities is an ethical challenge yet to be discovered.

2. The Longing for Security and the Challenge of Freedom

In addition to the socio-economic aspects on national and international levels, the security issue seems to be having yet another impact. It is from globalized terrorism that there emanates a serious political-ethical problem both within European societies and in the United States. What must be observed in the aftermath of 9/11 is an astonishing political disposition to limit personal freedom for the sake of presumed security interests—such as the limitation of freedom of press, freedom of assembly, the violation of the private sphere, of data protection, etc. No doubt one can imagine certain situations that urgently require serious limitations of individual rights. But at present there seems to be a tendency to put those rights into question quite easily and without any sufficient proof of the effectiveness of the measures taken for the sake of security interests.

In terms of political ethics this means: (1) The relation between human rights as basic rights of citizens and the necessary limitation of freedom by the legitimate power of the state seems to be imbalanced. (2) Values of democratic culture and the transparency of political strategies for the citizens as an important condition for a basic confidence in the state are being endangered.[13] (3) People's longing for feeling safe seems to make them believe all too easily in a promise of security, which might be, at least partly, a populist illusion. (4) There is an urgent need to strengthen the awareness of freedom as a good and as an ethical value—not in a limited individualistic and merely formal sense, but as a means of leading one's own life responsibly and of acting soundly as a citizen.

Christian political ethics must be aware of these tendencies and critically comment on what is going on in the field of law and political decision making. Furthermore it seems to be an issue for educational ethics (as a field of research of Catholic social ethics which recently seems to have been becoming of greater interest).[14] We must reflect on the objectives and ends of education as a responsibility to be taken not only by parents and families but also by various actors in the public sphere.

3. The Reality of War and the Challenge of Peace

When in 1989/90 the Berlin Wall and the Iron Curtain broke down within a short period, a vivid hope arose that this could be not only the definite end of the Cold War but the beginning of a new era of peace. Instead, there followed times of violence and war in the south of Europe—with the breakdown of the former Yugoslavia—and soon after in the Middle East with the wars in Afghanistan and in Iraq. The ethical impacts of war have come to be a major issue in European ethical reflection.

What really has been happening is the development of a new stage of ethical reflection on conflict and peace, which can be described as a shift from just war to *just peace*. The main idea behind this more than marginal modification is not only to define sharp conditions for an eventual justification of war, but to reflect on societal conditions to prevent violence and war, on the measures to be taken and the chances of peace-building in post-war situations to overcome the sources and consequences of violence (including gender aspects) in a sustainable way.[15] Thus the reflection on war and peace becomes more closely linked with developmental issues, socio-economic and ecological issues, and even education.

4. The Political and Cultural Need to Integrate a Plurality of Identities

In addition to its economic and social aspects the European process of integration has brought up certain cultural and religious changes within European societies which are of great ethical relevance. Thus, for example, the theme of the 2004 Congress of the *Societas ethica*, an ecumenical association of ethicists (theologians and philosophers) was "Pluralism in Europe."[16] Modern European societies are shaped by a great variety of identities in terms of religious beliefs and worldviews. Let me very briefly point out two aspects of the multifaceted religious image of present European societies and its ethical impacts.

First, we have to realize that Christianity in itself reveals manifold images on the European level: Due to different paths of political history and development of thought there are deeply rooted differences between the Western Christian traditions, on the one hand, and the Orthodox churches and their theologies, on the other hand. The way of thinking about the state, about the relationship between the church and the state, as well as between the church and modern society, about whether or not a Christian social teaching has developed, differ between "Eastern" and "Western" Christianity in Europe and produce relevant consequences in the European integration process. The process of shaping the European Union's constitutional treaty with its hopeless debate on whether or not the religious or spiritual heritage as a source of common basic values may be read as symptomatic of the differences existing even between traditionally Christian countries in Europe.[17] This reveals an important ethical challenge that requires great efforts to increase mutual understanding and to build up a common platform of ecumenically shaped Christian political ethics.[18]

Second, the fact that there is a growing Muslim population (with origins in different parts of the Islamic world) in many European countries not only provokes certain conflicts between social groups but also the need to fight certain (at times racist) prejudices that sometimes erupt violently. Moreover, the presence of a strong Muslim minority whose members demand the right to express their Muslim identity in the public sphere causes specific institutional conflicts in European societies. On the one hand they refer to the implications of the right to religious freedom and the neutrality of the secular state. On the other hand they are related to the broader issue of integration, which, as closely linked as it is to religion, is rather a political and societal challenge than an exclusively religious one.[19]

These very short remarks may give a first idea as to what seem to be the major socio-ethical challenges:

What we urgently need is an intensified discussion of the implications and limits of religious freedom as both an individual and a corporative right. That implies the necessity to reflect on the position of the Christian churches in relation to other religious organizations within a secular state. In order to clarify the public role and influence the Catholic Church may claim to hold, she has to reflect more deeply her institutional position within a pluralist society.

We have to concern ourselves with the integration issue, which, in our European societies, is related to the problem of racism.[20] Research has to be intensified in order to develop ethical guidelines for integration policies and for sound strategies that can help us to deal with the related problems of racism (anti-Semitism, anti-Islamism, xenophobia) and radicalism (namely, the growing problem of right-wing extremism in several European societies) on the one hand, and social exclusion and mistrust in the political institutions on the other hand.

In addition, there is a strong need to develop concepts of education (on all levels, including universities) that help students to build rooted and open-minded identities ready to meet "others" without being afraid of losing their own roots. Catholic ethics with its biblically rooted anthropological foundations may be a rich source to nourish such educational concepts—if it is brought forth in a way that encourages dialogue. Since the Catholic Church has been an important actor in the field of schooling, universities, and in other areas of education, this is in fact a focal point of Christian practice and cultural engagement.[21]

All these issues, among others, are treated in several new research initiatives and university centers that recently have been established, such as the Center for Intercultural Ethics at the University of Tilburg (Netherlands) and the Center for Interreligious Studies at the University of Bamberg (Germany).

Both are, of course, interdisciplinary institutions, but with a strong accent on ethical research and with a high level of commitment on the part of Catholic ethicists.[22]

5. The Challenge to Create a Fundamental Ethical Consensus within Pluralist Societies

Rather than drawing a conclusion, I would like to raise another question which seems to be a truly fundamental issue within modern (Christian) political ethics and therefore underlying all mentioned issues: Is there—or can there be reformulated—a common ground, a fundamental consensus of values and ethical principles within pluralist and secular societies in terms of cultural belonging, religious beliefs, or worldviews? And how do we have to bring forth our own convictions and contributions to make them a relevant voice within a multivoiced concert of ethical conceptions, theories of justice, and ideas of a good life?[23]

6. Some Hopes for the Future

To make Catholic ethics an influential factor within the process of turning Europe into a political union and a space of peaceful cultural exchange we need to improve our communication in a way that allows a fruitful discourse with other worldviews, be they secularly or religiously shaped. This is a question of both the identity and the relevance of Catholic faith and its ethical impacts.

The more we succeed in developing an *ecumenical ethical discourse* which includes the Orthodox churches in the Eastern European countries, the more Christians will become able to contribute together to the solution of the urgent problems of living together in a multifaceted Europe in terms of cultural identities and religious beliefs or worldviews.

One very basic hope is that if Christians learn to speak up with a common voice in European societies, they will contribute more to the cultivation of respect for the life and worth of each individual whatever his or her ethnic, cultural, and religious background and convictions may be. And this indeed seems to me a major need in a European society that is shaped by deep social disparities and unequal chances of participation and personal development.

Piotr Mazurkiewicz

On Stem Cells and Homophobia

I propose to look at the moral challenges facing the Catholic Church in Europe seen from the perspective of certain actions taken by the European Parliament this year. I would not like to suggest that this is the mainstream of the activities of the European Parliament, but since I was invited to provoke discussion, I found these examples very provocative. The first challenge is the EP *resolution on homophobia,* adopted by the Parliament on January 18, 2006.[1] Another is the *resolution on the increase of racist and homophobic violence in Europe* of June 15, 2006.[2] The third challenge is the vote of June 15, 2006, on the *Seventh Framework Programme,* under which the EU should fund research with human embryos and embryonic stem cells.[3]

In the first of the documents, the very definition of homophobia raises fundamental questions. It reads as follows: "homophobia can be defined as an irrational fear of and aversion to homosexuality and of lesbian, gay, bisexual and transgender (LGBT) people based on prejudice, similar to racism, xenophobia, anti-Semitism and sexism."[4] Among manifestations of homophobia, the authors mention murder, acts of physical violence, together with hate speech, ridicule, or verbal violence. They also refer to the banning of gay parades as well as to the fact that in some Member States, partners of the same sex cannot enjoy all the rights and protections that married opposite-sex partners do, including recognition of same-sex families.[5]

In spite of all the appeals for "sound and clear definitions,"[6] the authors of the first resolution chose to adopt a very broad, and through this, a very ideological description of homophobia. It applies equally to real manifestations of discrimination and to a situation where legal (meaning not punished by law) same-sex unions do not enjoy legal protection and privileges that are due to heterosexual marriages under a national legal system.

The very structure of the term "homophobia" is interesting. It contains a measure of manipulative potential. The Greek root *homos* in this word (meaning identical, the same) is probably associated by most Europeans, not so well versed in Greek, with the Latin *homo* (man). The Greek *phobos,* which means fear (from which the new-Latin *phobia* is derived to describe the state of fear in persons suffering from neuropathy), suggests that the pejorative moral judgment of homosexual behavior or disagreement to legal privileges for such relationships is only an outcome of irrational prejudice.[7] Therefore, persons who do not share the same opinion as the authors of the text should be treated or perhaps even subjected to compulsory therapy, since Member States are urged to step up the fight against homophobia through administrative, judicial, and legislative means.[8] Until recently, it was homosexuality that was seen as a condition of illness; now the authors of the resolution suggest taking more or less the same approach towards the disapproval of homosexual behavior. This has very significant bearing on public life by blocking all rational discourse of the issue. Given that all forms of criticism, according to the authors of the resolution, are founded only on negative emotions, it is virtually impossible to take any rational arguments from the opponents. Therefore, persons who have different views on the issue, regardless of their scholarly achievements, are seen as persons driven solely by prejudice. Hence, they should have no right to spell out their views or to participate in a public debate.

It is by no means a coincidence that homophobia was placed on the same list next to racism, xenophobia, and anti-Semitism. The authors of the *resolution on the increase of racist and homophobic violence in Europe* clearly wish to extend the understanding of the notion "discrimination" onto this new area. At the same time they expect that Member States shall "reinforce criminal law measures aimed at the approximation of the penalties for such offences throughout the EU."[9] The object of such actions is to make the conviction about homosexuality being a deviation from the norm, a shameful relic out of place in the mainstream political debate and also an opinion that cannot possibly be professed by civilized persons of different views, as much as other phenomena on this list are rightly banned as inadmissible.[10] The authors also believe the reasons of public order, religious freedom, and the right to conscientious objection are not sufficient grounds to make the view opposite to the one they profess palatable and legal in public.[11]

Little wonder that Cardinal Joseph Ratzinger expressed the following concern: "The concept of discrimination is ever more extended, and so the prohibition of discrimination can be increasingly transformed into a limitation of the freedom of opinion and religious liberty. Very soon it will not be possible to state that homosexuality, as the Catholic Church teaches, is an objective disorder in the structuring of human existence."[12] If the very word "homophobia" means that moral evaluation of homosexual behavior is banned, then the teaching of the Catholic Church in Member States should be legally prohibited, and the church should be seen as a stronghold of "homophobic conservatism." Thus, the case of Rocco Buttiglione, commenting on the fact that his candidacy for the position of EU commissioner was rejected, remarks: "They wanted to humiliate one Christian in order to threaten all others. They wanted to demonstrate that it is not a coincidence that the invocation of God was excluded from the Constitution, conversely, that this lie is a manifestation of another faith, an atheist relativistic and anti-Christian faith. But there is more to it. A powerful lobby in Brussels wants to impose on all Member States the recognition of marriage between same-sex persons and an active promotion of homosexual lifestyle by the State."[13]

Also the example of Poland can be mentioned here, the country libelled by the resolution of June 15, 2006, and charged with racism, anti-Semitism, and homophobia (which happened merely a few days after the enthusiastic greeting accorded in Poland to Pope Benedict XVI). In Poland, during a legal gay manifestation the participants shouted out the following slogan; "Giertych do wora. Wór do jeziora" ("Let's put Giertych in a sack. Let's' throw him to a lake"). Roman Giertych is at present the minister of education, whereas the sack and the lake are allusions to how Father Jerzy Popieluszko was murdered by the communist regime. Therefore, a question can arise: is the ban against preaching Catholic thought and attempts to intimidate Catholics not a manifestation of discrimination? Is it not a grave discrimination undermining the first of all freedoms, religious freedom?

At this juncture, it is worth recalling what the so-called homophobic teaching of the Catholic Church is about, for instance what we read in the *Catechism* (2358): "The number of men and women who have deep-seated homosexual tendencies is not negligible. This inclination, which is objectively disordered, constitutes for most of them a trial. They must be accepted with respect, compassion, and sensitivity. Every sign of unjust discrimination in their regard should be avoided." In the letter *Homosexualitatis problema* by the Congregation for Doctrine of the Faith, we find the following: "It is deplorable that homosexual persons have been and are the object of violent malice in speech or in action. Such treatment deserves condemnation from the Church's pastors wherever it occurs. It reveals a kind of disregard for others which endangers the most fundamental principles of a healthy society. The intrinsic dignity of each person must always be respected in word, in action and in law."[14]

One must see a difference between respect for a person regardless of his or her sexual orientation and a demand to have same-sex unions legally recognized and to grant them privileges, including the right to adopt a child. The legal system that grants same-sex unions the status of a legal institution—according to the official teaching of the church—is contrary to reason. Bias in this direction means "going beyond the framework of history of human morality."[15] "Allowing children to be adopted by persons living in such unions would actually mean doing violence to these children, in the sense that their condition of dependency would be used to place them in an environment that is not conducive to their full human development."[16] Such an ethical assessment of the postulates raised by the gay community makes it necessary for Catholics to oppose the attempts of granting legal recognition to homosexual unions and to equal legal treatment of homosexual unions and marriages together with the enjoyment of rights that are vested in marriages. In a situation when a state has already made such a move, Catholics have a duty to oppose this law in a clear and unequivocal way. Should such obviously unjust laws be taken on board, everyone can resort to the right to conscientious objection.[17]

Another European problem is illustrated by the consent expressed by the European Parliament on June 15, 2006 to the EU funding of research on human embryos and human embryonic cells within the *Seventh Framework Programme* on scientific research and development. The basic problem consists in the manner in which a human embryo is treated: as a kind of object, an object of experiments which can be destroyed in the course of them. This opens the door to the instrumentalization of human life, which is a flagrant violation of human dignity. It is against the *Charter of Fundamental Rights,* which contains the following provision: "Human dignity is inviolable. It must be respected and protected."[18]

Moreover, the vote of the EP raises fundamental objections as to the compliance of their decision with the EU overriding the principle of subsidiarity. The European Union is expected to provide funding for research which is incompatible with national legal systems in place in many Member States. The area that provokes such controversy: the regulation of ethical questions belongs solely to the competency of Member States. Some of them have safeguarded this fact through the protocols and declarations attached to their accession treaties. The decision of the EP, incompatible with the position of the Legal Commission of the EP, is an attempt at bypassing the subject since formally it only pertains to scientific research and how it is funded. Despite all the provisions contained therein as to the respect of national law, it can be construed as a means to promote measures not allowed by national law. As a result, ethical questions should be resolved by decisions of an economic nature. Research which is unlawful under national law should be financed from the EU budget, and this from the contributions of the states where such research is illegal.

This brings us to a very sensitive problem of using the European Parliament to exercise pressure on Member States to change national law. It applies equally to research with embryos and to the guarantee that same-sex relations enjoy the same rights granted to heterosexual marriages. Pierre de Charentenay notes that this is an attempt "to impose a particular moral conception on the European Union as a whole without respect for the diversity which is written into the very heart of the European system. With a very specific idea in mind, . . . (they) wish to impose the most liberal moral concepts practiced in Northern Europe. They are using the platform of the European Parliament for very specific campaigns. Parliament thus becomes a steamroller to push through a particular moral view that will destabilise local cultures and the long-held ways of life in the various countries of the EU. Such behaviour discredits the role of the European Parliament."[19]

The above problems are a manifestation of a deeper cultural crisis that plagues Europe, the crisis defined by Cardinal Ratzinger as "the West's almost pathological hatred of itself."[20] The purpose of many activities taken by various groups of Europeans is to turn around the paradigm of the vision of man and culture. The phenomenon is rightly encapsulated by what Nietzsche called "the revaluation of all values." This may probably correspond to the condition termed by doctors "the self-aggression of an immunologic system"; such a system when subject to strong irritation cannot see the difference between the alien and itself and attacks anything at random.

The promotion of gay culture should not be viewed as a stand-alone phenomenon isolated from a broader context. What we see in Europe today is a dramatic crisis of marriage and family, which once underpinned the development of Europe's culture. This is expressed by both the undermining of the indissolubility of marriage and by the more and more universal recognition of cohabitation of men and women, which is not founded on the legal institution of marriage. The striving to devaluate marriage through the undermining of its definition is only one of many symptoms of such a broader crisis.

The endeavor to revaluate everything around us relies to a great extent on the individualist concept of a person which is gaining ground in the public awareness. Its meaning is fairly well caught in the following passage from Louis de Bonald:

> The philosophy of the previous [eighteenth] century had only man and the universe before its eyes, and not the society. On the one hand—and here I can resort to a colloquial culinary term—it "chopped" states and families without making out fathers, mothers, children, lords, servants, authorities, civil servants nor subjects, just people, i.e. individuals, each having his/ her own vested rights but not persons interrelated with each other. . . . On the other hand—it urged us to love mankind alone.

Tzvetan Todorov adds the following comment to the above passage: "Such a broad proposition excludes any genuine attachment. The very idea of a social contract: the attempt to found everything on the will of bargaining individuals is tainted with an 'individualist' and deeply misleading concept of mankind."[21] The presumption that society was established as a result of a social contract between adult, autonomous, rational beings previously isolated from one another is a convenient tool facilitating all kinds of reforms, but it easily crushes all axiological foundations of social life. Usually it fails to sufficiently take into account the good of persons who do not fit in the anthropological description of this kind—especially children. Thus, all the rules of social life, including ethical norms, are only fruits of negotiations between the founding fathers in the moment of transition from the "natural state" to the "social one." Under changing circumstances, all of them can be freely renegotiated. The implicit atheist presumption easily escapes people's attention but is often seen as mandatory as a precondition to be admitted to participation in public discourse, under the guise of absolute necessity to guarantee its neutrality.

John Paul II mentioned "existential fragmentation," as a result of which humanity is left all alone on the forum of life.[22] It is also in this context, that the exhortation about Europe mentions the term "fear." One could, therefore, say with a measure of perfidiousness that a phobia of a homophobia is a fruit of many other even more serious phobias. In the first place, it is related to "chrystophobia" as it was described by Joseph Weiler, a symptomatic fear of Christianity. In its extremity, it fuels the attempts to obliterate Christianity and all traces of Christian heritage from the public space. In the second place, this involves the fear of the future, which, once torn away from the past, seems to be very bleak and uncertain. This is also why there is a universal unwillingness to procreate. Calling new persons to being when one fails to see enough reasons for living and the purpose of one's own life seems to be a crime. Therefore, we see dramatically low birth rates, an unwillingness to get married, to take on lasting commitments vis-à-vis another person; hence there is "a temptation to dim hope."[23]

What can the church attempt to do? First, given the new challenges, the more precise teaching of the Catholic Church is provided on these issues. Second, through the Commission of the Episcopates of the European Community (*COMECE*) and through the national conferences of bishops, it lobbies in favor of solutions compatible with the rightful mind. Third, it spreads the word among the faithful. But the true hope for Europe will shine only once, as we read in the title of the exhortation; Europe rediscovers the person of Jesus Christ.

What might be surprising, as we read in the *Pastoral Instruction on Theology and Secularisation* in Spain, is that not only lay people but theologians also can have problems with the correct understanding of the mystery of Jesus Christ.[24] Thus, as the Spanish bishops suggest, quite often theologians follow the worldly way of approaching contemporary challenges rather than the magisterium. Consequently, they can be coresponsible for the effects of secularization's processes. This is a very hard diagnosis, some can say even unfair; but if there is a particle of truth in it, the rediscovery of the whole truth of the person of Jesus Christ and his relation with the church might be very helpful also.

Latin America

Ronaldo Zacharias (Brazil)
Dreaming to a New Moral Theology for Brazil

Sebastian Mier, S.J. (Mexico)
Hope in the Midst of Enormous Challenges in Mexico

Tony Mifsud, S.J. (Chile)
*Moral Reflection in Latin America: Challenges and
Proposals within the Chilean Reality*

The enormous complexity of Latin America is caught by the writings of three theological ethicists reflecting on the situation of their specific nations: Brazil, Mexico, and Chile. While poverty and the influence of globalization run through each essay, they differ considerably in the challenges, theological resources, and strategic proposals that each one describes.

With near-brutal honesty, Ronaldo Zacharias provides a picture of the moral life in Brazil: an insensitivity to social exclusion, cultural uprootedness, dehumanizing poverty, with the attendant emergence of religious fundamentalism. Theological ethics is in the meantime often distant from reality, parsing unobserved norms, and needing to find greater interdisciplinary engagements. Finally, Zacharias recognizes a phenomenom that cannot be ignored, that is, the way Brazilian Catholics differentiate their fidelity to worship from their adherence to magisterial moral teachings. Known as the *"jeitinho brasileiro,"* it constitutes a kind of social blessing to formal disobedience. The people then have a strategy "that allows a predominantly Catholic country to find no moral problem in loving the Church while paying little attention to some of its official teachings." He notes: "As mediators between the voice of the teaching authority of the church and the needs of the faithful, our position as moral theologians becomes very unsettling and destabilized: we are called to reconcile these two different worlds, but we do not know how to achieve equilibrium in the midst of such disequilibrium."

Sebastian Mier's essay is considerably different from Zacharias's. Mier points to many similar problems: corruption, poverty, moral compromise. But his essay, written very much in the context of liberation theology, drinks hopefully from the richness of the Word of God, the power of the Spirit, and the solidarity of the People of God. Still, these resources allow him to face the specific economic, social, and cultural challenges that face Mexico as it confronts a globalizing world that takes so much from Mexico leaving it with little alternatives to look elsewhere.

Finally, Tony Mifsud reflects on life in Chile and finds a progressive individualization that resists the claims of tradition (moral, familial, religious, social) and attempts to forge new conditions for possible relatedness predominantly through consumption. Like Giacometti figures, Chileans are seen as no longer connected to the common good or more specifically to the poor neighbor; likewise their only association with the church is in its spiritual sustenance but not in its moral or social claims. Mifsud proposes three tasks for today's theological ethicist (1) to reflect more deeply on the alienation of the other by looking not primarily to poverty but rather to the causes of social inequity; (2) to articulate a sexual ethics so as to meet the needs of contemporary society unfamiliar with meaningful discourse on love, unable to express the significance of commitment, and bewildered by the claims of marriage; and (3) to forge a renewed sense of Christian identity that helps individuals to see their incorporation into the Body of Christ.

Ronaldo Zacharias, S.D.B.

Dreaming of a New Moral Theology for Brazil

A lthough this is a panel focusing on the continent of Latin America, I speak as a representative of the Brazilian experience.[1] Certainly, the problems facing Brazil are the same, to a greater or lesser degree, as those of other Latin American countries. At the risk of overstating generalizations in ways that do not do justice to a wide variety of contexts, I have chosen to opt for a more restricted and realistic approach.[2]

An Overview of the Major Moral Challenges in Brazil

1. A Lack of Sensitivity to the Phenomena of Social Exclusion

We live in a context of institutionalized injustice: there are scandals in every sphere of society. Both the state and the politicians are immersed in a sea of corruption. They have no specific goals (for social reform). They limit themselves to the development of plans that favor economic growth and the well-being of the economic system. They negotiate agreements in response to the interests of pressure groups. We can see with our own eyes and feel with our own hands the weakening of the state and the undermining of the very reasons why many political parties came into existence. Serving economic interests along with their own, elected and appointed officials ignore the importance of developing socially responsible governmental programs. Politics have been identified as a propitious place for thieves and robbers. The credibility of both the state and the nation's politicians has fallen to an all-time low. In and of itself, this problem is shocking. However, an even more shocking problem is the indifference that characterizes people's attitudes toward the lack of morality in politics, the ways in which everything that deals with public welfare is ridiculed, and the total lack of any sensitivity to corruption and its social consequences. Political scandals have become entertainment spectacles for the general public.[3]

2. Dehumanizing Forms of Poverty

Poverty, in all of its dehumanizing forms, has become a scourge that is manifested in many different ways: the lack of food, housing, work, health care, and basic respect for the human dignity of every person. The country stands by watching as extreme forms of poverty give rise to a series of explosive social upheavals. The globalization of misery places before us a challenge of incalculable proportions: How do we begin to respond to the needs of the excluded, the marginalized, and those who have lost everything? Attracted to the large cities as to "promised lands," the vast majority of Brazilians has had no opportunity to learn what it means to be a citizen, an engaged member of the city. As the populations of cities have increased, the cities themselves have expanded. Materially speaking, they mirror the structure of Brazilian society: divided, disorganized, improvised, and juxtaposed. Our cities are exploding: those who are able escape from the cities, run away to build their man-made countryside paradises far from the urban centers, convincing themselves that the farther they are from urban realities, the better. The irony is that in order to secure their escape, they make use of the best resources the municipality has to offer. Those without resources, they flood into the cities, but have at their disposal nothing from which to build but leftovers. Violence explodes. The state loses control of the situation. Organized crime occupies increasingly more social space of its own and imposes itself as a powerful social force that seeks to gain control of the cities.[4]

3. Cultural Uprootedness

We live in a context in which all kinds of objects have been and continue to be manipulated by the dominant scientific culture. The only limit to scientific research is the time needed to invent something newer, and this time grows shorter every day. Science gives power, creates power, and becomes the primary power. This power, however, is not in the hands of scientists but in those of groups with economic interests. Once science, like culture, is transformed into a commodity with economic value, the market determines that which has worth and that which does not, what to produce and what to discard, who deserves to stay and who is dispensable. The fatal blow comes when science is controlled by interest groups and culture becomes nothing more than a folkloric object of curiosity, a tourist attraction. When this occurs, science ceases to be at the service of the people and culture ceases to be an expression of the people's identity. In such circumstances, a question arises: what does inculturation mean? By accepting science and its economic advantages as our top priority, we relegate culture to a secondary role and function. This seems to be the posture that many people have assumed.

However, while people integrate themselves into the dominant culture believing that they will be better able to control their lives, in actuality, the dominant culture confines them to the margins of progress.[5]

4. The Attraction of Religious Fundamentalism

We are living in a period of ever-increasing religious fundamentalisms. Such forms of fundamentalism absolutize doctrines, customs, and rituals. They adopt and adhere to certain historical expressions as unchanging and unquestionable. In the process of advancing such positions, fundamentalists seek to give a definitive, immutable, and sacred form to religious institutions. While taking notice of this phenomenon, little is done with regard to understanding the challenge that it poses. As a consequence, we find ourselves unable to understand the reasons why there is simultaneously a proliferation of new sects, churches, and movements *and* an attraction to traditional morality and uncompromising ethical stances that oftentimes are vague with regard to their content, but extremely precise regarding their form. If, on the one hand, the proliferation of sects, churches, and movements is driven by the diverse desires and needs of the people, it is curious that on the other hand, the phenomenon is a long way from being able to give expression to greater commitments with the people and the broader society. What is at stake here is not the sincerity with which people engage in their search for God. Rather, it is the role that such approaches to morality and theological ethics have in the defining, directing, and supporting of a project supposedly in the service and defense of life, a project that has so little to do with the characteristics of life itself, namely: flexibility, adaptability, change, and transformation.[6]

5. Understanding Theological Ethics on Its Own Terms

Many times, in teaching theological ethics, we worry more about the correct formulation of an objective set of norms and directives for action than with the people themselves and their decisions as moral agents carrying the weight of their concrete historical realities and social contexts. In and of themselves, the cool rationality of a set of objective norms or the uncritical echoing of an abstract formula does not lead anyone anywhere. All too often, prudence unfortunately ends up being a mantle of fear and cowardice and, therefore, ceases to occupy an important place in our work as moral theologians and, consequently, in the ethical education of the people we seek to form and serve. As walking encyclopedias of theological ethics, we are of little use if, by fear or cowardice, instead of assuming the role of the Good Samaritan we leave those seriously injured by thieves to die in the streets. It is important to recognize that not infrequently, whether within or in the name of the church, we communicate our knowledge with an exaggerated arrogance that annoys people instead of helping them on their life journey.[7]

6. The Need for an Interdisciplinary Approach

New problems always emerge, and we need to be attentive to them if we want our proposals and projects to be meaningful. However, the meaningfulness of any proposal or project depends today on the degree to which interdisciplinary perspectives are taken into consideration. If paying attention to new problems is important, our paying attention to new approaches is even more important. Today, a significant number of biblical scholars, church historians, and systematic theologians, along with scholars and specialists from other disciplines, are in a position to serve as allies of moral theologians, considering the fact that many of them incorporate into their work an emphasis on ethics. We need to pay attention to their work in the same way that we pay attention to the magisterium of the church. What the magisterium says is important, but if the whole of our proposals and projects is limited only to what the magisterium says, we run the risk of failing to make connections, or worse, we end up transmitting signals that cannot be received by others and, therefore, impossible to take into consideration.[8]

7. The Task of Rethinking Theological Ethics

Most of our ethicists in Brazil have had a European theological education. Without losing the capacity to set our theologies in dialogue with theologies produced in other contexts, we need to attend to the production and articulation of our own theologies in order to contribute to the process of rethinking theological ethics. When we talk about the task before us, we run the risk of assuming that such a task belongs exclusively to us, the moral theologians. Obviously, we have a specific responsibility to engage in this work. This fact is undeniable. But to think that the rethinking of theological ethics depends only on us is a delusion. Thanks to liberation theology, we have come to recognize that the phenomenon of exclusion is a challenge—both for those who are excluded as well as for those who exclude. This lesson serves us well as we undertake the task of rethinking theological ethics. If our ecclesial community excludes people due to its way of formulating and presenting the ethical demands of the gospel, then it has the moral duty to rethink its practice in the light of the actions of Jesus. Such rethinking cannot happen in a vacuum. The ecclesial community needs to be open and to hear the voices of those who are or who feel excluded. This implies placing people at the center of its thought and letting them voice their needs, difficulties, dreams, and hopes. If we trust that the "seeds of the Word" are everywhere, then we cannot ignore the fact that those people who are or who feel excluded may find ways of embodying certain values even in contexts that fall short of the evangelical ideal.[9]

8. A Phenomenon That Cannot Be Ignored

Although Brazil is a predominantly Catholic country, being Catholic in Brazil—even a practicing Catholic—while living outside the norms of the church's magisterium, are experiences that are not mutually exclusive. This is a reality that cannot be ignored. To properly understand our role as ethicists in such a context, we must come to terms with a life skill developed by the Brazilian people known as *"jeitinho brasileiro."* This phenomenon is characterized by finding creative solutions. It provides us with insights into ways of dealing with the difficulty of accepting as normative pretentious approaches to ethics that claim to be universal. In prioritizing the emotional rather than the intellectual, the human aspects of the relationship rather than the institutional ones, the *"jeitinho"* can be described both as a "special" way—expressed through the transgression of the norm or through the conciliation between wit and ability—of resolving a problem or a difficulty or forbidden situation, *and* as a creative solution to an eventual emergency. Such a strategy so permeates the Brazilian culture that it is impossible to understand how people react to the norms of the church without taking it into account. The *"jeitinho brasileiro"* constitutes a kind of social blessing to formal disobedience. And it is such a strategy that allows a predominantly Catholic country to find no moral problem in loving the church while paying little attention to some of its official teachings. There is no doubt that the sense of ecclesiality and of communion among the people of God is compromised in this context. As the distance between the magisterium of the church and the faithful increases, the credibility and meaningfulness of the teachings of the church in terms of contemporary sensibility are put at risk. The result is that we have two completely different worlds, with their irreconcilable sensibilities and radically distinct values. As mediators between the voice of the teaching authority of the church and the needs of the faithful, our position as moral theologians becomes very unsettling and destabilized: we are called to reconcile these two different worlds, but we do not know how to achieve equilibrium in the midst of such disequilibrium.[10]

How Are Moral Theologians Addressing These Problems?

It is very difficult to give a general answer to this question that is equally valid for all of those who have been working in the field of theological ethics. I prefer to point out some aspects that will provide a broad panoramic view of the problems that we face in addressing the problems just mentioned.

- The majority of our moral theologians in Brazil teach in seminaries. Although this is not a problem, the moral questions we address tend to relate directly to the formation of future ministers. The questions themselves tend to be considered from an ecclesiastical perspective.
- The vast majority of our moral theologians have other activities for which they are responsible in addition to seminary teaching. Immersed in administrative concerns and problems, the time that they have at their disposal is used to prepare their classes. Very few have the opportunity, in terms of time and freedom from other responsibilities, to write and to do research.
- Because of these circumstances, most of us have no time to develop a proposal much less to rethink our theology. We run the risk of engaging in a discourse that is far from reality, from the necessary dialogue with culture and science, and from the moral agents who should be the subjects of our discourse. The consequence is the tendency to reduce morality to its deontological dimension.
- Even though they are few, some of our moral theologians have made significant strides in engaging the challenges and the changes of our time, in offering critical assistance and advice during times of crisis, in approaching some specific moral problems in a multidisciplinary way, in confronting reality and faith. But it is very interesting to note that several of our moral theologians have moved into the field of bioethics and do not want to invest their time and effort in the development of more meaningful approaches to fundamental moral theology, social ethics, and sexual ethics. This may be a sign that what most of us want in terms of teaching or writing in the area of theological ethics can be found (or at least favored) by a field that, in itself, demands dialogue, and openness to science and culture.
- We need to pay attention to the cultural dynamics that drive most of the social processes. In facing culture wars, we lack the ability to reveal the mystical dimension of Christian ethics.
- We fail to deepen the understanding of the eschatological dimension of moral life as we tend to delegate to spirituality the ethical demands of faith, hope, and charity.
- A great challenge today: to reconcile the construction of justice with the attention that must be given to cultural processes and interreligious dialogue.

The Sources That Have Been Employed

It is impossible to deny that there is an abundance of literature representative of the theological disciplines that includes literary and historical-critical approaches to Scripture, that concentrates on the systematic interpretation of Scripture and tradition, and that analyzes human action from anthropological, psychological, social, and cultural perspectives. In other words, diversity of methods and approaches is a given when looking for continuity among Scripture, church history, systematic theology, and theological ethics.

Unfortunately, our interdisciplinary efforts are barred by the rigidity of the curriculum, its consequent fragmentation, and by the fact that we count on a few professors who work primarily from a unitary perspective of theological knowledge.

We lack sources produced in Brazil. We still have as reference texts works produced in other contexts. At the same time, we also lack consistent access to adequate bibliographies (national or international).

The number of moral theologians and of those who are pursuing higher degrees are increasing among us. But we also notice that almost 100 percent are priests or religious. Lay women and men, despite their significance in the church, are underrepresented among us.

Since 1977, national meetings of moral theologians have taken place in Brazil every year. These meetings provide opportunities to discuss, to study, to exchange experiences, especially regarding academic teaching. The Brazilian Society of Moral Theology was founded (twenty-nine years ago) to guarantee the intellectual and affective articulation of moral theology. In the golden years of liberation theology, our society was deeply committed to producing a theological ethics for the Latin American continent. Currently, it is the place where we encounter strength to continue believing in our work with and for the church.

Because of changes that have taken place in the Brazilian church during recent decades (a new face of the church was the result of the pontificate of John Paul II), it has become increasingly more difficult to dialogue with some church authorities. There is, generally speaking, a lack of trust and sincerity among theologians and authorities of the church. To demand loyalty without giving it and to underestimate the value of reciprocity are articles that are very difficult to sell in the marketplace of relationships. The consequences tend to be evident.

Perspectives for the Future

Many are the perspectives one could take with regard to the future. As I was listing some of the possibilities, I was reminded of a poem written by a young woman student of moral theology—Luzenir Maria Caixeta—who gave a presentation at the conclusion of the Third Latin American Meeting on Moral Theology.[11] Putting aside what I have written, I decided to take the risk of creating space where this poem could be given voice. I am convinced that if we really want our work within the church to be significant and prophetic, the words written by Luzenir hold far greater potential than mine for offering us some clues as to how we might think about where to direct our efforts in the development of a meaningful theological ethics.

I dream of a theology
that moves between the imminent and transcendent,
but that defines itself the imminent commitment
to produce and reproduce life on the planet.
A theology that begins with a unified vision of the human person,
situated in history.
A theology that is palpable and sensitive,
with a Latin-American face:
the face of a poor person,
the face of a woman,
the face of a black person and an indigenous person,
the face of a lay person,
the face of a young person. . . .
A theology with the scent of sweat from work and from love,
enhanced by the color
of different cultures and sciences;
marked, in sum, by intersubjectivity,
by interdisciplinary work,
by plurality,
by reciprocity.
A theology capable of bringing together
scientific rigor with its many rules,
epistomologies, hermeneutics, and methods,
with the quotidian experiences of its subjects and interlocutors,
with its life of scarcity and abundance,
of the struggle for survival,
of feasts, pleasures, sorrows,
of resistance and the sharing of solidarity,
of neighborhood shops and so many loves!
A collective theology, constructed by everyone
and recognized by all as their own.
I carry this theology in my womb, my skin, and my hair.
I need it to live and to survive.
I dream to live, with dignity, by the fruit of such theological labors!
Could this be the profile of Moral Theology
at the dawn of the Third Millennium?

Sebastian Mier, S.J.

Hope in the Midst of Enormous Challenges in Mexico

L et me say from the outset that I do not claim to offer an in-depth view of the subject, but rather a significant and reasoned contribution with emphasis on the Mexican perspective.

With regard to the challenges: from the beginning of liberation theology in Latin America, it was clear that the important thing is not theology itself but the real liberation of the people, a full and integral life for them. Theology must make a contribution to that liberation in daily life, a contribution that we theologians offer toward the coming of the reign of God. So the main challenges to moral theology are not doctrinal or academic issues but the ones our people face in trying to live fully.

Moral theologians have become aware then of a close connection among the branches of theology; thus ethical reflection draws rich nourishment from biblical and systematic theology, and its motivation goes hand in hand with spirituality.[1]

The Fundamental Challenges

With regard to the challenges, let me briefly recall that for centuries our continent has been suffering a situation of misery and subjection to foreign powers; and that in the past three decades the model of globalization imposed by the neoliberal system has further expanded the gap between a few people of great wealth, power, and means of communication—even greater than that of many in the first world—and the large majorities who lack the basics, often even the minimal necessities of food, health, housing, education, and even dignified employment.[2]

This situation has produced an enormous emigration from the countryside to the cities, and also to the United States—which requires free access for its capital and exports but restricts access for workers, thus forcing them to emigrate under extremely unfavorable, "illegal" conditions, often at risk of their lives. Broadening the focus, we must recognize that Central American migrants in Mexico are often treated as unfairly as the U.S. policy we denounce.[3]

On the political side we see the frustration of the population vis-à-vis rulers who are subject to transnational economic power on the one hand, and on the other are more concerned with personal and partisan interests than with the good of the people; this is especially evident in their appalling infighting and high levels of corruption. This still prevails, although later on I shall point out significant changes.

Furthermore the mass media have acquired tremendous power, distracting and manipulating the multitudes on one hand, and using their enormous influence in favor of neoliberal business people and governments on the other.

Paths to Solutions in the Life of the People

In the face of these large issues, and other important ones in the background, solutions must come—and to some extent are already coming—not so much from reflection as from action in all areas of society.

One of these, at the continental level, is the establishment of the World Social Forum. From its beginnings in Brazil, it has resonated very widely in Latin America and on other continents. It has undergone changes in its most concrete objectives, headquarters, and types of gathering. It has succeeded in bringing together hundreds of thousands of representatives from organizations that are struggling in every area of society to improve living conditions for their people. Within this "relatively large" number,[4] there is a wide range of goals and methods as well as success in achieving their objectives. They are a vivid manifestation of hope in action.[5]

In our country, the Indian organization Zapatista Army of National Liberation (EZLN) stands out. Its roots are in the evangelizing work of the diocese of San Cristóbal de las Casas; later it was influenced by other social movements and decided to "rise up in arms" against an obstinate, devious system of injustice on January 1, 1994. Facing military repression, large sectors of Mexican society cried out in search of a way out through dialogue; since then the Zapatistas themselves have sought to use other tactics, in cooperation with many Mexican organizations and with the solidarity of numerous groups in other countries and continents, where they have taken on a noteworthy symbolic meaning.

In general we should note that Brazil (Lula 2002), Argentina (Kirchner 2003), Uruguay ("Tabaré" 2004), Bolivia (Evo Morales 2006), and Chile (Bachelet 2006) have brought to the presidency persons more representative of the true interests of their people. This does not mean that all the problems are solved: these persons are still strongly subject to national and international, economic and political forces, which still have ways of imposing conditions and will not hesitate if necessary to use more persuasive military arguments. They also face varying degrees of problems within their parties. But they do represent significant achievements from the combined efforts of ethical-"scientific" reflection[6] and sociopolitical organization.

As I have just mentioned, it is undeniable that reflection has an important role in illuminating people's intelligence, and in orienting and motivating their hearts. This is where we find the role of ethics in general and theological ethics in particular. Although it is not as quickly effective as we would like and as the situation of the majorities requires, it has helped to awaken people's conscience and strengthen their spirit to move forward toward the "reign of God."

The Resources of Theological Ethics

In confronting these great challenges we rely mainly on three rich resources: the word of God, the power of the Spirit, and the wisdom of the people.

The word of Jesus stands out in the midst of God's revelation. Indeed, the prophetic clarity and boldness of the Gospels are renewed when we hear them again in the context of the daily, loving solidarity of the people. We have been reminded that "the Spirit of the Lord has anointed us to bring good news to the poor . . . and to let the oppressed go free" (Luke 4:16–26); that "I desire mercy and not sacrifice" (Matt 9:13, 12:7); that the authentic way of life is the love of God the Father rather than riches and power and ideology, and that it is shown by caring for the multitudes who fall into the hands of robbers on the Jericho road (Luke 10:25–37); that "the sabbath was made for humankind, and not humankind for the sabbath" (Mark 2:27—an "anthropocentric" note introduced by the son of God himself); that we will be known as his disciples if we have love for one another (John 13:35); that we will be blessed if we have the spirit of the poor, if we hunger for justice, and if we are persecuted for the sake of justice (Matt 5:1–12); that true worship and the sacraments must be at the service of love, and that he requires love and justice of us (Matt 25:31–46).

We have thus a whole series of simple and profound teachings which we confess as divine, and which must inspire every theological and ethical effort even if they lack philosophical subtlety and academic documentation. This does not mean that philosophy and the university have nothing to say, but it does mean they are not the dominant force in Christian faith.

The words we have recalled give concrete shape to a central symbol of the Synoptic Gospels that has profoundly inspired our theology: the reign of God. Jesus declares it at hand, considers it the center of his mission, and teaches us in the Lord's prayer to long for it. The reign of God means acknowledging God as the Father, who lives among us as brothers and sisters in love and service, in liberation from all sin and oppression, in the fulfillment of justice which renews by communicating abundant life. All this is already present in history and open to eschatological fulfillment.[7]

These are only a few of the fundamental elements in the Gospels; there are also fruitful resources in other books of both the Old and the New Testaments.[8]

This understanding of the centrality of the Father's kingdom has many relevant implications for theological ethics, of which I will mention two: first, Jesus' invitation "to be with him, and to be sent out" to collaborate in his mission (Mark 3:14), which we have described as following Jesus, each in our own historical circumstances; second, the reign of God is not the same as the church but is a broader reality; the church is not an end but a means, albeit an important one.[9]

Based on these two implications, we believe that the power of the Spirit moves us to be open and courageous—open to all the manifestations of truth within the church and outside it. Faithfulness to the revealed word is not limited to reciting the magisterium; nor is it jealous of contributions from other religions, philosophies, or sciences; nor does it need to demonstrate its superiority over them. On the contrary it admires and incorporates them with full respect for cultural diversity, giving thanks to the source of all truth, which "blows where it chooses" (John 3:8) and which is known by its fruits and is courageous in defense of the humiliated, in the face of threats from the powerful.[10]

"The people" are not perfect; but they also have received wisdom from the One who has revealed himself to the little ones (Matt 11:25). We Latin American theologians are learning to enter into dialogue with these sources of popular wisdom, which is often more lived than articulated. One of the main sources is the religion of the people, which is now being revalued after a crisis in the first years after Vatican Council II; the Mother of God plays a central role, and in Mexico, Tonantzin Guadalupe.[11] Others include the everyday life of the people with their survival mechanisms, their rich human sense of community celebration, their demonstrations and struggles of every kind. In closer relation to the church, the ecclesial base communities play an important part.[12] More recently—especially because of the high awareness built up by the 500th anniversary of the arrival of the Europeans—there have been contributions from the indigenous peoples, and more specifically, Indian theology.[13]

More Specific Challenges

With this as a panoramic context and basis, let us move on to some specific challenges and the way in which we are confronting them.

In the Economic and Political Fields

The great transnational corporations, and to some extent all capitalists, are demanding absolute freedom of the market and independence from economic laws. We in turn are stubbornly denouncing all greed, the bedazzlement of technology, and the savagery of competitiveness. We are saying that the workers and the natural environment are not made for riches, but that the economy is made to serve human beings; the resources of Mother Earth are meant to serve not the ambitions of the wealthy but the needs of all her children. We say this in spite of the deafness and cynicism of the powerful and the relative weakness of our voices.

We also recognize the enormous and laborious task of continued dialogue with science and technology in search of solutions that are not only voluntaristic—because mere denunciation and good will are not enough—but effective. (In this respect we often go beyond simple ethics; service to life and the liberation of the people do not have clearly defined boundaries.)[14]

The simple life of the indigenous peoples reminds us that their goal is not an unlimited increase of technical progress, comfort, and money, but basically "health, home, clothing and sustenance," and now also dignified employment.[15]

Politicians no longer use the discourse of absolute monarchs; they have learned the language of formal democracy and even of service to the people, which shows some progress in ethical terms. But the political practice of many of them is full of personal ambition for money and power, gained by many means: lies, manipulation, corruption, impunity, the cooptation or elimination of opponents, among others. To a large extent the political parties are made up of such people, and have drawn deep skepticism from many sectors of the population.

This leaves ethics facing the challenge of devalued language, and theologians facing problems of coherent living, since "clericalism" in its many guises bears witness against them.[16]

In the search for viable models we also need dialogue with science, technology, and successful experience. Here the example of indigenous authorities shows us a structure of true service; far from being paid or enriched, they work overtime to attend to community affairs, while at the same time they carry on their regular occupations and save their money to organize the annual saint's day festivities.[17]

In the Cultural Spheres

Here the problems are much more complex. On the one hand, each of the many cultures on our continent is evolving; on the other, there are closer relationships among them, and together they are subjected to whatever comes from the "first world," especially the United States. The growing currents of migration add to this complexity. Together these factors have led to a "crisis of values," which has become even sharper since the council. A crisis does not necessarily mean decline, as many believe; it does mean profound changes, in which it is hard to distinguish between "the wheat and the weeds."

The role of women is a clear example. "Before the council," everything was clear and simple; now we recognize that this "accustomed order" entailed—along with personal and social values—many forms of discrimination and injustice must be overcome. But it is not clear how to preserve the values and overcome the injustice in families, in the church, and in other social spheres. This makes it difficult to reach useful agreement on "rights and duties," so to speak. And if it is hard to agree on the "guiding light," obviously it is even harder to find the path leading us to the light.[18]

There are many other challenges to ethics in the areas of sexuality (its meaning; its relationship to affection, commitment, and procreation; homosexuality, with its more or less coercive commercial connotations); family relationships (among adults, children, and the aging; single mothers; their ecclesial and social dimensions); and bioethics (the depersonalization of abortion, the distribution of resources, the commercialization of traditional medicine, genetic engineering, ecological issues). At present these are debated in many magazines, and for the poor majorities in Latin America they raise special circumstances that we cannot overlook. We also face other important issues for the life of our people which are not receiving the needed attention in the areas of schooling and informal education, interpersonal communication (where the proliferation of psychotherapies is symptomatic of many problems), and religious practice (changes in the sacraments, new "ecumenisms," etc.).

In the face of these issues, the gospel presents the fundamental criterion of the dignity of every human person and the option for the humiliated ones whose liberation we are to seek; on this basis we are in continuing dialogue with different persons and groups who share that criterion.

Toward a Grateful, Energetic, and Patient Hope

In the economic and political areas there is basic agreement among those of us who share a humanistic ethic—believers and secular people. The more difficult problems arise at the level of method (finding more effective ways) and social organization (gathering sufficient power to carry out a project of justice). By contrast, in the cultural and religious areas the specifically ethical issues are far from evoking consensus; a sincere and dialogical search is needed, respectful of the diversity of cultures and beliefs.

In the area of mass communication we have a combination of economic-political issues on one hand, and cultural issues on the other. Again, there is wider "humanistic" agreement on the economic and political side (denouncing all oppression but unable to overcome it); on the cultural side the differences are greater, and therefore also the need for ethical dialogue.

Certainly the challenges—coming from the present reality of our peoples, moving toward the reign of God—are enormous, almost crushing; equally great is the power that has brought us thus far and moves us forward. God the Mother-Father is present throughout our history in the many "servants of Yahweh," whose prototype is Jesus, son of God and Mary, a peasant woman of Nazareth. Jesus continues to reveal to us a God who is more all-loving than all-powerful, whose "omnipotence" is manifest in an invincible love that leads him to full, humble, and liberating self-giving, to the point of death and resurrection. And the power of his Spirit remains present in many persons and communities.

He has placed us with his people and has given us the gift of a merciful, solidarity and liberating theology, with all its limitations. That theology has made its contributions and must continue working with confidence and dedication, and also with patience, since—although the calamities of the people are enormous—the divine rhythms are slower than our eagerness. The resurrected One and his Spirit carry history forward in a mysterious way that enlightens and nourishes us, but does not offer all the solutions right away. We shall go on seeking those solutions with the people, in our many services and ministries—among them that of moral theology—collaborating with people inside and outside the church.

Tony Mifsud, S.J.

Moral Reflection in Latin America

Challenges and Proposals within the Chilean Reality

The establishment of a neoliberal *economic* model, the *political* transition from dictatorship to democracy, and the *globalization* which has challenged traditional values have produced such rapid and profound social change in Chile that we are experiencing not only the future but the present as an enormous challenge. For example, the permanent social division, which prevents equal access to the benefits that are produced, remains in force although the context has changed. Chile is making progress, but goods and services are not equitably distributed among its citizens; one sector is totally marginalized.[1]

Challenges

1. An Asocial Individualization

The society is undergoing a profound *cultural change*.[2] The problem is not so much the loss of old social models, but rather the weakness of the new imaginary collectives that fail to shape a shared *we*. Modernization is not only changing countries externally, but also the physiognomy of society. The globalizing process (in which the global affects the local and the local can only be fully understood in a global perspective), the reshaping of the *nation-*state (in which the identification of the people with the state is overcome by the logic of neoliberalism), the logic of the *market* (in which social recognition is related to purchasing power), and the modernization of communications (the presence of a virtual reality which has changed our notion of public space) are all radically changing the context in which the society develops.

But the most striking feature of the present society is *the process of individualization*. Today's individuals distance themselves from inherited traditions and affirm their right to define for themselves what they want to do with their lives. This process can lead to a reformulation of social relationships, but it may also result in an asocial mentality. Individualization, as a social category, implies a more intentional self-development by individual subjects, the right to self-determination, to be the protagonists of their own biography, to be themselves. Therefore, this concept is not the same as egoism (an ethical category) or apathy (a political category).

Nevertheless, this need to build one's own identity is not based on support from the society, because individuals do not consider themselves interpreted or represented by social systems; therefore their process of individualization tends to move toward ethical individualism, since they feel increasingly distant and marginalized from the present-day organization of society.

This brief and necessarily incomplete picture of the society is not catastrophic; it simply reflects the *changing times*, in which the great challenge is to give new meaning and shape to the social fabric in line with new experiences and the emerging contemporary context. This is only possible insofar as we recognize tradition (the past that shapes collective identity over time), discern current trends (encouraging new expressions of values and critically analyzing the obstacles), and build a shared social project (a future that is the responsibility of the whole citizenry). This task cannot be carried out through confrontation (with intolerance toward whatever is different), nor by denying the weight of the past (which forms a part of the present), but through dialogue (separate identities respecting their differences in order to find common spaces in which to live together).

2. The Socio-cultural Context

We have gone from the modern age of critical reason (the masters of suspicion: Nietzsche, Freud, and Marx) to the present-day sense of *enjoyment* based on consumption (sensationalism, eroticism, foolhardiness, drug trips, etc.). Thinking is out of style; enjoyment and good times are in, because tomorrow is another day.

Secularization came later to Chile than to Europe, mainly because the military dictatorship was economically liberal and conservative in values (indeed the debates over divorce, abortion, euthanasia, and homosexuality began after the transition to democracy).

The level of secularization (meaning the decline of religion) in today's society has been exaggerated. The very uncertainties, risks, and doubts caused by modernity itself have contributed to the growth of *religiosity*. But Catholicism has ceased to be the central feature of national identity; it remains an important element among others, but not the only or most decisive one. Religion has lost its central role in society; thus the process of secularization has led mainly to a progressive loss of religious influence in the most important spheres of social life. In this sense, Chilean secularization has not brought religion or religious feeling to an end, but rather to a loss of centrality with the arrival of pluralism. At the same time, this religiosity is more *massive* than *communitarian*, more *therapeutic* than transformational, more *cosmic* than socially committed, focused more on a vague, faceless *divinity* than on a personal God.

Consumer culture is very present in today's society. What is new is that today many people have access to goods and services that were out of their reach a few years ago, the exclusive privilege of the elites. Consumption is more than purchasing power, because it is related to identity itself. That is, by possessing or acquiring certain things people project their own selves onto those things. Their identity is formed, in part, by the opinions and expectations of other people who are important to them. Thus having things means belonging to a group, and being recognized by it. They feel they are somebody because they have something. This is reinforced by a society that recognizes people on the basis of their purchasing power. So it is not only a personal problem but basically a social and cultural one.

There is also a *cultural malaise* because, in the midst of economic growth and increased consumption, citizens tend to feel insecure and unhappy under increased levels of stress, indebtedness, urban overcrowding and pollution, and increased crime. They suffer a lack of complementarity between modernity and subjectivity, so that the individual feels ever more vulnerable and less significant in this new context.

3. The Ecclesial Context

Although there is still a deep-rooted Christian-Catholic tradition, we can identify a series of changes: (a) a larger *number* of Catholics; (b) the church as an institution has ceased to be the *center* (significant actor) in society; (c) it is publicly *questioned* by some of its own members; and (d) the *norm* (not its fulfillment but its content) is questioned.[3]

Nevertheless, people declare themselves as *religious* (over 90 percent believe in God) although not necessarily as church members (the crisis of identification with institutions, typical of postmodernity). Several indicators suggest that they are in a period of personal searching for spirituality, transcendence, and community, although many of them do not seek it in institutional religion. The emphasis is on personal searching over received tradition; the de-institutionalization and privatization of religion are increasing.

With respect to *moral conduct* in Chile, while Catholics strongly disapprove of homosexuality, adultery, drugs and abortion, there is substantial approval of contraception, divorce, and premarital cohabitation by young people.

With respect to the official declarations of the church, questions are raised about their *style* (judgmental), *content* (which is not accepted), *legitimacy* (invasion of private life), and *reasoning* (unconvincing ecclesial reasons). Thus the problem is not only lack of compliance with the norms, but questioning the norms and those who establish them, who are generally considered to be outside the realm of concrete, everyday life.

Finally, in the context of a market culture with individualistic features, there is an apparent diminution of ethical concern around the discourse of *poverty* and its causes, which in earlier times led to reflection that was conflictive and confrontational but also creative, innovative, and motivating. At the same time, there is more discourse on the theme of solidarity which goes beyond mere paternalism and social indifference.

Previously, ethical efforts were basically directed toward proving the existence of massive poverty and exploring its causes, challenging the old assumption that poverty was simply a natural, random phenomenon. Thus poverty was seen as having concrete, historical causes, and overcoming poverty as an ethical challenge involving human freedom and responsibility in the social context.

But in today's society there is less confrontation over that topic, since the facts are now undeniable; rather we tend to see a division between those who have responded to this reality with commitment and those who simply remain indifferent as a result of the prevailing individualism. In place of the Parable of the Final Judgment (Matt 25:31–46) as ethical paradigm, we have the Parable of the Rich Man and Lazarus (Luke 16:19–31). In other words, social concerns tend not to be considered as an integral part of society's values agenda.

Proposals

The present challenges to ethical reflection suggest three priority concerns: (a) cultural inequality as a cause of economic poverty; (b) the need to reformulate an ethic of sexuality; and (c) a dialogue with society from the perspective of religious experience.

1. To Move from the Question of Poverty to the Issue of Inequality

Neoliberal economic policies have succeeded in reducing the poverty index, but social inequality remains.[4] One of the main causes of this difference is the variation in social capital by families and in access to different levels of educational institutions. The absence of a broad, solid middle class also generates an economically vulnerable sector of the population, for whom any unforeseen situation (sickness, job loss) or economic crisis leads to a return of poverty. Within this floating population there is no certain way to measure progress in terms of simple indicators, since they are unstable over time.

A large part of the inequality is related to large *salary* differences, which in turn reflect an unequal distribution in the quantity and quality of *education*, differences of *gender*, and gaps between formal and informal *employment* and between *rural* and *urban* income.[5] The greatest educational differences begin with preschool education, which later affects the development of more complex skills.

The precariousness of most wages, the strong classism which favors some social classes (membership in a social group outweighs meritocracy in the labor field),[6] a deficient public education which tends to reproduce social inequalities and generate new ones, the massive presence of informal labor without social security, and the unequal access to health systems are among the factors in an economic and cultural context that hinders the effort to overcome poverty.

To be sure, democratic governments have given priority to social policies; but we must ask whether these are focused on situations of poverty (a market economy for those with purchasing power; state subsidies for everyone else), or on creating social conditions that can mitigate the inequalities—for instance, by improving the quality of public education, developing the basic skills for incorporation in the workforce, and decisive support for the small and micro-enterprises which employ 80 percent of the work force.

2. Toward a Reformulation of an Ethic of Sexuality

There is an increasing perception (correct or not; the perception itself is important) of an official Catholic Church totally changed from the days of military dictatorship, now primarily concerned with the topic of sexuality.

This has produced a growing loss of identification with the church as an institution, together with an incipient loss of social credibility from the onslaught of reports about cases of pedophilia at both the national and international level. A growing number of Catholics now see the official church as a point of reference but not for membership (Catholics who declare themselves nonpracticing). This loss of identification is also part of the postmodern mentality, one feature of which is criticism of all institutions.

The fact that a sexual ethic propounded by the Catholic Church is widely ignored, especially by a significant group of young people, raises a series of questions.[7] On one hand we see youth identifying sexual relations (the act) with love (the value that gives human significance to the act), without an institutional reference point; at the same time, what love means to them is not specified (a feeling that may pass, or a choice for life—changeable or committed over time?). In other words, what is the specific meaning of the sexual relationship? What does it mean between two persons? This is very important, since otherwise the sexual relationship is reduced to a purely physical fusion rather than a meaningful encounter between two persons.

On the other hand, we see a significant failure to understand the religious content that should underlie, and justify, the positions propounded by the church. So we must ask if there is an adequate pedagogy capable of reaching today's youth. Is the pedagogy normative and judgmental, or persuasive and engaging? Does it address young people's freedom, or is it imposed on them? Does it follow a developmental educational style that moves from teaching a norm to formation in discernment?

We must also explore the critique of the church as old-fashioned on matters of sexual ethics. This may mean that the church is giving yesterday's answers to today's questions, that is, failing to recognize cultural change. But does this refer to its message (the content of its teaching), or to its presentation (style and reasoning)? It is most important to avoid two extremes: dismissing the criticism without serious consideration, or adapting to today's fashion without exploring the sources of Christian ethics. The possibility of applying the *sensus fidelium* in the moral arena is worth considering. Obviously this would not mean a simple majority demand, but a deep conviction of faith in which people "from the bishops to the last faithful lay people" (St. Augustine) "give universal consent in matters of faith and custom."[8]

Should we not take more seriously the affirmation of *Gaudium et Spes* (no. 33), that the church "does not always have at hand an answer to every question"? We need to reflect seriously on the importance of maintaining the ideal, but also on human weakness. How should we respond to concrete situations of error or failure in marriage? The urgency of this challenge is that every situation requires a pastoral solution. There is an increasingly urgent need for serious theological and moral debate over burning issues (without condemning or imposing prohibitions in advance), because otherwise we will create a two-track way of thinking between official and alternative discourse. Finally, in the realm of sexuality we must avoid a reductive norm focused on corporeal acts, and explore more deeply in the direction of feelings and motivation.

3. Forging Christian Identity and Dialogue

In his first encyclical *Deus caritas est* (December 25, 2005), Benedict XVI describes Christian vocation in terms very relevant to the relationship between ethical discourse and Christian experience. "*We have come to believe in God's love*: in these words the Christian can express the fundamental decision of his life. Being Christian is not the result of an ethical choice or a lofty idea, but the encounter with an event, a person, which gives life a new horizon and a decisive direction" (no. 1).

In the context of this "intrinsic and indivisible nexus between faith and morality,"[9] there has been a tendency, influenced by Kant (the *ought to be* of the categorical imperative),[10] to move preferentially *from morality to faith*; that is, compliance in order to earn a reward, or obedience in order to assure salvation. This focus has often generated a strong sense of guilt (compliance with the *ought to be* as the reference point of religious self-esteem), and a normative-legalistic approach (the *ought to be* without further justification). Furthermore, Catholicism is generally associated with the moral dimension of Christianity. Indeed our pluralistic society usually identifies the Catholic Church with its ethical positions, especially in the areas of sexuality and bioethics (especially abortion and euthanasia).

But Christianity is not primarily a moral system but basically a realm of *transcendent meaning* (faith) and *celebration* (hope), which lead to a specific *way of life* (charity). Christian ethical action consists precisely in the mediation of charity in a context of deep faith in the action of the Spirit.

Christian ethics, expressed in life and in words, needs to reclaim its *theological home*;[11] it needs the context of meaning to motivate a corresponding change of lifestyle in history. A morality of meaning can provide the basis for an ethics of obligation as an expression of its coherence and integrity; a morality of content (following the person of Christ, guided by the action of the Spirit, in the building of the kingdom of the Father) can provide the basis for the basic motivation for acting and thinking ethically from the viewpoint of faith.[12]

Giving preference to an ethical approach that grows out of faith, or out of a faith-based morality, leads to a relationship of coherence and integrity in everyday life, in the context of gratuitousness which offers the responsibility of an ethics motivated by constant reference to the person of Jesus of Nazareth, proclaimed as the Christ by God the Father.[13]

But this approach does not lead to moralizing faith (reducing religion to moral compliance), nor to a religious fundamentalism of morality (rejecting ethical reasoning in favor of moral fideism), nor to a sectarian morality (incapable of entering into dialogue with other forms of ethics). On the contrary, it highlights the need for *a faith expressed in concrete works*,[14] avoiding the temptation of spiritualism without commitment. Ethical action verifies (*verum facit*—makes true) the spiritual experience.[15] It is not about earning faith through works, but about the need for works to express gratitude for— and coherence with—the gift of faith.

Therefore one of the great challenges in the formulation of Christian ethics—in the context of a society that is traditionally Christian, but increasingly pluralistic in its thinking and way of living—is this: the elaboration of a *theological reasoning* (identity) and a *reasoned and reasonable presentation* (dialogue) in order to offer today's society an alternative project, inspired by the gospel.

North America

David Hollenbach, S.J. (United States)
Catholic Ethics in a World Church: A U.S. View

Jean Porter (United States)
Due Process and the Rule of Law: A Moral/Theological Challenge

Kenneth R. Melchin (Canada)
The Challenge of World Poverty: Continuity and Change in Theological Ethics from a Canadian Perspective

David Hollenbach begins his essay with a timely case: his experience of leading the faculty in opposing his (Jesuit) university's honoring the U.S. secretary of state Condoleezza Rice as its commencement speaker and recipient of an honorary doctor of laws degree. Hollenbach narrates how the local archdiocesan newspaper editorialized in favor of Rice's presence at the event, suggesting that if the speaker had been in favor of policies permitting abortion, objection to her presence would have been appropriate. But since war is not immoral in every case, objection to honoring Rice was a "political disagreement, not one of dogma or doctrine." Using this case as a basis, he explores three outstanding challenges for U.S. Catholic theological ethicists: the need to avoid single issue politics; the need to take context and circumstances seriously; and the need to understand and challenge the singular power of the United States. To this last point, one that was continuously raised at the Padua conference, Hollenbach refers us to Kwame Anthony Appiah's "rooted cosmopolitanism." This "cosmopolitan approach," Hollenbach writes, "takes the humanity of all persons with moral seriousness and resists division of the world into us versus them. At the same time, a genuinely cosmopolitan approach is deeply interested in understanding people as they are, so it recognizes the particularities that make peoples and cultures different from one another."

Jean Porter focuses on the continuous erosion of due process in the United States (and elsewhere), particularly in safeguarding the rights of persons. Porter is motivated by the actions of the present administration in the United States, where domestic surveillance, criminal detention without charges or representation, and now even the practice of torture are some of the most dangerous and explicit challenges to the rule of law. She examines this phenomenon by recalling that theological claims in the twelfth century established a code of law in the church in which personal rights existed for the sake of the flourishment of the common good. This original, theological claim prompts Porter to wonder why theologians do not see a similar need to revisit and theologically critique the on-going diminishment of legal procedures. She also asks whether the type of responsibility and accountability canonical models once developed by the church are able to survive in the contemporary Roman Catholic ecclesial governance structures where accountability generally diminishes the higher one rises in the hierarchy.

Kenneth Melchin argues that Catholic social teaching (CST) enjoys very little attention in Canada and that the hierarchy rarely teach it or call the Canadian church to heed it. Melchin obviously wants to see a reversal on this matter, but is also concerned that some might claim that the CST does not square with the tradition on usury that was the central social teaching of the church from 1150–1750. Is there any continuity between the usury tradition and the more recent CST? Turning to the legacy of the great Canadian theologian Bernard Lonergan so as to consider the nature of theological continuity and development, Melchin invokes Lonergan's notion of "doctrine" and makes a strong case that the pillars of charity and justice so fortifying in the tradition of usury are equally evident in the more recent CST. So as to develop CST further, he concludes turning to Canadian theologians Gregory Baum and Christopher Lind to show how their writings on Community Economic Development (CED) advances CST's vision and its search for a "third way" between free-market capitalism and state socialism.

David Hollenbach, S.J.

Catholic Ethics in a World Church

A U.S. View

My comments on the challenges facing Catholic social ethics in the United States today begin with the case of a recent controversy at the university where I teach. At its graduation ceremony on May 22, 2006, Boston College invited U.S. Secretary of State Condoleezza Rice to be the main speaker and to receive an honorary doctor of laws degree. Along with another social ethicist on the faculty, I prepared a letter protesting this invitation, which stated: "On the levels of both moral principle and practical moral judgment, Secretary Rice's approach to international affairs is in fundamental conflict with Boston College's commitment to the values of the Catholic and Jesuit traditions and is inconsistent with the humanistic values that inspire the university's work."[1] This statement was signed by over two hundred other professors. The administration of the university clearly disagreed with our position, since the honorary degree was granted and Secretary Rice gave the address. Further, the newspaper of the Archdiocese of Boston editorialized in favor of Rice's presence at the event. They suggested that if the speaker had been in favor of policies permitting abortion, embryonic stem cell research, or euthanasia, objection to her presence would have been appropriate. But since war is not immoral in every case and since "Catholic doctrine allows for consideration of the particular circumstances of each case," objection to honoring Rice was a "political disagreement, not one of dogma or doctrine."[2] Here, the archdiocesan paper was echoing a statement of the then Cardinal Josef Ratzinger in a letter to Cardinal Theodore McCarrick on the relation of Catholic morality to politics in the midst of the U. S. election in 2004: "There may be a legitimate diversity of opinion even among Catholics about waging war and applying the death penalty, but not however with regard to abortion and euthanasia."[3]

From reflection on this controversy I want to highlight three ethical challenges facing the Catholic community, responses by theologians to these challenges, and several of my hopes for moral theology in the United States today.

The Challenge of Single-Issue Ethics and Politics

First, the controversy reveals a deep-seated tendency, sometimes supported by the magisterium, to make the ethics of sex and reproduction more important matters in Catholic moral concern than are questions of social ethics such as war, human rights, torture, or economic justice. One bishop has called abortion "the issue that trumps all other issues."[4] This statement implies that Catholics should be publicly engaged on the single ethical/political issue of abortion in a way that far outstrips involvement with other moral concerns. Abortion and euthanasia are certainly important moral questions. Both sex and reproduction also raise major ethical challenges today and need careful reflection.[5] These issues, however, are surely not the only questions that are important in lives shaped by Catholic faith. Thus in the United States today is a real danger that the prophets' challenge to bring justice to the poor and Jesus' call to be peacemakers will be lost from the life of the church by an approach that focuses in a one-sided and oversimplified way on matters related to sex, reproduction, and the protection of human life in medical contexts. The issues of war, the human rights not to be tortured and not to be imprisoned without trial, and economic justice are also matters on which "a well-formed Christian conscience does not permit one to vote for a political program or an individual law which contradicts the fundamental contents of faith and morals."[6] Single-issue ethics leading to single-issue politics has become a major challenge facing the Catholic church in the United States today.[7]

The most influential response to this challenge so far has been the effort of the late Cardinal Joseph Bernardin, with the help of moral theologian J. Bryan Hehir, to articulate a "consistent ethic of life." Bernardin sought to form an ethical stance toward American public life based on respect for human dignity and human life in a consistent way. He insisted on such respect across an array of practical questions, ranging from respect for the unborn and those facing terminal illness, to efforts to eliminate poverty, to provision of adequate health care for all, to a human-rights based approach to the needs of developing countries, to a critical engagement with U.S. military and strategic policy.[8]

This effort to advance a consistent ethic has parallels in recent discussions of human rights in both secular and religious analysis, where it has been increasingly stressed that all human rights are interdependent. The full range of human rights, including rights to life and personal security, political rights classically expressed in democratic self-government, and economic rights to the fulfillment of the most basic economic needs of the poor, are all essential parts of a unified stance defending the full dignity of the person.[9] An empirical argument has also been advanced recently in the United States for the interconnection of the rights to life and to the fulfillment of basic economic needs. It has been pointed out that a decline in the number of abortions in the United States during the 1990s accompanied the improvement of the economic conditions faced by pregnant women, while the reverse has occurred since 2000.[10] In an analogous way, some have argued that protecting people's rights not to be subject to terrorist attacks is linked, at least indirectly, with overcoming the social and economic marginalization of peoples tempted to terrorist tactics in the Middle East and elsewhere. Thus both normative and empirical considerations suggest that an inclusive approach to the full range of human rights is needed, and that narrow focus on one issue or right will be counterproductive. In addition, I would argue that attention to all the dimensions of human dignity in an interdependent community is required in a Catholic ethic that places high value on promoting the full common good of all people in society.[11] My hope is that arguments for such an inclusive approach will be developed further and an inclusive and consistent ethic will become the guiding framework for Catholic engagement in public life in the United States. Seeing social ethics as an integral and indispensable part of the Catholic moral contribution to life in the United States is one of the greatest challenges faced by the church today. I hope that we theologians will work vigorously to bring about a creative response to this challenge.

The Challenge to Take Context and Circumstances Seriously

A second challenge is how to understand the relation of basic moral principles and virtues to the complex social and political context of the United States and global society today. A relatively small but influential group of theologians and bishops today suggest that ethical conclusions can be drawn about issues such as abortion or euthanasia independent of serious consideration of the context or circumstances within such actions can occur. At the same time, these thinkers argue that context and circumstances should play a determining role in the conclusions reached about ethics of war or capital punishment. Thus, they suggest that the ethics of abortion and euthanasia are matters of faith while judgments about war or capital punishment are largely political. This is another way of removing issues of social ethics from the heart of Christian identity.

In my judgment, assessment of context and circumstances must play a role in forming the ethical judgments reached about particular examples of all of these practices. Thus contemporary embryological knowledge about the process of fetal development must be taken fully into account in assessing the morality of a particular case of abortion. Such assessment requires careful attention to the stage of pregnancy at which it occurs. In addition, reaching conclusions about a particular civil law dealing with abortion demands assessment of the context of alternative legislative actions and other political issues.

Careful consideration of context and alternatives is taken for granted in moral argument about the morality of war. Judgments about a particular military action are certainly not matters of eternal truth, so they should be made with intellectual modesty and caution. The importance of context in all particular judgments about war, however, does not mean that all conclusions about a conflict are equally acceptable from a Christian standpoint. There are degrees of connection between prudential judgments about concrete cases and the central requirements of Christian identity. Some prudential judgments are much closer to the heart of being a Christian than are others.[12] Therefore, the fact that a judgment about the morality of the U.S. war in Iraq is not a matter of eternal Christian doctrine does not mean all ethical judgments about the war are equally acceptable. Indeed, I believe the just-war norms point strongly to the conclusion that the Iraq war is unjust and should, therefore, be opposed by faithful Christians. The fact that this conclusion is not dogma does not mean Christians are free simply to set it aside as a matter of political preference or ideology. Similarly, acknowledging the importance of circumstances certainly does not mean that all abortions are justifiable. But it does mean that that the decisions of individual women facing threatening pregnancies and the judgments of legislators and citizens dealing with the law and politics of abortion cannot be assessed by appealing solely to allegedly timeless and absolute prohibitions.

The Catholic community in the United States is thus challenged to move beyond an illusory quest for certitude that keeps moral engagement restricted to the domain of sexual and medical ethics narrowly understood. Catholics are called to recognize that very important issues of Christian identity are often involved in responses to war, poverty, and other social ethical issues. Theologians are responding to these challenges by providing the detailed analysis of how the values at stake in these matters can be realized in diverse contexts, developing an appropriately careful casuistry across a range of practical issues.[13] My hope is that this very traditional task of moral theology will be taken seriously enough to enable the church to respond much more effectively to the complex realities of U.S. society.

The Challenge of the Power of the United States

Third, the case of Secretary Rice at Boston College reveals one way that Catholics in the United States have not yet adequately come to grips with the fact that they are citizens of the world's most powerful nation. Some supported Rice receiving an honorary degree at Boston College's commencement because her presence would add stature to the university. This motivation may be a vestige of the days when U.S. Catholics were largely poor immigrants who sought to advance their status in U.S. culture and who needed to show that they were patriotic American citizens. Though there are many new immigrants among U.S. Catholics today, American Catholics today are among the most highly educated, richest, and most influential U.S. citizens.[14] In my judgment, these educated, wealthy, and influential Catholics need more careful reflection on how their Christian identity should be lived out in the midst of the culture of American power and wealth. Because their country is so dominant a force on the world stage today, Catholic citizens must determine where they stand in relation to this power.

In fact, the United States is the most powerful country in the world. Some speak of American hegemony over much of the rest of the world; others speak of the United States as an empire. This power is evident militarily. The United States spends more on defense than all the other nations of the world combined.[15] Were the United States to use the military power it possesses, it is difficult to imagine it being defeated in an actual military conflict. Further, the U.S. National Security Strategy of 2002 affirmed that the United States intends not only to retain this predominant power but to prevent potential adversaries from "surpassing, or equaling" its power.[16] This military-political power is assessed positively by some. For example, the neoconservative commentator Charles Krauthammer has observed that in the United States "We run a uniquely benign imperium."[17] Some Catholic conservatives have supported this view.[18] On the other hand, Andrew Bacevich, a Catholic former military officer who has become a strong critic of the direction of U.S. policy, argues that if it continues on its present course of military dominance "America will surely share the fate of all those who in ages past have looked to war and military power to fulfill their destiny."[19] American Catholics need to become seriously engaged in assessing the relation between their faith and the issues raised by their country's military power. The same can be said about the relation between Christian faith and the economic and cultural influence or hegemony exercised by the United States.

Several stances within theology can be observed in response to this challenge of the relation between Catholicism and U.S. power. Some theologians have adopted a strongly countercultural posture that seeks to place distance between the Catholic and civic communities in the United States. For example, William Cavanaugh has called the church to become involved in a "counter-politics" that is sharply discontinuous with the world of ordinary political activity.[20] This theological stance represents the posture of resistance to war and injustice long associated with the Catholic Worker movement in the United States and given a new systematic expression by the so-called Radical Orthodoxy movement originating in the United Kingdom.[21] This approach envisions the church as a community whose way of life contrasts sharply with the violence and injustice of secular politics. It rejects the charge that it withdraws from the world in a sectarian way. Rather, it sees the church and especially its liturgy as providing an alternative way of life that calls the world to a more peaceful and just way of acting.

A sharp alternative to the church-as-contrast society approach is advocated by those who argue that secular politics is properly based on reason rather than directly on Scripture or theology. Thinkers as diverse as Pope Benedict XVI, J. Bryan Hehir, and George Weigel reject a direct move from theology and ecclesiology to social ethics, or from a vision of the kingdom of God to what secular politics should seek to achieve.[22] Such a move risks reducing the reign of God to a secular political agenda. Or, inversely, it can undervalue the integrity of the political order as created by God and jeopardize the legitimate autonomy of politics from control by the church.

In my view, social ethics should be based neither on theology and ecclesiology in an unmediated way, nor purely on a rational, natural law foundation. Neither approach will be adequate for developing an effective vision of the role of the Catholic community that addresses the realities of power and pluralism in the United States of today. On the one hand, a purely theological response to American power will be incapable of effective engagement with the pluralistic contexts of the church in the United States. On the other hand, the hegemonic power of the United States can so easily distort what appears to be reasonable that the challenge of the gospel needs to be heard continually if the church is to remain true to its authentic social mission.[23] At the same time the gospel must be brought into intelligent dialogue with the plural communities and forms of thought that are so obviously present both within U.S. society and globally.

In other words, Catholic social ethics needs to be grounded in the particularity and distinctiveness of Christian belief, while it is simultaneously engaged in wide-ranging dialogue and interaction with the diverse modes of thinking and cultures in which it is immersed.[24] This task is analogous to the political/cultural stance toward our pluralistic and increasingly interdependent world that Kwame Anthony Appiah has called "rooted cosmopolitanism."[25] A cosmopolitan approach takes the humanity of all persons with moral seriousness and resists division of the world into us versus them. At the same time, a genuinely cosmopolitan approach is deeply interested in understanding people as they are, so it recognizes the particularities that make peoples and cultures different from one another. Further, a genuine cosmopolitan recognizes that she is rooted in a particular tradition that both makes her who she is and at the same time enables her to affirm the people and appreciate the values that come from other traditions. Such a rooted cosmopolitan can thus be a patriot who celebrates her own culture while simultaneously affirming the human dignity and rights of people from traditions and cultures that are different. In an analogous way, Catholic social ethics must be deeply rooted in the traditions of Israel and of Jesus, while being open to reasoned interaction with persons from other traditions. Such an ethic can affirm both the distinctiveness of the prophets' call to justice for the poor and Jesus call to be peacemakers, while simultaneously supporting universal human rights for all people. One might call this universal humanism rooted in Christian distinctiveness.

My hope is that such an approach to social ethics can lead U.S. Catholics to be sufficiently faithful to the distinctiveness of their Christian faith that they can challenge the hegemonic impulses of contemporary American politics and culture. The cosmopolitan aspect of such a social posture will also enable Catholic ethics to support a vigorous pursuit of human rights and justice for all, and to resist the ways that the temptations of imperial power can distort the ethical claims of reason in a chauvinistic way. At the same time, an ethic that is self-critically rooted in American identity will enable Catholics to bring the message of the gospel to bear on the actual challenges facing them as citizens of the United States, rather then simply standing against or outside of the American situation. Such a universalism rooted in the distinctive and powerful call of the gospel of Jesus Christ is essential if U.S. Catholics are to make genuine contributions to justice and peace in a world where their country exerts increasingly dominant power. It is my hope that such an ethic can be further advanced through the conversations emanating from this conference.

Jean Porter

Due Process and the Rule of Law

A Moral/Theological Challenge

What is the most important moral challenge facing the North American continent today? Strictly interpreted, this question would be impossible to answer. In just a little over five years, the new century has presented us with so many challenges that it is almost impossible to take them all in—much less, to identify one as *the* most important. Yet this question does prompt us to focus on issues that call for particular attention, because of their far-reaching impact, or the distinctively theological questions that they raise, or both together. In what follows, I want to examine one such issue, which in my view has not yet received the sustained attention that it merits from theologians and Christian ethicists.

What I have in mind is an emerging pattern of disregard, or worse, outright rejection of a fundamental ideal of the rule of law—including above all elementary requirements of due process, together with norms of consistency, transparency, and other elements of what might be described as an ideal of proper legality. The dangers posed by world terrorism and violence have created a climate in which authoritarian rule and the disregard of individual rights seem to many to be not only justified but necessary.[1] Eminent jurists argue that the president has the power to act without regard to congressional constraints or judicial review, provided only that he does so in virtue of his powers as commander in chief, in time of war—and since we are now apparently always at war, this proves to be no constraint at all. U.S. citizens and foreign nationals are being held incommunicado, without even being charged with a crime, much less being given an opportunity to answer the charges against them or to receive a hearing before an impartial tribunal. Government officials, on the command of the president, have carried out clandestine electronic surveillance domestically, in defiance of explicit laws and without regard to even the minimal kinds of accountability built into those laws. Worst of all, the practice of torture has recently been defended in principle and incorporated into the practices of the United States.[2]

To a very considerable extent, the responsibility for these and similar practices rests with President Bush, Vice-President Cheney, and other members of the executive branch of the U.S. government. These practices have been challenged almost from the beginning, both by government officials and by a wide cross-section of the general public. In *Hamdan v. Rumsfeld*, decided on June 29, 2006, the Supreme Court struck down the system of secret tribunals set up for the detainees at Guantanamo Bay. Yet it would be unwise to take too much comfort from these developments. What the courts have given, the courts can take away, especially since our judiciary is deeply divided on these matters. What is more, the current U.S. administration could not have acted as it has done without the broad support, or at least the acquiescence, of congress and the general public. While there is considerable, and growing, opposition to the administration's policies in this regard, it can also count on widespread public support for what are seen as pro-active efforts to preserve public safety, together with widespread indifference to the claims of proper legality.

Yet, as the legal scholar Bruce Ackerman has recently observed, even the worst terrorist attack would not threaten the existence of the United States as a political community—that is, it would not destroy the government, or the political and social ideals that our government, at its best, embodies.[3] The real danger is that we ourselves will undermine our political institutions and ideals in our response to those attacks. To the extent that we have acquiesced in the ongoing disregard of due process, that is just what we have done. And this, I want to suggest, presents a moral—as well as a political and legal—challenge.

The claims of due process and proper legality are not mere abstractions or technicalities, but expressions of a fundamental right to an active, publicly acknowledged and protected voice in one's encounters with the community acting through its political representatives. Those who are denied due process are treated unfairly, subject to unjust harm, and denied fundamental rights. They are, in short, subject to moral wrongs that should concern us all. By the same token, the disregard of claims of due process and proper legality undermine our integrity as a particular kind of moral community, one which—at its best—aspires to an ideal of political authority grounded in reasonable principles and shared consensus rather than an arbitrary will backed up by the use of force.

In making these observations, I do not want to imply that other societies lack their own distinctive ways of embodying public reasonableness and equity, and I most certainly do not want to claim that only Western or Christian cultures can sustain such ideals. The practices that sustain due process and proper legality in Western societies are inextricably bound up with the broader legal systems distinctive to those societies, and it is not always clear what meaning these practices could or would have apart from these systems. More specifically, these systems are characterized by the relative autonomy of legal structures from more general moral considerations, as well as broadly pragmatic concerns, and this autonomy, in turn, appears to be inextricably bound up with the centralized and bureaucratic character of these societies. We should not be surprised to find that considerations of legal procedure play a different role in societies organized along different lines and possessing very different forms of legal arrangements. Of course, such societies can and do embody ideals of public reasonableness and equity in their own distinctive ways, which will not always resemble our own expressions of these ideals.[4] Nonetheless, within the moral ecology of Western societies, public reasonableness and equity have long been embodied in practices of due process and respect for the rule of law, and it is difficult to see how these ideals can be sustained within this context if these practices are undermined.

In my view, moral theologians have been slow to identify the disregard of due process and the rule of law as a distinctively moral issue. Again, I do not want to imply that there have been no such responses, or to minimize their importance. Many Christian theologians and social ethicists, together with fellow citizens across a wide spectrum of religious and ideological views, have objected to the denial of due process and related practices. At the same time, however, the broader issues raised by these practices, namely, the subtle yet pervasive erosion of ideals of legality, constraint, and accountability, have been overshadowed to some extent by their more egregious manifestations, particularly torture.[5] What is more, even the most socially engaged Christians have not always taken account of the distinctively theological values at stake in maintaining ideals of due process and fundamental legality. And yet, within American and European societies, the ideals and practices of due process can be traced, in key part if not entirely, to a social/historical trajectory that has its immediate origins in the expansion and reform of European and church laws beginning in the late eleventh century. As such, they are deeply rooted in a theological vision of the human person and the kinds of respect that are due to him or her, as one whose judgment and freedom are the truest image of God in the visible creation.

As the legal historian Kenneth Pennington (among others) has argued, the idea of judicial due process began to emerge in the early twelfth century as one result of the gradual abandonment of the procedures of trial by ordeal and their replacement by what were manifestly human judgments on the part of judges or juries.[6] The growing reliance on human judgment—rather than the ostensibly divine judgments manifested through the ordeal—prompted the thought that judicial processes should take account of, and as far as possible safeguard against the fallibility and sinfulness of human judges, while at the same time paying due respect to the claims of litigants and the accused. The papal court, with its insistence on observing the *ordo judiciarius* in all ecclesiastical judicial procedures, played a central role in this process, and correlatively, canon lawyers in the twelfth and thirteenth centuries laid much of the foundation for defending and elaborating due process. The early twelfth-century canon lawyer Paucapalea offers a rhetorical defense of due process by appealing to the most persuasive considerations known to his society—namely, the practice of God himself, as manifested at the very origins of human history. As Pennington remarks, "He noted that the *ordo judiciarius* originated in paradise when Adam pleaded innocent to the Lord's accusation. . . . Paucapalea's point is subtle but would not be lost on later jurists: even though God is omniscient, he too must summon defendants and hear their pleas."[7] A little later, the canon lawyer Stephen of Tournai offered the first definition of the *ordo*, including a summons in due form to a court having proper jurisdiction, a right on the part of the defendant to some delay, requirements that the accusation be put in writing and that witnesses be brought forward, that a presumption of innocence be maintained until formal conviction, and that the final decision be rendered in writing.[8] While these requirements are not exactly equivalent to our own ideas of due process, they reflect the same broad purposes, namely, that judicial procedures be carried out in accordance with established formal processes, set up in such a way as to safeguard the right of the accused to confront the case against him and to respond to it before being convicted.

The ecclesiastical roots of due process have long been obscured, but perhaps the time has come to reclaim them—at least for those of us who reflect on these issues from the standpoint of Catholic moral theology. At the same time, if we—and here I mean specifically we as Catholic theologians—are to undertake this reclamation, we will first need to engage in a process of self-examination. There are real questions about the extent to which the structures and practices of the Roman Catholic Church today reflect our own best ideals of due process and proper legality. I am thinking not so much in this context of denials of due process—although I think we do have problems in this regard—as of the authoritarian, "top-down" structures of church governance, culminating in the papacy itself.[9] For many, this style of governance reflects divine will or theological necessity, and as such, it is beyond critique. This perception is reinforced by a tendency, widespread among critics as well as defenders of current church structures, to assume that the Catholic Church has always been governed in this fashion.

Yet, as Francis Oakley and other historians have recently argued, current structures of church governance are by no means inevitable—at least, not if history is any guide. Far from reflecting ancient Christian ideals or prejudices, these structures reflect a distinctively modern option for a kind of monarchial rule, over against the more constitutional model offered by the conciliarist movement that emerged in the late medieval period. The hallmark of this movement lay in its insistence, in Oakley's words, that the "communal and corporate dimension" of the church requires institutional expression, most notably through "the assembly of general councils representing the entire community of the faithful and not necessarily limited in their voting membership, therefore, to the ranks of the episcopate alone."[10] This model of church governance is not necessarily democratic, but it does at least provide for boundaries and systems of accountability for the exercise of ecclesiastical power—thus at least creating an institutional context hospitable to ideals of due process and respect for law.

This is significant, because whatever may be said in defense of the papacy as currently constituted, it is difficult to see how the concentration of nearly all juridical power in the hands of one individual can be consistent with a commitment to a rule of law. What is more, the authoritarian ethos generated by our structures of church governance cannot be limited to internal church affairs; it inevitably spills over into our attitudes toward political authorities as well. As Oakley remarks, arguments that the church, being divinely instituted, is not just one polity among others "are almost always deployed in an attempt to vindicate highly authoritarian ecclesial structures or practices that have altogether too much in common with those of secular authoritarian or even totalitarian regimes."[11] In any case, we—meaning here, committed Catholics in North American democracies—find ourselves in an awkward position, committed to respect for law, democracy, and political equality in the public sphere, while at the same time (at least tacitly) endorsing an authoritarian style of government in the church community. At best, this situation generates an objective tension between two very different ideals of political and communal life. At worst, it fosters attitudes of authoritarian paternalism, leading to a disregard for niceties of procedure in the face of vital and urgent social goals—and it is worth emphasizing that these attitudes can be found right across the spectrum of political and ecclesial stances, among liberals and conservatives alike.

Let me end on a more positive note. There is at least one context within which ideals of due process and proper legality are once again salient for Catholics across the political spectrum. I am referring to the extensive conversations generated by the sex abuses scandals over the past decade—conversations that are already beginning to bear fruit in the form of institutional creation and reformation, albeit it on a small scale.[12] This sort of inquiry cannot proceed very far without raising the very issues of due process and respect for law that I have identified, and indeed these issues are already moving to the forefront of the conversation. This is a very hopeful development, both for the church and for the wider society. We have much to learn from our fellow citizens as we reflect on what it means to be a church of law in the service of grace. By the same token we have much to offer in defense of fundamental ideals of due process and legality, especially once we have re-appropriated the lessons of our own tradition and begun to put them into practice in our own common life as a church community.

Kenneth R. Melchin

The Challenge of World Poverty

Continuity and Change in Theological Ethics from a Canadian Perspective

In June 2006, Canadian newspaper headlines announced that 1 billion people around the world now live in horrific poverty in urban slums.[1] Many Catholics know this reality intimately. I am Canadian, and my focus is on the tragic absence in Canada of a strong and clear public voice of the Catholic tradition on world poverty. My interest is in exploring some theological reasons behind this situation and offering ways theologians can promote directions for change.

The public perception in Canada is that the voice of religion is the voice of the politically conservative right.[2] Traditionally, issues of poverty and social justice have been championed by the political left, but in North America, the left is perceived as the voice of secularism.[3] Statistics show that social justice ranks at the bottom of ministry priorities in Canadian Christian churches.[4] Canadian Catholic Church leaders are heard speaking strongly on topics like marriage and the family, but on world poverty their voices are weak and diffuse. In past decades, theologians like Gregory Baum have devoted considerable effort to raising awareness of social justice among Catholics.[5] Within the Canadian bishops' Social Affairs Commission, Tony Clark and Joe Gunn have worked tirelessly to cultivate interest in social justice. But their work has not received support. In the past four years, only 2 of the 209 "Media Releases" of the Canadian Conference of Catholic Bishops and only 7 of their 129 "Public Statements" focus on world poverty.[6] Given this, Canadians are left believing that religion means political conservatism, and Catholics do not feel the call of their faith tradition on world poverty.

I believe the roots of this problem include theological and methodological issues. Catholic Church leaders are rightly concerned with fidelity to tradition. This can pose problems, however, when they are not clear about their tradition. Theologians such as David Hollenbach, Charles Curran, Donal Dorr, and Michael Schuck have worked to promote the Catholic social encyclical tradition that has come to be known as Catholic Social Thought (CST).[7] This is principally a twentieth-century tradition that focuses on Catholic Church documents since Leo XIII's *Rerum Novarum* (1891). Schuck situates the origins of CST in Catholic responses to industrialization in 1740, and Curran and Hollenbach identify biblical and Thomistic roots of CST. What is interesting, however, is that CST makes little reference to the tradition on poverty and economic justice that dominated the Catholic world for six-hundred years, from 1150 until 1750, the tradition on usury.

For six centuries, church teaching on poverty and economic justice was defined by the usury tradition. Now, however, we are embarrassed by the usury tradition. How can we think that it could be wrong to receive interest on our bank deposits? We feel we were mistaken on the ethics of lending, and theologians like John Noonan and John Thiel pronounce that the teaching on usury has been overturned.[8] What are Catholic Church leaders to make of this apparent discontinuity and reversal? Is CST a recent upstart? Are we to believe that the church went astray in its ethical reflection on economic justice? If so, how can we trust that the church's recent teaching on poverty belongs to its oldest, most reliable traditions?

I would like to help answer some of these questions by arguing for doctrinal continuity unifying the CST and usury traditions. I argue that despite change on particular ethical issues, there is a deeper continuity linking the two traditions that reflects the oldest and most authentic tradition of the church on poverty and economic justice. To speak of continuity and change in ethical doctrine, however, requires some preliminary reflection on what is meant by doctrine and doctrinal development.

Doctrinal Development

The topic of doctrinal development has attracted considerable attention in Catholic theology.[9] In 1999, the Catholic Theological Society of America made it the theme of its annual convention. John Noonan and Richard McCormick offered historical examples of changes in the church's ethical doctrine, and they proposed criteria for understanding how such change could be understood as authentic and reasonable.[10] They also noted, however, that to speak of development is to speak not simply of change, but of continuity. As Cathleen Kaveny argued, for change to be truly development, it must build upon past teaching and carry it forward. Moreover, there are diverse models of doctrinal development, and so arguing critically for doctrinal development requires arguing critically on behalf of a framework or model.[11]

I propose drawing upon a particular understanding of *doctrine* rooted in the work of Bernard Lonergan. Lonergan distinguishes various functional specialties in theology as methodical steps in the process of working through theological issues.[12] The eight specialties are rooted in the operations of human understanding, and doctrines function on the level of verification and judgment. They are judgments of truth and value we can trust because they emerge from the authentic tradition of the Church. In Lonergan's words, they emerge from the foundations of religious, moral, and intellectual conversion. Doctrines, as understood here, are not first principles in a logical argument, nor are they abstract statements that entail concrete applications in a purely logical sense. Rather, they are judgments that function to point us in reliable directions in our work of theological retrieval and innovation.

Judgments come to function as doctrines not simply because they are traditional, but because they are authentic; they are judged time and again throughout history to be rooted in a state of character or virtue that has been transformed religiously, morally, and intellectually. I suggest that this approach is reflected in Noonan's own efforts to rethink continuity in moral doctrine in terms of "experientially grounded insight into Christ."[13]

What is interesting, however, is that doctrines affirm truth without delimiting the range of further insights that can be discovered, verified, revised, corrected, and developed in the light of this truth. This subsequent work of innovation and verification is the task of systematics. Doctrines function to provide direction and guidance in living and in the search for insights, and they do this by affirming *that* something is true or truly valuable. On their own, however, they do not supplant or short circuit the ongoing work of innovation in answering the novel challenges of the age. They do not tell us *what* the doctrine might mean with respect to a particular context, experience, or question. In ethics, doctrines can remain valid, even when new contexts and challenges call for new and different answers to new and different ethical questions. Through the centuries, we can rely on doctrines, even as we pursue vigorously the innovative work of systematics. As we explore how doctrines are to be lived out in ever new cultural and historical contexts, we can expect this innovation to give rise to differentiations and transpositions that will be felt, eventually, in new doctrinal formulations.[14] What remains firm through the differentiations and transpositions, however, is the dynamism provided by the doctrines themselves.

What doctrines provide is an orientation that guides Catholics in their living and guides theologians in their work of innovation and verification. They provide indicators, lines of questioning, and directions for commitment in the pursuit of knowledge and justice. They provide a horizon of caring and valuing for the empirical and ethical inquiry of systematics. While systematics admits diversity, debate, and ongoing verification, doctrines provide direction and guidance. Church leaders can rely on doctrines, and they can appeal to the results of systematics as probably verified opinion to guide policy and action. On issues belonging to systematics, church leaders can admit cultural and contextual differences as well as respectful disagreement. They can look forward to innovation in settling old questions, correcting errors, and answering new questions as they arise. With doctrines they can exercise leadership and call Catholics to commitment and action.

Doctrinal Continuity Through the Usury and CST Traditions

I suggest this model can help clarify some thinking related to Catholic tradition and world poverty. John Noonan has provided a detailed historical analysis of usury. Over the years, Noonan's work has been cited to show that ethical teaching can change.[15] He also argues, however, that his work supports the argument for continuity,[16] and I suggest we can discern doctrinal continuity unifying the usury and CST traditions.

Noonan argues that the two pillars supporting the usury tradition throughout its history were the values of charity and justice.[17] The first of these, charity, provided the religious foundations that set the tradition in motion.[18] The authoritative Old Testament texts situate usury in the context of responsibility to the poor. Lending to the poor is an obligation rooted in religious faith, and usury meant exploiting the vulnerability of the poor for personal gain.[19] From the earliest days of the scholastic tradition, usurers were those who profited from the hardship of the poor.[20] When Urban III cites the text of Luke 6:35 in support of the condemnation, usury becomes a violation of the highest obligations of Christian charity.[21]

The challenges presented by diverse commercial transactions, however, required understanding what exactly counted as usury. To meet these challenges, the scholastics invoked the second pillar of the tradition, the natural law foundations of justice.[22] Money has a nature and purpose, and justice requires action in keeping with this purpose.[23] The strongest formulation of this purpose was Aquinas's.[24] He argued that, with consumer goods, ownership cannot be separated from use because goods become the user's when they are used up or consumed. Unlike farms or livestock, consumer goods cannot be used time and again to produce other things. Such is the case with usury. Thus, the price of ownership is repayment of the principal, and there is no moral justification for an additional charge for use.

Aquinas's argument established an ethical tradition of differentiating functions of money and grounding obligations of justice in insights into natural purpose. Moreover, I argue that it establishes a distinction between ethical obligations attached to consumer and producer transactions that remains valid today. This distinction is reflected in our contemporary understanding of the public responsibilities of business in organizing economic life.[25] And I suggest it is most clearly articulated in Lonergan's economics, with his distinction between consumer and producer circuits and his analysis of diverse ethical obligations rooted in the various phases of these circuits.[26] Eventually, church leaders recognized that diverse types of commercial transactions called for diverse ethical judgments on lending, and the result was a growing recognition that many types of transactions could admit and even require the charging of interest. Yet Noonan shows how the progressive ethical justification of various forms of interest was rooted in this same work of discerning and differentiating natural purpose in the service of justice.[27]

What remained constant and authoritative through the tradition were the obligations of charity and the natural law foundations of justice. What emerged was a more empirically grounded and differentiated understanding of what this required of Christians. We now acknowledge newer ways of understanding the ethics of particular types of lending. Yet Noonan's argument shows how the two pillars of charity and justice endured even as they laid the grounds for the newer arguments that would develop Catholic ethical thought. I suggest these pillars have functioned doctrinally in Lonergan's sense of the term, and the innovative work of differentiation and transposition can be understood as the work of systematics.

I suggest that these two doctrinal pillars remain authoritative today, and can be observed guiding and directing the innovative work of systematics in contemporary Catholic Social Thought. The first of these, the virtue of charity with its ethical obligation to the poor, finds expression in the principle of "the option for the poor."[28] Catholic theologians such as Donal Dorr, Stephen Pope, and Patrick Byrne argue that God's own solidarity with victims of sin calls us to action in the face of poverty and structural injustice.[29] Living out this call is not only our initiative, it is participation in God's own redemptive work, and rooted in the most authentic tradition of the church. Yet discerning what this requires of us requires considerable innovation and diversity, and we can observe in their work the task of systematics, differentiating and transposing doctrine in relation to diverse questions and contexts.

The second pillar of justice, I suggest, is captured in the principle of "the common good."[30] David Hollenbach argues that the common good is a structure of social relations that is a good in itself and essential for the flourishing of persons.[31] In its modern form, the common good is constituted by the shared speech and cooperative action of self-determining citizens. As a framework for discerning ethical obligations related to poverty and economic justice, it calls for the analysis of structures of interdependence and solidarity that ground the conditions for the full and free participation of all.[32] I believe we can observe in Hollenbach's analysis a differentiated and transposed version of Aquinas's natural law foundations of economic justice. The ethical argument proceeds from the analysis of the "nature" or structure of the common good to the discernment of how this structure serves the highest purpose of the human person, and this framework grounds ethical obligations for promoting economic justice. I suggest we observe here an example of what Jean Porter calls a "process of dialectic interpretation" in continuity with the work of the scholastic natural law tradition on usury.[33]

New Directions

I argue that Catholics can rest confident supporting the work of theologians who promote CST in response to the challenges of world poverty and economic justice. One of the most creative directions in this work is Community Economic Development (CED).[34] Canadian theologians Gregory Baum and Christopher Lind see CED as advancing CST's common-good vision and its search for a "third way" between free-market capitalism and state socialism. Baum situates CED within Karl Polanyi's call for a morally informed economy where market transactions are re-embedded in the webs of social and cultural relations that form communities.[35] Lind draws on a community economy framework to analyze the crisis in Canadian agriculture that has arisen due to the forces of globalization.[36] Internationally, CED theorists and practitioners point to the Grameen Bank and the Mondragon Cooperative in the Basque region of Spain as examples of CED's success in combating poverty.[37] And historians trace the roots of CED to Catholic pioneers such as Moses Coady who were inspired by early social encyclicals to develop the cooperative movement in Canada and around the world.[38]

A second direction in advancing CST on poverty and economic justice is the work of rethinking the purpose of business.[39] Over the past decade, Catholic theologians such as Daniel Finn and Dennis McCann have worked with economists and management theorists such as Charles Clark and Michael Naughton to explore how CST can inform an ethically and theologically based approach to business and economics curricula at Catholic universities.[40] They argue that business has a "common good" purpose that must redefine the way we do business in the world economy. Business's purpose can no longer be understood simply as returning a profit to shareholders. Rather, business has a purpose that grounds ethical obligations of justice, equity, and the alleviation of poverty. Furthermore, the ethical work of business goes forward within a market framework that must be understood not as a mechanism of self-interest but as a "moral ecology" of ethically responsible actors.[41]

I suggest that understanding functional specialization can help theologians differentiate and support both tradition and innovation in all areas of Catholic ethics. On poverty and economic justice, I suggest that the two pillars of charity and justice function doctrinally to ground continuity and unify the traditions of usury and Catholic Social Thought. Most important, this work can help church leaders speak out loudly and clearly from the most authentic tradition of the church on one of the great challenges of the millennium, world poverty.

Part III

The Central Themes

I. Hermeneutics and the Sources of Theological Ethics

Robert Gascoigne (Australia)
Suffering and Theological Ethics: Intimidation and Hope

Maureen Junker-Kenny (Ireland)
Hermeneutics and the Sources of Theological Ethics

Dionisio M. Miranda, s.v.d. (Philippines)
What Will You Have Me Do for You?
(Theological Ethics Agenda from an Asian Perspective)

The three essays in this section take us in different directions. On the one hand, the universality of suffering allows Robert Gascoigne to focus on the centrality of this shared experience as a source for theological ethics, wherever. On the other hand, Dionisio Miranda argues that the uniqueness of the Asian context makes the particular culture and history themselves sources for ethics. Maureen Junker-Kenny engages both of these claims and provides an over-all foundational examination of the specificity of the hermeneutical and the universality of the deonotological.

Since experience is a source for theological ethics, Robert Gascoigne turns to the experience of suffering, which poses the greatest challenge to ethical reflection. Suffering, above all, "threatens to render Christian proclamation null and void, to overwhelm our attempts to envision a life of goodness and hope and to understand the complex threads of human experience as held together by a God-given dignity. Yet, although it is suffering that most confounds our search for ethical intelligibility, it is likewise suffering that is the most profound source of insight and conversion." Suffering then prompts us to be drawn more deeply into the mystery of Christ's redeeming love manifested in human experience. These two powers of suffering to intimidate and make silent on one hand, and to reveal and convert, on the other, allows us to "appreciate" suffering as a distinctive source of theological ethics. Yet, in our contemporary situation in which we are called to eliminate as best we can the causes of human suffering, we are contradicted by the fact that we have been the cause of such enormous suffering. For this reason theological ethics, in reflecting on human suffering, turns inevitably to a conversion that responds to suffering through compassion, that is, "an active identification with the sufferer in his or her pain." Gascoigne concludes: "Compassion can lead to hope, when sorrow and outrage at human suffering provoke an intense sense of our true nature and destiny, of the dissonance between present pain and how God wants us to live as dwellers in the Kingdom."

Maureen Junker-Kenny begins her essay examining each of the four sources of the theological ethical tradition: Scripture, tradition, experience, and the sciences and finds that hermeneutics play a significant role within each of the four sources of Christian ethics. Therein she argues for the inevitability of hermeneutics for a Scripture-based ethics and for its culture-specific, culture-transforming interpretation. The claim, however, that it is a sufficient approach on its own needs to be rejected for philosophical and theological reasons. The only way to keep it from degenerating into an ethnocentric, particularistic ethos of a specific community is to introduce the deontological, unconditional, universal level of morality. She concludes with a Catholic "both/and" project of developing a universalism that is not maintained at the cost of particularity, by engaging Paul Ricoeur in the discovery of "inchoate universals."

At the heart of his very radical essay, Dionisio Miranda argues "that the poor need to become the sources and hermeneutics of Asian theological ethics." Though Miranda focuses on the local, it is precisely the universals that he critiques. For instance, he writes, "Universally, a primary principle of ethics is to do good and to avoid evil. Uncritically elaborated Christian versions of the same, however, can orient action almost exclusively toward the caritative and palliative, traditional approaches too effete for the challenges of constructing a new civilization of love, or of building a solid order of human rights." His essay stands then as making the claims of Junker-Kenny feasible only in the context of a mutually dynamic dialectic wherein the universal and particular are continually engaged and critiqued. Miranda argues thus that together with the poor, local culture and history "are primary sources of our moral discernment." In this way the theological ethicist can only *do* theological ethics by emulating Jesus and asking of the poor, "What will you have me do for you?" In this way, "we are dared to source our theological questions from the existential ones they raise; to shape our questions in conjunction with their frames, to find answers that will satisfy not only our minds but also their hearts."

Robert Gascoigne

Suffering and Theological Ethics

Intimidation and Hope

It is a commonplace of contemporary theology that human experience is a source of theological reflection—this is especially clear in ethics, which reflects on our experience of the good in the light of the Christian faith tradition. In the field of human experience, it is the experience of suffering which poses the greatest challenge to ethical reflection. It is suffering, above all, which threatens to render Christian proclamation null and void, to overwhelm our attempts to envision a life of goodness and hope and to understand the complex threads of human experience as held together by a God-given dignity. Yet, although it is suffering that most confounds our search for ethical intelligibility, it is likewise suffering that is the most profound source of insight and conversion. It is through the encounter with suffering that theological ethics is drawn into an ever-deeper response to the mystery of Christ's redeeming love manifested in human experience. This paper will attempt to sketch these aspects of suffering as a source of theological ethics: both its power to intimidate, to strike dumb, and its power to reveal and convert, in the light of faith in the redeeming suffering of Christ.

In so many ways, suffering has an overwhelming character, especially in our own times, since the development of technology has given the opportunity for inflicting suffering and death on an unimaginable scale—and technology has also given us the opportunity to record that suffering and to make us chillingly aware of its horror and enormity. This suffering threatens to overwhelm all our systems of meaning, our human attempts to develop and reinforce ethical insights and shared minimum standards of ethical behavior. Especially when this suffering is inflicted by human beings on their fellows, it threatens to reduce all efforts at ethical communication and education to flimsy irrelevance: when members of cultures and communities that have been exposed to Christian preaching for centuries are nevertheless guilty of such atrocities, what hope is there for Christian ethics as a project which seeks not only to understand human life in the light of the Gospel but also to teach and to convert, to help shape human communities?

The power of suffering to numb and repel sympathy and intelligibility is summed up in Isaiah's description of the suffering servant: "He was despised and rejected by others . . . as one from whom others hide their faces" (Isaiah 53:3).[1] How can theological ethics help to overcome this alienating power of suffering in Church and society? In what ways has it been tempted to "hide its face" from the dreadful visage of human suffering?

At one level, this "despising and rejecting" was evident in rationalizations of suffering that betrayed a scandalous indifference: rationalizations that accepted social suffering as inevitable, expressed in preaching that exhorted those who suffered to bear their lot in life as a preparation for the world to come. So many Catholic reactions to the plight of the working classes in the early nineteenth century displayed this response, relinquishing hope of finding a humane ethical solution to the plight of the victims of the social and economic revolution, and consoling them only with thoughts of the next world.[2] The ways in which these responses gave credence to the atheistic rejection of religion as a dehumanizing and alienating ideology are very well known.[3] The tragic inadequacy of this response became, of course, a powerful stimulus to conversion, leading to the development of the tradition of modern Catholic social teaching.[4] Yet how many other contexts of human suffering have been responded to too late because we have preferred to "hide our faces" from suffering that makes such demands on our sympathy, on our willingness to understand, and to act with understanding?

Nevertheless, the awareness of the failure of the church to respond in a timely and adequate way to the ethical crisis of European industrialization has been a spur to theological ethics to be open to and aware of human suffering, especially the suffering of the marginalized and voiceless. Thankfully, we are much less likely to hear the rationalizations and alienating theodicy that characterized some nineteenth-century preaching and theology. These have largely been overcome by a theology that is predicated on a far greater sense of Christian responsibility for and within historical change.[5] Contemporary theological ethics does not view the elimination of suffering as its overriding goal: it knows that some suffering must be borne as part of our reverence for the goods of creation, especially the sanctity of innocent human life. Yet, within this context, it attempts to reach out to the boundaries of human possibility in eradicating the causes of suffering. Chastened by the failure of the church's earlier responses to the crises of social change, it seeks to bring the light of the gospel to human suffering in ways that avoid the rationalizations and consequent indifference of the past.

Yet an ethics that avoids such rationalizations is thereby confronted with the sheer overwhelming reality of human suffering, and a theology that seeks to give a voice to the voiceless and marginalized risks being overwhelmed by the sound of lamentation. By overcoming false responses and exposing itself to the sound of suffering it risks being stunned into silence. In this case theology would no longer "despise and reject" but would still "hide its face" out of a sense of sheer inadequacy before those who weep for their children, and "refuse to be consoled, because they are no more" (Matt 2:18).[6]

Today this overwhelming, intractable character of human suffering is manifested in the sheer scale and complexity of interconnected geopolitical challenges: terrorism, nuclear weapons, fundamentalist religion, fossil fuels, global poverty, and the environment, to name only some aspects of our situation. Such an unprecedented array of urgent and interdependent issues makes the most stringent demands on ethics: how can it find the resources of courage and understanding to shed light on our contemporary situation? How can it resist the temptation to "hide its face" from this and rest content with the responses it has already developed for more familiar problems? How can these contemporary forms of suffering become a source of new life in theological ethics, rather than a source of intimidation?

Reading the Scriptures in the light of this intimidating and baffling field of experience, we can identify with the disciples on the road to Emmaus, whose own political ethics was summed up in the despairing cry, "We had hoped that he was the one to redeem Israel" (Luke 24:21). The shattering of this hope, as they conceived it, the sheer overwhelming unintelligibility of the events that had just occurred, is the context for Jesus' response: "Was it not necessary that the Messiah should suffer these things and then enter into his glory?" (24:26).[7] The overwhelming power of suffering, rendering experience unintelligible, is the very place where the meaning of redemption is revealed, "beginning with Moses and all the prophets." Perhaps the creedal affirmation of Jesus' "descent into hell" can be understood in a similar way: the death of the Messiah comprehends and redeems all the hells of human suffering.[8] None of them is untouchable by compassion, courage, and understanding that seek to follow the Messiah in discipleship.

This witness of Scripture and tradition affirms that the power of God's redeeming love can be found within all suffering: for theological ethics, this conviction of faith can express itself in the courage to confront suffering, not as a power that strikes us dumb, but as a call to conversion.[9] Countless human testimonies—Christian and otherwise— speak of the encounter with suffering as a path to conversion: the precious fragility of the human person is recognized most clearly in the midst of its desecration, its value experienced most profoundly in the pain of its loss.[10] For Christian ethics, the faith-inspired act of seeking Christ's redeeming love in the midst of unintelligible suffering is the beginning of a conversion that may bring a new realm of meaning into ethical awareness. The wretchedness of the exploited working class provoked a conversion that has gradually expressed itself in a social ethics that is now a constitutive dimension of Catholic tradition. In similar ways, the feminist movement and environmental ethics are realms of ethical meaning and insight that have developed from the experience of conversion in the face of exclusion and desecration.

How can the theological response to suffering avoid new and subtler rationalizations, finding meaning in what for many simply causes bitterness and despair? Suffering itself is meaningless, yet it can be the occasion for moral and spiritual insight. What is crucial is that the response to suffering begins with compassion, an active identification with the sufferer in his or her pain. Compassion can lead to hope, when sorrow and outrage at human suffering provoke an intense sense of our true nature and destiny, of the dissonance between present pain and how God wants us to live as dwellers in the kingdom. This hopeful vision of our true destiny can give the confidence to seek understanding, rather than to succumb to despair at the scale of human suffering. In this sense, compassionate solidarity with suffering can lead to new understandings of human situations and of social change. The task of theological ethics is to be able to develop these insights in ways that are always based in an attentiveness to those who suffer and inspired by hope for a community based in human dignity. This challenge faces us in the continuing attempt to develop an ethics of economic justice, gender equality, and environmental awareness—and it is bound to constantly re-emerge in other contexts of which we are now scarcely aware.

In a hermeneutical sense, these developments are examples of the ways in which a response to experience, inspired and empowered by tradition, can develop the scope and meaning of that tradition itself.[11] In his *Salvifici Doloris*, reflecting on the affirmation of the writer of the Letter to the Colossians that "in my flesh I am completing what is lacking in Christ's afflictions for the sake of his body, that is, the church" (1:24), John Paul II writes that "in the mystery of the Church as his Body, Christ has in a sense opened his own redemptive suffering to all human suffering. In so far as a man [*sic*] becomes a sharer in Christ's sufferings—in any part of the world and at any time in history—to that extent he in his own way completes the suffering through which Christ accomplished the Redemption of the world" (SD 24).[12] Analogously, insofar as the conversion which this suffering inspires enables theological ethics to respond more deeply to the "joys and hopes, griefs and anxieties" (*Gaudium et Spes* 1) of the human condition, to this extent it discovers the meaning and scope of Christ's redemption in new and unpredictable ways.

Unlike the disciples on the way to Emmaus, we live in the light of the resurrection and know that Christ has already "descended into hell" on our behalf. Like them, however, we both recognize him "in the breaking of the bread" and at the same time must go forward without his immediate visible companionship. Suffering will always retain its power to intimidate and strike dumb, but we engage in Christian theological ethics in the faith that the hope of conversion—and with it the light of love and insight—can spring from the desolation of pain.

Maureen Junker-Kenny

Hermeneutics and the Sources of Theological Ethics

The sources of theological ethics include

- Scripture,
- its reception and interpretation in the practice of Christian communities and in the traditions of theological thinking,
- a philosophical, general concept of the "normatively human,"
- human sciences to interpret human experience in its agency and receptivity, its institutions and practices.[1]

My two fellow panelists from Australia and from the Philippines are exploring different aspects of human experience. Robert Gascoigne discovers in the encounter with the ongoing challenge of *avoidable suffering* the possibility of "a path to conversion: the precious fragility of the human person is recognized most clearly in the midst of its desecration."[2] A similar step from the vulnerability to the unconditional value of the human person can be found in the Universal Declaration of Human Rights of 1948 which shows the traces of its origin in the experiences of trauma of the Holocaust and of the Second World War.

Dionisio Miranda points out the specifically *Asian* challenges posed to a church-linked ethics by *poverty, cultural pluralism, and religious diversity.* Compared to the urgency of questions of everyday survival and respectful co-existence, many a debate in Western Roman Catholic theological ethics must seem remote and irrelevant. Yet I would like to show that in some of its current systematic reflections it amounts to more than a "dying tradition" or an "import" that threatens other cultures.[3] By making the case both for and against the hermeneutical approach from a context-transcendent, universalist position, I want to defend the possibility of a culturally sensitive, nondismissive universalism in ethics, which to me is also the hallmark of its Catholic understanding.

First, I will show the inevitability of hermeneutics for a Scripture-based ethics and for its culture-specific, culture-transforming interpretation. Second, my aim is to point out the inherent limits of a *merely* hermeneutical or prudential understanding of ethics. The only way to keep it from degenerating into an ethnocentric or ecclesiocentric ethos-ethic of an Aristotelian or ecclesial communitarianism is to introduce the deontological, unconditional, universal level of morality. I shall conclude with the project of developing a universalism that is not maintained at the cost of particularity (i.e., especially at the cost of non-Western cultures, worldviews, life forms, and self-understandings), engaging with Paul Ricoeur in the discovery of "inchoate universals."[4]

I. The Inevitability of Hermeneutics

There is no alternative to including hermeneutics into one's approach to Christian ethics with regard to each of the above mentioned sources, with the Bible and Christian tradition as theological bases, and both the "normatively human" and the social sciences as philosophical and interpretive resources.

Scripture and Tradition

The task for systematic theology to account for the identity of the Christian faith can be described only in hermeneutical terms. Hermeneutics is needed for theological reasons: The Christian truth is given by God. God's self-revelation is witnessed to in—but not identical with—Scripture, where we encounter it in an already-interpreted form. To establish the continuity of that faith in the ensuing traditions, the identity of its truth in the changing forms of its ongoing reception, one needs to reconstruct the ways in which the question of salvation was posed in each era and culture. Instead of a steady process of linear unfolding, one has to reckon with processes of translation and transformation which we try to identify from the vantage point of the present faith of the church.[5] This contemporary horizon comes to us, however, only in its particular local form. I speak here from the tradition of Latin Christianity which developed an understanding of theology as *scientia*, as distinct from theology as commentary on a sacred text, as wisdom, or as praxis, as Robert Schreiter points out in his helpful classification based on a sociological analysis of cultural forms of knowledge.[6] Thus, as Thomas Pröpper concludes, the reconstruction of the tradition of Jesus and its critical contemporary appropriation go together.

Dionisio Miranda's well-founded description of the task of moral theology exemplifies how the present local vantage point and the definition of the essence of the Christian faith interconnect:

> If moral theology is essentially the systematic search for the will of God made manifest in Jesus Christ, a will for life in its fullness, its routine extinction or degradation poses a continuing question for the ethicist's conscience. For Asia-Pacific the primary content or subject matter of Theological Ethics cannot but be the issues of justice, peace and integrity of creation provoked by poverty.[7]

The *contemporary vantage point* for defining the content to which Christian ethics is to attend comes out clearly in identifying "justice, peace and integrity of creation" as primary concerns. The *theological designation* of moral theology as exploring "the will of God made manifest in Jesus Christ, a will for life in its fullness" is based on a number of assumptions and interpretive decisions. It presupposes an understanding of Jesus's mission, death, and resurrection, of God as the power that rescues from death, and of the human person as answerable and accountable to the manifest will of God. More specific hermeneutical questions arise for each of these. For example, was Jesus motivated by a creation or by an exodus spirituality? Does his critique of Zion have a bearing on how we are to understand the Christian church and those outside of it?[8]

Image of the Human Person and Human Sciences

Hermeneutical expertise is also required in tracing the development of the view of the human person from antiquity to the present day, and to work out a position within current competing anthropologies with their different underlying presuppositions.

How one reconstructs the genealogy of the "normatively human" depends on these assumptions. One will have to take sides and argue for one's position. For instance, can one speak of a genealogy of practical reason that sees the concept of moral agency as historically originating in the monotheistic understanding of the human person *coram Deo*, as the discourse ethicist Jürgen Habermas does? Or should one follow Nietzsche in judging Platonism, Christianity, Kantianism, and socialism as "slave moralities" that interrupted the previous natural noble order of strong versus weak? Is the modern emphasis on freedom a counterposition to the Nominalist insistence on divine omnipotence, the arbitrary use of which called for shelter in a concept of human autonomy, as the philosopher Hans Blumenberg has claimed? Or is freedom the core of what *imago Dei* signifies and thus a consequence of the Christian experience of the divine-human relationship?

It is helpful that a critical social theorist such as Jürgen Habermas clarifies in the debate between different concepts of the human that since "also secular knowledge concedes to religious convictions an epistemic status that is not simply (*schlechthin*) irrational . . . , naturalistic world views do not by any means enjoy a prima facie priority over competing world view (*weltanschaulichen*) or religious conceptions."[9]

Since the "normatively human" is not restricted to conceptions of the human person as an individual but includes the dimensions of society and of justice, current discussions that lead into a hermeneutics of culture need to be addressed: for example, how to establish priorities in the order of goods (Michael Walzer), the relationship between justice as distribution and as recognition (Nancy Frazer, Axel Honneth), and between goods and capabilities (Amartya Sen, John Rawls). Sen's criticism of Rawls is that

> the orientation toward primary goods must be given up in favour of an orientation toward a person's capabilities to realize certain human functionings. . . . An equal distribution or measurement of resources according to primary goods does not do justice to unequal persons who can utilize these goods differently on account of unequal capabilities . . . e.g., handicapped persons . . . the difference principle requires and permits a stronger, discursive contextualisation.[10]

Not only capabilities have to be factored into schemes of distributive justice. Also the primary goods on which resource allocation is premised are a matter of debate. For example: Having landed in Italy, "*la mère des arts*," according to my French *Guide Michelin*, one wonders how it is possible to leave out from a list of "primary goods" the striving for beauty. Those provided by John Rawls—"rights and liberties, opportunities and powers, income and wealth . . . a sense of one's own worth"[11] indicate an individualistic culture that prizes the ability to choose as the prime expression of freedom. A different anthropology would start with human dignity as the first justified expectation to the social system and as the basic condition of any life plan that can be called "rational" in a noncalculating sense. All these ongoing debates make it clear that the exploration of the third source, the 'normatively human,' opens up into the realm of cultural hermeneutics.

Human Sciences

Finally, regarding the fourth source, the human sciences should not be taken just as value-free analytical tools, but as themselves constituting products and mirrors of their specific cultures, as the Protestant practical theologian Friedrich Schweitzer has pointed out.[12] This insight raises the question of how "culture" and the "experiences" that the human sciences reflect on relate to each other? Which, then, is more foundational? Are elementary human experiences cross-culturally the same, just like basic needs seem to be? Or are experiences such as pain, bereavement, intimacy, childhood and subsequent stages of life, fulfilment in work, parental joy, and concern encountered in such culture- and gender-specific ways that these are more foundational than the allegedly universal experiences? Such questions cannot simply be put to the test in empirical enquiries. Instead, they first call for a conceptual framework that does not foreclose multiple perceptions and varied interpretations. For example, if one uses a Foucauldian framework to analyze the interaction between children and adults, it will be difficult to discover any other dimension than that of power on either side. The possibility of mutual learning does not appear on the horizon, since every move can only express one thing: domination or submission. The basic decision, as Paul Ricoeur pointed out in his final book, is whether one reconstructs human life and its institutions in terms of recognition, or in terms of struggle for biological self-preservation in a hostile world.[13] If it is true that the dividing line between either a Hegelian or a Hobbesian, between a Kantian or a Nietzschean reconstruction will resurface in the basic assumptions of domain-specific theories, the philosophical and ethical intellectual decision that informs the individual empirical human sciences needs to be highlighted. The contributory role of philosophy within the human sciences has equally been pointed out by Jürgen Habermas. It acts as a "stand-in" (*Platzhalter*) for universalist questions.[14] However, his readiness to reduce it to the method of theories that can be falsified has been criticized as giving up what is specific to philosophy: its nonempirical, reflective, transcendental procedure of inquiry.

The evidence adduced so far by mentioning some of the ongoing debates in social philosophy justifies the conclusion that hermeneutics plays a significant role within each of the four sources of Christian ethics. The claim, however, that it is a sufficient approach on its own needs to be rejected for philosophical and theological reasons.

II. The Limits of a Hermeneutical Approach to Ethics

The inside perspective of the hermeneutical understanding of ethics as a biographical or cultural ordering of life goals or goods supplies a dimension missing both in moral systems that are centered on obligation alone and in theological systems that are focused on God's revelation and command. Yet taken as a complete and self-sufficient alternative, the hermeneutical approach misses out on the significance of the unconditional in the realm of morality (a), and of the givenness of God's truth (b).

(a) Deontology and Hermeneutics

The drawback of a pure "ethos-ethics" is that it can only recommend prudential values. The bias in favor of the existing ethos of the culture and its institutions tends to dissolve the dialectics between community and individual whose subjectivity and individual gift of conscience are distrusted. The concept of human dignity, if it is reached, does not denote the idea of unrepeatable and irreplaceable singularity that a noncontextual understanding of morality as an unconditional act of freedom implies.

> Kant is the first philosopher to give the status of a universal to the unrepeatable, that which is special and cannot be exchanged . . . the battle for a self-definition of human beings in which the unconditional, the realm of ends, is brought to bear against the extending power of means and interchangeable techniques of power, spans an arch from Cicero to Kant.[15]

The Cambridge philosopher Onora O'Neill's critique of neo-Aristotelian hermeneutical approaches is pertinent also for churches. It can be related to Dionisio Miranda's warning of sinful social structures, many of which are cultural.[16]

> The failings of particularist accounts of (practical) reasoning lie . . . in their assumption that reasoning need be followable only by a restricted audience who already share quite specific norms or practices, sensibilities or commitments.
>
> Although particularist reasoning can allow for the revisability of norms or of commitments across time, in the light of other norms and commitments (. . . it is not, contrary to some critics, intrinsically conservative), it cannot allow for the thought that one stretch of practical reasoning may have multiple and differing audiences. Particularist reasoning is intrinsically "insiders'" reasoning. Depending on context, it might be said to be ethnocentric (more flatteringly: communitarian) or simply egocentric (more flatteringly: authentic). Vindication of action is taken not to work across whatever borders there may be between "insiders" and "outsiders": it is reasoning for those who have internalised a given way of thought or life and its norms or traditions, its sensibilities, attachments or commitments.[17]

This is why the hermeneutical approach needs to be linked to the deontological and universalist level. Paul Ricoeur's ethics shows how the "grid of the norms" forms a necessary second step that derives from Kant, to watch critically over the Aristotelian first level of "*aiming at the 'good life' with and for others, in just institutions.*"[18] Equally, the ethos-independent role of legality to which Jean Porter pointed so decisively in her contribution from the North American Continental Panel at the Padua conference needs a deon-tological foundation that goes beyond a communitarian understanding of the scope of ethics.[19]

(b) Theological Truth and Hermeneutics

In the first section, I supported the theological approach of a hermeneutical understanding of the truth given to us in Scripture. However, just as in philo-sophical ethics, the role of hermeneutics has to be restricted also for theo-logical reasons. This need becomes obvious whenever the current context appears to be all-defining. It is then no longer possible to see the "text" as a counterpart and summons, as critique, resistance, and promise that needs to be safeguarded over against the present culture in which it is read and recon-structed. It is true that the text has been mediated to our time through its his-tory of reception which has "added" to it—and part of the ongoing reception, unfortunately, is to undo some of its previous ideological uses. The histories of colonialism and of patriarchy are clear examples for today's critical work of deconstruction and reconstruction.

Yet, there is a need for balance, which the Protestant theologian Lewis Mudge has expressed as follows:

> It is not merely a question of adaptation or application of the gospel to circumstances, but rather fundamental differences of perspective, diver-gent ways of conceiving what the gospel is about. When pluralism reaches a certain point, contextuality begins to become more important than tradition, more important than any ideal or essential unity the faith may possess. How far along this path is it legitimate to go?[20]

This question reaches a practical edge with many issues in domain-specific ethics that cannot be found in the Bible, such as the genetic engineering of crops, of new human races, or of enhanced offspring. But apart from the specific argumentations called for in each of these issues, the foundational question of how to judge what is a justified and authentic Christian witness has to be addressed. On the one hand, it is important to stress that what is given are not just religious forms of human self-expression that provide the-ology with the material for its investigations. In the self-understanding of the Christian faith, God's self-communication in the person of Jesus is the truth that inspires the subsequent religious experiences of his followers. On the other hand, the Christian understanding of God's revelation includes the promise of the Spirit in introducing us to and helping us to re-interpret the truth of Jesus within our own cultural conditions. This freedom to forge new syntheses in the spirit of Christ marks an important difference with another type of monotheistic faith, such as Islam, where the Qu'ran constitutes the complete word of God. Thus, the insight that Scripture is an already-interpreted form of God's incarnated word that calls for transmission into other languages does not mean that the Bible is being reduced to a merely human invention. It is the task of a theology of cultures to appreciate the new richness of Christian practices and understandings in the world church and to spell out the abiding unity within the current forms of discipleship.[21]

III. Towards an Inchoative Universalism

I want to conclude with two final thoughts on the relationship between universality and particularity. First, it does not have to be an either/or.

The philosopher and sociologist Hans Joas locates the origin of values that support and regenerate norms in what he calls "experiences of self-transcendence and self-transformation," as, for example, in religions. He shows that the particularity of the traditions that enable these experiences does not need to be at odds with the universality of principles:

(N)o culture can manage without a definite, particular value system and a definite, particular interpretation of the world. "Particular" here does not, of course, mean "particularistic"; cultural distinctiveness does not lead to an inability to take universalistic points of view into account. On the contrary, the questions are: which particular cultural traditions from the point of view of the universality of the right be most readily adhered to, and how can other cultural traditions be creatively continued and reshaped from this point of view?[22]

Different cultures can offer mutual help to encourage one another beyond their own unseen ethnocentrisms. John May's and Linda Hogan's attempt to find anchoring points for the concept of human dignity and human rights in non-Western cultures shows how the universal is embedded in the particular,[23] and that particular features of a culture can be judged in the light of the universal, for example, justice, or the integrity of nonhuman nature.

Second, reconciliations between global and particular cultures can only happen if particular cultures see themselves as global citizens, wish to be part of a larger whole, and unfold their resources to contribute what only *they* can offer. This vision applies to cultures just as much as to local churches whose riches are a necessary part of a full account of Catholicity. The systematic theologian Margit Eckholt reminds us of two conditions that are needed: "in the face of the multiple life-destroying conquests, of occidental modernity and of a universalism equated with occidental thinking: . . . the capability to empathize with histories of suffering, discontinuities, otherness, and the working out of structures of dialogue in which the recognition of the other becomes concrete."[24]

Catholic moral thinking should be universalist thinking, based on the universality of God's salvific will first manifested in creation. Its trust that human reason and freedom survived the Fall should fuel its interest in the diverse forms that the specific cultural appropriations of the message of salvation continue to take.

Finally, the root and benchmark of this universalist thinking which leads to a culture of recognition—which in turn implies rights, not just charity—is a particular understanding of justice as attentiveness to what Robert Gascoigne in his essay calls "the precious fragility of the human person." It is crucial for the kind of universalist understanding I am endorsing that this root is to be kept alive, and not deemed superseded. It stems from the prophet Isaiah in whose heritage Jesus understood his ministry:

The bruised reed he does not break,
Nor quench the wavering flame. (Isa 42:3)

Dionisio M. Miranda, S.V.D.

What Will You Have Me Do for You?

The Theological Ethics Agenda from an Asian Perspective

Were the world a global village of 100 persons, so certain statistics show, 61 would be Asian, 13 African, 12 European, 8 South American (with Mexico), 5 Americans and Canadians, and 1 from Oceania. Religion-wise, 32 would be Christians, 19 Muslims, 13 Hindus, 12 Shamanist-animist, 6 Buddhist, 4 Bahai and similar groups, 1 Jewish; 15 would have no religion. Other data indicate that 20 percent of the highest-income countries account for 86 percent of total private consumption expenditures, while the poorest 20 percent account for a minuscule 1.3 percent; to cite one illustration, the richest fifth consumes 45 percent of all meat and fish, while the poorest fifth consumes only 5 percent. Such data constitute an excellent starting point to locate the declared concerns of this conference. They define a context and in the process outline theological priorities[1] for the ethicist in the broad socio-political construct that comes under the name of "Asia."

Although Asia seems to participate only desultorily in the global conversation among theological ethicists, a closer look reveals a significant on-going exchange in certain circles, all on different concerns and with different intensities. Even the most superficial analysis of contexts should explain the consensus that Asian theological ethics should, and indeed cannot, pose the same questions raised elsewhere. Among many, therefore, these three tasks have become indisputable, namely, (a) to unlearn or at least prescind from the Western mode of doing theological ethics imbibed from earlier training;[2] (b) to explore and develop suitable ways of doing theological ethics in the absence of local models on one hand and the plethora of competing foreign models on the other; and (c) to engage its audiences in the spirit of "prophetic dialogue," to borrow a contemporary concept in mission studies.[3]

Two helpful cues are proposed by the Federation of Asian Bishops' Conferences (FABC), in whose light certain generalizations, even if drawn primarily out of the experience of the Philippine church, may not be inapplicable to most other parts of the region. From the very outset FABC has framed its responses to religious questions in correlation with what it considered as the three most important traits of our "continent," a world that is home to a multiplicity of cultures, of populations marked in many cases by extreme poverty, of manifold groups belonging to a variety of religious traditions. Asian churches engaged in a three-fold dialogue with poor peoples, cultures, and religions are urged to do so through the pastoral method of "see, judge, act,"[4] a methodology that cannot but have an impact on regional moral theology as well.[5] In this essay three large themes will be woven together summarily: the three questions posed to theological ethics by this conference, the methodology reshaping Asian theological ethics, and the concerns of hermeneutics and sources of this panel.

A. Generalized Poverty as Moral Challenge

Increasingly FABC's invitation to its theologians to pay more attention to local realities has been taken seriously; past theological ethics were glaringly incongruous in their detachment from the burning issues of the zone.[6] For economic, language, and other reasons the only available manual regionally for at least two decades was that of Karl-Heinz Pesche,[7] yet from its content one would never guess that it was born in or meant for Asia. Even today contemporary preferences for moral scrutiny remain limited and predictable, running repeatedly through largely overwritten themes. And yet, if Christian ethics is at core the methodic search for the humanizing will of God, a will for life in its fullness made manifest in Jesus Christ, the routine extinction or degradation of human life through the absence or denial of basic needs like food, water, and shelter cannot but be its primary content or subject matter, as the gospel itself is witness. As long, therefore, as governments, capitalist ideology, mass media, and whatever other force conspire to keep God's poor from being seen, heard, and responded to seriously in their quest for the full life, the task of Asian theological ethics must be to keep them from succeeding.

An Asian theological ethics that not only perceives but grapples with poverty and survival issues instinctively looks for allies in the West, but searches in vain for guidance from First World literature. Much of Western ethics, in the verdict of its own theologians, has become bourgeois, indifferent to Third World problems such as land reform, state violence, human trafficking, brain drain, labor migration, cultural conflicts, religious persecution, biopiracy, international debt, to cite some of the more prominent. Some are paralyzed by the panoply of challenges, painfully aware that Asian matrices (be these social, economic, political, and so on) are so myriad and complex that common problems like conflict of interest, corporate responsibility, graft and corruption, unilateralism, and so on cannot be asked in the same forms nor "acted on" with universal principles or standard approaches. Finally and inexplicably, despite the urgency and intensity of issues such as starvation, epidemics, and displacement, the rest refuse to dialogue with theologies whose methods and solutions bring those of the church herself into question, look on them with suspicion, or blunt their implications. Absent the infrastructure, institutions and resources of research and scholarship that the West so takes for granted, the local theological ethicist must often act the generalist, cobbling responses on the wing to constantly mutating problems, a point that I will develop further in later paragraphs.

It is never enough that Christian ethics "notices" those whom others would rather not, and "looks" preferentially at their concerns; its added task is to ensure that the poor—whatever dehumanized faces they may wear as women, children, migrants, indigenous, handicapped, elderly, enslaved, indebted, oppressed, and so on—be encountered less as objects of pity but more as interacting subjects, invited in fact to participate as advocates or "associate judges" of their causes. Rather than some arcane dispute in the tradition between unrecognizable unknowns, it is the ongoing history of suffering under inequality and violence of living and dying human beings that cries to heaven for answers. That struggle has begun to bear fruit in local literature, which is increasingly more experience based in content and committed to their audiences.[8]

Even as he commended the rich young man for his religious compliance, Jesus left no doubt that without its validation in humanist consequences in favor of the poor, no type of religious perfection can guarantee salvation (Luke 18:18–30). Generalized poverty is a challenge to the extent that it invites us to make the poor an indispensable element of our religious and moral reflection. We are dared to source our theological questions from the existential ones they raise, to shape our questions in conjunction with their frames, to find answers that will satisfy not only our minds but also their hearts. It is in that sense that the poor need to become the sources and hermeneutics of Asian theological ethics.

B. Cultural Pluralism as Ethical Challenge

The theological ethicist is continuously reminded by his own milieu that Asia is a continent of many ethos, rendering moral inculturation an inevitable challenge and indispensable response to context.[9] Because of a difference in temper and the systemic alienation of Asian theological ethics from its counterparts, inculturation will need to consider indigenization as hermeneutics and use culture and history more as prisms.

Universally, a primary principle of ethics is to do good and to avoid evil. Uncritically elaborated Christian versions of the same, however, can orient action almost exclusively toward the caritative and palliative, traditional approaches too effete for the challenges of constructing a new civilization of love, or of building a solid order of human rights. Surely the gospel ethic is also about resistance to evil, nonviolent but resolute, and the conquest of evil by and with good? Why—it is often wondered in Asia—are Christian ethicists so swift to condemn evil (in the very special and narrow senses of sexual and reproductive ethics), and yet are notoriously inhibited in providing effective guidance on the promotion of structures of grace in place of sinful social, political and economic structures—many of them cultural and colonial? Why has ethics become so identified with the negative and judgmental but rarely with the inspirational and constructive?

Since fundamental ethics, the prism through which Western morality analyzes issues and responds to them, is itself in crisis due to hermeneutical challenges to the tradition,[10] Asian theological ethicists are hesitant to acculturate to an obsolescent heritage or to import it into one's idiom; one might just as well justify pouring old wine into fragile wineskins. Issues of poverty, which the West considers practically passé, are everyday challenges; the culture issues that the West interprets in "postmodern" ways fail to connect with many premodern cultures; the advance of secularization resonates differently with long-standing religious traditions. Those who insist on replicating Western discourses on Asian soil should not wonder that theological ethics is often seen askance as an esoteric debate among an exclusive club, intelligible if at all only to Christian audiences, meaningless to the vast majority, unremarkable in its results, and mediocre in its effective witness.

After a year of teaching I shifted from English to the vernacular in order to remedy what I assumed was a mere linguistic shortcoming, only to make a disconcerting discovery that was to change my approach to systematic ethics radically. Communicating moral theology not to, but out of, local culture entails as much hermeneutical as pedagogical considerations; reconceptualizing conscience, for example, is not a question of semantics alone but of culture itself.[11] For the theoretically inclined, therefore, *Ephpheta!* is a formidable challenge to the ethical aphasia of one's culture, a summons to exegete its moral vocabulary, to construe its inchoate frameworks, to test the connections between categories that issue in different imperatives illegible outside their matrix, in short, to configure the ethical strands of the cultural ethics so that the indigenous agent can face each moral issue in all its pristine force and immediacy.

Jesus' prophetic dialogue with the crowds, his disciples, and religious critics is instructive of how inculturated and contextual ethics can occur: he claimed the good he found in his culture and history, yet harbored no illusions about their sinfulness as well. Despite the importance of local culture and history accepted by other disciplines as powerful conditionings in terms of paradigms and models, values and norms, institutions and patterns,[12] theological ethics has yet to give both their due, and they remain two of the most underexamined influences not only on personal conscience but on the social structures and systems that constitute the context of moral challenges to the same. Neither is sheer context; both are primary sources of our moral discernment. More than adjunct topics such as multiculturalism, inculturation, and the like, culture and history are evolving today into prisms for reading politics, sexuality, health, economics, and other moral issues. In dialogue with the Syro-Phoenician woman (Mark 7:24–30) Jesus illustrates what it means to be drawn out of reflex ethnocentrism simply by allowing oneself to be vulnerable to the universal despair of the human over a loved one's suffering and pain.

C. Religious Diversity as Ethical Challenge

In a continent of long-established religions and ethical systems, some antedating the Christian, the Asian theological ethicist is challenged unremittingly to dialogue at two interwoven levels simultaneously: the religious and the moral, each more complex than the other. Unlike the continent of the baptized but mostly social Christians of South America, and unlike the continent of secularized and self-declared post-Christian Europe, but only somewhat like Africa with regard to biocosmic religions and Islam, Asia as a continent was never at all Christian and sees little incentive for becoming such soon. Introductory texts on mission in Asia point to the complexities of the religious dialogue, without even crossing the moral threshold.[13] In my view, the book exploring explicitly the dialogue between Christianity and other religions at the moral, ethical, and meta-ethical levels has yet to be written. All these might account for the curious omission of moral theology among the disciplines to be inculturated by the church in the continent.[14]

(a) Intellectual Inns or Religious Homes? What difference or contribution does faith make to morality? One way of establishing a handle on the question in Western ethics is to consider the nodal question, often raised but just as often set aside: What is the call, mission, test, and fulfillment of theological ethics as a discipline, particularly in an age of secularization and pluralism? The fundamental problem of "theological ethics" can then be posed as follows: what is ethics all about, and what does theology have to do with it? Correspondingly the problem of "moral theology" would be what theology is all about, and what morality should flow from it. Since Vatican II, Christian ethics has shed much of its extremely philosophical cast as autonomous ethics and has consciously reacquired more of its biblical foundations, pastoral perspectives, and spiritual dimensions.[15] The new integration of ethics with theology (whether one opts for a theocentric vision as demanded by one's faith[16] or chooses to bring autonomous ethics to its theological home[17]) retrieves the original sense of "giving a moral account of one's faith." Yet one wonders if such syntheses offer greater credibility for post-Christianity, which seems to have turned its attention elsewhere, such as in a global ethics.[18]

For the theological ethicist from Asia, the question presents itself differently. If it was legitimate for Augustine to seek enlightenment in Plato, and Thomas in Aristotle, why should Asian ethicists be suspect when they venture into theoretical explorations of their own legal, sapiential, and prophetic traditions, be these Hindu, Buddhist, Confucian, or Muslim, much as Jesus did for Judaism? If inculturation means finding our own voice, why should not interreligious dialogue likewise mean drinking from our own wells? Primal, tribal, or biocosmic religions present peculiar challenges. In the absence of official interlocutors and faced with an amorphous system, the Christian moralist is forced to listen even more closely to "the groans of culture," to recast an image from Paul, since this primordial and widespread system of belief has proved quite resilient, as shown in issues of health or the environment.[19] Bioethics in the non-Western mode, to give one example, will need to retrieve the more immediate and important health issues involving ethnomedical beliefs and public policies as much as it needs to keep apace with sophisticated biotechnological problems posed by medical science.

(b) Moral Skepticism vis-à-vis Moral Authoritativeness. Given few prospects that Christian belief will find a home in Asia, the challenge to theological ethics as Christian praxis becomes even more acute. In most places of Asia the church was and continues to be a tiny minority (e.g., Mongolia, Thailand, Bangladesh, Kampuchea, Laos, Japan, Korea), tolerated in some (India, Indonesia), persecuted in others (e.g., China, Vietnam). In the atypical case where Catholics are a majority, the Philippine hierarchy's authority and credibility are sometimes challenged whenever it asserts its right to speak in the public arena.[20] The fact that isolated missionaries objected to and offered their lives in protest against the colonial policies and the fact that John Paul II apologized for the sins of the West do not erase the larger fact that Christianity became rooted in parts of Asia despite its abysmal record and the deafening silence of its moral theologians as a whole. Having tasted bitter fruits from its first encounters, Asia expects not more theological words but convincing witness, such as those of Blessed Teresa of Calcutta.

The questions being posed to Christianity are whether it is a truly redemptive religion, or an ethos that offers a more satisfactory meaning, not in an afterlife but in the here and now. While Asians are not unimpressed by the analytical sophistication of Western theological ethics, there is a greater desire for transformational commitments, a demand for orthopraxis rather than orthodoxy. If the Christian God of love is so totally different from the Asian gods of power, this conviction has to be made credible in the same ways that Jesus demonstrated. Non-Christians are drawn to Jesus because his ethics were so coherent with his vision of the reign of God. Essentially, in a region where the ethos emphasizes being over doing, the *proprium* or *specificum* of Christian ethics must be sought in discipleship, and theological ethics is precisely at its evangelical best when it becomes good news, offering salvation for the oppressed and redemption for oppressors.

D. Measuring Up to the Challenges

When the blind man was presented to him (Luke 18:35–43), Jesus posed what to bystanders must have seemed an astoundingly obtuse question—the man, as everyone could see, was blind. What else could he have asked for but sight? Elsewhere well-meaning people assume that slum-dwellers, for example, must want housing; social scientists know that jobs often take precedence in their wish lists. The point is no matter how patent the theological ethics agenda may seem to us ethicists, wisdom urges some hermeneutical suspicion as we ask the poor, the outcast, the stranger, and the nonbeliever, respectfully and without presumption, "what will you have me do for you?" Theological ethics, after all, was made for God's people, and not God's people for theological ethics.

Moral theology is a contextual-dialogical project. Assuming, then, that we have correctly identified the real needs of theological ethics in Asia according to its intended beneficiaries, the next question is how, or perhaps even whether, its practitioners can face up to those challenges. There are daunting difficulties for Christian ethicists, let alone Catholic ethicists, in establishing a common agenda, language, methodology, organization, personnel, and resources, as mirrored in the very history of the FABC (which held its first assembly only in 1974) and its theological arm. To foster indigenous Asian theologies relevant to its peoples, FABC founded the Theological Advisory Commission (TAC) in 1987, and only elevated it to the Office of Theological Concerns (OTC) in 1997.

Clearer insight may be possible by focusing on one case example. In the Philippines all we have are oral testimonies of the formation of an association of theologians in the 1960s and 1970s, but no recoverable record of its composition or activities. In the 1980s there was a renewed attempt to gather theologians (first systematic, then including biblical, finally inviting "even" moralists) into a forum. In the 1990s Jaime Cardinal Sin pushed to organize a consortium of theological schools so that the inchoate voices of Asia could finally have the opportunity to articulate its unique concerns and with greater sensitivity to context. Institutionally the express purpose was to be able to issue doctorates of sacred theology out of Asia—a factor that led to Loyola School of Theology's becoming the country's only other pontifical university aside from the University of Santo Tomas. It is a fervent hope that recent associations and new journals will survive their birthing pains. Many seminaries are able to maintain continuity of programs only because the religious congregations sponsoring them are able to share professors internationally. This situation obtaining in the Philippines, arguably one among the better positioned to lead theological education in the area, speaks volumes of what the situation of Catholic theological ethics in particular can be in other places, barring the subcontinent of India, which can boast of a functional, if young, Association of Moral Theologians.

Content-wise most curricula basically divide into two parts. General moral theology presents a pale reflection of the divisions found in theology as such, between academic and pastoral, magisterial and popular, international and regional emphases. In general foreign professors and local understudies show a more global focus, only a few natives aimed explicitly at local accents. Special moral theology follows either the manual division for comprehensiveness, or emphasizes special topics such as sexual ethics or bioethics. Social issues are distributed along the second half of the Decalogue with the traditional emphasis on inherited debates, or approached along the perspectives of justice, peace, and liberation, and the integrity of creation. It is in the latter format that classical morals have been enriched by other theological currents, such as liberationist, feminist, environmental, and cultural theologies. In effect, it is mostly at the casuistic level that some general trending of leanings can be identified: institutional or magisterial, anti-institutional and occasionally dissident, and finally highly contextual advocacies. Never bound to the separation of moral from general theology or even one particular schema, Protestants have always begun from the theological, and have thus more readily explored morally inspired political theologies such as revolutionary, *dalit, minjung,* or struggle theology.

Catholic Philippines has very few professionally trained theological ethicists, only a handful who teach full-time, and still less who publish. Clerics are often saddled with too many administrative jobs, formative duties, and pastoral concerns competing with their main profession; lay professors have to contend further with the practical demands of survival and concerns of family. Ultimately both are unable to concentrate on their professional concerns or to design programs better suited for theological education or relevant apprenticeship, reducing their teaching to homework or schoolwork, leaving no space to fieldwork. Where they are able to pursue certain interests, the urgency of the local and the looseness of their ties with colleagues prevent them from expanding their visions and activities to broader planes. Furthermore, professional development requires libraries, resources, and congresses like the present that Third World countries can only dream of. Hence, a challenge to the community of theological ethicists is to explore how First World institutes can share their human resources with the rest of the world, establishing some kind of network, coordination, and collaboration at international, regional, or national levels. Solidarity can extend to other resources: the contrast between the freeware model of Linux, IBM, Wikipedia, and others and the proprietary model of Microsoft invites us to reconsider whether our approach to intellectual property rights with regard to moral literature may not replicate some of the contradictions we moralists presume to resolve for others.

Apart from rare accounts of how they came to be and grew into moral theologians (think of Enrico Chiavacci, Bernard Häring, Charles Curran), one rarely comes across sustained and systematic reflections on this question: What is the call, mission, and fulfillment of the theological ethicist? Helpful as some historical studies may be,[21] the existential questions remain. Should s/he be a moral educator or technical analyst, a guide or consultant, a counselor or model?[22] Should s/he be the critic and prophet, asking tough but unanswerable questions? Is the call that of leadership, focused more on persons than ideas, ready and willing to assume the costs of discipleship? Is advocacy the mission, such as affirmative action in favor of underrepresented sectors, accenting inchoate voices, promoting more vertical rather than horizontal communication? Should the role be animation and support from afar, or hands-on activism? If the magisterium can justifiably see itself as the guardian of moral orthodoxy, does it follow that ethicists are to be its moral police? If ethicists are to be the conscience of the world, at what levels should that occur and how? Clearly much depends on how the theological ethicist defines his role, a matter on which we have yet to arrive at a consensus.[23]

Our part of the world is replete with issues too important to be left unaddressed in the absence of professional moralists, themselves a rare species. For theological ethics to have even minimal influence it will have to cast its net wider. Fortunately for the church, the Spirit has supplied other partners, beginning with the official voices of the bishops, as individuals and in conference, speaking to particular issues and comprehensive themes.[24] Filling up the theologico-ethical void are colleagues from allied theological disciplines[25] and related fields. Finally, there are the lay advocates in movements, ideologies, or parties, linking and networking with, for example, Amnesty International or Transparency International. In a real sense, it is the conscientious laity who keeps most of the moral debates alive, whether in newspaper columns, TV talk shows, or coffee shops. We are in stronger company when we see the challenges and responses as belonging to the larger People of God rather than to a restricted group of specialists. This flock, little as it is, can take faith in and pin its hopes on the Master who reassures us that he accompanies us on our way. Always.

II. Sensus Fidelium and Moral Discernment

Paul Valadier, S.J. (France)
Has the Concept of Sensus Fidelium *Fallen into Desuetude?*

Nathanaël Yaovi Soédé (Ivory Coast)
The Sensus Fidelium *and Moral Discernment: The Principle of Inculturation and of Love*

Giuseppe Angelini (Italy)
The Sensus Fidelium *and Moral Discernment*

Paul Valadier begins his essay describing how the *sensus fidelium* is rooted in the ancient tradition of the church, validated and promulgated from there through Vatican II's *Lumen Gentium*. The teachings acknowledge the constitutive role that the *sensus fidelium* has in helping the church hierarchy to formulate and articulate its magisterium. *Sensus fidelium* is not simply a polling of the faithful to know what they believe; rather it is the intelligibility of the faith as it arises from the faithful. In this way, the magisterium of the hierarchy is really only possible to the extent that it expresses the faith that has been received. Without it, the laity becomes passive and the hierarchy remote, leading to a gulf of suspicion on both sides of the divide. Valadier argues that there are present indications, especially in hierarchical teachings, of a suspicion of the *sensus fidelium,* because it might lead to dissent, but he argues that generally speaking any failure of the hierarchy to convince the faithful of the rightness of their teaching may not be due to a disobedient temper in the faithful but rather a failure of the hierarchy to understand the faith of the church. Because of these suspicions, Valadier suggests that the leadership encourage the whole church into a more dynamic, honest, and respectful discourse so as to better discern the faith being and needing to be expressed.

"Inculturation and love: this is what must provide structure and inspiration to our understanding of the faith, so that theological reflection (especially in the ethical field) may generate a living knowledge of God. It is essential that inculturation and love shape the discussion of the various problems connected with the magisterium and moral discernment." In this way

Nathaniel Soédé, having provided several insights, closes his essay, but here
we consider three. First, *sensus fidelium* can serve as a continuous catalyst to
help the baptized to mature into disciples of Christ. Second, magisterial
teachers must be very attentive to the inculturated needs in the local expression of the *sensus fidelium*. Soédé asks of the hierarchy: "Are they aware
that these Christians find themselves (whether consciously or not) in a foreign country, when they translate their faith into a philosophical, theological, liturgical, or legal language which expresses, not so much the catholicity
of the church, as the Western form which this catholicity takes in the Third
World countries which groan under the neocolonial yoke of the West?"
Finally, if we really want an authentic teaching then we must let our teaching be shaped by the roots, the radicality, of our local community, because
there we will find the Spirit

Giuseppe Angelini believes that *sensus fidelium* was not part of the history
of moral theology from its inception at Trent even until Vatican II. Then, in
the wake of Vatican II, "in response to unsatisfactory aspects of the responses
given by the magisterium to the new moral problems, especially those concerning the sphere of sexual behavior, modern theology makes a precise accusation: the magisterium ignores the *sensus fidelium*." Angelini proposes
another strategy: "What we basically lack today is not in fact a reference to
the *sensus fidelium* in the documents of the magisterium but rather the elaboration of an effective *sensus fidelium*, a common *sentire* on the part of
believers with regard to the new problems of choice with which they are confronted by the changed context of society." Angelini argues that many equate
sensus fidelium with a public opinion mediated by mass media and often
expressing a collective of individual assertions of personal autonomy. He
rather looks to the Scriptures, for instance, the preaching of the apostles after
Pentecost, when the hearers of the word find their hearts penetrated which
in turn leads to their conversion and lives of faithful believers. These believing consciences ought to be the point of departure for trying to discover and
express the common *sentire* appropriate to moral theology.

Paul Valadier, S.J.

Has the Concept of *Sensus Fidelium* Fallen into Desuetude?

The concept of *sensus fidelium* plays a central role in Catholic Christian theology. It is one way of doing justice to the scriptural theme of the common priesthood of the faithful (according to 1 Pet 2:17 and numerous other passages in the New Testament, e.g., 1 Cor 12:4–11 and Eph 4:4–6), and it permits us to express the idea that through baptism, the Holy Spirit is poured out on all who believe in Christ, in fulfillment of the promise that God made to the prophets of the old covenant (especially Jeremiah and Ezekiel). Accordingly, this concept embraces the idea of the effective realization of the new covenant in the share in God's gift which is given to all the baptized; it also alludes to the idea that the entire believing community follows the teaching of Christ, and to the translation of this teaching into their lives.

In its Dogmatic Constitution on the Church, the magisterium of Vatican II offered a classic formulation of this *sensus fidelium*: "The whole body of the faithful who have an anointing that comes from the Holy One [cf. 1 John 2:20 and 27] cannot err in matters of belief. This characteristic is shown in the supernatural appreciation of the faith (*sensus fidei*) of the whole people, when, 'from the bishops to the last of the faithful' [St Augustine], they manifest a universal consent in matters of faith and morals. . . . The people unfailingly adheres to this faith, penetrates it more deeply with right judgment, and applies it more fully in daily life" (*Lumen Gentium*, no. 12).

Through its quotation from St Augustine, the council bases its affirmation on a long series of fathers of the church who either alluded to this *sensus fidelium* or demonstrated its importance. We recall also the statement of the phrase of Vincent de Lérins in his *Commonitorium* (Patrologia Latina 50, 615–66): "that which has been believed everywhere, always, and by everyone" constitutes the contents of this *sensus* which is shared in the church. In modern times, we owe the most powerful theological illustration of this traditional theme to Cardinal Newman,[1] who based his arguments on the strong resistance of the Christian people to Arianism at a time when the great majority of the hierarchy let themselves be seduced by the heretical theses.

He also shows how Marian devotion developed on the basis of this *sensus fidelium,* which led the faithful, without any dogmatic prescription in the strict sense of the term or any imposition "from above," to develop the veneration of the Mother of God and even to believe in the assumption of the Virgin to join her Son in glory—something that became a dogma only much later, in 1950! It was thanks to a very acute perception of its own faith that the believing people intuitively sensed the place of Mary in the dispensation of salvation even before there was any scholarly formulation of this, or any explicit theology backed up by technical arguments.

I have recalled these basic data briefly and in an allusive manner only because I wish to note and deplore the fact that such a fundamental subject has very frequently been the object of suspicion, or at least that it has not enjoyed the place and the importance in the church's life and thought that is in fact its due. The intention of the present essay is to show the price that the church must pay in terms of its internal vitality and its missionary elan if we accept the minimalization of this theme.

It is not difficult to see that the concept of *sensus fidelium* awakens mistrust, especially on the part of the Roman hierarchy. For example, the *Instruction on the Ecclesial Vocation of the Theologian,* promulgated by the Congregation for the Doctrine of the Faith in 1990, expresses considerable reservations on this subject; indeed, it denies in n. 27 that there is a plurality of "magisteria" in the church—an affirmation by Thomas Aquinas which the text rejects without offering any arguments. This plurality indicates that not everything comes "from above"; rather, a healthy ecclesiological approach will take account of the faith that is shared by all, and of the internal diversity of the Body of Christ, especially on the level of charisms. And every proposition that comes from the ecclesiastical magisterium must necessarily be "received" by the people of God if it is to have the power of conviction and of life. Instead of taking its stand on the consensus of a common faith, this Roman document insists almost exclusively on the place of the ecclesiastical hierarchy in the regulation and affirmation of the faith. Despite the very clear words of *Lumen Gentium* that I have quoted above, this text, permeated by an attitude of suspicion, repristinates an astonishing lack of trust vis-à-vis the church. The *sensus fidelium* is suspected here of justifying "dissent." And so the text discredits it and would prefer to see it forgotten.[2] Nevertheless, I should like to show that this desuetude or devaluation leads to a weakening (to put it mildly) of the moral positions of the Catholic Church. I limit my remarks to the field of moral theology; I say nothing here about dogma or liturgy. It is urgent to restore all its pertinence to a concept which is entirely traditional, and indeed very ancient.

First of all, this concept says a great deal about the faith of the church. To remove it from the field of theology is to inflict injury on the Catholic sense of a faith which is shared by the entire body of the faithful since it is received from the Holy Spirit through baptism and confirmation. It is also to suppose that the Spirit dwells only in an elite (or in experts capable of controlling the faith of the others), instead of being spread abroad over all the baptized—as if God were miserly with his gifts. Accordingly, the suspicion that is cast on this concept does harm to a right sense of the church, dividing it into a church that teaches and a church that is taught. This is a fairly recent distinction made in canon law; it is juridical, rather than genuinely theological. It suggests that the teaching church "knows" without requiring to be taught. It suggests that in matters of morality, the teaching church has no need to seek information about the complexity of the problems involved and has a kind of specific intuition with regard to solutions which are so difficult and hazardous. And this makes the hierarchy the proprietors of a Christian faith and life that would not need to be deepened all the time (as is the case with every Christian). The magisterium would not need to seek information about ethical problems, although these can be intractable—or quite simply new.

At the same time, the others, the so-called taught church, are assigned to a passivity that is a basic contradiction of their Christian vocation; worse still, it is supposed that they lack a moral conscience or skill in discernment, as if they were incapable of discerning in their human and ecclesial experience what is necessary for a life in keeping with the Spirit of Christ.

It is indeed true that the faithful have this experience in the church, not in splendid isolation. But it is equally true that whenever a word from the magisterium is to be accepted, this presupposes that the faithful are capable of making a moral judgment on the words and instructions that they receive. It is only in this way that they can make such words genuinely their own and "follow" them in the Spirit—not merely according to the letter. This is why the recent council insists so strongly on the "faithful Christians" (*christifideles*), thanks to a very necessary reevaluation of the role of the laity in the church and in the world. They are not a passive flock of sheep! They have a vital share in the ecclesial consciousness, and they bear witness to Christ in the world.

We should add that if the praxis of the *sensus fidelium* were taken seriously—and this is not the case today—this would establish a possibility of "reception" or "recognition" in the genuinely philosophical sense of this concept, which has been well analyzed by the philosopher Axel Honneth in his book *La lutte pour la reconnaissance* (1992). This assumes *inter alia* that one who speaks or teaches will seek to grasp the reaction of the one whom he is addressing, to find out about his agreements or his reservations, to discover whether his own remarks have been well received, and whether they seem capable of summoning people to a life that is truly in accord with the gospel. This means that one emerges *ipso facto* from the solitude that surrounds everyone in authority; one looks for some kind of test of the validity and pertinence of one's remarks; one guards against the dangers of an authoritarianism that is utterly contrary to an ecclesial life formed by the precepts and practices of the Sermon on the Mount; and one gives oneself the chance to discern the relevance of the teaching one has imparted.

If the ecclesiastical magisterium fails to undertake this task, it isolates itself and speaks on its own, cutting off the necessary contact and the reciprocal interchanges that ensure the health of every word that is shared between human beings. Ultimately, it speaks only for itself, unceasingly repeating or quoting its own self, as if to confirm the existence of an ecclesial reception that is, in fact, lacking. It is not in the least surprising that such a message is "inappropriate." It *cannot* be "appropriate," because the church's magisterium thinks that it is enough for it to make pronouncements, without bothering to ask whether the faithful recognize the message—and recognize *themselves* in it—that is, whether they find their faith in it and welcome the good news that they hear as something good and rewarding. This is the source of the widespread perception that the ecclesiastical magisterium does not know whether people are listening to it and that this is why it is forced to repeat the same ideas, which are put forward again and again, but never genuinely received. The magisterium feels compelled to raise its voice, thereby forgetting that a Truth which is not heard or received or recognized, but is merely repeated with stubborn obstinacy, becomes inaudible and loses its character of Truth.

The failure to practice the *sensus fidelium,* especially in the field of morality, thus isolates the magisterium and prevents it from being heard. It devalues the official pronouncements of the church, which become sterile and may even be contested openly by many of the faithful, who have the impression that although the message they hear is "authorized," it lacks all credibility. An isolation of this kind promotes dissent, disregard of the church's moral teaching, and an indifference vis-à-vis what the church says, because the pronouncements show no sign that the church cares about the effective reception of its message. This leads to serious and highly disturbing divisions within the church, or even to schism. If the believer cannot see how the church's moral discourse (especially in matters of sexuality) truly concerns his own life, he will be tempted to withdraw into his own shell. This favors individualism and thus shatters the communion of the church.

It is too often forgotten that "dissent" is not necessarily the fruit of disobedience on the part of believers or theologians. In many cases, it is the by-product of an authoritarianism that is incapable of offering a theological justification of its positions. This dissent ought to alert the hierarchy to its own inability to make itself heard, and thus to the crisis of authority that the hierarchy itself engenders by its own praxis; nor should it forget that it is both incorrect and disrespectful to apply the term "dissidence" (a very strong word with grave implications in the political and the spiritual spheres) to every formulation of criticism or questioning of the positions taken by the ecclesiastical magisterium. This ill-will and injustice are further evidence of a deafness that cuts off those in authority from the ecclesial community and locks them into their own inability to communicate—and hence to hand on the Word.

The only way out of this impasse is to accept debate and discussion more honestly than is common today. The Roman Instruction sees there only the seeds of dissent, but in fact the opposite is true: it is debate that permits consent, a better understanding of the teaching, and its acceptance by the faithful. The goal of the *sensus fidelium* is to allow the faithful to "recognize their own lives" in the teaching that is proposed to them, and thus to make it their own. We could also add the important point that a climate of greater honesty and freedom of speech would help the magisterium to formulate the message better. The "teaching church" (if I may be permitted to use this inappropriate expression) would discover that it too was being taught—and this would mean speaking a word that was more audible, a word based on serious arguments rather than on the anthropological vacuities that take up so much space in the countless documents about the married couple, sexuality, new medical practices, or economic questions. This is because the concept of *sensus fidelium* envisages a lively dialogue between those who take part in the life of the church, not only the descent from "on high" of imperative propositions that are to be received by an inert crowd. It is this lively dialogue, this "wonderful exchange," that makes mutual understanding possible. How can we overlook the fact that on moral issues, it is difficult even to hear what the other person is saying, let alone to *understand* his words? It takes time to make oneself heard; one must consider the objections that may be made in order to formulate one's ideas more precisely and make them more acceptable to one's listener—and that does not in the least mean watering them down or making them lukewarm. Every moral discourse presupposes a lengthy work of reciprocal listening, of considering what the other has to say, and of clarifying what I myself wish to say.

This was the case with the documents published in the 1970s and 1980s by the bishops of the United States of America when they spoke out on economic matters and on disarmament. They organized a systematic consultation of the great Catholic institutions (parishes, universities, etc.). This did not weaken or compromise the credit of the ecclesiastical authority, but rather enhanced it, since there was general agreement that these public and official positions were "received" and enjoyed a large measure of assent on the part of the ecclesial community. Injunctions that fall from above are much more likely not to be heard at all, or else to be misunderstood. The wisdom of the church instructs us, by means of this concept of the *sensus fidelium*, to abandon a unilateral discourse that bears the marks of heteronomy, or even of indifference vis-à-vis its recipients. It obliges us to listen to one another. It leads us to take seriously the community of the faithful, that is, the church itself.

This concept entails a difficult and costly process, and this is doubtless one of the reasons why it is minimized or caricatured. For example, the claim

that those who speak of the *sensus fidelium* are introducing purely sociological considerations into the church, or that passing opinions (so easily
manipulated) are being made the criterion of truth, is clearly nothing more
than a cynical maneuver to devalue a traditional concept that is essential to
the life of the church. And this concept is a long-term indicator of truth, since
it is linked to the idea of nonreception. When a moral teaching is met with
reservations and criticisms, and the faithful refuse to accept it over a long
period, this is an obvious sign that something is wrong with the teaching.
This does not necessarily mean that it is false; it may even contain much
truth. But the fact that it is not received, or received only poorly, demands
an act of discernment by the church's magisterium. This nonreception by the
faithful may mean that the message is badly formulated and its arguments
unconvincing. What then is the reason for the reluctance on the part of the
faithful? Is it because of their sinful lives and their attitude of disobedience?
Or is it because they cannot understand formulations that are defective, rigid,
unilateral? And is the whole fault necessarily theirs?

This necessary discernment entails investigating the reluctance of the people of God (or of a large portion of it), and reexamining the reasons that
underlie the message of the magisterium. In many spheres, the persistent
refusal to listen seriously to the reactions of the people is not a sign that all
the truth is on the side of the magisterium, and that the faithful are merely
being disobedient; an elementary discernment may lead one to the conclusion
that the people of God, in whom the Spirit dwells, does not recognize its
own life in a particular teaching (in whole or in part), and that this is why it
cannot receive the teaching. A persistent refusal to listen helps devalue the
teaching that is set forth. When there is no genuine adherence to the teaching, the faithful are left to their own devices. Lacking orientation, they con-
form to the environment in which they live. And this means that the
magisterium has failed to perform its essential role.

I hope that I have indicated the capital importance of the *sensus fidelium*
for a vital ecclesial life that is in accordance with the gospel. An authoritarian theology thinks that it can get on perfectly well without the *sensus
fidelium,* but such a theology makes no real contribution to the living of the
truth of the gospel—it shatters the unity of the church and isolates the magisterium in a remoteness where it loses its credibility and drains the life of the
people of God, who are abandoned to their own whims and to an uncontrolled subjectivity. To accept the demands implied in this expression would
be a great contribution to the vitality of the church and to both its internal
unity and its external mission, because this would bear witness to a community that was alive—not to an administration that was deaf to the lives of
the faithful. It would lend credibility to the message which the church proclaims, because it would make this message legible and comprehensible,
showing that it is not the private property of anyone, but gives life and hope
to an entire ecclesial community.[3]

Nathanaël Yaovi Soédé

The *Sensus Fidelium* and Moral Discernment

The Principle of Inculturation and of Love

Introduction

The magisterium carries out its mission in an attitude of respect vis-à-vis the principle of inculturation, which is inseparable from the Word of God and from the tradition of which the magisterium possesses the *depositum*.[1] We can however note that, historically speaking, this principle has been realized principally on the basis of the questions and the philosophical and theological data of the Western and Eastern churches: inculturation has allowed the local churches of West and East to put forward questions that have strongly influenced the teaching of the magisterium. This teaching has not only addressed questions posed in the societies and the Christian communities of the North; it has also adopted in a specific manner the concepts and the most expressive anthropological and theological ideas of their culture. The churches of the other cultures must be aware of this fact, if they are to find the theological courage to elaborate analyses of problems and reflections that can likewise offer the magisterium some small fishes and pieces of bread (cf. John 6:6–12) that can provide the nourishment of the Word for the life of the faithful who are in their care, within the communion of the universal church.

In this context, what are we to say about the *sensus fidelium* and moral discernment? With Meinrad Hebga, we are aware that in the non-Western churches, "we too must learn to set our own indelible seal on the same religion (the Catholic faith), no longer elevating to the rank of divine revelation the Aristotelian-Thomistic philosophy, German or Anglo-Saxon Protestant thinking, or the usages and customs of Gaul, the Greco-Roman world, Portugal, Spain, or Germany, which were 'christianized'—if not indeed divinized—by Europe."[2]

In this essay, I shall speak of one aspect of this responsibility, namely, the widespread problems concerning the theology of the *sensus fidelium* and moral discernment today. We shall demonstrate that the *sensus fidelium* and moral discernment pose at every point the question of the responsibility and the formation of the baptized Christians, and the problem of inculturation and of love.

The Responsibility of the Faithful and of the Church

The *sensus fidelium* is a *locus theologicus* that invites us to reveal to baptized Christians and to the local churches, in communion with the universal church, their charism with regard to the understanding of Scripture and to the knowledge and proclamation of the truth of the faith. All too often, formation and reflection on the identity and the vocation of the faithful have centered on their life of communion with Christ in fidelity to the commandments; the Christian witness was understood as the kind of conduct necessary in order to be the light of the world and to share, alongside the clergy, in the proclamation of the gospel. In this way, the laity too would have their share in the teaching function of the pastors of the church.[3]

The concept of *sensus fidelium* summons pastors and theologians to help the laity grasp and put into practice, in an effective and enlightened manner, their charism with regard to the understanding of Scripture and to the knowledge and proclamation of the truth of the faith. This task is particularly urgent in the churches in the Third World. My remarks will address the topic of the inculturation of the anthropological foundations of the *sensus fidelium* and of moral discernment.

According to the foundations of African anthropology, the human person is a "being life" (*être-vie*), that is, a life that exists as relationship (between the individual and the community: an "I/we" that attaches us to the cosmos and to God), as being, and as action in order to conquer death and let life spread out through the world.[4] We would therefore say that the *sensus fidelium* allows us to see above all that the baptized person is a "christified" life. Through baptism, the risen Lord animates the one who belongs to him, by means of the Spirit whom he poured out on his disciples on the very day of his victory over death. In himself, the living one, he makes the baptized person a "being life" who bears in herself or himself what Christ is. In his death that conquered death, he manifested fully to the world what he is, namely, love. In his first encyclical, Pope Benedict XVI writes of the identity of God as "love" and speaks of the depths of his love in Christ.

"God is love" (1 John 4:16). His love for the world led God's Son to surrender himself to death in order to uproot from the heart of the "being life" (i.e., the human person) the hatred which is evil and to deliver that one from sin and death. When the "being life" are baptized, they put on Christ. In Christ, they are a life that finds its authentic identity and its responsibility in

God. As such, they are members of the body which is the church—a body made visible through his testimony of love. Baptized persons affirm their identity and nourish and strengthen their "Christified being life" when they accept their vocation and are profoundly united to the church which comes together and proclaims, celebrates, and lives its faith as a community that forms the family of God.[5] As members of the church, and as a manifestation of the church in their own persons, the faithful exercise their own specific charism in authentic communion with Christ and with his church.

This means that the so-called *sensus fidelium* is in fact what we might call a *sensus fidelium ecclesiaeque.* The expression *sensus fidelium* is not a radical expression of the communal dimension of the subjects in their relation to the church. In the context of African inculturation, it fails to state that since the baptized person, the believer, is a "being life" and a believer who has come to faith in Christ, he or she is also an ecclesial "I." The relational and ecclesial dimension of the identity of the baptized person would never occur to one who hears the expression *sensus fidelium.* This phrase has become classical; but the Graeco-Latin anthropology that constitutes the philosophical foundation of this term insists less strongly than African anthropology on the communal dimension of the person. The translation of this relational existence of the human person into the concept of "being life" obliges the theologian to underscore this dimension on the christological or ecclesiological level.

Let me briefly make this point: in those cultures that affirm that the human person is life and in relationship, it is helpful to speak, not of the *sensus fidelium,* but of the *sensus fidelium ecclesiaeque,* which includes the former phrase within itself and expresses its openness to all the dimensions and all the forces in the church.

The expression *sensus fidelium ecclesiaeque* signals that it is as a son or daughter of the church, in and with the church, that the believer shares in the function of the magisterium, in which indeed the whole church participates. This is not a charism only of believers who are exceptional members of the church, nor of disciples in some secondary zone who take their place in the church after the ordained ministers. This phrase invites the faithful to become aware of their ecclesial existence and to promote the growth of that body and family which is the church, in celebrating and bearing witness to their faith.

For its part, the magisterium must consider the faithful as full members of the church, responsible subjects, disciples of Christ, who are baptized and therefore share in the power of the hierarchy. This means that they have a contribution to make to the magisterium in the sphere of the knowledge and proclamation in history of that faith which was received from the apostles. Bénézet Bujo emphasizes the communal dimension of the African concept of moral discernment.[6] He shows that the African mode of deliberating through dialogue, that is, the *palaver,* which involves all the members of the group in the decisive choices with regard to community life in the field of social and religious beliefs and practices, is a valuable element that can promote a genuine *sensus fidelium ecclesiaeque* in relationships between the magisterium and the laity.

Accordingly, the magisterium must bring the faithful to adulthood in the faith, in order to make them capable of responding fully to their baptismal vocation. In its teaching about the witness and the commitment of the laity in the church, the magisterium must devote more attention to making baptized persons adults whose formation and whose life of faith will make effective and fruitful their exercise of the *sensus fidelium ecclesiaeque.*

The Formation of the Laity and the Exercise of the Mission of the Magisterium in the Field of Inculturation

The faithful are no longer simple consumers of the pronouncements of the magisterium. The same is true of the Christian communities in relation to the bishop and priests, and of the local churches in relation to the universal church.

For their part, the laity must attach equal value to their human and Christian formation and to their life of communion with Christ, so that they may make their faith more fruitful and the action of the local churches more prophetic, in a full spirit of freedom. Their critical function and their moral discernment find in their faith and in their action the necessary strength to move on from practices, beliefs, and a language of faith that are not anchored in their own lives.

This means that the laity will not remain on the level of people with a "spiritual" flair. When they emerge from the realm of popular piety, they will permit the magisterium to offer the whole church the possibility of confessing and celebrating a faith that bears the marks of the unexpected revelation of the mystery of the kingdom to the "little ones"—and of the efforts of these "little ones" to acquire an authentic knowledge of Christ.

In the churches with a non-Western culture, the various efforts to achieve inculturation, in fidelity to Rome, express the desire of the Christian communities to live their faith in a profound manner. At the same time, these efforts show us the humility of God.[7] God does not try to impose his own will. Rather, he respects the freedom of those whom he has placed at the head of his church, and he hopes that all his children will celebrate the faith and confess his name in their own languages—in keeping with the liturgical norms and the teaching of the magisterium, and in such a way that they affirm that his kingdom is at work in the heart of their lives.

The *sensus fidelium ecclesiaeque* is expressed in our churches in Africa, Asia, etc., through the endeavors and the powerlessness of the baptized persons and of the basic ecclesial communities in the sphere of inculturation. Are the magisteria of the local bishops and the episcopal conferences, and the Roman magisterium, capable of displaying sufficient openness to this problem in their dealings with their sons and daughters? Are they aware that these Christians find themselves (whether consciously or not) in a foreign country, when they translate their faith into a philosophical, theological, liturgical, or legal language that expresses not so much the catholicity of the church as the Western form that this catholicity takes in the Third World countries that groan under the neocolonial yoke of the West?

There exists a *sensus fidelium ecclesiaeque* that makes itself known through the needs felt in the sphere of inculturation by those local churches which have not yet succeeded in imprinting their own socio-cultural seal on the faith that they received from the West. It is imperative that we listen to this *sensus fidelium ecclesiaeque* if we want the magisterium to have a radical function of serving the Spirit—"radical" in the etymological sense of this term—by listening to what he says to the local Christian communities.[8]

In the first centuries of the church, the apostles and their successors permitted the faithful, the theologians, and the pastors to cast into the mold of the Greco-Roman culture an inheritance that up to then had been expressed in the language of Palestine. Yesterday, the magisterium liberated the churches of the West from a burden when it disentangled them from the Jewish culture. What of today? We may legitimately ask whether the magisterium is not imposing on oppressed peoples the same burden when it refuses to give the churches of Africa, Latin America, Asia, etc., a free hand in the matter of inculturation.

We must ask here whether the magisterium is de facto sufficiently attentive to all those aspects of inculturation in the life of the local churches which invite us to discover and welcome the new faces assumed by the *sensus fidelium ecclesiaeque.*

Reflection on this *sensus fidelium ecclesiaeque* and moral discernment can no longer center on the question of the competence or authority of the magisterium in the very complicated questions of the moral conscience, of liberty, of autonomy, of sexuality, or of the Christian's relationship to politics (in the Gallican sense of this word); nor on the question of what one must believe about God or about the mystery of the faith with regard to the Trinity, the Virgin Mary, etc.

The *sensus fidelium ecclesiaeque* raises problems of inculturation that we overlook when the debate about moral discernment is narrowed down in the traditional manner. It indicates that the task of the magisterium is to summon pastors to an ecclesiological, dogmatic, pastoral, and moral discernment.

The Essential Point Today: Inculturation and Love

Inculturation broadens the context within which the *sensus fidelium ecclesiaeque* is to be put into practice, for this is not concerned only with the project of rooting the gospel in the culture and the life of the baptized, but also with helping them to accept and to live the law of love.

The *sensus fidelium ecclesiaeque* asks theologians and the magisterium to try to find out what is required in order that the faithful and the Christian communities may be masters and witnesses of that love which is God, the love made manifest in Jesus Christ as the life that triumphs over sin and death, wherever this love is present in the world.

The *sensus fidelium ecclesiaeque* implies here the *sensus mundi*. The world that bears the mark of the salvation wrought by Christ who descended into the depths, the world in which the Spirit is at work, is a place where persons of good will, even if not themselves baptized, can contribute to making known and living the truth of the faith. Their contribution may be smaller than that of the baptized, but it is no less real.

Some dimensions of the mystery of the God who is love have not yet been put into words. As Vatican II says, the magisterium, the theologians, and the faithful will discover in the world the signs of the times, voices that must be listened to, so that we will understand these dimensions more deeply and teach them to others. In this perspective, the *sensus fidelium ecclesiaeque* demands from the magisterium a discernment about the inculturation and the love that are to be lived by the baptized in the world.

The ideals of unity and peace, attempts to promote development, the situations of cultural alienation and of political-economic domination, conflicts and wars—all these require of the magisterium an increased commitment to the work of interpretation and teaching, thereby helping people to celebrate and live the name of Jesus Christ—a name that tells us not only who God is in himself but also who he is as love for the world. The baptized must manifest this love to the world, so that others too may come to know him and love him.

The *sensus fidelium ecclesiaeque* of those peoples who are abandoned to a subhuman poverty, and of the other peoples of the earth—whether or not they profit from the structures of sin that characterize the world economic order—is a matter of urgent concern to theologians and to the magisterium. In this field, the successors of the apostles will have to proclaim dogmas about faith in the name of the God who does not compromise with the one who exploits his brother, heaps up wealth so that he may enjoy worldly goods, or despises the poor and the stranger. The exercise of the magisterial function or the infallibility of the church cannot be restricted to the proclamation of articles of faith about the Trinity, the immaculate conception of the Virgin Mary, and so on.

When the conciliar decree *Gaudium et Spes* speaks of the presence of the baptized in the world, it emphasizes that the revelation of the mystery of God in Christ, and the entire service of the church which has the task of making this revelation known, can be summed up in love. It is therefore necessary that the exercise of the *sensus fidelium ecclesiaeque* make a contribution, in the words of the Second Vatican Council, to sharing "with others the mystery of God's heavenly love"[9] in the heart of today's world.

This is a complex matter; it suffices here to recall the need to awaken people's consciences to the ideals of unity, of lasting development, and of peace. We must pay heed to the protests of nations and of local churches against situations of injustice and against the westernization and alienation of their people and their world.

The questions that are raised, the failures and the successes in working to establish an order of peace and love within the nations and the church, demand a fundamental moral discernment on the part of theologians and the magisterium. Faith and reason must be joined to love; and this is why the final coping stone is placed on the encyclical *Fides et Ratio* of John Paul II by the encyclical *Deus Caritas Est* of Benedict XVI. In this way, the relationship to the gospel and to the *depositum fidei* always has the threefold (yet also single) objective of making known the truth of the faith, of letting the faith be lived in truth, and of helping it find expression in the life or the cultural language of the faithful and of the social and ecclesial communities.

Since all the disciples will be judged in terms of their readiness to confess in truth the name of Christ (Luke 6:46–48; Matt 7:21; 25:31–46), both magisterium and theologians will endeavor to discern whether what they have to say about the *sensus fidelium ecclesiaeque* goes to the heart of the matter, namely, the love of God and of human beings. For only so can the signs of the kingdom be manifested effectively (Luke 7:18–22; 10:26–28; Matt 7:18–22).

In this context, the *sensus fidelium ecclesiaeque* and moral discernment are above all an invitation to discover what morality is. Discernment takes account of this and thereby itself becomes moral, that is, open to the commandment of love or to the praxis of the beatitudes.[10]

The teaching of the magisterium and theological thinking will be attentive to the importance of the basic ethical commitment in the life of the baptized, to see whether or not this indicates a basic adult moral conscience in which the values of love and of life in Christ can bear fruit.

Is not the discourse about the bread of eternal life (John 6:1ff.) an appeal to collect the little loaves and fishes, the talents of those who minister in the fields of ethics or of Catholic moral theology, in order to reflect, to announce, and to prepare a welcome in people's hearts for a gospel that obligates Christians everywhere to work genuinely so that no one on earth may be the victim of subhuman living conditions and a subhuman moral life? That no one may die of sicknesses for which other persons possess medicines? That no one may sink under the weight of prejudices and distress, whether through his own fault or through a failure of love on the part of others? That no one may be incapable of expressing the faith in his own culture, in and with his local church (and naturally, in communion with the universal church)?

The theologians and the magisterium ought to promote the emergence of churches that are not "under the guardianship" of local sister churches in the West—for the simple reason that the theological, liturgical, spiritual, and legal responses that the Western churches have made to the Christian faith have been confused in the universal church with the truth of the faith itself, the truth of the life of faith, and the truth of the celebration of the life of faith which must be proclaimed to all the peoples.

An authentic personal and ecclesial moral discernment obligates the faithful and the Christian communities to become the agents of "Christianities" which, as in the West, put down their roots in the culture of the people and become living expressions of theological, liturgical, legal, and pastoral pluralism within the unity of the faith.

Conclusion

There is no other moral discernment than that which is bestowed on the baptized so that they may live according to the law of love, helping them make their understanding of the faith and their life of faith a service of that love according to which we will be judged at the end of our lives. Catholic moral theology must liberate itself from all those problems which do not support the commitment of the faithful to bring about the signs of the kingdom of love. Similarly, the magisterium must liberate itself from everything that could lead it to construct churches in the Third World modeled on the regulations and institutions of Western Christianity, preventing those local churches from hearing and putting into practice what the Spirit says to their churches—in communion with all the churches of the *catholica* and with the successor of Peter.

In this context, the magisterium will listen in a new manner and place itself at the service of the *sensus fidelium ecclesiaeque* of all the local churches, drawing closer to these. It will not treat their members like infants who exist only to obey. It will regard them as brothers and sisters in love, in the knowledge of the truth, and in testimony to the gospel. And they can call it "our brother the magisterium," just as they confess "Christ our brother."[11] The link of brotherhood in Christ permits the magisterium, the theologians, and the baptized to unite in the service of love and of inculturation.

Inculturation and love: this is what must provide structure and inspiration to our understanding of the faith, so that theological reflection (especially in the ethical field) may generate a living knowledge of God. It is essential that inculturation and love shape the discussion of the various problems connected with the magisterium and moral discernment. In this way, Christian ethics could help pastors become better witnesses to the gospel, who proclaim the name of Jesus Christ to the baptized and help them to confess it. It is Christ who sends them out as artisans of his kingdom in our world, and it is their mission to free the world from the iron law of exploitation and from all forms of sin.[12]

Giuseppe Angelini

The *Sensus Fidelium* and Moral Discernment

The importance that the *sensus fidelium* may and should receive in theological reflection poses different problems with regard to the topics of Christian moral theology from those which are *de facto* discussed with regard to the topics of dogmatic or systematic theology. The category of *sensus fidelium* was in fact elaborated with specific reference to issues *de fede* rather than issues *de moribus*. And we must rethink in depth the account that has been given of the distinction between the two spheres of theology— faith and morals.

As is well known, moral theology was detached from the central body of theology—that is, from what was called *theologia scholastica* in the sixteenth century—as a result of concrete pastoral needs. More precisely, it was detached as one chapter of Catholic reflection, with the intention of ensuring the professional preparation of priests as ministers of the fourth sacrament. For centuries, this sacrament had taken the "modern" form of the confession of sins followed by the absolution of the penitent, and the Council of Trent set out with technical precision the canons relating to confession of this kind. The council demanded a discernment that certainly went beyond the assumed capacities of the penitents. But this discernment also went beyond the capacities of the priests, and this was why a special professional preparation was needed. The *theologia moralis* took the form of casuistry, that is, a training in the discernment of sins. It was held that the theoretical categories previously elaborated by scholasticism were appropriate for such a training, since it was believed (mistakenly) that they did not require any further theoretical developments.[1]

I may note in passing that a similar model is found at the birth of other new chapters in theology. At their origin, we find the emergence of new problems and tasks, and of new questions which of their nature would have prompted the theoretical rethinking of theology as a whole; instead, the attempt was made to respond by simply adding one new chapter. This branch was detached from the trunk of scholastic theology, but it was thought that one could use the conceptual instruments available to the old theology in order to promote the growth of the new discipline. Here I refer in particular to ascetic and mystical theology, then to spiritual theology, and finally to pastoral theology.

The fact remains that the low theoretical profile of the new discipline called *theologia moralis* entailed the potential for a substantial suppression of fundamental reflection on moral topics. This suppression was all the more serious in that it happened at the beginning of the modern cultural period, which asked questions of objective macroscopic significance for moral theological reflection. The marginal position of moral theology with respect to the questions raised by the new forms of philosophical thinking and the new forms of living together in society form the background to the confused and vague character of the *aggiornamento* in the wake of Vatican II. Only in this very recent period has the category of *sensus fidelium* made a genuine appearance on the stage of moral theology. In response to unsatisfactory aspects of the responses given by the magisterium to the new moral problems, especially those concerning the sphere of sexual behavior, modern theology makes a precise accusation: the magisterium ignores the *sensus fidelium*.

The thesis that I shall try to illustrate advocates a different diagnosis. What we basically lack today is not in fact a reference to the *sensus fidelium* in the documents of the magisterium, but rather the elaboration of an effective *sensus fidelium*, a common *sentire* on the part of believers with regard to the new problems of choice with which they are confronted by the changed context of society. The primary task of theology is to clarify the reasons for such a deficiency and then to propose potential remedies.

* * *

It is significant that recent debates within the church—and hence, in theology too—have frequently appealed to the *sensus fidelium.*[2] This has mostly happened with a polemical intention (as I have remarked), against the background of the widespread dissent that enormous sectors of the Catholic public have displayed vis-à-vis certain teachings of the papal magisterium, typically those referring to moral and disciplinary matters. The theologians were often the spokesmen of this Catholic dissent, especially in the years following Vatican II.[3] They expressed critical positions vis-à-vis the magisterium, especially on moral matters.[4] In this context, the appeal to the *sensus fidelium* took on the highly dubious form of a demand by the laity that their rights be granted them.[5]

The most serious question posed by the present historical situation of Catholicism with regard to the forms taken by the moral conscience of the laity[6] is in reality the definition of the appropriate *sentire* of faith in today's civil and religious situation, in which the primary task is the formation of a moral conscience. In this context, the appeal to the *sensus fidelium* risks being a verbal sleight-of-hand which allows us to avoid the real question. Do the attitudes of the faithful with regard to their daily conduct genuinely put into practice the *sensus fidei*? Do the conditions exist in which it is possible to ascertain the *sensus fidelium*? Or do their attitudes display an insidious (and unquestioned) dependence of the Christian conscience on the commonplaces of secular culture?

This culture promotes a separation between faith and conduct, since it understands faith only as an interior attitude about which nothing meaningful can be said. With regard to external behavior, it adheres to secular criteria that are resolutely pragmatic and hence make no reference to the radical attitude of faith. Can public opinion—to which appeal is made in order to ascertain the contents of the alleged *sensus fidelium*—truly be called *ecclesial* public opinion, and hence function as evidence of the attitude of the church as a whole? Is it not rather the case that it simply takes the form of a public *opinion* which is distorted by the suspect mediation of the public means of communication?[7] This doubt is particularly urgent in countries such as Italy, with a long Catholic tradition, because everyone here thinks himself qualified to say what is Christian.

* * *

The category of *sensus fidelium* designates an authority that is undoubtedly relevant to all theological thinking; but it has not yet proved possible to make a precise conceptual definition of this authority. In order to determine the true meaning of this category, we must adopt a perspective that is very different from that currently in vogue. We certainly cannot think of the *sensus fidelium* as something existing antecedently to the praxis of ecclesial relationships, something that the church's ministry would therefore be obliged to recognize as a normative authority in questions of pastoral praxis. The concept of *sensus fidelium* designates a contribution that the *sentire* of the faithful can and must give, down through the ages, to the identification of what is Christian. This contribution is certainly necessary today; indeed, in one sense it is more necessary than ever, and the reason for this increased urgency lies in the rapid social and cultural transformation that makes less unequivocal the pointers offered by the long tradition of Christian morals. And yet, this contribution is not only more urgent today; it also seems more problematic. Let me mention two particularly important factors here.

The first factor is the media of mass communication, which I have already mentioned. These promote systematically distorted processes of the formation of public opinion, processes that are remote from the attitudes of individuals since they tend by their very nature to give a privileged position to declamatory perspectives that completely ignore the conscience of the individual. Every minister of the church, who is called in virtue of his ministry to encounter the conscience of individuals, has innumerable opportunities to observe the gap between the language that the individual speaks and his true attitudes, or his *conscience*.[8] The individual tends almost inexorably to use a language that is offered to him by public communication—and which seems unable to say what he in fact *feels*.

The second systemic factor is connected to those forms of the knowledge of the human person that enjoy the highest authority today in the public sphere. I refer here to the knowledge offered by the human sciences and by philosophy. For a long time now, this knowledge has decreed the substantial suppression of the moral question,[9] which however continues inexorably to confront the conscience of the individual.

It is important to state explicitly that the moral question cannot in any way be reduced to the question of what is licit or illicit, that is, to the question of law. It must be understood more radically as the question posed by the objective necessity for the individual to recognize the *good,* or the *good cause* to which he may dedicate his life (since otherwise it would be lost). It is only this good cause that can authorize the exercise of his freedom. The greatest threat that hangs over the freedom of everyone who lives in the opulent West today is certainly not caused by economic misery or coercion. Rather, it is generated by the enormous difficulties which he or she experiences in truly positing an unconditional act of the *will*.[10]

* * *

In the last thirty years, we have experienced in my country a surprising return of *ethics,* while *morality* remains rigorously suppressed.[11] *Ethics* is concerned with justice in societal relationships, not with my immediate neighborhood; it has a fundamental interest in procedures. *Morality* ought to be concerned precisely with the relationships between neighbors, through which the individual acquires self-knowledge from the very beginning of his life. In these relationships, his own identity is always involved.

Moral knowledge has by its very nature a religious connotation, since it points us to the authority of the *sacred,* of that which deserves unconditional devotion. The *sensus fidei* can make a decisive contribution to the elaboration of moral knowledge; but if it is to achieve this, it must take on an objective form in the context of the church. It must take on the form of the *sensus fidelium*—indeed, of the *consensus fidelium.* Here, the service rendered by theology is absolutely necessary.

We can make a more precise distinction between two levels of service that theology must render to the formation of the *sensus fidei,* a theoretical and/or fundamental service and a service with a practical, historical character. Obviously, these two are very closely linked. It is clear that contemporary theology finds it very difficult to comprehend the *sensus fidei,* and hence to help this develop into the *sensus fidelium.* But this is largely the fault of the inadequate theological categories with which it works: even today, it is the excessively intellectual perspective of the theological tradition that dictates a priori how we approach this subject.

It is only in the modern period that the idea of the *sensus fidelium* was elaborated, against the background of the problems posed by the exercise of the ecclesial magisterium. More precisely, it was elaborated in connection with the definition of the dogmas of the Immaculate Conception and the Assumption of Mary. It is well known that there is very little support for these dogmas in the biblical texts and the literary documents belonging to the most ancient tradition, but they had a certain attestation in the praxis of the common faith, so that the reference to the *sensus fidelium* served to make good this defect. The earliest elaboration of this idea took for granted an understanding of the Christian revelation which later developments have rightly corrected—I refer here above all to developments in biblical research and to the fundamental theological reflection that found its reception at Vatican II in *Dei Verbum*. All theologians today would agree that it was necessary to overcome the "doctrinalistic" idea of revelation, which reduced it to a series of propositions. Today, just as in earlier epochs of the church's history, the common *sentire* of the faith cannot be ascertained by means of a mere registration of the propositions by means of which this faith is professed.

The appeal to the idea of the *sensus fidelium* with regard to moral issues, or with regard to the tasks that are incumbent on the church's magisterium in moral matters, is much more recent, and became genuinely significant only thanks to the lengthy and painful conflict about *Humanae vitae*. The forms in which this appeal is made are based on the idea that the *sensus fidelium* exists antecedently to its application to any one specific moral issue.

* * *

I myself believe that the idea of the *sensus fidelium* requires a new definition when it is employed with reference to questions of mores. And this renewed definition would in turn renew its use with reference to the *res de fide* or (to use the conventional language) with reference to questions of dogma.

Here, an observation of a formal character is necessary. The idea of the *sensus fidelium* refers to the conscience of the faithful, and more precisely to the testimony that this conscience bears to Christian truth. We certainly cannot assume that this attestation immediately takes on a verbal form, articulated in a series of propositions; rather, it is realized by means of ways of *sentire*. We must therefore clarify what *sentire* means, and what the *sensus* of the faith is, for otherwise we cannot explain how the *sensus fidelium* can be translated into propositions. This task appears complex, and theologians have in fact devoted very little attention to it.

The task of clarification requires theology to introduce the concept of the *believing conscience*. As we hear *ad nauseam* today, faith in its most original sense does not consist in holding this or that proposition to be true, that is, in the assent to individual propositions, but rather in that act whereby the subject consents to his or her own vocation, to a divine plan that refers specifically to this individual person.

I have the impression that theologians in general today broadly accept the position that faith must be thought of in so-called *personalistic* terms. This, however, is only a program; it still awaits its full elaboration. The contemporary attempts at presenting a personalistic concept of faith tend in the direction of a purely fiducialist conception, like that which is dear above all to the Protestant theological tradition, or that which is dear to the postmodern forms of the believing conscience. In order to overcome this fiducialist understanding of faith, we must recall the concept of the believing conscience and its essential work of mediation in praxis.

All I can do here is suggest an initial step toward the elaboration of such a concept. Our starting point is the very effective formulations by Luke in the Acts of the Apostles. He tells us that those who heard the words of Peter on the day of Pentecost *felt that their hearts were pierced.* This was how they realized that his preaching concerned them personally and brought to light a truth that was genuinely inscribed on their *heart* but hidden from their eyes—and indeed, a truth denied by the forms that their consciousness had adopted under pressure from the social context. The preaching necessarily led to a conversion. The perception of the indubitable relevance of the words they had heard was not sufficient to tell them which new path they should take; it was clear that they had to make a choice, but it was not yet clear what that choice should be. The initial form of their choice has therefore an interrogative form. They ask *Peter and the other apostles, "Brethren, what must we do?"* (Acts 2:37). The comprehensive perception of the truth of the gospel precedes the understanding both of that truth and of what precise conduct it demands. The initial evidential character of this truth must be given a specific definition by means of renewed reflection on all those things that once seemed well known, but now no longer seem so.

The faith of the people in Jerusalem undergoes a process analogous to that of the faith of Jesus' first disciples. Here I refer above all to the narrative of John. When they hear the prophetic proclamation of the Baptist, two of his disciples begin to follow Jesus, and when he explicitly asks them about this choice, *What are you seeking?*, they reply: *Rabbi, where do you live?* Jesus does not give them his address. Rather, he summons them to follow him: *Come and see. So they went and saw where he lived, and they spent that day with him* (John 1:38ff.). These brief formulations indicate very well the original structure of faith in Christ: it is only by means of a real journey that we can reach the place where we dwell, or even learn where it is. Those who wish to become disciples must pass through this apprenticeship.

The Fourth Gospel expresses more explicitly the necessity of this journey when Jesus says to the Jews who have come to faith in him: *If you remain faithful to my word, you will be truly my disciples. You will know the truth, and the truth will set you free* (John 8:31f.). A faith that develops only on the basis of a word that one has heard, a word that appears convincing, is not true faith. The real knowledge of the truth presupposes that we put the word into practice. Only thus will the conversion of our life, and of the very being of the believer, be brought about: *you will be truly my disciples.*

* * *

The formal structure that I have set out with reference to Christian conversion corresponds to the original structure of the practical experience of everyone under heaven, and thus to the original structural of the moral form of life. Most of the theoretical proposals of the philosophical tradition, and also of contemporary reflection, bear the marks of an *idealistic* conception of norms that makes it impossible to see the need for a mediation of these norms in praxis. In order to be genuinely a categorical imperative, the moral imperative ought to be defined in abstraction from any reference to the concrete and contingent circumstances of the subject. In reality, however, it is only the evidence revealed in the course of a genuine journey—the journey that permits the conscience to emerge—that proclaims the commandment.

In the perspective of the Christian faith, one absolutely characteristic aspect of the moral imperative is precisely its reference to a specific history. We see this already in the case of the law given on Sinai, which takes up well-known norms that were proposed by the common ethos but gives them a new meaning by placing them within the framework of the exodus, a surprising event that is a new beginning for the journey of life.

The exodus reveals a truth that ought always to have been known: at the beginning of the journey of life there stands the grace of God. Precisely because it comes first, his grace is *worth even more than life itself* (Ps 63:4). The link between the imperative of the law and the event of grace, which is indicated from the very outset, is defined more precisely through the prophetic and sapiential criticism of the forms that the journey of *this people* takes in history. The law, which was given at the beginning, can find the fulfillment of its truth only at the coming of the One who fulfills the law. Faithfulness to the testament of Jesus, to the *new and eternal covenant*, is realized in the genuine praxis of the relationship of friendship that he establishes among his disciples.[12]

These two aspects must always be borne in mind. The commandment of Jesus takes up an earlier covenant that the Creator himself had instituted among all creatures, and which necessarily adopted those forms of life in common that are attested by the customs of every people. Nevertheless, faith in the Gospel of Jesus brings about a new understanding and a critical comprehension of something that everyone already knows. This believing and critical adoption of the tradition of the children of Adam finds its definition precisely by means of the forms of ecclesial communion, which must give a form to that *sensus fidei* which determines the initial proclamation of the gospel, thereby equipping it to serve as a criterion of moral discernment.

The theoretical clarification of this formal structure of the relationship between faith and morality is necessary for the concrete historical discernment which appears particularly difficult in the situation of a post-modern society. This is necessary, but not enough. With the aid of renewed conceptual instruments, we must discern the forms that human relationships should take today.[13]

III. The Challenge of Pluralism and the Future of Moral Theology

Eberhard Schockenhoff (Germany)
The Challenge of Pluralism

Lisa Sowle Cahill (United States)
Moral Theology: From Evolutionary to Revolutionary Change

Márcio Fabri dos Anjos (Brazil)
Community and Pluralism: Challenges to Moral Theology

Eberhard Schockenhoff outlines two agenda in his paper. First he discusses pluralism as an essential characteristic of the modern world, "the intellectual 'calling card' of the modern age." There he discusses the reality of political pluralism arguing that just as contemporary society entertains Catholic social teaching as amenable to the ends of modern pluralism so too it ought to consider and not reject outright Catholic moral teaching regarding individual responsibility. The church's "public function of advocacy in favor of the weak and those without rights is in fact demanded by the rules governing societal and political pluralism, since this pluralism must not be confused with an ethical relativism." Second, he turns to the legitimacy of pluralism in theological ethics. He names three contemporary causes: the plurality of perspectives from which moral philosophical questions are posed in a postmetaphysical age; the time lag affecting societal challenges to the various world religions; and the divergent evaluations of empirical issues. He then turns to an argument in its favor:

> As the eschatological revelation of the love of God, the message of the Gospel claims not only to be valid for particular cultural spheres and periods in human history, but to be the definitive word of God about the human person, a word possessing a breadth and fullness that go beyond every historical form in which the attempt is made to realize it. This eschatological claim by the word of God means that it is never possible for any one intellectual approach in theology to grasp exhaustively the fullness of revelation.

210

Lisa Sowle Cahill engages the concept of pluralism by first talking about two types of challenges facing theological ethics. The evolutionary challenge occurs within traditional structures and attempts to expand the tradition on a host of topics from HIV/AIDS prevention strategies to questions about end-of-life issues. This challenge both expands concepts of authority to include issues of integrity and one's solidarity with the poor and insists on all ethical judgments occurring within a social context. Revolutionary challenge is the challenge of cultural pluralism. "It requires us to grasp and express *simultaneously* two paradoxical facts. *One*, moral truth is contingent on concrete moral practices with a specific historical, cultural or multicultural character. Yet, *two*, moral truth is not simply 'constructed' by cultures or traditions, but refers in some way to shared human goods, values, and bonds." For Cahill, this is the search across cultures (a "transversalism") for a realistically more just world as a tangible ground for hope for those who live under the weight of deplorable inequities.

Márcio Fabri dos Anjos locates his topic within the nexus of moral theology and the Christian community. Arguing that the task of moral theology is to shape and guide the Christian community, Fabri sees pluralism as a constitutive insight for the task of moral theology today in the face of the leveling process of globalization that diminishes the subject, the culture, and the context, leaving each to be a stand-alone individual. "The density of the concept of subject enters a crisis with the depersonalizing process of the global economy and its methods of production; global pluralism weakens the consciousness of the people, annulling the participatory power of the subject." Not only are we called then to insist on the intersubjectivty and relationality of all persons but in formulating a moral anthropology of our time, we need to recognize anew the People of God. "Affirming the community as people of God leads to an affirmation of the people as subjects of their own history, which in turn leads to a critique of whatever curtails their freedom to participate in their own destiny." In short, to be truly counter-cultural in a time of globalized autonomous detachment we must insist on the nature of the human as needing to be in solidarity with the poor, or else we shall never see ourselves in the image of God.

Eberhard Schockenhoff

The Challenge of Pluralism

1. Pluralism as an Essential Characteristic of the Modern World

Pluralism is a fundamental characteristic of our times, leaving its imprint on virtually every dimension of the world in which we live. Premodern societies were held together by the "brackets" of a unified interpretation of the world and by shared moral views which imposed themselves on the individual in myth and religion, ethics and teaching; but the modern period is characterized by the disintegration of stable forms of living, systems of knowledge, and forms of dominion. Instead of a hierarchically structured universe in which politics, law, and morality reflected the unity of a cosmic ordering, we have a polycentric universe that is defined by the lack of one dominant structural principle and by a plurality of perspectives that enjoy equal status. As a concept, "pluralism" denotes not a mere arbitrary multiplicity, but the juxtaposition in equality of points of view, perspectives, and interpretative elements with no overarching principle of unity. Since the individual elements compete with one another, pluralism—as the intellectual "calling card" of the modern age—displays an explicitly antagonistic structure: the various perspectives that offer an interpretation of the world are locked in combat. They are marked by discord and conflicting interests, and refuse to let themselves be integrated into a higher synthesis in which the antitheses might be reconciled.

At the beginning of the twentieth century, William James called the modern world a "pluralistic universe" constituted by an infinite number of natural and social elements that are changing all the time, and which thus lead to ever new configurations, relationships, and structures. Here there is no longer any fixed point that could offer a safe epistemological starting point; rather, the individual must integrate into her/his own private interpretation of the world perspectives that offer mutually contrary orientations. Obviously, this antagonistic situation contains a high potential for conflict; in order that a productive cooperation may be achieved in professional work, in academic life and economics, in politics and in society, the theory of modernity complements pluralism by the requirement of tolerance and of

cooperation in sharing work. The normative foundations of modern pluralism also include the fact that it is not only accepted as an empirical circum-
stance but is also acknowledged as the intellectual point of departure of the
modern age.[1] The multiplicity and variety of mutually contrary standpoints
must be approved and affirmed by everyone, since this is the necessary
reverse side of the principle of freedom—and the modern world is generated
precisely by the acknowledgment of this freedom.[2]

Among the various forms of pluralism produced in the process of differentiation that gave birth to the modern world, a particular challenge is posed
to theological ethics by *religious* pluralism (the plurality of religions and confessions that coexist contemporaneously in a society), *political* pluralism (the
competition between political groups and programs for influence and
power), *ethical* pluralism (the plurality of competing convictions about values and lifestyles), and the *epistemic* pluralism of academic discourse.

2. The Political Pluralism of Democratic Societies

Contemporary political theory sees societal and political pluralism as one
necessary epiphenomenon of a state with a neutral worldview. Unlike the
Greek *polis* and the premodern forms of society, the modern state is no
longer constructed on the foundation of a structure of truth and virtues. It
limits itself to guaranteeing an external structure of peace which ensures freedom, safety, and justice for all citizens and thereby offers the framework
within which the plural forces of society can develop freely. Political pluralism and the plurality of convictions and worldviews are meant to protect the
citizens in their freedom to take part as full equals in the process whereby the
political will is formed. This means that pluralism is not its own legitimation;
rather, it finds its basic legitimation in the ethical principles of freedom and
equality and in the equal participation of all in the cultural, social, and political life of the community of the state.

Catholic social doctrine and the church's magisterium emphasize today
the importance of societal and political pluralism in permitting a free democracy to function. At the Second Vatican Council, the Catholic Church
acknowledged the basic democratic freedoms of opinion, of religion, of conscience, and of coalition—freedoms against which the church had resolutely
fought in the nineteenth century—as individual rights of each human being,
with their roots in his dignity as a person. Thereby the Church also implicitly admitted the right and the necessity of a political pluralism that permits
everyone to exercise these rights and so to take part in political activity.

The political pluralism of democratic societies is, however, neither unlimited nor devoid of any presuppositions; nor may it be confused with an unrestrained antagonism of individual political, cultural, and economic interests.

Rather, modern democracy is itself based on presuppositions that are not subject to the arbitrary acknowledgment of individual groups and world-views. A democratic state under the rule of law must be neutral in terms of worldview, but this principle must not lead in practice to an indifferent equidistance vis-à-vis all the moral convictions that are de facto lived out in society, nor to a refusal to lay down reliable boundary conditions within which the moral, cultural, and economic activity of its citizens can freely unfold. If the state—founded on the distinction between law and morality—is to function as the guarantor of a free democratic ordering that respects the claim to social justice, it cannot simply understand itself as value-neutral when it is confronted by a plurality of existential standpoints on the part of its citizens. We are faced with a growing ethical pluralism; if there is no longer any sphere of law (not even in the core area of domestic life) that the state keeps immune from changing majorities and the enforcement of indi-vidual interests, then it endangers the very foundations of its own legitima-tion. And without these foundations, it cannot retain the trust of its citizens in the long term.

In addition to the responsibility to promote the common good, the pro-tection of human dignity and human rights is an especially important polit-ical task. As rights to personal defense, as rights to make claims within the context of society, and as rights to participation in cultural life, human rights are an expression of citizens' mutual acknowledgment as fundamentally equal members of the political community. "This is why they denote claims to which every human person as such is entitled. They belong to that dimen-sion over which a legitimate pluralism has no hold; this is owed to the human person by every legal and civic ordering—and *a fortiori* by a pluralistic democracy."[3] Accordingly, the neutrality in terms of worldview that is of constitutive importance for a democracy is not the same thing as indiffer-ence to moral values. The latter is incompatible with a living democracy that exercises vigilance over its own inherent risks. A pluralistic democracy that respects the claims of freedom and justice is viable in the long term only if it continues to respect its obligations vis-à-vis the basic moral values that it embodies—and its political and legal institutions must protect these values. In his encyclical *Evangelium Vitae,* Pope John Paul II identifies the founda-tions that exist a priori to all activity on the part of the state as the dignity of the human person, the inviolable rights of this person, the solidarity of individuals, and the common good that provides orientation for both indi-viduals and groups in society in their endeavor to realize their own good in a pluralistic situation of mutual antagonism.[4]

To the extent that these moral postulates emphasize the obligation to pro-mote peace and social justice, tolerance and intercultural openness, they gen-erally meet with broad assent in democratic societies. The Catholic Church is accepted as a moral "watchman," above all in the field of social ethics, in a manner compatible with the pluralistic processes by which a political will is formed in democracies. On the other hand, when the church recalls basic ethical norms in the sphere of personal responsibility for the life one leads, this is usually rejected. The objection is that a pluralistic society cannot base its legislation on the internal morality of one particular community of faith. This accusation belongs to the standard repertoire of moral argumentation when a response is sought to the increasingly acute moral conflicts with which pluralistic societies are confronted today. This accusation, however, overlooks the fact that such conflicts by no means always concern *only* questions about a personal lifestyle—topics that enlightened individuals could decide within the framework of a legitimate pluralism, free from external interference. Since abortion, research into the human embryo, and many procedures of modern reproductive medicine affect the rights of third parties, pluralistic societies are confronted here with elementary problems of justice that they cannot leave to the arbitrary choices of individual citizens. Unlike other collisions of values that occur within the framework of a legitimate pluralism, questions of justice can be decided only on a basis that exists a priori to the cultural preferences of individual groups and safeguards the rights of all involved parties.[5]

In an open society, divergent moral views in the sphere of the individual conduct of life can remain undecided for as long those who practice this behavior do not infringe the human rights of other persons by exercising what they see as their own right. Where, however, ethical conflicts concern the acknowledgment and enforcement of elementary rights, one cannot avoid them by employing the pluralistic rule about conflicts which states that each one should follow his own convictions, without imposing these on other persons. The obligation to practice justice vis-à-vis third parties who are affected by my behavior cannot be abolished by a mere appeal to tolerance and toleration. This means that when theologians and the church intervene in the democratic process whereby a political will is formed in pluralistic societies, and raise their voices against abortion and euthanasia, defending the rights of the human person from conception to a natural death, they are not demanding that the state protect their own ethos or the religious feelings of their own believers. Rather, they are demanding that each human being enjoy protection from the very beginning of his individual existence. The theologians and the church are not promoting their own private agenda here, nor are they seeking to claim any special privileges for themselves; for in the open competition of pluralistic ideas, programs, and opinions, no one is entitled to such privileges. Rather, the theologians and the church are assuming the function of an advocate on behalf of the weak and those without rights, those who have no voice of their own, in order that their existential perspectives and rights may be perceived and accepted by those who are stronger and seek to enforce their own views.

This public function of advocacy in favor of the weak and those without rights is in fact demanded by the rules governing societal and political pluralism, since this pluralism must not be confused with ethical relativism.[6] An unrestricted plurality of opinions and of political views (even among Catholics) expresses the *life* that exists in pluralistic societies, and indeed constitutes their inherent richness. But this political and cultural pluralism presupposes a framework of fundamental things held in common, within which it can flourish to the benefit of all the citizens; if pluralism becomes an absolute value, it will destroy this framework. This is why a legitimate political and cultural pluralism must not be confused with a pluralism of moral principles and basic values, which regards the various values as options that are all equally acceptable. And it is then a matter of indifference which option one chooses, since all these values have become meaningless. Political theory too states that when pluralism is envisaged as a one-sided, nondialectic concept that places the emphasis on that which is individual rather than on that which is held in common, on plurality rather than on unity, and on competition rather than on the obligation to solidarity, it destroys the bases of legitimation which are its normative substance.

In addition to varying views on issues of domestic and foreign policies (e.g., the integration of minorities, strategies to combat terrorism, paths to safeguard peace), pluralism also reigns in principle in issues of economic and social policies (e.g., the kind of tax system that is desirable, the level of social security, the future of the health system). Although there is a broad consensus about the goals of political activity in these fields, the concrete strategies that ought to be adopted remain often a matter of dispute.

3. The Legitimacy of Pluralism in Theology

Let us now take a further step in our reflections on the significance of pluralism for theological ethics and ask what the function of pluralism for this discipline might be. We move from a consideration *ab extra* of the societal environment of the church to the internal perspective of faith. In our first step, we analyzed the altered context in terms of the history of ideas and of mentalities, which has an impact on theological work in the various societies to which we belong; now, we ask how the internal theological pluralism should be evaluated. The theological problem of the relationship between unity and plurality, which takes the form in exegesis of the question of the unity of pluriform biblical theologies on the basis of the biblical canon, confronts us in ethics with regard to the believers' testimony to the gospel in their lives. How is it possible to establish a mutual communication among the various existential forms and praxes in which the Christians in Asia, Africa, and Latin America, in the industrialized societies of North America, and in southern, central, and eastern Europe live their faith day by day, in such a way that these not only represent the plurality of their own cultures but also bind together their various forms of expression to form one pluriform testimony of the entire church to the truth of the gospel? And what is the relationship within theological reflection between the various intellectual approaches of discourse ethics, the natural law theory, liberation theory, and the intercultural comparison of forms of ethos? How is it possible to show that, despite all their differences, they can all serve the basic questions of Christian ethics, which are everywhere the same? What individual conduct of life, and what common activity, are considered by the believers of the various local churches to be an answer to the moral conflicts in their societies?

(a) Reasons for the Process of Differentiation in Theological Ethics

In order to understand the enduring legitimacy of the theological pluralism which is a typical manifestation of our discipline today, we must analyze the reasons for the postconciliar process of differentiation within academic theology. We must distinguish three factors that were decisively important in the genesis of an irreversible pluralism in theological ethics. First, like Catholic theology as a whole, our own discipline too presupposes the disintegration of a unified metaphysical form of thought which in the age of neoscholasticism guaranteed that the same questions would be posed, the same methodology would be followed in seeking solutions, and answers with identical contents would be given. The structures of thinking and language in neoscholasticism made it possible for Catholic theology everywhere in the world to work on the same problems with the same intellectual instruments. This structure began to crack open even during the council, but it was only in the following decades that the real reception of the problems and the possibilities of expression of the modern moral philosophers took place.

The great tradition of European philosophy supplied a basis in traditional metaphysics and anthropology, but it is no longer possible to rely on this when we endeavor to show that the Christian ethic teaches a morality leading to an authentic human existence, a morality that helps develop the basic human capacities and is the right response to the basic needs of each one of us—needs that are anchored in that which makes us human. If theological ethics is to respond to the council's demand for an academic exposition of the basic concerns of Christian ethics on the same level of seriousness as contemporary philosophical trends, we also need to assimilate the philosophical trends of the twentieth century (phenomenology, linguistic philosophy, analytical ethics, discourse ethics) and to engage in debate with a utilitarian approach to ethics. In addition, a polycentric world perspective requires that we assimilate the cultural forms of language and thought that have led in the non-European traditions to a different accentuation in the evaluation of basic anthropological phenomena such as the relatedness of human existence to community, the significance of popular piety, the position of older persons in societal structures, and the meaning of bodiliness, of sexuality, and of the transmission of life. These tasks necessitate a greater diversification of theological-ethical approaches.

The pluralism within Catholic moral theology that this entails is the logical consequence of developments to which the council itself gave the green light, although an inner momentum took these developments beyond what the council had envisaged in a situation that was still dominated by neoscholasticism and the theology of the Roman school. Ultimately, the right of the non-European linguistic and cultural spheres to develop their own expressions of Christian thought and life within the one world-church derives from the structure of the one church of Jesus Christ as a *communio* that lives in and on the basis of the many local churches throughout the world. We should also note that from the perspective of the theology of history, the pluralism in theology that has arisen in the last decades presents the appearance of fragmentation and disintegration, with no unifying perspective, *only* in a direct comparison with the tendencies towards uniformity in the construction of the neoscholastic system; in a larger historical context, it can be seen that Catholic theology in earlier epochs was marked by a greater internal plurality of schools and styles of thought, and that precisely this plurality constituted the intellectual riches of the church.

In the preceding paragraph, I have sketched one reason for the contemporary theological pluralism in the church, based on the very nature of theology's task. There is another, more pragmatic reason for this pluralism. Within the canon of the theological disciplines, theological ethics has in a preeminent manner the task of confronting the specific challenges that are linked to the societal, economic, and cultural developments in the individual countries, and the varying tempo of these developments means that theologians face different priorities when they endeavor to respond to the needs of their own societies at any given time. The pluralism generated by the different cultural and social questions entails a time lag. This, however, is only one aspect of the world situation today. It is surely no less important to note that the world is confronted everywhere and at the same time by the same ethical challenges, thanks to scientific and technological progress in the modern life sciences. Despite the common elements in the questions that the cultural and intellectual disciplines pose about the nature of the human person, of the world, and of history, a greater measure of particularity has been preserved in these areas, since they are always linked to specific contexts; but the rationality inherent in the natural sciences bears no specific cultural imprint and is everywhere the same. This is why today's world situation is marked to an unprecedented extent by the emergence of a uniform technological-scientific civilization that poses the same ethical questions everywhere. In the field of bioethics, Asian theology reflects on problems comparable to those studied by North American and European theology, because they are all confronted in their own societies by the onward march of a utilitarian and pragmatic way of looking at things which largely dominates the international bioethical debate.

One final reason why today's theological-ethical pluralism is a legitimate development of our discipline is related to what the council called the autonomy of the inner-worldly specialist areas. Since the individual normative affirmations of ethics are based on mixed judgments, to which the empirical knowledge of the human and social sciences makes its contribution, a wider spectrum of answers is inevitable. This means that different theologians, while equally conscientious in their work, will find different solutions to one and the same question. This is the reason why a wider spectrum of answers and solutions, all equally justified, coexist within theological ethics.

(b) The Fundamental Legitimacy of Pluralism in Theology

The reasons I have indicated for the plural constitution of theological ethics—the plurality of perspectives from which moral philosophical questions are posed in a postmetaphysical age; the time lag affecting societal challenges to the various world religions; and the divergent evaluations of empirical issues—can help explain why the process of differentiation began after the council, and why we still see this differentiation today. But we can fully comprehend the justification of a legitimate pluralism in the field of theological ethics only when we see that this is derived from the scientific-theoretical character of theology as an academic discipline dealing with faith and revelation.

The right and the boundaries of a legitimate theological-ethical pluralism can be defined only when we bear in mind the task proper to our discipline, namely, the elaboration of a theory of the conduct of human life under the claim made by the gospel. As the eschatological revelation of the love of God, the message of the gospel claims not only to be valid for particular cultural spheres and periods in human history, but to be the definitive word of God about the human person, a word possessing a breadth and fullness that go beyond every historical form in which the attempt is made to realize it. This eschatological claim by the word of God means that it is never possible for any one intellectual approach in theology to grasp exhaustively the fullness of revelation.

(c) The Boundaries of a Legitimate Pluralism within Theology

This means that both the fullness of the word of God and the variety of the groups to whom it is to be proclaimed demand a plurality of styles of thinking and forms of reflection. Pope Benedict XVI has observed that there are as many paths to God as there are human beings; and this makes a theological pluralism legitimate in the sphere of Christian ethics. At the same time, however, we can see the point at which a legitimate plurality of intellectual approaches is distinguished from an arbitrary pluralism, and we can see the border post at which one could succumb to an indifferent juxtaposition and antagonism of the various perspectives. A genuine plurality of standpoints and perspectives comes into existence only where these are differing views about one and the same question; a mere disparate congeries of viewpoints does not suffice to generate an academic discipline with an inherently plural constitution. A pluralism in which people join together in seeking and asking questions is not merely the result of adding together the various individual perspectives of those taking part; rather, plural questions complement one another in such a way that they constitute a pluralism in theological ethics *only* when they are studying a common topic and the plural perspectives cooperate in the attempt to analyze this.[7] And all these perspectives must submit to judgment by the common criterion: can they plausibly explain to their own time and culture what it means to love God and one's neighbor?[8]

Lisa Sowle Cahill

Moral Theology

From Evolutionary to Revolutionary Change

It is an immense responsibility to come before hundreds of colleagues from dozens of countries and attempt to address the "challenge of pluralism." We *are* the face of pluralism. I therefore take up my task with a great sense of humility. But I am also extremely hopeful, because I look forward to the dialogue ahead. Together we can find the courage to overcome the limits of our individual perspectives and confront the problems of our world. Humility, courage, and hope—these no doubt are the most essential virtues of moral theologians in today's "world church."

I want to address two key ways in which pluralism has especially challenged Catholic moral theology since the Second Vatican Council. I will refer to the first challenge as *evolutionary*. It comes from within the Roman Catholic tradition. It is a challenge to change and adapt the discipline of moral theology in light of a new pluralism of sources and of theologians, stemming from openness to the modern world, to Scripture, and to the role of the laity. The second challenge must be called *revolutionary*, and goes beyond the Catholic tradition. It is a radical challenge to reexamine the very terms and conditions of moral theology in light of the heightened cultural pluralism introduced by globalization and the birth of new theologies on every continent and in many faiths.

The first, evolutionary, challenge concerns the received neoscholastic "system" of moral theology, which works with a framework of supposedly rational principles that can be applied universally to cases. This familiar system is derived from one particular understanding of "natural law," and involves principles and concepts such as double effect, intrinsically evil acts, principle of totality, material and formal cooperation, and probabilism. Pluralism has challenged this system "from within" in the sense that, in the middle of the twentieth century, moral theologians applying the principles began to see that many results, while authoritatively confirmed by the magisterium, did not correspond to the moral experience of most people. Nor were they sensitive to prudent pastoral practice. As Thomas Aquinas said, moral truth concerns "contingent matters," and carries much more uncertainty and variety than do matters of speculative reason.[1] Moral knowing occurs through an exercise of the practical reason, guided by the virtue of prudence.

Appreciating this fact, moral theologians such as Josef Fuchs, Bruno Schüller, Richard McCormick, and Charles E. Curran began to question whether what moral theology had claimed to know in the past was absolutely certain. Special targets of criticism were the principle of double effect and the concept of "intrinsic evil." Their questions were evolutionary in that they did not reject these traditional principles and concepts altogether but began to propose new meanings. These interpretations were guided in great part by practical problems such as artificial birth control.[2] Revisions were proposed, many controversial and still hotly debated. Examples are the reinterpretation of double effect as "proportionalism,"[3] the debates about exactly when an embryo becomes a person, the definition of artificial nutrition and hydration as an ordinary or extraordinary means of life support, and the permissibility of using condoms to prevent AIDS.[4] Although the first advocates of change in moral theology were priests and seminary professors, the involvement of lay people, especially women, in moral theology, as well as the movement of moral theology beyond the seminary setting to universities, contributed greatly to these potential evolutions of traditional moral theology.

One important aspect of this first evolutionary challenge is the fact that the source of authority in moral theology has begun to shift, or at least expand. Authoritative traditions and teachings are still important of course. The weight or degree of their authority, however, depends much more on the lived experience of individual persons, of Catholic Christian communities, and on corresponding developments in the field of moral theology itself. Authority now requires the power to illumine our real situations and guide us toward more humane relationships and practices that respect human dignity and the common good, and express a gospel-informed "preferential option for the poor." And discernment of who or what has authority is a much more communal and practical process today than in generations past.

Another important aspect of the evolutionary challenge is the fact that moral theologians have noted discrepancies between the way analysis typically operates in the so-called personal and social spheres. Theologians, especially feminist moral theologians, insist that moral actions cannot be isolated from social contexts.[5] These contexts introduce great contingency and complexity to moral decision making. All moral theology must take into account not only individual choices but the practices and institutions in which agency takes shape. This insight prepares the way for the second, *revolutionary*, challenge of pluralism to moral theology.

The revolutionary challenge is the challenge of cultural pluralism—a much more radical challenge. Worldwide communications media make us more aware than ever before of the extent of human variety and differences, as well as the frequency of clashes and conflicts among cultures and peoples. Cultural pluralism questions the very premises of the discourse of moral theology. Is there really a "natural law" applying to everyone? Can moral analysis be "objective" and "rational"? Do "human dignity" and "the common good" mean the same thing around the world? Is it even possible any more to speak of "truth"? Moral theology is challenged by the apparent fragmentation of experience into myriad incommensurable value systems, and by the proliferation of "different" and "new" voices who assert their right to speak in their own names and for their own contexts—be it Brazil, Ghana, Croatia, India, Vietnam, Lebanon, or Trinidad.[6] In this vein, postmodern and deconstructive philosophy and cultural criticism have greatly influenced contemporary moral theology. Few Catholic moral theologians have given up the search for truth. Yet many participants in this conference on "Catholic Theological Ethics in the World Church" (Padua, 2006) have insisted that no one has a universal perspective on truth and that truth must be sought and known practically—and thus differently—in different contexts.

The revolutionary challenge of cultural pluralism is one of the most immense challenges we face in the next few decades. It requires us to grasp and express *simultaneously* two paradoxical facts. *One,* moral truth is contingent on concrete moral practices with a specific historical, cultural, or multicultural character. Yet, *two,* moral truth is not simply "constructed" by cultures or traditions but refers in some way to shared human goods, values, and bonds. The first fact, the practical nature of moral truth, corresponds to the practical character of moral reason and moral responsibility as well as to the beauty and value of diverse forms of human life and culture. The second fact, that truth is in some sense "objective," corresponds to the reality of human interdependence and to the possibility of our being in solidarity with one another to relieve human suffering.

Theologians and philosophers who completely reject the idea of objective and universal truth rightly resist all the forms of "cultural hegemony" that underwrite oppressive and discriminatory systems of racism, sexism, and what we might term "Westernism" with its liberal individualism and penchant for economic and military violence. Yet manifold moral issues in "the world church" demand cooperative problem solving and conflict resolution, and even the ability to identify problems and name immorality in a "global" way. Examples are violence against women and children, extreme poverty, environmental degradation, terrorism, torture, preemptive war, and the sacrifice of AIDS victims to the profits of drug companies. Only if any given cultural practice or institution can be held to a higher standard can moral theology criticize and demand change in practices that undermine people's basic needs and dignity.

One positive legacy of our natural law tradition is to give us a basis on which to commit ourselves to dialogue about what divides us, on the assumption that our shared humanity will support practical agreements about how to resolve specific threats to the common good. No meaningful consensus will ever be "derived" in a top-down fashion from abstract principles, nor will it ever be comprehensive, perfect, or revision free. Our approach to moral truth, as practical, will always be inductive, incremental, participatory, and culturally nuanced as to the specifics of good moral practice.

The feminist legal theorist Hillary Charlesworth proposes a model of *"transversalism"* rather than "universalism" for moral understanding across cultures.[7] Transversalism is a process of mutually empathetic and critical communication, in which participants cross imaginatively into one another's territories, express their own values and assertions, listen to others, modify their own claims, try to reach agreement on the moral nonnegotiables, and honestly criticize the shortcomings of all cultural systems. A "transversal" approach was the aim of the Padua conference and its participants—who listened, challenged, reconsidered, and reached greater understanding through the process.

A clear message of the conference dialogue is that it is important for moral theologians—both within the church and as social agents—to make sure that transversal exchange is a process in which everyone can be involved. An intervention from Tina Astorga (Philippines) reminded us that it is important that the dialogue of moral theology not be controlled by social or intellectual elites. Teresia Hinga (Kenya) urged that we not only recognize the agency and voice of "grassroots" women and give credit to their solutions to problems, but that they also be viewed as theologians in their own right. In the discussion following a plenary panel on North America, Stephen Pope (United States) called for an analysis of power. Unbalanced power and misuse of power obviously lead to social injustices, but they also lead to distorted apprehensions of the truth. Unless discourses about morality, society, and politics are fully and freely participatory, then knowledge about these realities and the obligations they entail will be partial at best, a self-serving lie at worst.

Moral uncertainties and conflicts will always remain, even if moral discourse gains inclusivity. For example, is ritual genital mutilation a form of violence against women? Should the livelihood of indigenous peoples be sacrificed to protect a rain forest or an endangered species? What is the difference between a terrorist and a freedom fighter? Exactly when do interrogation tactics become torture? How immediate does a threat have to be to justify an act of military self-defense? And what is the justified limit of the profits that a drug company is entitled to make? These questions cannot be answered in an absolute and final way, but this does not mean that we are left with uncritical "pluralism."

Human beings everywhere share physical and even psychological characteristics. Every culture and every person values family, food, clean water, shelter, and freedom from fear of violence and illness. After all, all cultures develop kinship, educational, and political systems to provide access to these goods and to ensure their availability, through material production, distribution systems, and social stability. There is actually very little cultural pluralism on *the most basic goods and needs* of persons and societies, things that every person wants for herself or himself and her or his valued family members.

But where cultural pluralism makes a huge and often negative moral difference is in defining *the systems of access* by which individuals and groups either do or do not obtain the goods their welfare and flourishing require. Access to goods is typically restricted. Every culture and institution known to humanity systematizes types of discrimination. Modern terms such as "human dignity," "full humanity," "democracy," "human rights," "equality," "solidarity," and "equal opportunity" are ways of challenging inequitable access patterns. Such language represents a social, political, and legal ethos in which participation in the common good and access to basic goods of society is universally shared, even though on many possible cultural models. This is the modern definition of social justice, and social justice is an indispensable constituent of contemporary moral theology.

In attacking injustices, moral theology as theology has an indispensable role to play. Basic goods and equitable access can be defined philosophically or "humanistically." These are not the special province of religion. But theologians also call attention to the wrongful tendencies of every society to allow domination or exclusion of some groups to serve the more powerful. Moral theologians call this "sin." To name "sin" is also to call for resistance and change. It is a sin to exclude women's voices or those of the poor from moral theology or politics. The Catholic Church itself has been guilty of this sin. To name sin and call for resistance is also to hold up a vision of a better future. Moral theologians have a special obligation to work for change in the moral practices of our Christian community and its institutions, and to make sure that Christians are catalysts for positive change, not obstructions to it. If the cooperative discernment of truth from within pluralism is the first "revolutionary" challenge to moral theology today, then a second and equally great challenge is to sustain a realistic hope that the human reality can be brought closer to the truths of love and justice. Sustaining hope in the contemporary world is also "revolutionary" because hope rejects the status quo. Hope does not accept that evil and violence are stronger than love and solidarity (Romans 8:35–39).

Moral theologians have access to Christian narratives and practices that provide pathways to the *conversion* of the *imagination*, the *emotions*, and the *moral dispositions*. Jesus' parables, his ministry, his death on a cross, his resurrection, and his sending of the Spirit shape the preferential option for the poor that should inform the church, the faith community in which we practice moral theology. The needs and goods of others become real and important to oneself, and shape communal and social behavior, as we retell parables such as the Prodigal Son (Luke 5:11–32), the Good Samaritan (Luke 10: 30–37), the Rich Man and Lazarus (Luke 16: 19–31), and the Last Judgment (Matt 25:31–46). From the stories of the woman with a hemorrhage who was healed by her faith (Luke 8:43–48), the Samaritan woman at the well (John 4: 7–30), the woman caught in adultery (John 8:1–11), and above all the witness of Mary Magdalene to the resurrection (John 20:1–18), we learn that Jesus reached out to women and to others who were marginalized or oppressed, and that women were important disciples and even apostles of the gospel.

Moral theology as theology offers grounds for hope that Christians can change their communities and societies for the better, despite the tragedy, evil, violence, and suffering that are all too plainly visible in our world. On one level, we see hope as a theological virtue, an eschatological gift that unites human aspirations to God's power of fulfillment. Too easily, however, theological hope can turn into passive despair about the fate of this world, as we await the rewards of "eternal life." Superficial, naïve, overly pious, or otherworldly hope is a luxury that only those who are not being ground down by life can afford. Feminist theologian Sharon Welch warns us not to succumb to "cultured despair"—an "erudite awareness of the extent and complexity of many forms of injustice" that paralyzes us and makes us unable to act in resistance to injustice.[8] Those whose suffering is great both need and deserve a more active, powerful sort of Christian hope.

A Kenyan theologian, Elias Omondi Opongo, interviewed liberation theologian Gustavo Gutiérrez for a book dealing with the difficulties of ending violence and rebuilding societies in situations of acute conflict, even despite histories of horrendous atrocities. In such cases, the guilt of mutual violence can be just as heavy an obstacle to peace as the pain of loss and victimhood. Opongo asked Gutiérrez about the challenge of keeping hope alive while working with people in such extreme situations. Gutiérrez replied, "On the one hand, hope is a gift, a grace of God, while on the other, people always expect something that leads to a possibility of change." "The Gospel demands the elimination of unjust social situations right now." Hope cannot just be an "empty hope" but must build on the possibility of "creating a new life" out of historical conditions. Active, engaged hope is hope that gives "some security for the possibility of change."[9]

While Christian hope is eschatological, it is also hope for the reign of God that "breaks into" our own reality. This kind of hope takes root whenever we, as individuals and as communities, become involved to take action to change our own situations and the situations of those whom we can empower or whose lives we can improve. Gutiérrez gives the examples of action through base Christian communities, parishes, youth groups, and community organizations. He believes that it is important for Christian theologians, church workers, and activists to help all people "realize their capacity to change the situation of suffering on the ground and create a new hope for themselves."[10] The author of 1 Peter tells Christians to give "an accounting for the hope that is in you" by our deeds—by forming communities of compassion, hospitality, and service that are not intimidated by evil (3:14–15, 4:8–10).

Those who write or cry out from the margins of society do not call for a relativist end to moral truth-telling but for the recognition of *their* true and full humanity, their agency, and their voices. It is not the right of theologians and academics (especially Western or North Atlantic academics) to succumb to the postmodern temptation to render moral judgment timid or irrelevant. We need a "transversal" sense of human values to invigorate our quest for justice. This sense of values has to be built up pluralistically and inclusively, by sharing practices as well as discourses. The practices that bring us together in mutual understanding are also the grounds of our hope.

In conclusion then, one revolutionary challenge to moral theology is to affirm and appreciate cultural pluralism with a critical consciousness that rejects any "cultural hegemony" of racism, sexism, neocolonialism, or militarism. Precisely this challenge also requires that we identify shared values. It calls moral theologians to *name truly* and *judge rightly* the essential conditions of a decent human life. A *second* revolutionary challenge to moral theologians is to *seek globally* and *cooperatively* the achievement of these conditions for everyone, nourishing hope that greater compassion and justice are attainable. Moral theology for the world church in the twenty-first century cannot be purely academic, theoretical, or scholarly. Neither may it be easily discouraged. Moral theologians must be engaged participants in the moral and social challenges they describe. As theologians, we must name oppressive conditions as sin, confront sin with the transforming narratives of the gospel, and seek concretely to enact the new relationships those narratives depict.

As moral theologians in a global church we must have our feet on the ground, as teachers, as church members, and even as researchers. We seek knowledge within our theological discipline, but we also can help sustain hope at the practical level by fostering action that unites people around common objectives. Concrete steps, however small, can begin to overcome divisions in favor of cooperation, encourage reconciliation by constructing histories of mutual endeavor, and convert the powerful to the satisfactions of life with and for others in just institutions.[11]

Márcio Fabri dos Anjos

Community and Pluralism

Challenges to Moral Theology

I shall approach this broad topic from the nexus between moral theology and the Christian community. Specifically, this nexus is the formulation of moral discourse in service to the community and its members. Certainly the discourse of moral theology is an academic discourse; therefore its use in society must be basically rational, and thus different from the discourse used within the Christian community. But I am aware that the Christian communities and their members are surrounded by globalized pluralism, and that among the challenges they face in that context are important, specific challenges to moral theology. This reflection will identify specifically Latin American approaches, but precisely because of the impact of globalization we can agree that this does not mean reducing them to an isolated experience.

1. Moral Theology and the Community of Disciples

The discussion of this theme should begin with a brief historical reference. The renewal initiated by the Second Vatican Council (1962–1965) has greatly improved the quality of the nexus between moral theology and the Christian community in general. As we know, Vatican II raised the issue of purifying the theological identity of moral theology in the face of excessive disciplinary and authoritarian normativity. In this context, the council's definition of Christian morality emphasized its scientific character, along with its affirmation of Scripture; its dimension of vocation and service in terms of love; and therefore, its demand to make love bear fruit on behalf of the life of the world.[1]

Among the aspects of conciliar renewal supported by this proposal is a re-encounter between the church and history, with its particular contexts and its challenges. By proposing an association among moral theology, Christian vocation, and discipleship, I am focusing the formulation of its ethical-theological discourse on the environment of the community of disciples, and on promoting fruitful practices within that community. This nexus of moral theology and the community is recognized in theology,[2] and it is accepted today that any formulation of the moral values that identify us must include the development of a community.[3]

The development of this impulse of conciliar renewal has led Christian reflection to see the reality of its contexts in a different way. Reflection in Latin America has been especially creative in developing new insights in recent decades. It began by discovering structures of injustice in social organizations, and at the same time started asking how deeply the privileges entailed by those structures had compromised the ecclesial community itself.[4] It went on to identify the face of the poor people in its midst, and the evangelical demand on the community to open itself fully to the poor.[5] This led to a clearer awareness of the different faces of poverty and exclusion present in the cultures, especially as caused by the dominant culture; and finally to the need for inculturation of the gospel.[6]

Without going too far afield, I must emphasize that in such a process, changes in ecclesial awareness have entailed changes in theological method itself. Analysis of the reality becomes a necessary step for reflection and for ethical proposals in action. The question arises with new force: What analytical methods do in fact permit a valid diagnosis of social constructs? Furthermore, it helps us understand that questions about the poor, poverty, and exclusion not only lead to a pastoral option to take steps for shared assistance and socio-structural transformation; they also require an epistemological shift, in which the question about the poor and excluded ones becomes the standpoint from which we do moral theology, and their needs are considered as theological criteria.[7]

Before it encountered the pluralism of today's world, this trajectory helped to clarify the real diversity of models of theological ethics,[8] since each model was developed in a different place. This highlights the importance (not only in the formulation but in the content of the discourse) of the difference, for example, between the "official" morality developed primarily by clerics, for seminary education, in academic thought structures; the morality that grows out of dialogues with the Ecclesial Base Communities;[9] and "popular" morality, also developed in its own way by grassroots community participants who want nothing to do with the official reasoning and criteria.[10] It is worth noting that in this process it becomes increasingly easy to see the importance of participation by a broad and diverse range of people in such theological formulation.

2. Christian Subjects in Globalized Pluralism

In order to understand the challenges of today's pluralism to moral theology, we would need to engage in a broader and more complex analysis of recent cultural trends than is possible in this essay. The changes in the way we produce consumer goods and tools; establish interpersonal, social, and environmental relationships; and establish meanings and understanding have been so radical that they amount to a new cultural condition.[11] But in keeping with our focus on Christian communities, let us point out just a few aspects of these communities in the context of that process, in relation to the ethical challenges.

Pluralism as Depoliticization

We might describe today's pluralism as emerging in a paradoxical way from the process of globalization. That is, the concept of globalization connotes increased proximity, uniformity, common systems throughout the globe; therefore it works against pluralism. Globalization, for example, in neoliberal economic terms, is presented precisely as a world system. Yet pluralism is involved in this process and appears as an ethical challenge in that it implies "a full depoliticization of the economy, which generates an appeal to a world governed only by the impersonal laws of the marketplace." Competition is established as a rule governing individuals and social groups. The world becomes plural mainly because each person is subjected to his/her own destiny. This pluralist logic, especially in the poor regions, aggravates inequalities and reduces opportunities for well-being. Millions of youth are left without work, which sets them from an early age on the bitter road to exclusion and disillusionment.[12]

Thus the face of pluralism is partly hidden by depoliticization, which directly affects the level of commitment among communities and among their members. Such pluralism demolishes the importance of social iniquities and unjust distinctions, precisely because it wipes out political responsibility. It causes the fragmentation of relationships of shared hope between people and communities. It leaves the marks of devastation in people's faces and in the biological and environmental processes of nature.

Pluralism as the Domestication of Intersubjectivity

The viewpoint of the subjects should also be considered in this political context. Subjectivity evokes the particularity of the subjects, both individuals and groups. This includes their desires and interests. The process of neoliberal globalization has a direct influence on subjectivities, spreading the roots of pluralism in the hearts of the subjects. To put it simply, this is done by putting consumer goods in front of the subjects and convincing them that their fulfillment as subjects depends on possessing such goods. This reduction fosters the dream of fulfillment in a subjective way, that is, within the self.

In global pluralism, the human need for relationships among subjects is understood in terms of economic intersubjectivity. G. W. F. Hegel mentions this relationship, and Adam Smith describes it in terms of characteristics that operate "beyond personal relationships and beyond the vital expressions of the subjects," because economic rationality is given priority over subjects. "In this process, the transcendence of subjects over the objective reality of their lives disappears; on the contrary, the disappearance of the subjects improves the efficiency of the system as a whole." It leads to a "systemic intersubjectivity" aimed at the production of goods and the accumulation of profits.[13]

3. Specific Challenges

These few observations have established a context in which to raise some specific challenges from pluralism for moral theology. Still in direct relationship to the Christian communities, we are initially confronted with a return to a morality strongly expressed in norms and disciplines, often by appealing to the authority governing it. Moral pluralism is certainly the main challenge that we try to meet in this way, by having a well-integrated community, with clear procedural norms and well-defined levels of power. Moral theology is developed according to a model fitting this premise, and for that reason there is an inclination to defend membership in the community rather than the Christian belief that underlies and upholds it.[14] This tendency significantly curtailed the expression of Christian morality in the development of ways of thinking and arguing that might lead to a crisis in these conditions for membership; some theologians paid a heavy price for even small disagreements in the midst of this tension.

Thus, we can see that pluralism challenges moral theology by challenging the identity of the Christian community within the new environment of subjectivity and in the midst of a plural society. Implied in the council's renewal of moral theology, mentioned above, is the proposal of a new ecclesiology, inspired in discipleship. José Comblin observes that this ecclesiology brought different repercussions in different world contexts. In Latin America and Africa it was especially influential in bringing theology closer to the life of the people and encouraging its transformation into projects for life.[15] But he emphasizes that the strength of this ecclesiological conception is nourished by the theology of the people of God and that this concept furnishes "the entrance gate for a Church of the poor" and encourages "the interaction of theologians" with other groups and levels of social life in transformation.[16]

Analyzing the scope of this concept, we can see that it is more than an interaction of theologians. Affirming the community as people of God leads to an affirmation of the people as subjects of their own history, which in turn leads to a critique of whatever curtails their freedom to participate in their own destiny. Although the concept of a people is in itself an imprecise, vague term, it becomes clearer to the extent that it creates awareness of their participation in their own destiny. This is the point of the critique of a moral theology developed along disciplinary lines, far removed from the lived experience of the people.[17]

Meanwhile, considering the impact of today's global pluralism on the subject, we can see that the challenge to the development of Christian morality is even greater. The density of the concept of subject enters a crisis with the depersonalizing process of the global economy and its methods of production; global pluralism weakens the consciousness of the people, annulling the participatory power of the subject.[18] This deepens the crisis and challenges moral theology to express itself in a way that empowers persons and groups as subjects of their history, in contrast to this global process that fragments the participation of the subjects—and in a way that favors the consciousness and practices of the subject, that contributes to the consciousness and practices of the people and of the community.

4. Tasks of Building Awareness and Commitment to the Other

The challenge of expressing Christian morality so as to empower the subject has become really crucial in our time, especially because the process of global pluralism can easily transform subjectivity into individualistic subjectivism. Thus, in setting goals for ethical formulation, we must give proper attention to the "construction of real intersubjectivity as a supreme ethical demand."[19] The affirmation of intersubjectivity in ethics today is evident well beyond theological discourse and is assumed even by those who do not identify with a religious confession when they affirm that "respect for the Other is an absolute, not a relative, value. It is even ontological, because I need the Other in order to be myself, and the Other needs me in order to be himself."[20] Thus intersubjectivity can be understood as an anthropological condition to be assumed, which makes it an ethical criterion.

Another extremely important challenge follows from this: the question whether a subject can be the subject of his/her own moral conscience. Indeed the consciousness of values develops within social relationships and is not exempt from the dominating influences that inhibit one's freedom. The contributions of Paulo Freire in this regard have been extremely suggestive vis-à-vis the formation and education of conscience; and they have made even clearer the resulting challenges for the formulation of moral theology.

Freire's fundamental concept, known as "conscientization," refers to a process in which the subject goes beyond a naïve, massified, or fanatical consciousness; the latter is "intransitive" because it cannot go beyond itself toward the other. In overcoming that situation, the subject gains critical consciousness to perceive the causes of the processes of his/her own history, even when doing so inspires fear. This process implies that even the oppressed person assumes critical consciousness. In Freire's account, critical consciousness presupposes critical transitivity, and thus becomes ethical by discovering the other and community relationships.[21]

The process of forming the conscience of the subject presents moral theology with the challenge of its pedagogical task in pluralistic times. It would be easy to discount this challenge at first sight, by appealing to the academic nature of the discourse of theological ethics. But what we see today in the processes of global pluralism is precisely the privileged status of knowledge, sheltered and focused in academic formulations and advanced research projects. In this process a great mass of people are relegated to being consumers of conclusions and products. Our challenge is not to do the same thing in ethical discourse and moral theology. The Christian communities and their members today are increasingly deprived of the elements for the formation of critical consciousness, for overcoming the massified consciousness imposed on them by the onslaught of commercial messages and propaganda. This requires more than having people who can translate academic language into pedagogical language. It means seeking a methodology for the formulation of academic discourse itself, which will facilitate the deconstruction of naïve consciousness in favor of the formation of critical consciousness with a transitive openness to the other and to the community.

5. Fear of the Other as Fear of Freedom

The process of building critical consciousness comes into difficulty in the subject him/herself. Paulo Freire speaks of the "fear of freedom" that leads to the breakdown of the curiosity and self-confidence that permit an encounter with one's own and the other's reality. In global pluralism, the fear of freedom manifests itself as a fear of losing power. Science and technology today strengthen subjects by placing ever more resources at their disposal. They strengthen subjects' dreams with appealing promises. In pluralism, this power, which on the one hand opens so many windows of communication, works in favor of self-sufficiency and self-absorption. It imposes a fear of imperfection, of vulnerability, and finally deprives the subjects of freedom by binding them to power itself.[22]

For ethical reflection this scenario raises a challenge to subjects, to recognize "that part of them that belongs to the others," and to enter into a "dynamic of trans-individuality, . . . the only dynamic today that can reverse the destructive effects of the isolation of individuals."[23] In other terms, ethical reflection faces the challenge of making manifest the ontological ties that bind us to one another and thus direct our freedom into a close interdependence rather than isolation. This is why we can say that "the issue of constructing a freedom-generating intersubjectivity is the central issue of (human) history."[24] This general anthropological foundation naturally leads to questions that are beyond the scope of this essay, about the theory and practice of social relations in all the areas where this task must be carried out.

In exploring these underlying anthropological questions, Christian reflection is critical of the search for freedom in the concentration of power within the subject him/herself. Rather, it contends that the freedom-generating process should occur in the development of a transitive, communicative, shared power that is capable of empowering the self and others together. Thus moral theology is challenged to become countercultural, against the concentration of power. This has been a constant challenge throughout human history, engaged in power conflicts as it obviously has always been; but today it takes on new meaning as a result of the scientific advances and the global pluralism that we have been discussing here.[25]

6. The Excluded, the Victims, and the Vulnerable as Critique and Criterion

How then, in a culture fascinated by power, can we argue persuasively that isolated and concentrated power is destructive and insane? How can we show that life in freedom is built by sharing power? We take these questions here as a challenge of pluralism based on the isolation of subjects. The most effective answer has been developed through the recovery of the voice of precisely those who are farthest away from power, that is, of the poor and excluded, and who being subjected to the power of exclusion are really victims. This theological emphasis on the cry of the poor and the victims has a strong basis in the reading of Scripture, and it has been thoroughly developed by Latin American theology.[26]

That cry first gives direction to two somewhat sociological questions. One is, How can the cry make itself heard by those who possess this exclusionary and victimizing power? The other refers to the consciousness of the victims and the poor themselves with regard to their condition. In past decades, one way of responding was to speak enthusiastically of the irruption of historical consciousness among the poor, which led them to organize themselves into social movements and ecclesial base communities.[27] Indeed there are visible signs of such organization, mainly in indigenous communities, in movements such as those struggling for land and housing, and in the ecclesial base communities. But as Comblin points out, this irruption is much more limited than people hoped; the poor have not even responded with the hoped-for enthusiasm to the church's option for the poor.[28]

This sociological reality highlights the difficulty of building a transitive critical consciousness and developing it into social commitment. It shows the difficulty but not the inappropriateness of the effort; to withdraw from such initiatives would mean abandoning the poor and the victims to their fate. With specific respect to the reflection of theological ethics, we can see here two important challenges with which I shall close this brief essay.

The first is the importance of constructing ethical theological dialogue in such a way that it can contribute to the formation of this consciousness, and to the direction of this consciousness toward transformative practices. In this perspective, the option for the poor persists in moral theology as a challenge to its methodological formulation. Without going into the full scope of this affirmation, we should recall the way in which ecclesial consciousness was awakened to a new perception of the evangelical centrality of the victims and the excluded ones in understanding the love of God, which led to the affirmation of their role as a criterion for ethical reflection and Christian practices. Enough time has passed since the tensions caused by the implications of the option for the poor that today we can accept the need for an ethical theological discourse that can unveil the forms of exclusionary power; a discourse that can help people hear the cry of the victims and the excluded ones; and that can, at the same time, help people open up their consciousness to critical transitivity, to intersubjectivity. Certainly in this regard the option for the poor suggests the need for at least a slightly more dialectical way of thinking in moral theology, in order to see the faces of the excluded ones, hear their cry, and contribute to a merciful and transformative consciousness.[29]

In this option, the discourse of theological ethics contributes to the self-realization in community of the excluded ones themselves, in overcoming their exclusion. As Enrique Dussel puts it, "the symmetry created among the victims by their arduous struggle for recognition, by the discovery of untruth (even when supported by the scientific method), of invalidity (of the formal, participatory-democratic process that decides the status of aware, critical and militant victims), and of ineffectiveness (in terms of technological, tactical or strategic feasibility) in the face of the hegemonic system, opens the doors to positive creativity in the formulation of possible utopias."[30]

The second challenge is similar to the first, but it highlights the need for ethical discourse in favor of the victims and excluded ones; a discourse conducted in the Christian community in the wider society. Pluralism tends to soften the harshness of inequality and the abuse of power. In that context, ethical discourse is challenged to maintain its critical force. J. B. Metz defines the task of theological reflection as being the bearer of an anamnetic rationality that prioritizes the memory of others' suffering (*memoria passionis*), as a critique of the inadequate rationality that prevails in global pluralism. He ends with a quotation from Theodore W. Adorno: "The necessity of letting sorrow speak is the condition of all truth."[31]

So we can say that the poor, the victims, and the excluded, simply by existing, represent a critique of global pluralism. Christian ethical reflection gathers them as subjects and as a condition that requires transformation in terms of ethical consciousness and inclusive practices. In doing so, it accepts the challenge of awakening hope and creativity for the building of transformative alternatives in the midst of global pluralism.

IV. Globalization and Justice

Enrico Chiavacci (Italy)
*Globalization and Justice: New Horizons for
  Moral Theology*

Vimal Tirimanna, C.Ss.R (Sri Lanka)
Globalization Needs to Count Human Persons

John Mary Waliggo (Uganda)
A Call for Prophetic Action

"May the Lord help us poor moral theologians!" So Enrico Chiavacci closes his elegantly written essay. In a series of four meditations, he leads us to four insights. First, globalization is both a new *technological possibility* with enormous capabilities for connecting the entire world, yet, as a de facto *structural reality,* it is marked by enormous domination, politically, socially, and economically by a few. Second, moral theology must proclaim the supreme commandment of love (*caritas*), properly understood. Herein is the relevance of the "common good" tradition for the emerging human family, and here we must overthrow the predominant and singular influence of the West so as to make space for a true human solidarity. Third, this charity must be expressed in justice and "a strict duty of justice incumbent upon the national and international institutions, as well as upon the individual members of this global community, to ensure that every human being has the basic conditions necessary for a life that is truly human: food, a place to live, health care, and schooling." Finally, justice is not only an economic principle. Chiavacci names three relevant issues that moralists must address regarding justice and the person: to help everyone entertain the fundamental decision in life (how do I include my neighbour in my project for a good life); to respect people's cultures; and to respect the uniqueness of each person.

Vimal Tirimanna proposes his main thesis: "Instead of concentrating on exclusively 'profit-making economics' as it happens now, a serious focusing on 'person-building economics' is called for, if globalization is to give benefits to all in a given society. Such an economics needs to be inclusively participatory of all persons in the microlevel (within a given country) and all states in the macrolevel (internationally), especially in decision making and

237

profit/benefit sharing." To arrive at it, he first notes that the global economy from 1492 to 1945 was already established as fairly fixed, but after World War II, the continuous development of international agencies secured the fact that the rules of the economic game were put into place to continue to favor the already rich nations at the expense of the already poor nations. To demonstrate this, he looks at trade relations and economic barriers and then by repeatedly turning to data from United Nations' annual *Human Development Reports*, he shows how repeatedly the call to drastically overhaul international economic policies remains unheeded. In this very real context, globalization does not in any way establish a series of just relations among nations, and as such is specifically designed to act otherwise.

John Mary Waliggo explores many positive dimensions to globalization in the world of justice, for example, the expansion of advocacy for human rights, the intention to eradicate threats to humanity from disease to illiteracy, the attempt to harness war and other massively destructive actions, the desire to more faithfully attend to the environment. Yet in each instance he finds abrupt breakdowns of plans that extend a common and more just destiny to all people. As he explores the negative side of globalization, he warns of "the first and most hideous injustice of globalization": that "people in the developing world are thus mere *recipients* of the already-laid-down agenda of current globalization. The recipients are told over and over again that they have no alternative but to accept it or gradually become isolated and die out!" This lack of bringing more inclusively all human beings to the global table leads him to consider many of the harms affecting the developing world today: HIV/AIDS, the brain drain, dumping, corruption. He concludes by calling for prophetic action, telling theological ethicists that we must more concretely work together to promote the specifics of our Catholic social teaching.

Enrico Chiavacci

Globalization and Justice

New Horizons for Moral Theology

I

" Globalization" is a new term with two different meanings: a new *technological possibility* and a *de facto structural reality* in the life of the human family as a whole.

A new possibility: from the 1970s onward, new technologies, silicon transmitters and electronics, have wholly eliminated space and time in the *communications* between human beings, whether individuals or groups, and this development is not yet finished—the widespread diffusion of the Internet is only a few years old. Besides this, the *physical contact* between people from remote regions is possible today at low cost and in a short time, but this began only in the 1970s with the introduction of "wide body" aircraft: in the 1950s, it took seven days to travel by ship from Europe to the United States, but today it takes seven hours in a tourist-class plane. We must add to this the massive emigration of people who flee misery and famine with every clandestine means at their disposition. Finally, today's ships have a capacity of 8,000 containers, so that the international *transport of goods* has very low costs per unit. This means that it costs more or less the same to purchase an item in the neighboring city or at the antipodes of the earth. The ideal of the "unity of the human family"—and the "human family" is itself a new term in juridical documents—which was proposed by documents of the United Nations and by the encyclical *Pacem in terris* is no longer purely utopian but a concrete possibility.

A structural reality: today, globalization means de facto an almost complete domination or control by very small public or private groups with economic or political interests. The political interests in developed countries are controlled by powerful groups with economic interests. In the poor countries, the governments are dominated, controlled, or blackmailed by the governments of the rich countries, while it is impossible for the frequent cases of corruption to be subjected to democratic controls, since the people are uneducated and have no independent means of communication, nor any pos-

239

sibility of joining forces with others and of organizing and mobilizing. On the technical level, the increasing concentration of immense amounts of capital is made necessary by the costs of research, development, and marketing of complex goods such as the media or transport systems. (For example, in the United States there were three producers of big civil aircraft, McDonnell Douglas, Boeing, and Lockheed, but Boeing is the only one left, since it bought up McDonnell Douglas a few years ago and Lockheed now produces only military planes.) Such a concentration is doubtless necessary. The problem is due to the concentration in *private* hands (e.g., of corporations or multinationals) because of financial interests that are exclusively private and aim only at the maximization of profit, irrespective of the human or environmental costs. Is *this* necessary, or indeed inevitable?

II

Moral theology, and social ethics in particular, must proclaim the supreme commandment of love (*caritas*). Thus, the virtue of justice too is—*and must be*—nothing else than the virtue of charity applied to any form of organized societal existence, such as the forms of social life in the various cultural spheres and epochs of the past and the present. This is the fundamental idea of the *bonum commune,* the "common good," which is typical of the entire Christian moral tradition.[1] In the West, where all the classical texts of Catholic moral theology have their origin, the dominant structure from the sixteenth century onward has been the sovereign national state, a structure that was exported by colonialism and imposed on a large part of the world. We may recall, for example, the absurdity of the borders imposed by the various colonial countries on Africa or the Middle East, borders sketched at a drawing board by the colonial powers without any correspondence to the social realities that existed on the ground. Throughout the twentieth century, the common good was (and still is) envisaged as the task of the governments of the individual sovereign states, and even the United Nations was born and structured as a sum of states and a pact between states.

Nevertheless, it is precisely in the two foundational texts of the United Nations, the 1945 *Charter* and the 1948 *Universal Declaration,* that we find the completely new idea of the "human family," which is generated by the central idea that every human being ought to have the same essential rights everywhere on earth.[2] The limited possibilities of communication prior to the advent of the new technologies, and the safeguarding of the traditions and rights of the individual states, have not allowed a broadening of this vision to include the human family in its unity—and this judgment applies to Catholic moral theology as well. *Today, however, traditional moral theology must come to terms with two new realities.*

First, academic discourse has left behind the old cultural anthropology with its central idea that Western culture was the only true culture (or at least, the most advanced culture) for the construction of the human family. In a similar way, the claims made on behalf of the theology that has been elaborated in the West must be relativized; see the splendid analysis by Bénézet Bujo.[3]

Second, the new technological possibilities offer the potential for active involvement to make the world a *spatium verae fraternitatis, (a space of true solidarity)* to borrow the phrase of *Gaudium et Spes*. The conciliar text speaks explicitly of *the birth of a new multicultural humanism*,[4] something that was in fact announced by all the texts in the New Testament.

This, then, is the urgent task for moral theology today. The common good cannot be considered as the good of one national community, but only as the good of every member or group of the human family. Unfortunately, the individualism that took root in the West in the sixteenth century has given birth to a kind of group individualism (of states, cultures, and religions) which has resulted in a "right to egoism." This is the real frontline on which moral theology must fight.

III

All this demands an approach to the subject of "justice" that is radically different from what we find in all the texts of moral theology, including those of the magisterium, in the last four centuries—an approach that still prevails today. It is not a new approach: it is already present in the Gospel, in all the fathers of the church,[5] and in St. Thomas. For example, the notion of private property (*aliud quasi proprium possidere*) in Thomas and the fathers is limited by the essential needs of the poor: if (Thomas writes: *si tamen*) the one who possesses does not give, the poor person who takes what is necessary is not a thief, because he is taking *what is already his own*.[6] A recurrent adage in the fathers says that the clothes or shoes that are gathering dust in your cupboard are not yours; they belong to the poor.

The profound transformation of economic and financial life between the fourteenth and the sixteenth century[7] (our checkbook was born near Florence in the fifteenth century) and above all the doctrine of John Locke about the innate right to property[8] generated the doctrine that everything that I have legitimately acquired is sacred and inviolable. It may sometimes be a duty of *charity* to give to the poor, but never a duty of *justice*.[9] In the United States, "charity" means "benevolent goodwill or generosity,"[10] and charity/love is generally considered as something separate from justice. This is reflected both in philosophy and in political praxis. Nor is this all. Today, personal wealth (even if the amount is modest) is regarded as a means of production of even more personal wealth, and so on *ad infinitum*. For the New Testament, this is real idolatry.

Contemporary moral theology has the duty to *overthrow this way of thinking*. Attention and care for every human person: these are the very essence of justice. It is a strict duty of justice incumbent on the national and international institutions, as well as on the individual members of this global community, to ensure that every human being has the basic conditions necessary for a life that is truly human: food, a place to live, health care, and schooling.

IV

Justice, however, is not only an economic theme.[11] We must give our neighbor not only money, but also attention, time, and more important forms of solidarity, especially the equality in dignity of every human being. This means respect for the different cultures, an equal respect and treatment of the rich and the poor, respect for life (and hence opposition to the death penalty!), respect and support for all the disabled, etc. Xenophobia, racism, workhouses that recall Dickens's *Oliver Twist* and are still exceedingly common today in the United States and in Italy—all these are symptoms of the individualism and egoism of individuals and of groups, as I have mentioned above.

The moral theologian faces deeper problems in connection with the theme of globalization and justice. Let me mention three that seem to me to be inescapable.

First, every human being is born and develops in a given societal framework with its cultural conditioning. No one is born and develops in a vacuum. Accordingly, the attitude that one takes toward one's neighbor is one—or indeed *the*—basic question for a moral life. I believe that the fundamental problems of the "social" dimension do not form part of applied ethics but of fundamental ethics. The basic decision is how I include my neighbor in my project for a good life: I can consider my neighbor as a help or a hindrance to my project, or else I can consider my neighbor as an essential part (a goal) of my project. I do not believe that it is possible to arrive at this decision by a process of rational deduction:[12] it must be considered a *primum ethicum*. For the Christian theologian, what is involved here is the call of God, the supreme call to charity that is present in every conscience, both that of the believer and that of the atheist, even if the latter does not know the author of this call.[13] This is the solemn affirmation of the council when it speaks of the task of moral theology: to declare the sublimity of the human vocation in Christ, namely, to bear fruit in charity for the life of the world.[14] Accordingly, Catholic moral theology is aware of a principle that is absolute and valid for every human being and can help in the construction of an ethic for the human family.

Second, it is also true that every human being is culturally conditioned by a series of data that he or she unconsciously receives from earliest infancy, and probably also by prenatal existence. These data are imprinted on the unconscious or subconscious memory (in the "shadowy zones"). They include the various languages with all their nuances (a *true* translation is impossible: at most, we may get an excellent interpretation), as well as the various systems of social relationships (in family, politics, marriage, economics, and education). These "data" are, in fact, structures, and one could define a culture as a complex and coherent system of structures. This is why different cultures inevitably produce different models of cooperation with other persons and different concrete modes of behavior by means of which we express and live our love and our service of others. It is clear that in the very recent epoch of globalization, the continuous and massive contacts between various cultures are leading to profound variations in every cultural system; but the stable principle that must be maintained is respect for every culture.[15]

Third, we must bear in mind that each human being is an unrepeatable *unicum*. Although each individual lives within his or her own cultural conditioning, each has a biography of his own, made up of encounters, things one has read, emotions, loves, and artistic experiences. In an epoch of globalization, this element is expanding. Dante and Shakespeare are well known and read in Japan and in Iran, and they provide every reader (even if only unconsciously) with food for reflection. Similarly, Western music is combined with African or Asian music, and each one, whether performer or listener, "reads" this in the light of his or her own unique sensitivity and personal experiences. This means that each human being must be welcomed and loved as he is, with his own culture and his own biography.

In consequence, the intersection between a possible ethical decision with foundations common to all persons and the diverse forms of living this decision in concrete everyday reality constitute a very serious problem for fundamental philosophical and theological moral discourse.[16] Applied ethics must take up the practical applications to the various spheres of social life (bioethics, nonviolence, ecology, sexuality, etc.).

Conclusion

Contemporary globalization poses the dramatic problem of how we are to live together as one single human family, with the same reciprocal love and care for one another. This, in turn, implies a question: What conditions must be met, if we are to live together in charity and justice, beyond all cultural diversity, and what must be respected in all the diversity? Our race has lived for hundreds of thousands of years on earth, but this is a *completely new* problem. The phenomenon of rapid and cheap movements of persons *en masse* is not yet thirty years old, and it is still developing in ever more complex forms—as yet, we know little of the potential developments of nanotechnology and robots. This means that the moral theologian must be patient! But his patience will be attentive and active, able to understand and to shed light on the difficult path that each human person takes toward God. May the Lord help us poor moral theologians![17]

Vimal Tirimanna, C.Ss.R

Globalization Needs to Count Human Persons

From an ethical perspective, what concerns us most is how globalization affects the human person. In a way, this ethical concern is the outcome of the need to solve the apparent contradiction between the efficiency of economic growth and human costs.[1] As such (and for brevity's sake), this paper will exclusively concentrate on economic globalization.

Reality, as It Is

From a Third World perspective, the predominant negative effect of globalization is the ever-widening unjust gap between the rich and the poor, both between countries and within countries. The main reason for this ever-widening gap is the "head start" that the rich developed nations had been enjoying since the fifteenth century, thanks to their colonizing of the contemporary developing, poor nations. As Tissa Balasuriya points out, between the years 1492 and 1945, the main characteristics of the present world order were already set in place,[2] which has given an undue advantage to the rich developed countries, at the expense of the poor developing countries; and so, when the "competition" of contemporary globalization was set afloat a couple of decades ago, this head start has enabled the former to enter into the arena of globalization with a never-ending upper hand in continuously and unilaterally calling the tune of today's globalization, too. Moreover, the resultant clout that those same nations enjoy in the decision making (through their agents in the World Bank, the International Monetary Fund and the World Trade Organization) with regard to the rules of the game, that is, the rules of globalization of market economies, has been at the root of the inequality in all spheres between the rich and poor nations. This unjust inequality continues even to this day. The United Nations' Human Development Report (HDR) of 1999, for example, says:

> Intergovernmental policy-making in today's global economy is in the hands of the major industrial powers and the international institutions

they control—the World Bank, the International Monetary Fund, the Bank of International Settlements. Their rule-making may create a secure environment for open markets (exclusively beneficial to them), but there are no countervailing rules to protect human rights and promote human development. And developing countries, with about 80% of the world's people but less than a fifth of global GDP (Gross Domestic Product), have little influence.[3]

So far, rich developed nations have not only exclusively wielded this clout of policy and decision making to their own advantage, but they have also enacted rules and regulations (especially in trade) that are advantageous to themselves.[4] The earlier Millennium Goals to attend to these discrepancies and to halve world poverty by 2015 are very far from being realized, especially after the disappointing summit meeting of the world leaders at the United Nations in September 2005.[5] The HDR of 2005 illustrates this point well.

Fairer trade rules would help, especially when it comes to market access. As we know, in most forms of taxation a simple principle of graduation applies: the more you earn, the more you pay. The trade policies of rich countries flip this principle on its head. The world's highest trade barriers are erected against some of its poorest countries: on average the trade barriers faced by developing countries exporting to rich countries are three to four times higher than those faced by rich countries when they trade with one another. Perverse graduation in trade policy extends to other areas. For example, the European Union sets great store by its commitment to open markets for the world's poorest countries. Yet its rules of origin, which govern eligibility for trade preferences, minimize opportunities for many of these countries.[6]

Within such a background, the obvious result is that in globalization, as we experience it today, we have "winners" and "losers." The pathetic part of this story is that if something serious is not done in the concrete level to check this injustice, the "winners" are going to continue to gain more and more, while the "losers" are going to continue to lose more and more. The scandalizing gap of inequality is ever widening, with each passing year, as the HDRs since 1990 have revealed so convincingly. The HDR of 2000, for example, says, "The distance between the incomes of the richest and poorest country was about 3 to 1 in 1820, 35 to 1 in 1950, 44 to 1 in 1973, and 71 to 1 in 1992."[7] When one realizes that the gains of the rich are at the expense of the poor, the ethical perspective of the issue becomes even more acute and serious. Some of the statistics of the 2005 HDR are startling:

• In 2003, 18 countries with a combined population of 460 million people registered lower scores on human development index (HDI) than in 1990—an unprecedented reversal.

- In the midst of an increasingly prosperous global economy, 10.7 million children every year do not live to see their fifth birthday, and more than 1 billion people survive in abject poverty on less than $1 a day.
- One-fifth of humanity live in countries where many people think nothing of spending $2 a day on a cappuccino. Another fifth of humanity survive on less than a $1 a day and live in countries where children die for want of a simple antimosquito net.
- The world's richest 500 individuals have a combined income greater than that of the poorest 416 million.
- 2.5 billion people (40 percent of world's population) living on less than $2 a day, account for 5 percent of global income. The richest 10 percent (almost all of whom live in high-income countries) account for 54 percent of global income.[8]

Reality, as It Ought to Be

Of course, the above are not opinions or ideals but statistics. Behind those statistics are human persons, and we know that human costs and miseries can never be captured fully by digits and numbers alone! As June O'Connor points out, whereas the chief development question of the past has been "how much is a nation producing?" the human development perspective of the United Nations' HDRs since 1990 have correctly focused on "how are its people faring?" Although this perspective takes growth in income to be a given and good, and the expansion of economic opportunities a value to be fostered, it conceives of these human values not as *ends* in themselves but as *means* to enhancing human capability broadly construed.[9] Accordingly, persons should be seen as *ends* not as *means* only. Obviously, such a perspective rejects an exclusive concentration on people as mere capital.[10] This concept of human development is very much in resonance with the magisterial teachings of social ethics, especially those of Pope Paul VI wherein development is perceived as "the total integral human development."[11] Acclaimed economic experts such as Amartya Sen, too, argue that development should be understood ultimately not as mere economic growth, industrialization, or modernization, which are at best "means," but as the expansion of people's "valuable capabilities and functionings."[12]

It is important to note here that even within the so-called success stories of globalization in countries such as China and India, the gap between the "haves" and the "have-nots" is ever widening, simply because the benefits of globalization never seem to seep down to the masses at the base of the social pyramid (as the basic norm of capitalism theoretically had presumed). Experts point out that in both these countries the contemporary globalization has failed to convert wealth creation and rising incomes into more rapid decline in child mortality. The inequality of deep-rooted human development is supposed to be at the heart of the problem.[13]

In view of the appalling inequality between the "haves" and the "have-nots," the following concrete ethical obligations become imperative. One needs to note here that the predominant guiding moral norm in stipulating these obligations is the good or the welfare of persons in a given society, that is, the common good:

- Persons need to be considered as primary in all decision making (that is, they are more important than profits). The fundamental human rights to life, food, shelter, medical care, education, etc., need to be catered to as the top-most priority of any globalization, especially in the removal of the barriers to free trade and closer integration of national economies.
- Today, in many developing countries, the government monopoly of companies and industries has not served the common good; instead, inefficiency, corruption, and debt have ensued. As such, privatization may be a good solution, but only if it enhances the efficiency of the companies and lowers prices of goods for consumers. Competition should result in these two by-products beneficial to the common good. For this to happen, we need a framework of responsibility and account-ability, within which both governments and multi-national corpora-tions could function.

It should be obvious that for these moral norms to be effectively in place, strong forms of governments are a must.[14] As the HDRs of 1999 and 2000 argue, if the genuine aspirations of the people are to be met, then, the estab-lishment of stronger forms of governance than are currently in place are nec-essary, governance that will protect the weak and regulate the strong in a given society so that opportunities, participation, and economic benefits are broadly accessed. The term "governance" here refers not exclusively to nation-state's government apparatus but to a coalition of parties that would include governments, but also multinational corporations, nongovernmental organizations, policy makers, trade unions, and other networks of people helping people.[15] Globalization of trade and financial transactions cannot remain unmanaged, they correctly argue, because these exchanges and the structures that house them are as destructive for the majority as they are ben-eficial to the minority.[16]

The "trickle-down theory" of Adam Smith (which is the fundamental eco-nomic theory of the agents of today's globalization) merely presumes that an "invisible hand" will make sure that the economic growth of a society will automatically make sure that the lower rungs of the same society too will benefit from such growth. As statistics above convincingly show, this has not happened in our lived reality, and as such, there is a crying need today to concentrate on justice as fairness, on distributive justice, to be precise, along the lines proposed by models of justice such as that of John Rawls,[17] of course, with all the adaptations and changes that a particular society demands of such a model. The main idea here is that the least advantaged of a given society are not overlooked, or still worse, marginalized.

Contrary to what capitalism advocates, markets, left to themselves, cannot function on their own; as things stand now, of course, they are already guided exclusively to the desired effects by those "invisible hands" of developed nations (and their agents) for their own benefit! Free-market economies need to be guided or regulated by human agents who are benevolent to the common good.[18] Thus, democratically elected governments need to have a say in guiding/regulating those economic policies for the welfare of their peoples, especially the most abandoned. In this sense, the relationship between governments and private transnational corporations has to be complementary, both working in partnership and recognizing that while markets are at the center of the economy, there is an important role for government to play, especially in ensuring the common good of a given society. Of course, this sort of relationship would necessarily demand "a global code of ethics," in and through which every participant and agent of globalization will be accountable and responsible.

At the same time, it is crucially important to respect the diversity of countries and the implications of such diversity in formulating economic strategies for various countries (that is, the strategies must be "contextually sensitive"[19]), and then, to allow each country to make its own decisions about its economy based on those diversities.

Each time and each country is different. Would other countries have met the same success if they had followed East Asia's strategy? Would the strategies that worked a quarter of a century ago work in today's global economy? Economists can disagree about the answers to these questions. But countries need to consider the alternatives and, through democratic political processes, make these choices for themselves. It should be—and it should have been— the task of the international economic institutions to provide countries the wherewithal to make these *informed* choices on their own, with an understanding of the consequences and risks of each. The essence of freedom is the right to make a choice—and to accept the responsibility that comes with it.[20]

Last but not least, we also need to take seriously the importance of cultivating a sense of an efficacious human solidarity in the contemporary world if we are to reap the benefits and evade the burdens of globalization equitably. For this to effectively happen, first of all, the present systems of global governance (for example, organizations such as the World Bank, the International Monetary Fund, the World Trade Organization, etc.) need to go through a radical change that would ensure the equal participation of both the rich and poor nations in such governance.[21]

Human beings are by nature interrelated, and, as Soosai Arokiasamy points out, understanding this very relational nature points to the way we can respond to the challenges, patterns, and structures of exclusion and move toward a world civilized and humanized through the discovery of interconnectedness, interrelatedness, and interdependence of everything and everyone and above all by solidarity.[22] Catholic social teaching instructs us that each of us is responsible for the other in this one human family.

This is what Catholic social teaching is concerned with: the responsibility of each human being to others. This responsibility is so great that it is part of our personal Christian identity, part of who we are. The Second Vatican Council reminds us of the overall design of God: when God decided to save us, it was not as mere individuals, without mutual bonds, but by uniting us as a single people. God gave us responsibility for one another.[23]

The terrorist attacks of September 11, 2001 and the Indian Ocean tsunami natural disaster in December 2004 have brought home with great force that we all share a single planet, and as such, for our survival as one human family, we need to be in solidarity.

We are a global community, and like all communities we have to follow some rules so that we can live together. These rules must be—and must be seen to be—fair and just, must pay due attention to the poor as well as the powerful, must reflect a basic sense of decency and social justice. In today's world, those rules have to be arrived at through democratic processes; the rules under which the governing bodies and authorities work must ensure that they will heed and respond to the desires and needs of all those affected by policies and decisions made in distant places.[24]

As the HDR of 2005 correctly says, "the critical requirement is for a framework under which WTO rules do more good and less harm for human development."[25] In view of what has already been said above, such a framework would necessarily imply the following:

- Since most of the developing countries are way behind their developed counterparts, it is imperative that in the former, there be some concrete welfare programs that render a helping hand to the most marginalized in those societies. In this sense, the structural adjustment programs (SAPS) should be for the benefit of the most abandoned or the least advantaged, and not to suffocate them further, as it happens now. Such SAPS should get the maximum possible encouragement and aid from the World Bank (this was the purpose for which it was originally founded) and from the developed countries.
- As one human family in solidarity, the network of globalization necessarily implies partnerships for the benefit of one another, especially, partnerships between the rich developed nations and the poor devel-

oping nations. As in any partnership, there are responsibilities and obligations on both sides. All participants (that is, "moral agents," in this context) of the globalization process need to be "co-responsible, co-culpable and co-obligatory"[26] for the decisions, implementations, and consequences pertaining to globalization. For example, developing countries have a responsibility to create an environment in which aid can yield optimal results; rich, developed countries, on their part, have an obligation to act on their commitments.

Conclusion

Today, one often hears the hackneyed phrase that globalization in itself is neither good nor bad, thus attributing a certain moral neutrality to it. But when one considers that globalization is man-made, that behind the decisions and policy making of globalization, there are human agents, then the moral responsibility of those agents of globalization cannot be easily waived off. As Ian Linden correctly points out, political economy is in the realm of human choice, unlike the weather beyond human agency, and thus, "a central realm of morality."[27] Moreover, this realization that it is man-made gives us the hope that the processes of globalization can be regulated and guided by human agents to maximize the benefits and to minimize the burdens; in other words, they can be regulated and guided to bridge the gap of unjust inequality between nations and within nations.

My main thesis in this rather brief paper is that instead of concentrating on exclusively "profit-making economics" as it happens now, a serious focusing on "person-building economics" is called for, if globalization is to give benefits to all in a given society. Such an economics needs to be inclusively participatory of all persons on the microlevel (within a given country) and all states in the macrolevel (internationally), especially in decision making and profit/benefit sharing. After all, economics is meant for persons, not vice-versa.

I conclude by quoting Joseph Stiglitz, the chief economist at the World Bank till 2000, and also the chairman of President Clinton's Council of Economic Advisors, and the winner of the Nobel Price for Economics in 2001:

> I believe that globalization—the removal of barriers to free trade and the closer integration of national economies—can be a force for good and that it has the *potential* to enrich everyone in the world, particularly the poor. But I also believe that if this is to be the case, the way globalization has been managed, including the international trade agreements that have played such a large role in removing those barriers and the policies that have been imposed on developing countries in the process of globalization, need to be radically rethought.[28]

Stiglitz goes on to say: "Globalization can be reshaped, and when it is, when it is properly, fairly run, with all countries having a voice in policies affecting them, there is a possibility that it will help create a new global economy in which growth is not only more sustainable and less volatile but the fruits of this growth are more equitably shared."[29]

It is only through democratic participation of all those involved, both rich and poor, the weak and the strong, the governments and multinational corporations (and other nongovernmental bodies) in the relevant decision-making bodies that the fruits of globalization can benefit our humanity as a whole. It is only through an inclusive, participatory globalization that we can begin to even think of bridging the unjust inequality gap between the "haves" and the "have-nots."

John Mary Waliggo

A Call for Prophetic Action

Introduction

The presentation is written from the perspective of the majority poor and vulnerable peoples of Africa whose cries against the negative aspects and consequences of globalization must be heard by the theologians of the world. The paper raises issues and questions on "Globalization and Justice"; it shows the response and silence on them by African theologians and suggests possible responses on the way forward.

Main Arguments

Although globalization has both positive and negative aspects, the negative greatly outweigh the positives and even make the positives highly suspected by the vulnerable or marginalized people of Africa.

The link between globalization and justice can only best be assessed by considering it from the perspective of the poor and the vulnerable of the world. That is where glaring injustices and inhuman treatment and consequences can clearly appear.

The current globalization, from the time of the fall of the Berlin Wall in 1988, can be understood only in the historical perspective of earlier globalization movements of slave trade, colonialism, neocolonialism, and the competition for political and economic control of the world between the two former super powers. The present globalization movement and process contains many features in common with all the preceding globalization movements. When scientific and technological work, research and innovations and economic and political theories are left to work alone without the well-researched guidelines and critical challenges and informed views of the Christian and other moral and ethical professionals, whose expertise is on the defense and promotion of humanity, the dignity of the human person, and justice and social justice, the results may often times be regrettable. This is where the omission and silence by the moral and ethical experts become truly catastrophic.

This conference should awaken all Catholic moral and ethical experts to rediscover the unique richness of Catholic social teaching both universal and local, and, building from it, to decide to become proactive and fully engaged in the current debate on globalization and justice in the world. The moral and ethical experts need a New Pentecost to attentively listen to the cries of the poor and the vulnerable; to feel and form unity with the poor and the victims in what is happening in their lives for them to realize true solidarity and liberation. We ought to bring the gospel values of justice and social justice, peace and peace making, equal human dignity and equality of human rights, and affirmative justice to the formerly marginalized groups.

If Catholic moral and ethical experts have no prophetic message to proclaim and no liberating action to undertake in this global movement, then we have a real intellectual crisis in our task and mission in the world today.

Key Concepts

Globalization

Globalization is a *two-edged sword*; it is seen and perceived by some and in some aspects as a *blessing,* but to others it is viewed and experienced as a curse. In dealing with it critically and professionally, it is very important to articulate the perspective from which a scholar or expert is analyzing its nature, impact, and consequences. Globalization in its current form is a movement, a process, an ideology conceived and nurtured in the developed countries, through scientific and technological researches, innovations and theories for the total control of the rest of the world and the realization of the dream or vision of a *"global village."*[1] The people in the developing world are thus mere *recipients* of the already laid down agenda of current globalization. The recipients are told over and over again that they have no alternative but to accept it or gradually become isolated and die out! This, in my view, is the first and most hideous injustice of globalization.

Justice and Social Justice

Justice demands that we should never do to others what we do not want others to do to us. It demands that each person, each community, each people, each continent be given what is due to them. Social justice goes further to demand full and affirmative justice to vulnerable people and groups, communities, and continents.[2] When the demands of justice and social justice are not met, then whatever is done by a new movement, process, or ideology is not only unjust but a hideous crime against humanity—which should be denounced in the name of Yahweh, the protector of the poor and the vulnerable.

The Role of a Catholic Theologian

Any theologian, particularly, the Catholic theologian, is and should be the contemporary and *vibrant prophet* who *critically, professionally,* and *objectively* analyzes society and humanity in a holistic manner and in God's name gives support to positive values and trends, while courageously denouncing negative ideologies, evils, and injustices in society and humanity. He or she should and must be committed to the protection and empowerment of humanity, particularly those peoples and communities who are victims of unjust systems, institutions, theories, practices, and circumstances. In fulfilling this role, we need prophetic witness, effective advocacy, meaningful networking, unity, solidarity, and the ability to be at the center of the debate and liberalizing action for humanity.

The Principle of the Centrality of Life in the African Worldview

My clear discovery is that all African theologians from all religious traditions accept and believe in the centrality of life.[3] Whatever gives, transmits, nurtures, saves, protects, promotes, heals, and sustains life is morally and ethically good. Whatever does the opposite in relation to life is evil and unacceptable. It is on the basis of this principle that I personally evaluate both the positive and negative aspects of globalization.

Globalization and Justice: The Positive Side

The current globalization has promoted several movements aimed at the empowerment, emancipation, and total liberation of sections of society, which have been hitherto discriminated upon, isolated, marginalized, and oppressed. It has done this through the powerful human rights movements targeting gender equality and equity, women's rights, children, persons with disabilities, youth, workers, persons living with HIV/AIDS, refugees, internally displaced persons, suspects, prisoners, ethnic and indigenous minorities, the very poor, illiterates, and other vulnerable groups. If we can direct this movement toward only positive values and fully link it with Catholic social teaching, the poor and the vulnerable will be defended.

Globalization has also encouraged the world movement for peace, security, stability, and democracy, advocating the use of peaceful means in resolving deadly conflicts through the skills of mediation, negotiation, arbitration, and reconciliation. The use of war, violent methods, and the conquest approach are being discouraged internationally,[4] although the U.S. invasion of Iraq without the official sanction of the United Nations greatly weakened this positive movement.

The world movement for the conservation of nature, environmental protection and promotion, if pursued genuinely, justly, and consistently by all actors, will promote life and oblige people and leaders to be stewards for the future. This movement, however, is being highly compromised because poor people are cruelly evicted from areas designated long ago as forest reserves, a policy neglected for many years and now being revived but without a human heart and with no worthy alternatives for the families evicted! It is also undermined when foreign investors take over national parks or beach reserves—leaving many people homeless. The culture of dumping toxic material from the developed world to the poor countries still continues unabated!

The global movement for the eradication of illiteracy, continuous human rights education, the eradication of the main killer diseases of children through mandatory and free immunization, and the control of other killer diseases such as malaria, cholera, and TB is seen and perceived as a positive and prolife movement. Even within this positive movement, many people in poor countries are highly suspicious of the validity of some methods and drugs being used and promoted in their countries. For example, in Uganda, DDT, which was banned as an antimalaria drug in the 1970s, is being reintroduced and endorsed as one of the best methods for fighting malaria! Ordinary people wonder what has changed in the last thirty years to make this drug be seen today as the best drug to fight malaria![5]

Globalization and Justice: Negative Aspects

Moral and Ethical Issues surrounding HIV/AIDS

One of the major lessons in history is that to know the cause of any problem, conflict, or disease is already halfway to the discovery of the proper solution or cure. Concerning HIV/AIDS, scientists have played down the need to establish the origin of the disease and continued to concentrate on finding a possible cure.[6] This has led to a lot of suspicion and distrust among those affected, especially those with dark skins, among whom HIV/AIDS is prevalent. HIV/AIDS has become a very big business the world over, in which numerous companies heavily invest. In the global control of the spread of HIV/AIDS, the global world is emphasizing almost exclusively the widespread distribution and use of condoms. Very few funds can be found for the promotion of abstinence, behavior change, emphasis on marriage and family counseling, etc.[7] In this so-called global village, some developed countries put a requirement of medical tests for HIV/AIDS before considering a visa application from people coming from poor countries. Is this not official stigma? Many of these issues are moral and ethical and should be debated openly in search of possible answers.

Economic Injustice

Under globalization the poor are becoming poorer, the rich richer.[8] The *foreign investor* has assumed all the characteristics of the former slave trader and colonialist, aiming at getting the highest profits possible with minimum or no social responsibilities whatsoever. This has been greatly supported by the new economic trends of privatization, liberalization of the economy, a free-market economy, and free-market foreign investment.[9] These processes have promoted corruption and led to the dispossession of many local people from their land in a rather cruel manner.

Silence must be broken on the unjust international terms of trade between the developed and poor countries; the unethical policies of many multinational companies, and the abuse of power and harsh conditions imposed by the World Bank and the International Monetary Fund on poor countries. These are structural sins that must be denounced by ethical theologians. Both morality and ecology can never allow the two extremes of abject poverty and affluence to live side by side.

Genetically Manufactured Foods and Seeds (GMF/S)

The GMF movement, condemned in several countries of Europe, is left free to expand and increase daily in other continents of the world. The aim of this movement is very suspect to many people. It appears to be targeting poor countries that have a high level of productivity of natural foods and tilting the balance in favor of developed countries to enable them to get full political and economic control. Theologians should look into this matter critically and carefully so that they can denounce any evil designs and adequately warn and protect God's people.[10]

Grand Corruption

Corruption may be divided into two forms. Petty corruption which involves petty amounts of money and is indeed rampart in many countries of the world. Then there is grand corruption, which involves colossal sums of money. Although petty corruption is morally and ethically evil, it is not as dangerous to a country's growth as the grand corruption that is intrinsically related to the globalization movement. Grand corruption takes place at a high national level, and the decisions made have grave repercussions. These evil transactions are happening daily before our very eyes. How can we put a stop to this grand corruption?[11] How can we make it very costly for any organization, company, or country that supports it? How do we empower simple and ordinary citizens to demand clear and accurate accountability and transparency from their leaders at the national and local levels?[12]

Brain Drainage from Developing Countries

Globalization has encouraged the movement of professionals to work in the developed world, while foreign experts who receive massive emoluments are recruited in poor countries. The major reasons why African experts do not return home are inadequate remuneration, possible political persecution, and the fear of returning home after so many years of absence and not knowing exactly how to start and fit into society. But these issues are not beyond solution. An atmosphere must be created for poor countries to retain and gain from the professionalism of their sons and daughters.[13]

The Subculture of Dumping Dangerous Items in Poor Countries

Besides dumping toxic and dangerous waste in poor countries, there is the dumping of substandard drugs and foods that have either expired or been declared unacceptable in the developed world[14] and a rife business in importing old clothes, used vehicles, and second-hand machinery, etc. Most of the poor countries are filled with these dumped goods and items. This process is based on the theory that the poor deserve anything that has been discarded in the society of the rich; anything that can alleviate their poverty; anything that can clearly show to them that they are inferior. Here is a challenge to moral and ethical experts. All people have been created in the very image and likeness of God. They have equal human dignity and equality of rights. Is it proper for some human beings to be treated as second-class because of their material poverty? Must these people accept this gesture as a genuine sign of generosity and solidarity? Can moral theologians develop a *holy anger* in denouncing this humiliation and ill treatment of God's poor people?[15]

Moral Relativism, Monoculture, and Unipolar Political Supremacy in a World of Pluralism

To effectively defend the human person and particularly the poor and vulnerable, it is necessary to believe in some basic and common moral, ethical, and human rights principles. It is within these principles that the gospel values and Catholic social teaching perform their central role in today's pluralist world.[16] Many trends of globalization, however, appear to be promoting a monosecularist culture in the presence of religious, cultural, philosophical, and political pluralism. This trend toward a monolithic culture and way of thinking is what is creating fear in Africa and on other developing continents.[17] Third World theologians since 1977 have expressed their opposition to such a trend. Just as the principles of democracy, human rights, and integral development serve as the pillars of good governance, so do the principles of ethics, morality, culture, and religion serve, in their pluralist nature, as the conscience of a nation and its people.[18] The two sets of principles support and reinforce each other. It is, therefore, legitimate pluralism and not monolithic culture that must be emphasized by information technology, moral and ethical discourse, and political ideologies. Several African theologians are struggling with this global challenge.[19]

What African Theologians are Doing about the Challenges

Most African theologians are teachers in public and private Catholic universities, and colleges of philosophy and theology. They use mainly three methods for critically engaging leaders and society on the challenges facing Africa. These are publications, theological conferences, and encouraging their students to do research on topical issues raised by globalization.

The centers, in my view, that are doing well and need support and encouragement include the ecumenical symposium of Eastern Africa Theologians (ESEAT), the Catholic University of Eastern Africa (CUEA), the Uganda Martyrs' University, Nkozi (UMU), the Social Sciences Faculty of Makerere University, Kampala (MUK), and several National Commissions of Justice and Peace.

The themes that have attracted greater attention are holistic inculturation, democracy and good governance, human rights, peace and peaceful resolution of conflicts, economic justice in the light of Catholic social teaching, corruption and the eroding ethical-moral-cultural values and norms, and the entire challenge of HIV and AIDS on peoples and societies.

The issues that are not adequately addressed include environmental protection, genetically manufactured foods and seeds, information technology, the entire area of biotechnology and the emerging new economic and political theories for the control of the world by the rich and powerful. These aspects have not been part of their training, and even now they are not part of the theological education in most African centers of theology.

Apart from the emerging African feminist theology, African theologies have not yet become a social movement exerting noticeable impact on public policy, giving a new direction in economic development, that can eradicate poverty and resist the negative aspects of globalization. Once African theologians discover that missing link between theology and concrete empowerment and liberation of the people of Africa, their theologies will become more relevant and people centered and lead to social action for liberation. African theology must include policy makers, economists, political leaders, and above all the very people whose problems, anxieties, and sense of helplessness are being theologically analyzed in view of a better future for the victims of globalization. The search for this missing link is the major task of all African theologians now and in the near future.[20]

The Way Forward

- As theologians, we should cast away fear, become more prophetic, and defend the victims of globalization basing ourselves on the principles of social justice as articulated by Catholic social teaching.
- We should encourage many more theologians to specialize in the major issues emerging under globalization so that they have a clear picture on which to inform those very processes and alert the rest on the gains or dangers contained in each.
- We need to remove from people the sense of helplessness in the face of globalization. Its forces can be controlled, resisted, and substituted once the people are empowered to critically judge the good and separate it from the bad or the negative. People have and can find worthy alternatives to negative globalization.
- We must ensure that God and religion, morality and ethics remain at the center of any globalization process. Theologians must inform national, continental, and international policies, laws, human rights conventions and programs designed for people, life, and humanity.
- Those theologians who have the intellectual formation necessary should critically engage the scientists and technologists of our age in order to ensure sanity in whatever is being researched, the moral responsibility of all who undertake research and those who invent new theories that affect humanity and the environment.
- None of the above can ever be achieved unless there is unity and solidarity among theologians and ethicists, the sharing of information through effective networking, and the ability to sensitize people and to work with them as we theologize and empower them to be active, vocal, and responsible citizens who fully participate in policy making and leadership at all levels of society.

Conclusion

A Christian is by nature and vocation an optimist. Even in this age of globalization the good, the noble, the just, the right, and the peaceful and beneficial will overcome evil, injustice, and oppression of the poor and the vulnerable. Ours are the mission and vision to ensure that this optimism is fully supported by our energies, minds, and plans of action.

Notes

Antonio Papisca

1. Original title: "Besoins du monde et signes des temps: le défi des droits humains."

Adela Cortina

1. This study forms part of the Proyecto de Investigación Científica y Desarrollo Tecnológico HUM2004-06633-CO2-01/FISO, financed by the Spanish Ministry of Education and Science and the FEDER Funds.

2. Thomas W. Pogge, "Priorities of Global Justice," in Thomas W. Pogge, ed., *Global Justice* (Oxford: Blackwell, 2001), 6–23.

3. Amartya Sen, *Development as Freedom* (New York: Anchor Books, 1999); Jesús Conill, *Horizontes de Economía Etica* (Madrid: Tecnos, 2004).

4. Alasdair MacIntyre, *After Virtue* (London: Duckworth, 1981), chap. 14.

5. Adela Cortina, "El Quehacer Público de la Etica Aplicada: Etica Cívica Transnacional," in Adela Cortina and Domingo García-Marzá, eds., *Razón Pública y Eticas Aplicadas* (Madrid: Tecnos, 2003), 13–44.

6. Amartya Sen, "Las Teorías del Desarrollo en el Siglo XXI," *Leviatán* 84 (2001): 65–84.

7. John Rawls, *A Theory of Justice* (London, Oxford University Press, 1971); *Political Liberalism* (New York: Columbia University Press, 1993); *Collected Papers* (Cambridge, Mass.: Harvard University Press, 1989).

8. David A. Crocker and S. Schwenke, *The Relevance of Development Ethics for USAID*, US Agency for International Development, 2005, http://www.iadb.org/etica/sp4321-i/DocHit-i.cfm?DocIndex=2254 (accessed Jan. 15, 2007).

9. Denis Goulet, *Etica del Desarrollo* (Barcelona: IEPAL/Estela, 1965); *Development Ethics: A Guide to Theory and Practice* (New York: Apex Press, 1995); Amartya Sen, *Development as Freedom*; David A. Crocker and S. Schwenke, *Relevance of Development Ethics*; Emilio Martínez, *Etica para el Desarrollo de los Pueblos* (Madrid: Trotta, 2000).

10. Denis Goulet, *Development Ethics at Work* (London and New York: Routledge, 2006).

11. Will Kymlicka, *Multicultural Citizenship* (Oxford: Clarendon Press, 1995).

12. Jesús Conill, *Horizontes de Economía Etica* (Madrid: Tecnos, 2004).

13. Milton Friedman, "The Social Responsibility of Business Is to Increase Its

Profits," in W. M. Hoffman and J. M. Moore, *Business Ethics* (New York: McGraw-Hill, 1990), 153–57.

14. Immanuel Kant, *Zum Ewigen Frieden*, in *Kants Werke* (Berlin: Walter de Gruyter, 1968), 8:366.

15. Karl Homman and F. Blome-Drees, *Wirtschaft- und Unternehmensethik* (Göttingen: Vandenhoeck & Ruprecht, 1992).

16. R. E. Freeman, *Strategic Management: A Stakeholder Approach* (London: Pitman, 1984); Th. Donaldson and Th. W. Dunfee, *Ties That Bind* (Cambridge, Mass.: Harvard Business School Press, 1999); Domingo García-Marzá, *Etica Empresarial* (Madrid: Trotta, 2004).

17. Adela Cortina, *Hasta un Pueblo de Demonios* (Madrid: Taurus, 1998).

18. Thomas H. Marshall, *Citizenship and Social Class* (London: Pluto Press, 1992).

19. Adela Cortina, *Ciudadanos del Mundo: Hacia una Teoría de la Ciudadanía* (Madrid: Alianza, 1997).

20. Daniel Miller, ed., *Acknowledging Consumption* (New York: Routledge, 1995); David A. Crocker and Toby Linden, eds., *Ethics of Consumption* (New York and Oxford: Rowman & Littlefield, 1998); Juliet B. Schor, *The Overspent American* (New York: Basic Books, 1998); Adela Cortina, *Por una Etica del Consumo: La Ciudadanía del Consumidor en un Mundo Global* (Madrid: Taurus, 2002).

21. C. B. Macpherson, *The Political Theory of Possessive Individualism* (Oxford: Clarendon Press, 1962).

22. Karl-Otto Apel, *Transformation der Philosophie*, 2 vols. (Frankfurt: Suhrkamp, 1973); Jürgen Habermas, *Theorie des kommunikativen Handelns*, 2 vols. (Frankfurt: Suhrkamp, 1981); Axel Honneth, *Kampf um Anerkennung* (Frankfurt: Suhrkamp, 1992); Adela Cortina, *Covenant and Contract: Politics, Ethics and Religion* (Leuven: Peeters, 2003); Paul Ricoeur, *Parcours de la Reconaissance* (Paris: Stock, 2004); Jesús Conill, *Etica Hermenéutica* (Madrid: Tecnos, 2006).

23. Thomas W. Pogge, ed., *Global Justice*; Joseph E. Stiglitz, *Globalization and Its Discontents* (New York: Norton, 2002); idem, *Making Globalization Work* (New York: Norton, 2006).

24. Adela Cortina, *Covenant and Contract*; Stefano Zamagni, "La Economía como si la Persona Contara," in *Stromata* 62, no. 1/2 (2006): 35–60.

Henk ten Have

1. Julian Huxley (first director-general of UNESCO), *UNESCO: Its Purpose and Its Philosophy* (Washington, D.C.: Public Affairs Press, 1947).

2. See "Report of the IBC on the Possibility of Elaborating a Universal Instrument in Bioethics," Paris, June 13, 2003, http://www.unesco.ru/files/docs/ shs/ibc reporteng.pdf (accessed Jan. 15, 2007).

3. See UNESCO, "Universal Declaration on Bioethics and Human Rights," http://portal.unesco.org/shs/en/ev.php-URL_ID=9049&URL_DO=DO_TOPIC& URL_SECTION=201.html (accessed Jan. 15, 2007).

4. *Evans v. The United Kingdom*, 6339/05 (2006) ECHR 200 (Strasbourg, March 7, 2006).

Mawuto R. Afan, O.P.

1. Sélim Abou, *L'identité culturelle* (Perrin: Presses de l'Université Saint-Joseph 2003).
2. Kä Mana, *Théologie africaine pour temps de crise: Christianisme et reconstruction de l'Afrique* (Paris: Karhala, 1993), 32–120.
3. Mawuto R. Afan, *La participation démocratique en Afrique: Ethique politique et engagement chrétien* (Fribourg and Paris: Cerf, 2001), 238–40.
4. B. Baertschi, *La valeur de la vie humaine et l'intégrité de la personne* (Paris: PUF, 1995).
5. See Mawuto R. Afan, *La participation démocratique*, 116–19.
6. K. Nkrumah used to say that socialism and communism were a kind of reaffirmation, in a contemporary language, of the principles of communalism. See Nkrumah, *Le conscientisme* (Paris: Présence Africaine, 1976).
7. H. Memel-Fotê, *L'esclavage lignager africain et l'anthropologie des droits de l'homme* (Paris: Collège de France, 1996), 15–16.
8. Y. Benot, *Idéologie des indépendances africaines* (Paris: Maspero, 1969).
9. See C. Taylor, *Philosophical Papers* (Cambridge: Cambridge University Press 1985), 292.
10. A. Karamaga et al., *L'Eglise d'Afrique: Pour une théologie de la reconstruction* (Nairobi: All Africa Conference of Churches, 1991).
11. Ibid., 30.
12. Ibid., 126.
13. See Mawuto R. Afan, *La participation démocratique*, 150–52.
14. This word translates ideas such as mutual aid, interdependence, and brotherhood. On the translation of this term, see V. Carraud, "Solidarité ou les traductions de l'idéologie," *Communio* 14 (1989): 106.
15. Jacob M. Agossou, *Le christianisme africain: Une fraternité au-delà de l'ethnie* (Paris: Karthala, 1987).
16. Paul Hazoume, *Le pacte de sang au Dahomey* (Paris: Travaux et mémoires de l'Institut d'Ethnologie, 1956), 11.
17. Jacob M. Agossou, "L'anthropologie africaine et la notion de personne," in *L'expérience africaine et les relations interpersonnelles*, Acts of the International Colloquium at Abidjan, September 16–20, 1980, special issue, *Savanes-forêts* (1982): 173–240.
18. Paul Ricoeur, *Soi-même comme un autre* (Paris: Seuil, 1990), 202.
19. A. Stamm, *La parole est un monde: Sagesses africaines* (Paris: Seuil, 1999).
20. B. Bujo, *The Ethical Dimension of Community: The African Model and the Dialogue between North and South* (Nairobi: Pauline Publications Africa, 1998).
21. E. Gellner, *Nation et nationalisme* (Paris: Payot 1989), 11–12.
22. M. Mbonimpa, *Ethnicité et démocratie en Afrique: L'homme tribal contre l'homme citoyen?* (Paris: L'Harmattan, 1994), 27 n. 14.
23. W. K. Okambawa, "The Construction of the New Jerusalem (Rev 21:1–5a)," *RUCAO* 19 (2003): 64.
24. Original title: "Les grands chantiers de l'éthique en Afrique de l'Ouest."

Laurenti Magesa

1. Any study of comparative religion will show this. For example, see Mircea Eliade and Ioan P. Couliano, *The Eliade Guide to World Religions* (San Francisco: HarperSanFrancisco, 1991); Ward J. Fellows, *Religions East and West* (New York: Holt, Rinehart & Winston, 1979); and John B. Noss, *Man's Religions* (New York: Macmillan, 1963).

2. See Nancy C. Ring et al., *Introduction to the Study of Religion* (New York: Orbis Books, 1998), 1–51.

3. For example, see V. Y. Mudimbe, *The Invention of Africa: Gnosis, Philosophy, and the Order of Knowledge* (Indianapolis: Indiana University Press, 1988); also idem, *The Idea of Africa* (Indianapolis: Indiana University Press, 1994).

4. See all the contributions in Peter Kanyandago, ed., *Marginalized Africa: An International Perspective* (Nairobi: Paulines Publications Africa, 2002).

5. See Peter Kanyandago, ed., *The Cries of the Poor in Africa: Questions and Responses for African Christianity* (Kisubi, Uganda: Marianum Press, 2002).

6. When several years ago President Thabo Mbeki of South Africa proposed poverty as also a reason for the spread of HIV/AIDS, there was an international outcry that he was ignoring the "real cause," sexual promiscuity, and was thus misleading the youth.

7. For example, see Nancy G. Wright and Donald Kill, *Ecological Healing: A Christian Vision* (New York: Orbis Books, 1993), 31–48.

8. See Mike Kuria, ed., *Talking Gender: Conversations with Kenyan Women Writers* (Nairobi: PJ. Kenya, 2003).

9. See Julius K. Nyerere, *Freedom and Socialism: A Selection from Writings and Speeches 1965–1967* (Dar es Salaam: Oxford University Press, 1968), 136–42; also idem, *Freedom and Development: A Selection from Writings and Speeches 1968–1973* (Dar es Salaam: Oxford University Press, 1973), 23–29.

10. For instance, see Jean-Marc Ela, *Le Cri de l'homme africain* (Paris: L'Harmattan, 1980) and idem, *Ma foi d'africain* (Paris: Karthala, 1985).

11. See Laurenti Magesa, *Anatomy of Inculturation: Transforming the Church in Africa* (New York: Orbis Books, 2004).

Sébastien Muyengo Mulombe

1. John Paul II, *Ecclesia in Africa* (Post-Synodal Apostolic Exhortation "On the Church in Africa and Its Evangelizing Mission Towards the Year 2000," September 14, 1995), no. 12. This encyclical is hereafter referred to as EIA. Quotations are from the official English text.

2. See "Le synode africain dix ans après: un 'bruit pour rien'?" (theological evening meetings organized by the periodical *Telema* in memory of Professor R. De Haës, Kinshasa, Congo, May 8–10, 2006, forthcoming).

3. See S. Muyengo Mulombe, "Le rôle de l'éducation dans la situation de crise," *Congo-Afrique* 353 (2001): 157–64.

4. S. Muyengo Mulombe, "Médecine et Bioéthique en Afrique," *Congo-Afrique* 350 (2000): 580–90.

5. Kä Mana, *L'Afrique va-t-elle mourir? Essai d'éthique politique* (Paris: Karthala, 1993).

6. Original title: "Défis éthiques de l'Eglise en Afrique."

Thomas Hong-Soon Han

1. World Audit, *World Democracy Table*, October 2005, http://www.world audit.org/ (accessed Jan. 15, 2007).

2. The Alan Guttmacher Institute (AGI), *Sharing Responsibility: Women, Society and Aboriton Worldwide* (New York: AGI, 1999), 53, appendix table 3.

3. World Health Organization, *Unsafe abortion: Global and Regional Estimates of the Incidence of Unsafe Abortion and Associated Mortality in 2000*, 4th ed. (Geneva: World Health Organization, 2004), http://www.who.int/reproductive-health/publications/unsafe_abortion_estimates_04/estimates.pdf (accessed Jan. 15, 2007), 13, table 3.

4. Amartya Sen, "Many Faces of Gender Inequality," *The Frontline* 18 (October 27, 2001), http://www.hinduonnet.com/fline/fl1822/18220040.htm (accessed Jan. 15, 2007).

5. Amartya Sen, "More Than 100 Million Women Are Missing," *New York Review of Books* 37, no. 20 (December 20, 1990): 61–66.

6. Ibid.

7. See the United Nations Population Division, *Abortion Policies: A Global Review* (New York: United Nations, 2002).

8. See John Paul II, *Memory and Identity* (New York: Rizzoli International Publications, 2005), 134–35.

9. See http://www.asianews.it (accessed Jan. 15, 2007); http://www. ucanews.com (accessed Jan. 15, 2007).

10. See *Agenzia Fides*, http://www.fides.org/index.php (accessed Jan. 15, 2007).

11. John Paul II, *Tertio Millennio Adveniente*, no. 37.

12. John Naisbitt, *Megatrends Asia* (London: Nicholas Brealey Publishing, 1997), 163.

13. See Ibid.

14. John Paul II, *Sollicitudo Rei Socialis*, no. 36.

15. Bertram I. Spector, ed., *Fighting Corruption in Developing Countries: Strategies and Analysis* (Bloomfield: Kumarian Press, 2005), 68.

16. See CNN.com, "China: On the Brink of a Moral Crisis?", August 14, 2001, http://edition.cnn.com/2001/WORLD/asiapcf/east/08/14/willy.column/index.html (accessed Jan. 15, 2007); the Epoch Times, "Fradulent Diplomas Sold by Communist Leadership Academy," June 23, 2004, http://en.epochtimes.com/news/4-6-23/22117.html (accessed Jan. 15, 2007).

17. Geeta Batra, Daniel Kaufmann, and Andrew H. W. Stone, *Voices of the Firms 2000: Investment Climate and Governance Findings of the World Business Environment Survey (WBES)* (Washington, D.C.: World Bank Group, 2002).

18. Transparency International, "Corruption Perceptions Index 2005," http://ww1.transparency.org/cpi/2005/2005.10.18.cpi.en.html (accessed Jan. 15, 2007).

19. See Transparency International, "Global Corruption Barometer 2005," http://www.transparency.org/policy_research/surveys_indices/global/gcb (accessed Jan. 15, 2007).

20. John Paul II, *Christifideles Laici*, no. 38.

21. John Paul II, *Centesimus Annus*, no. 38.

22. John Paul II, *Evangelium Vitae*, no. 70.

23. John Paul II, *Christifideles Laici*, no. 38.

24. See *Gaudium et Spes*, no. 27.

25. John Paul II, *Christifideles Laici*, no. 39.

26. John Paul II, "Religious Freedom: Condition for Peace," Message for World Day of Peace, January 1, 1988, http://www.vatican.va/holy_father/john_paul_ii/messages/peace/documents/hf_jp-ii_mes_19871208_xxi-world-day-for-peace_en.html (accessed Jan. 15, 2007).

27. See John Paul II, *Sollicitudo Rei Socialis*, no. 37.

28. See Paolo Mauro, "The Effects of Corruption on Growth, Investment, and Government Expenditure: A Cross-Country Analysis," in *Corruption and the Global Economy*, ed. Kimberly Ann Elliott (Washington, D.C.: Institute for International Economics, 1997).

29. Lun Yu, *The Analects of Confucius*, 12:22.

30. Matt. 7:12.

31. *Analects*, 12:2.

32. Udana-Varga 5:18. See http://www.scarboromissions.ca/Interfaith_dialogue/sacred_texts_comparison.doc (accessed Jan. 15, 2007).

33. See Catholic Bishops' Conference of Korea, *CBCK Newsletter*, various issues.

34. Catholic Bishops' Conference of Korea, *Statement of the Catholic Church in Korea on the Embryonic Stem Cell Research of Dr. Hwang Woo-suk*, "A Human Embryo Is a Life: We Were All Embryos," *CBCK Newsletter* 51 (Summer 2005).

35. John Paul II, *Centesimus Annus*, no. 57.

36. Benedict XVI, general audience, June 28, 2006, http://benedictumxvi.va/holy_father/benedict_xvi/audiences/2006/documents/hf_ben-vi_aud_20060628_en.html (accessed Jan. 15, 2007).

Agnes M. Brazal

1. Anthony Giddens, *Beyond Left and Right: The Future of Radical Politics* (Stanford: Stanford University Press, 1994), 4–5.

2. Maruja Asis, *Understanding International Migration in Asia* (Quezon City: Scalabrini Migration Center, 2005), 16–17.

3. Among the issues non-Muslims in Malaysia are facing are the unequal allocation ratio for building places of worship, shortage of consecrated burial grounds, conversion of non-Muslim minors, prohibition in the use of certain words, problems of missionaries with immigration authorities, control of mission schools, etc. See Maureen Chew, *The Journey of the Catholic Church in Malaysia 1511–1996* (Kuala Lumpur: Catholic Research Centre, 2000), 264–88.

4. Franz Magnis-Suseno, S.J., "Religious Freedom in Indonesia: Situation and Prospects," http://www.sedos.org/english/Suseno.htm (accessed Jan. 15, 2007).

5. Hong Kong's largest group of foreigners are the domestic workers (numbering

217,000–237,000), while 41.5 percent of the migrant work force in Taiwan in 2004 were foreign domestic workers and caregivers. See Asis, *Understanding International Migration*, 21.

6. Intan Darmawati, "Ecclesia of Women in Indonesia: Facing the Challenge of State Violence Against Women," in *Ecclesia of Women in Asia: Gathering the Voices of the Silenced*, ed. Evelyn Monteiro and Antoinette Gutzler (Delhi: ISPCK, 2005), 46–49.

7. Dominador Bombongan, Jr., "From Dependency to Globalization: A Changed Context for Liberation Theology," *Hapag* 1, no. 2 (2004): 33–63.

8. See Dennis Gonzalez, "Modernity and Post-traditional Society: Some Insights from Anthony Giddens, *MST Review* 3, no. 1 (1999): 71–82; Dominador Bombongan, Jr., "Catholicity in the Context of Globalization: A Test Case for Pluralism in the Church," in *Fundamentalism and Pluralism in the Church*, ed. Dennis Gonzalez (Manila: Dakateo, 2004), 172–93; Percy Bacani, "A New Model of Matrimony and Celibacy in the Context of Globalization," *Religious Life in Asia* 5, no. 1 (January-March 2003): 26–35; Agnes Brazal, "Reinventing *Pakikipagkapwa*: An Exploration of its Potential for Promoting Respect for Plurality and Difference," in *Fundamentalism and Pluralism in the Church*, 50–70; J. B. Banawiratma, S.J., "Religions in Indonesian Pluralistic Society in the Era of Globalization: A Christian Perspective," *Voices from the Third World* 22, no. 1 (June 1999): 36–48.

9. Giddens, *Beyond Left and Right*, 159–63.

10. Eduard Kimman, "Asian Christian Communities and Economic Growth," in *Religions, Development and Liberation*, ed. Roberto Papin and Vincenzo Buonomo (Manila: New City, 1993), 210, 217.

11. Bacani, "A New Model of Matrimony and Celibacy," 32.

12. Aloysius Cartagenas, "The State of the Nation and Its Implications to the Church's Social Praxis," *Talad* (2001): 123.

13. Roland Robertson, *Globalization: Social Theory and Global Culture* (London: Sage, 1992), 61, 69.

14. Fausto Gomez, "Globalization: Ethical and Christian Perspective," *Religious Life Asia* 3, no. 2 (April-June, 2001): 63.

15. Romeo Intengan, "Moral and Spiritual Imperatives on Peace and Development," http://www.mindanaopeaceweavers.org/pdf/moral_imperatives-intengan.pdf (accessed June 2006).

16. Fausto Gomez, "St. Thomas Aquinas: Justice, Property and the Poor," *Philippiniana Sacra* 30, no. 89 (May-August, 1995): 251–76.

17. Fausto Gomez, "The Holy Eucharist and Commitment to Justice and Solidarity," *Philippiniana Sacra* 22, no. 66 (Sept.-Dec. 1987): 403–20.

18. Dionisio Miranda, "Towards an Ethics of Genetically Modified Organisms," *Diwa* (November 1999): 108–26. Roland Tuazon also stresses with Gibson Winter the significance of root metaphors that underlie our ethical thinking and applies this to the issue of biotech food. See Tuazon, "Biotech Food, the Solution to World Hunger? A Socio-Ethical Consideration on the Introduction of Genetically Modified Organisms (GMOs) to Agriculture," *Hapag* 1, no. 1 (2004): 129–39.

19. "BISA I: Final Reflections of the First Asian Bishops' Institute for Social Action (1–15 March, 1974)," in *For All the Peoples of Asia: Federation of Asian Bishops' Conferences' Documents from, 1970 to 1991*, vol. 1, ed. Gaudencio Rosales and Catalino G. Arevalo (Quezon City: Claretian Publications, 1992), 199–202.

20. Felix Wilfred, *From the Dusty Soil: Contextual Reinterpretation of Christianity* (Madras: University of Madras, 1995).

21. Carlos Ronquillo, "Moral Responsibility in Asia: A Proposed Approach," *MST Review* 3, no. 2 (2000): 217–35.

22. J. B. Banawiratma, "Gender Concern: A Male Perspective in Wholistic Paradigm," *Voices from the Third World* 24, no. 1 (June 2001): 137.

23. J. B. Banawiratma and J. Müller, "Contextual Social Theology: An Indonesian Model," *East Asian Pastoral Review* 36, no. 1–2 (1999): 17, 102–3.

24. Cristina Astorga, "Natural or Artificial: Re-examining the Morality of Birth Regulation Methods in Relation to SDM," *Landas* 17, no. 2 (2003): 270–82. In an article published in 2005, I proposed as well the decriminalization of prostitution in the Philippine context, using the lens of tragedy and the "tragic moral situation" as a way of dealing with issues where the choice is not between the absolute good and evil but which state policy can best minimize suffering of impoverished women. See Agnes M. Brazal, "Decriminalizing Prostitution in the Philippines: A Christian Response to the Tragic?" in *Ecclesia of Women in Asia: Gathering the Voices of the Silenced*, ed. Evelyn Monteiro and Antoinette Gutzler (Delhi: ISPCK, 2005), 3–21.

25. Graziano Battistella, *The Human Rights of Migrants* (Quezon City: Scalabrini Migration Center, 2005), 15.

26. Roland Tuazon, "Human Rights and/or Religious Ethical Values: Examining an Ambivalent Relationship," *Hapag* 2, no. 1 (2005): 73.

27. J. B. Banawiratma and J. Müller, "Contextual Social Theology: An Indonesian Model," *East Asian Pastoral Review* 36, no. 1–2 (1999): 103.

28. Amartya Sen, "Universal Truths: Human Rights and the Westernizing Illusion," *Harvard International Review* 20, no. 3 (Summer, 1998): 40–43, http://www.mtholyoke.edu/acad/intrel/asian%20values/sen.htm (accessed June 2006).

29. Battistella, *The Human Rights of Migrants*, 20.

30. Agnes M. Brazal, "Cultural Rights of Migrants: A Philosophico-Theological Exploration," in *Faith on the Move: Towards a Theology of Migration in Asia*, ed. Fabio Baggio, Agnes M. Brazal, and Edwin Corros (forthcoming, n.d.).

31. Brazal, "Reinventing *Pakikipagkapwa*," 56–57.

32. The list of such institutions includes the Faculty of Theology of Sanata Dharma University, Yogyakarta in Indonesia, and the Maryhill School of Theology and St. Vincent's School of Theology and the Inter-Congregational Theological Center in the Philippines.

33. Synod of Bishops, *Justice in the World* (Manila: Saint Paul Publications, n.d.), 21.

34. Bishops' Institute for Lay Apostolate (BILA) on Women, "III Final Statement," in *For All the Peoples of Asia: FABC Documents from 1997 to 2001*, vol. 3, ed. Franz-Josef Eilers (Quezon City: Claretian, 2002), 79–82.

Clement Campos, C.Ss.R.

1. FABC, "Evangelization in Modern Day Asia," nos. 9–24, in *For All the Peoples of Asia: Federation of Asian Bishops' Conferences from 1970–1991*, vol. 1, ed.

Gaudencio Rosales and C. G. Arevalo (Quezon City, Philippines: Claretian Publications, 1992), 14–16.

2. T. K. Oomen, *State and Society in India: Studies in Nation Building* (New Delhi: Sage Publications: 1990), 126.

3. K. M. Mathew, ed., *Manorama Yearbook 2006* (Kottayam: Malayala Monorama Press, 2006), 507.

4. See M. Victor Louis Anthuvan, *The Dynamics and Impact of Globalization: A Subaltern Perspective* (Madurai: Amirtham Publications, 2006), 266, 271.

5. See http://www.navdanya.org/news/04july15.htm (accessed July 1, 2006).

6. John Chathanatt, "Reclaiming our Vintage Values: This Hour of the Economic History of India," *Jeevadhara* 26, no. 156 (November 1996): 435–56. See also I. John Mohan Razu, "An Ethical Critique of Asia's Globalizing Economy," in *Towards a Just Economic Order*, ed. John Mohan Razu (Bangalore: NBCLC, n.d.g.), 9–26.

7. George Mathew Nalunnakkal, *Green Liberation: Towards an Integral Ecotheology* (Delhi: ISPCK, 1999), 18–54. See also the articles of Ipe M. Ipe, "Economic Crisis and Agenda for Mission," and Philip P. Eapen, "Poverty and Environmental Degradation," in *Ecological Challenges and Christian Mission*, ed. Krickwin C. Marak and Atul Y. Aghamkar (Delhi: ISPCK, 1998), 9–38.

8. See the two issues of *Jeevadhara* dedicated to ecological issues, *Jeevadhara* 18, no. 103 (January 1988) and *Jeevadhara* 21, no. 126 (November 1991), and the statement of the Indian Theological Association, "Ecological Crisis: An Indian Christian Response," in Jacob Parapally, ed., *Theologizing in Context: Statements of the Indian Theological Association* (Bangalore: Dharmaram Publications, 2002), 252–64.

9. S. Arokiasamy, "Liberation Ethics of Ecology," *Jeevadhara* 28, no. 103 (January 1988): 32–39.

10. See Philip K. J., "A Theological and Ethical Response to Water Crisis in theTribal Areas of Plachimada," in *Waters of Life and Death: Ethical and Theological Responses to Contemporary Water Crises*, ed. Sam P. Mathew and Chandran Paul Martin (Delhi: ISPCK, 2005), 68–91. See also Ajit Muricken, "Source of Life for Sale in Bottles: Trade in Water Services," *Integral Liberation* 9, no. 2 (June 2005).

11. Akash Acharya and Kent Ranson, "Health Care Financing for the Poor," *The Economic and Political Weekly* 40, no. 38 (September 7, 2005): 4141.

12. See *Health for All Now! The People's Health Source Book* (Chennai: AID-India, 2004), 10–60.

13. See http://www.nacoonline.org/fnlapil06rprt.pdf (accessed July 1, 2006).

14. Xavier Ilango, "Morality from a Dalit Perspective," *Jeevadhara* 28, no. 168 (November 1998): 426–40.

15. *L'Osservatore Romano, Weekly Edition in English* 21, no. 1945 (May 24, 2006): 5.

16. S. Arokiasamy and F. Podimattam, eds., *Social Sin: Its Challenges to Christian Life* (Bangalore: Claretian Publications, 1991).

17. See *Populorum Progressio*, no. 30; and *Centesimus Annus*, no. 52.

18. See Vimal Tirimanna, *Catholic Teaching on Violence, War and Peace in our Contemporary World* (Bangalore: Asian Trading Corporation, 2006); George Therukaattil, "Violence: Moral theological Perspectives," *Jnanadeepa* 6, no. 1 (January 2003): 121–37.

19. Felix Wilfred, "Asia and Human Rights in the Age of Globalization," *Vaiharai* 5, no. 1 (March 2000): 44–45.

20. See S. Arokiasamy, "Human Rights: Collective, Societal and Liberational Perspectives," *Jeevadhara* 21, no. 121 (January 1991): 53–62; George V. Lobo, *Human Rights in the Indian Context* (New Delhi: Commission for Justice, Peace, and Development, Catholic Bishops' Conference of India, 1991); Aloysius Pieris, "Human Rights Language and Liberation Theology," *Vidyajyoti Journal of Theological Reflection* 51, no. 11 (November 1988): 522–36.

21. Joseph Fonseca, *Marriage in India* (Bangalore: Redemptorist Publications, 1989).

22. One example is Felix Podimattam, who has written prolifically in this area. See, for example, his books: *Sex in Marriage and Morals* (Delhi: Media House, 1999); and *Sex Ethics: Critical Issue for the Third Millennium* (Delhi: Media House, 1999).

23. See Astrid Lobo Gajiwala, "My Marriage Is Not a Sacrament," *Vidyajyoti Journal of Theological Reflection* 53 (1989): 381–85.

24. See George Lobo, *Moral and Pastoral Questions* (Anand, Gujarat: Gujarat Sahitya Prakash, 1985), 159–72; and Gerwin van Leeuwen, "Mixed Marriages: A Sharing on Our Pastoral Approach to Mixed Marriages," *Word and Worship* 13, no. 4 (April 1980): 121–28.

25. Karl H. Peschke, *Christian Ethics: Moral Theology in the Light of Vatican II*, vol. 1: *General Moral Theology*, rev. ed. (Bangalore: Theological Publications in India, 1991); and *Christian Ethics: Moral Theology in the Light of Vatican II*, vol. 2: *Special Moral Theology*, rev. ed. (Bangalore: Theological Publications in India, 1992).

26. S. Arokiasamy, "Sarvodaya through Antodaya: The Liberation of the Poor in the Contextualization of Morals," *Vidyajyoti Journal of Theological Reflection* 51, no. 11 (November 1987): 545–64; see also Xavier Ilango, "Theology from a Dalit Perspective."

27. *Gaudium et Spes*, no. 16.

Marciano Vidal, C.Ss.R.

1. Philippe Delhaye, "L'Utilisation des Textes du Vatican II en Théologie Morale," *Revue Théologique de Louvain* 2 (1971): 422.

2. Louis Vereecke, "Historia de la Teología Moral," in *Nuevo Diccionario de Teología Moral* (Madrid: Paulinas, 1992): 841–42.

3. There are several monographic studies on this confrontation: Sergio Bastianel, *Autonomía Moral del Credente* (Brescia: Morcelliana, 1980); Vincent MacNamara, *Faith and Ethics: Recent Roman Catholicism* (Dublín: Gill & Macmillan, 1983); Eduoardo López Azpitarte, *La Etica Cristiana: ¿Fe o Razón? Discusiones en Torno a su Fundamento* (Santander: Sal Terrae, 1988); Eric Gaziaux, *L'autonomie en Moral: Au Croisement de la Philosophie et de la Théologie* (Leuven: Leuven University Press, 1998).

4. See Josef Ratzinger et al., *Prinzipien Christlicher Ethik* (Freiburg: Johannes Verlag Einsiedeln, 1975); Bernhard Stöckle, *Grenzen der Autonomen Moral* (Munich: Ktisel, 1974); Karl Hilpert, "Die Theologische Ethik und der Autonomie-Anspruch," *Münchener Theologische Zeitschrift* 28 (1977): 329–66; Joachim Piegsa, "Autonomie, Moral und Glaubensethik," *Münchener Theologische Zeitschrift* 29 (1978): 20–35.

5. Alfons Auer has added a useful appendix to the Italian translation of his work, in which he reviews the controversy surrounding the concept of autonomy in Catholic moral theology: "La controversa recezione del concetto di autonomia nell'etica teologica cattolica," in Alfons Auer, *Morale Autonoma e Fe Cristiana* (Cinisello Balsamo: Paoline, 1991), 211–48.

6. Yves Congar, "Réflexion et propos sur l'originalité d'une ethique chrétienne," *Studia Moralia* 15 (1977): 40.

7. Hans Urs von Balthasar, "Nueve Tesis (Documento aprobado 'in forma generica') por la Comisión Teológica Internacional," in Comisión Teológica Internacional, *Documentos 1969–1996* (Madrid, 1998): 89–90.

8. Walter Kasper, "Autonomie und Theonomie: Zur Ortestimmung des Christentums in der Modernen Welt," in Helmut Weber and Dietmar Mieth, eds., *Anspruch der Wirklichkeit und Christlicher Glaube: Probleme und Wege Theologischer Ethik Heute* (Düsseldorf: Patmos, 1980), 37–38.

9. Among the most significant reviews of the theological-moral literature in Europe are "La Teologia Morale in Europa Occidentale," by various authors, in *Rivista di Teologia Morale* 29 (1997), n. 116, 465–94; James Keenan and Thomas Kopfensteiner, "Moral Theology Out of Western Europe," *Theological Studies* 59 (1998): 107–35.

10. Vincente Gómez Mier, *La Refundación de la Moral Católica: El Cambio de Matriz Disciplinar Después del Concilio Vaticano II* (Estella: Verbo Divino, 1995). In a contrary view, Alberto Bonandi, after a summary and quite simplified review of four models of moral theology, in "Modelli di Teologia Morale nel Ventesimo Secolo," *Teologia* 24 (1999): 89–138, 206–43, concludes that the new moral-theological positions are still situated within the neoscholastic paradigm (239). He has incorporated this study in his book *Il Difficile Rinnovamento: Percorsi Fondamentali della Teologia Morale Postconciliare* (Assisi: Cittadella, 2003). Numerous commentators have criticized the partiality of some of his affirmations, and the lack of information on numerous aspects.

11. For the twenty-five-year review, see Marciano Vidal and Fabriciano Ferrero, "25 Años de Reflexión Moral, 1970–1995," *Moralia* 19 (1996): 141–74.

12. For the twenty-five-year review, see *Rivista di Teologia Morale* 25.100 (1993).

13. See *Moralia* 19.70-71 (1996).

14. For the fifty-year review, see Jean-Paul Durand, "La Revue a Cinquante Ans!" *Le Supplément* 200 (1997): 3–6. See Gérard Mathon, "L'evolution de la Théologie Morale dans l'Espace Francophone d'après la Revue 'Le Supplément,' 1947–1996," *Le Supplément* 203 (1997): 5–46.

15. See Pier David Guenzi, "Seminario Atism: la Teología Morale in Italia a 40 anni dal Concilio Vaticano II," *Rivista di Teologia Morale* 37.148 (2005): 415–19.

16. Marciano Vidal, "Secularización y Moral Cristiana," in Jesús Equiza, ed., *Diez Palabras Claves sobre Secularización* (Estrella: Verbo Divino, 2002), 347–81.

17. Andres Torres Queiruga, "Moral y Relixión: Da Moral Relixiosa á Visión Relixiosa da Moral," *Encrucillada* 28 (2004), 2–23.

18. Dietmar Mieth, "Theologie: Profile und Entwicklungstendenzen im Internazionalen Umfeld," *Bulletin ET* 7 (1996): 25.

19. John Paul II, "Carta a los Obispos Franceses con Ocasión del I Centenario de

la Ley de Separación entre el Estado Francés y la Iglesia" (February 11, 2005), in *Ecclesia* 3.248 (March 12, 2005): 33–36.

20. Benedict XVI, "Discurso al Presidente de la República Italiana" (June 24, 2005), *Ecclesia* 3.264 (July 2, 2005): 34–35.

21. See Christoph Baumgartner, "¿Etica Teológica sin Teología? Sobre la Valorización de la Reflexión Etico-teológica acerca de las Exigencias Morales del Pluralismo con Respecto a su Relación con la Teología," *Concilium* 315 (2006): 61–73.

22. Hans Küng, *Proyecto de una Etica Mundial* (Madrid, 1992).

23. "Tertio millennio ineunte," 55. In Latin: "*nomen pacis et monitum ad pacem.*" *AAS* 93 (2001): 306.

24. Enda McDonagh, "God as Stranger in Ethics," *Bulletin ET* 6 (1995): 37–43.

Marianne Heimbach-Steins

1. I thank Kerstin Clark, M.A., for her advice on the English translation, Andreas Barthel for preparing the secondary literature, and Dr Alexander Filipovic for helpful discussions.

2. For a first idea about the variety of topics within the field of (Catholic) biomedical ethics, see Konrad Hilpert and Dietmar Mieth, eds., *Kriterien biomedizinischer Ethik: Theologische Beiträge zum gesellschaftlichen Diskurs. Quaestiones Disputatae*, vol. 217 (Freiburg: Herder, 2006); Frank Haldemann, Hugues Poltier, and Simone Romagnoli, eds., *La Bioéthique au carrefour des disciplines: Hommage à Alberto Bondolfi à lòccasion de son 60ᵉ anniversaire* (Bern: Peter Lang, 2006).

3. See the Proceedings of the Fifth International Congress of the European Society for Catholic Theology (2004): "Gespenster der Angst in Europa. Provokation der Theologie," Bulletin ET, *Zeitschrift für Theologie in Europa* 15, no. 2 (2004).

4. Norbert Brieskorn and Johannes Wallacher, eds., *Arbeit im Umbruch: Sozialethische Maßstäbe für die Arbeitswelt von morgen. Globale Solidarität— Schritte zu einer neuen Weltkultur*, vol. 3 (Stuttgart, 1999).

5. For data, see http://www.unfpa.org/swp/swpmain.htm (accessed Aug. 7, 2006); Second Report on Poverty and Richness of the German Government (2005), http://www.bmas.bund.de/ BMAS/Navigation/Soziale-Sicherung/berichte, did=89972.html (accessed July 27, 2006).

6. See Matthias Möhring-Hesse, *Die demokratische Ordnung der Verteilung: Eine Theorie der sozialen Gerechtigkeit* (New York: Campus, 2000); Heinrich Bedford-Strohm, *Vorrang für die Armen: Auf dem Weg zu einer theologischen Theorie der Gerechtigkeit. Öffentliche Theologie*, vol. 4 (Gütersloh: Kaiser, 1993); Matthias Tschirf et al., eds., *Was bleibt an sozialer Gerechtigkeit? Gesellschaft und Katholische Soziallehre im neuen Jahrtausend* (Vienna: Verlag Österreich, 2000).

7. Friedhelm Hengsbach, S.J., "Eine amerikanische Herausforderung," in *Gegen Unmenschlichkeit in der Wirtschaft: Der Hirtenbrief der katholischen Bischöfe der USA "Wirtschaftliche Gerechtigkeit für alle,"* ed. Friedhelm Hengsbach, S.J. (Freiburg: Herder, 1987), 201–318; idem, *Für eine Zukunft in Solidarität und Gerechtigkeit: Wort des Rates der Evangelischen Kirche in Deutschland und der Deutschen Bischofskonferenz zur wirtschaftlichen und sozialen Lage in Deutschland.*

Eingeleitet und kommentiert von Marianne Heimbach-Steins und Andreas Lienkamp (eds.) unter Mitarbeit von Gerhard Kruip und Stefan Lunte (Munich, 1997). The document itself is also available online in English, French, Italian, and Spanish at http://dbk.de/schriften/fs_schriften.html (accessed July 27, 2006).

8. See Marianne Heimbach-Steins, *Menschenrechte in Gesellschaft und Kirche: Lernprozesse—Konfliktfelder—Zukunftschancen* (Mainz, 2001); Konrad Hilpert, *Menschenrechte und Theologie: Forschungsbeiträge zur ethischen Dimension der Menschenrechte. Studien zur theologischen Ethik*, vol. 85 (Freiburg im Bresgau/Fribourg (CH): 2001); Thomas Hoppe, *Menschenrechte im Spannungsfeld von Freiheit, Gleichheit und Solidarität: Grundlagen eines internationalen Ethos zwischen universalem Geltungsanspruch und Partikularitätsverdacht* (Stuttgart: 2002); Dieter Witschen, *Christliche Ethik der Menschenrechte: Systematische Studien. Studien der Moraltheologie*, vol. 28 (Münster: Lit, 2002).

9. See Group of Lisbon, *Limits to Competition* (Cambridge, Mass.: MIT Press, 1995).

10. Werner Veith, *Intergenerationelle Gerechtigkeit: Ein Beitrag zur sozialethischen Theoriebildung* (Stuttgart: Kohlhammer, 2006); Johannes Müller and Michael Reder, eds., *Der Mensch vor der Herausforderung nachhaltiger Solidarität. Globale Solidarität—Schritte zu einer neuen Weltkultur* (Stuttgart, 2003); Markus Vogt, *Globale Nachbarschaft: Christliche Sozialethik vor neuen Herausforderungen. Benediktbeurer Hochschulschriften*, vol. 16 (Munich: Don Bosco, 2000); Markus Vogt, "Natürliche Ressourcen und intergenerationelle Gerechtigkeit," in *Christliche Sozialethik: Ein Lehrbuch*, vol. 2, ed. Marianne Heimbach-Steins (Regensburg: 2005), 137–62.

11. See Johannes Müller and Johannes Wallacher, "Die Europäische Union unter dem Anspruch globaler Solidarität," in *Ideen für Europa: Christliche Perspektiven der Europapolitik: Forum Religion und Sozialkultur Abteilung A*, vol. 9, ed. Walter Fürst et al. (Münster, 2004), 305–28.

12. The series "Globale Solidarität—Schritte zu einer neuen Weltkultur," published by the research project of the Rottendorf-Stiftung at the Jesuit Hochschule für Philosophie in Munich, covers a number of remarkable contributions to the mentioned issues in its volumes.

13. See Hans F. Zacher, ed., *Democracy: Reality and Responsibility. The Proceedings of the Sixth Plenary Session of the Pontifical Academy of Social Sciences, 23–26 February 2000* (Vatican City: Pontifical Academy of Social Sciences, 2001); Antonio Autiero, ed., *Ethik und Demokratie: 28. Internationaler Fachkongress für Moraltheologie und Sozialethik (Münster, Sep 1997)* (Münster: Lit, 1998).

14. See Karl Gabriel, ed., *Bildung und Bildungspolitik: Jahrbuch für Christliche Sozialwissenschaften*, vol. 40 (Münster: 1999); Marianne Heimbach-Steins and Gerhard Kruip, eds., *Bildung und Beteiligungsgerechtigkeit: Sozialethische Sondierungen* (Bielefeld, 2003); the editors of this volume have recently started a socio-ethical research-project on the right to education; see www.menschenrecht-auf-bildung.de (accessed July 27, 2006).

15. See the pastoral letter of the German bishops' conference, "A Just Peace," September 27, 2000, German, English, or French text, http://dbk.de/schriften/fs_schriften.html (accessed July 27, 2006); Johannes Müller and Matthias Kiefer, eds., *Globalisierung der Gewalt: Weltweite Solidarität angesichts neuer Fronten globaler*

(Un-)Sicherheit. Globale Solidarität—Schritte zu einer neuen Weltkultur, vol. 12 (Stuttgart, 2005).

16. See Societas Ethica, the European Society for Research in Ethics, ed., *Pluralism in Europe? Annual Report 2004* (Annual Conference; Ljubljana, Slovenia, August 25–29, 2004).

17. See Joseph H. H. Weiler, *Un'Europa cristiana: Un saggio esplorativo* (Milan: Rizzoli, 2003).

18. For a first overview, see Ingeborg Gabriel, Alexandros Papaderos, and Ulrich H. J. Körtner, *Perspektiven ökumenischer Sozialethik: Der Auftrag der Kirchen im größeren Europa* (Mainz, 2005).

19. See Brigitte Maréchal et al., *Muslims in the Enlarged Europe: Religion and Society* (Leiden: Brill, 2003); Jamal Malik, ed., *Muslims in Europe: From the Margin to the Centre* (Münster: Lit, 2004).

20. See Marie-Jo Thiel, ed., *Europe, spiritualités et culture face au racisme* (Paris/Münster, 2004).

21. See Marianne Heimbach-Steins, "Education for World Citizens in the Face of Dependency, Insecurity and Loss of Control," *Studies in Christian Ethics* 19, no. 1 (2006), 63–80, esp. 66–70.

22. For further information, see www.tilburguniversity.nl.faculties/tft/cie/ (accessed July 27, 2006) and www.zis.uni-bamberg.de (accessed July 27, 2006).

23. See the proceedings of the conference of the Internationale Vereinigung für Moraltheologie und Sozialethik, Berlin 2003; Andreas Lob-Hüdepohl, ed., *Ethik im Konflikt der Überzeugungen. Studien zur theologischen Ethik*, vol. 105 (Freiburg im Bresgau, Fribourg (CH), 2004).

Piotr Mazurkiewicz

1. The European Parliament, "Resolution on Homophobia in Europe," http://www.europarl.europa.eu/sides/getDoc.do?pubRef=-//EP//TEXT+TA+P6-TA-2006-0018+0+DOC+XML+V0//EN (accessed Jan. 15, 2007).

2. The European Parliament, "Resolution on the Increase in Racist and Homophobic Violence in Europe," http://www.europarl.europa.eu/sides/ getDoc.do?pubRef=-//EP//TEXT+TA+P6-TA-2006-0273+0+DOC+XML+V0//EN (accessed Jan. 15, 2007).

3. The European Parliament, "European Parliament Legislative Resolution on the Proposal for a Decision of the European Parliament and of the Council Concerning the Seventh Framework Programme of the European Community for Research, Technological Development and Demonstration Activities (2007 to 2013)," http://www.europarl.europa.eu /sides/getDoc.do?pubRef=-//EP//TEXT+TA+P6-TA-2006-0265+0+DOC+XML+V0// EN&language=EN (accessed Jan. 15, 2007). Hereafter referred to as the "Seventh Framework Programme."

4. "Resolution on Homophobia in Europe," A.

5. Ibid., E, F.

6. "Resolution on the Increase of Racist and Homophobic Violence in Europe," 17.

7. Ibid., A.

8. "Resolution on Homophobia in Europe," 5.

9. "Resolution on the Increase of Racist and Homophobic Violence in Europe," 1.

10. Tomasz Wiścicki, "Kościół, homoseksualizm, człowiek i . . . kultura," *Więź* 569, no. 3 (March 2006): 87–88.

11. "Resolution on Homophobia in Europe," B.

12. Joseph Ratzinger, "The Europe of Benedict in the crisis of cultures," http://www. tcrnews2.com/BenedictXVIC.html (accessed Jan. 15, 2007).

13. Rocco Buttiglione, *Prymat sumienia w polityce* (*The primacy of conscience in politics*) (Poznań: Księgarnia w. Wojciecha Publishing House, 2005), 19.

14. Congregation for the Doctrine of the Faith, "Letter to the Bishops of the Catholic Church on the Pastoral Care of Homosexual Persons," http://www. vatican.va/roman_curia/congregations/cfaith/documents/rc_con_cfaith_doc_1986 1001_ homosexual-persons_en.html, 10 (accessed Jan. 15, 2007).

15. Joseph Ratzinger, *Europa, jej podwaliny dzisiaj i jutro* (*Europe: Its Spiritual Foundations of Yesterday, Today, and Tomorrow*) (Kielce: Publishing House Jedność, 2005), 30.

16. Congregation for the Doctrine of the Faith, "Considerations Regarding Proposals to Give Legal Recognition to Unions Between Homosexual Persons," http://www.vatican.va/roman_curia/congregations/cfaith/documents/rc_con_cfaith_doc_ 20030731_homosexual-unions_en.html, 7 (accessed Jan. 15, 2007).

17. Congregation for the Doctrine of the Faith, "Considerations Regarding Proposals to Give Legal Recognition to Unions Between Homosexual Persons," 5.

18. *Charter of Fundamental Rights*, http://ec.europa.eu/justice_home/unit/charte /index_en.html, article 1 (accessed Jan. 15, 2007).

19. Pierre de Charentenay, "Rights and Respect for Diversity," *Europe Infos* 45, no. 1 (January 2003), http://www.comece.org/comece.taf?_function=ei_ new&sub_ id=7&id= 36&language=en (accessed Jan. 15, 2007).

20. Ratzinger, *Europa, jej podwaliny dzisiaj i jutro* (*Europe: Its Spiritual Foundations of Yesterday, Today, and Tomorrow*), 31.

21. Louis de Bonald, *Mélanges littéraies, politiques et philosophiques*, vol. 2. Quoted in Tzvetan Todorov, *Ogród niedoskonały* (*An imperfect Garden*) (Warsaw: Spółdzielnia Wydawnicza Czytelnik, 2003), 22.

22. John Paul II, "Ecclesia in Europa," http://www.vatican.va/holy_father/ john_paul_ii/apost_exhortations/documents/hf_jp-ii_exh_20030628_ecclesia-in-europa_en.html, 8 (accessed Jan. 15, 2007).

23. John Paul II, "Ecclesia in Europa, 7.

24. Conferencia Episcopal Española, "Teología y secularización en España. A los cuarenta años de la clausura del Concilio Vaticano II," Instrucción Pastoral, Madrid, March 30, 2006," http://www.conferenciaepiscopal.es/documentos/Conferencia/ teologia.htm (accessed Jan. 15, 2007).

Ronaldo Zacharias, S.D.B.

1. I am grateful for the contributions of those with whom I consulted: Francisco Catão, João A. Konzen, Jose Antonio Trasferetti, Jose Roque Junges, Luiz Augusto de Mattos, Márcio Fabri dos Anjos, Nilo Agostini, Nilo Ribeiro, and Orestes Carlinhos Fistarol. To all of them, my sincere gratitude.

2. Another initial observation that I would like to make before beginning my presentation deals with the mission of this conference as stated in the following words: "We should pursue a way of proceeding that reflects our local cultures and engages in cross-cultural conversations, motivated by mercy and care." I am aware that what I am bringing to this dialogue is but one ethicist's perspective that has been enhanced and enriched by the contributions of the Brazilian ethicists mentioned below. Without any pretentiousness on my part, I understand my role to be one of furthering the exchange of ideas and insights.

3. José Comblin, *O neoliberalismo: Ideologia dominante na virada do século*, 2nd ed. (Petrópolis: Vozes, 2000); José Comblin, *Cristãos rumo ao século XXI: nova caminhada de libertação*, 2nd ed. (São Paulo: Paulus, 1996); Jung Mo Sung, *Deus numa economia sem coração: Pobreza e neoliberalismo, um desafio à evangelização* (São Paulo: Paulinas, 1992); Marcos Arruda and Leonardo Boff, *Globalização: Desafios socioeconômicos, éticos e educativos. Uma visão a partir do Sul* (Petrópolis: Vozes, 2000); Júlio de Santa Ana, *O amor e as paixões. Crítica teológica à Economia Política. Teologia Moral na América Latina*, vol. 5 (Aparecida: Santuário, 1989).

4. José Comblin, *Os desafios da cidade no século XXI* (São Paulo: Paulus, 2002); José Comblin, *Cristãos rumo ao século XXI: nova caminhada de libertação*, 2nd ed. (São Paulo: Paulus, 1996); Jung Mo Sung, *A idolatria do capital e a morte dos pobres: uma reflexão teológica a partir da dívida externa* (São Paulo: Paulinas, 1989); Jung Mo Sung, "Fundamentalismo econômico," *Estudos de Religião* 10, no. 11 (1995): 101–8; Jung Mo Sung, "Exclusão social: um tema teológico?," *Estudos de Religião* 11, no. 13 (1997): 134–58; Jung Mo Sung, "Violência e ação pastoral," *Convergência* 37, no. 350 (2002): 103–14; João Batista Libânio, "Globalização na perspectiva da fé," *Perspectiva Teológica* 35, no. 95 (2003): 95–103; João Batista Libânio, *As lógicas da cidade: O impacto sobre a fé e sob o impacto da fé*, 2nd ed. (São Paulo: Loyola, 2002); Nilo Agostini, "A cidade e a evangelização," *Convergência* 35, no. 336 (2000): 471–88.

5. José Comblin, *Cristãos rumo ao século XXI: nova caminhada de libertação*, 2nd ed. (São Paulo: Paulus, 1996); José Comblin, *Teologia da cidade* (São Paulo: Paulinas, 1991); Luiz Carlos Susin, "Cultura e inculturação," *Revista de Catequese* 13, no. 52 (1990): 15–21; Afonso Maria Ligório Soares, "Inculturação ou sincretismo? Considerações acerca de algumas opções terminológicas," *Revista de Cultura Teológica* 9, no. 37 (2001): 87–102; Márcio Fabri dos Anjos, ed., *Teologia da inculturação e inculturação da teologia* (Petrópolis: Vozes; São Paulo: SOTER, 1995); Márcio Fabri dos Anjos, ed., *Inculturação: desafios de hoje* (Petrópolis: Vozes; São Paulo: SOTER, 1994); Nilo Agostini, "O instituído e sua construção ética: teologia moral ante os desafios da inculturação," *Revista Eclesiástica Brasileira* 61, no. 242 (2001): 389–408; Leonardo Boff, *Virtudes para um outro mundo possível*, vol. I: *Hospitalidade: direito e dever de todos* (Petrópolis: Vozes, 2005); Leonardo Boff, *Saber cuidar: Ética do humano—compaixão pela terra*, 6th ed. (Petrópolis: Vozes, 2000); Márcio Fabri dos Anjos, ed., *Teologia Moral e cultura. Teologia Moral na América Latina*, vol. 8 (Aparecida: Santuário, 1992); Antônio Moser, "Moral e cultura: entre o diálogo e o etnocentrismo," in *Teologia Moral e cultura*, ed. Márcio Fabri dos Anjos (Aparecida: Santuário, 1992), 65–80; Luiza Etsuko Tomita, Marcelo Barros and José Maria Vigil, ed., *Teologia Latino-Americana pluralista da libertação* (São Paulo: Paulinas, 2006).

6. José Comblin, "A teologia das religiões a partir da América Latina," in *Pluralismo e Libertação: Por uma teologia latino-americana pluralista a partir da fé cristã*, ed. Luiza E. Tomita, Marcelo Barros, and José María Vigil (São Paulo: Loyola/ASETT EATWOT, 2005), 47–70; Alberto Antoniazzi, "Por que o panorama religioso no Brasil mudou tanto?" *Horizonte* 3, no 5 (2004): 13–39; José Oscar Beozzo, "Grandes questões da caminhada do Cristianismo na América Latina e Caribe," *Religião e Cultura* 3, no. 5 (2004): 27–65; José Oscar Beozzo, "Vaticano II e as transformações culturais na América Latina e no Caribe," *Religião e Cultura* 4, no. 8 (2005): 57–102; Clodovis Boff, "Carismáticos e libertadores na Igreja," *Revista Eclesiástica Brasileira* 60, no. 237 (2000): 36–53; Leonardo Boff, *Fundamentalismo: A globalização e o futuro da humanidade* (Rio de Janeiro: Sextante, 2002); Francisco Catão and Magno Vilela, *O monopólio do sagrado* (São Paulo: Bestseller/Círculo do Livro, 1994); João Batista Libânio, *Crer num mundo de muitas crenças e pouca libertação* (São Paulo: Paulinas; Valencia: Siquem, 2003); Carlos Josaphat, "Globalização, religião, mídia e mercado," *Religião e Cultura* 3, no. 5 (2004): 91–110.

7. José Roque Junges, *Evento Cristo e ação humana: Temas fundamentais de ética teológica* (São Leopoldo: UNISINOS, 2001); João Aloysio Konzen, *Ética teológica fundamental* (São Paulo: Paulinas, 2001); Leonardo Boff, *Ética e Moral: A busca dos fundamentos* (Petrópolis: Vozes, 2003); Carlos Josaphat, *Moral, amor e humor* (Rio de Janeiro: Nova Era, 1997); Paulo Sérgio Lopes Gonçalves, "A relação entre teologia e espiritualidade cristã," *Revista de Cultura Teológica* 6, no. 24 (1998): 37–58; José Trasferetti and Paulo Sérgio Lopes Gonçalves, eds., *Teologia na pós-modernidade: Abordagens epistemológica, sistemática e teórico-prática* (São Paulo: Paulinas, 2003); Antônio Moser and Bernardino Leers, *Teologia Moral: impasses e alternativas*, vol. 3: *A Libertação na História*, 2nd ed. (São Paulo: Vozes, 1988).

8. Márcio Fabri dos Anjos, ed., *Articulação da Teologia Moral na América Latina. Teologia Moral na América Latina*, vol. 2 (Aparecida: Santuário, 1987); Luiz Carlos Susin, "Fazer teologia em tempos de globalização. Nota sobre método em Teologia," *Perspectiva Teológica* 31, no. 83 (1999): 97–108; Leonardo Boff, *Igreja: carisma e poder. Ensaios de Eclesiologia Militante* (São Paulo: Ática, 1994); Clodovis Boff, *Teoria do método teológico*, 2nd ed. (Petrópolis: Vozes, 1999); Márcio Fabri dos Anjos, ed., *Teologia e novos paradigmas* (São Paulo: Loyola/SOTER, 1996); Bernardino Leers, *Moral cristã e autoridade do Magistério eclesiástico: conflito-diálogo. Teologia Moral na América Latina*, vol. 7 (Aparecida: Santuário 1991); Márcio Fabri dos Anjos, ed., *Ética na relação entre Igreja e sociedade. Teologia Moral na América Latina*, vol. 10 (Aparecida: Santuário, 1994); Alberto Antoniazzi, João Batista Libânio and José S. Fernandes, eds., *Novas fronteiras da moral no Brasil: Teologia Moral na América Latina*, vol. 9 (Aparecida: Santuário, 1992); Fábio Konder Comparato, *Ética: direito, moral e religião no mundo moderno* (São Paulo: Companhia das Letras, 2006); Antônio Moser, *Teologia Moral: questões vitais* (Petrópolis: Vozes, 2004); Antônio Moser, *Teologia Moral: Desafios atuais* (Petrópolis: Vozes, 1991); Comissão Episcopal de Doutrina (CED-CNBB), *A Teologia Moral em meio a evoluções históricas. Subsídios Doutrinais da CNBB 2* (São Paulo: Paulinas, 1992); Conferência Nacional dos Bispos do Brasil, *Ética: pessoa e sociedade. 31ª Assembléia Geral (Itaici-SP, 1993). Documentos da CNBB 50* (São Paulo: Paulinas, 1993).

9. Márcio Fabri dos Anjos, ed., *Teologia e novos paradigmas* (São Paulo: Loyola/ SOTER, 1996); Leonardo Boff, *Novas fronteiras da Igreja: O futuro de um povo a caminho* (Campinas: Verus, 2004); Leonardo Boff, *Ethos mundial: um consenso mínimo entre os humanos* (Rio de Janeiro: Sextante, 2003); Francisco A. C. Catão, *A pedagogia ética* (Petrópolis: Vozes, 1995); José Roque Junges, *Evento Cristo e ação humana: Temas fundamentais de ética teológica* (São Leopoldo: UNISINOS, 2001); Nilo Agostini, *Introdução à Teologia Moral: O grande "sim" de Deus à vida*, 2nd ed. (Petrópolis: Vozes, 2005); Nilo Agostini, *Ética e evangelização: A dinâmica da alteridade na recriação da moral*, 2nd ed. (Petrópolis: Vozes, 1994); Nilo Agostini, *Ética cristã: Vivência comunitária da fé* (Petrópolis: Vozes, 2003); Leonardo Boff and Frei Betto, *Mística e espiritualidade* (Rio de Janeiro: Rocco, 1994); Leonardo Boff, ed., *A Teologia da Libertação: Balanço e perspectivas* (São Paulo: Ática, 1996); Leonardo Boff, *Ética e eco-espiritualidade* (Campinas: Verus, 2003); Leonardo Boff, *Civilização planetária: Desafios à sociedade e ao cristianismo* (Rio de Janeiro: Sextante, 2003); Luiz Carlos Susin, ed., *O mar se abriu: Trinta anos de teologia na América Latina* (São Paulo: Loyola/SOTER, 2000); Jung Mo Sung, *Sementes de esperança: A fé em um mundo em crise* (Petrópolis: Vozes, 2005); Hugo Assmann and Jung Mo Sung, *Competência e sensibilidade solidária: Educar para a esperança* (Petrópolis: Vozes, 2000); Maria Clara Lucchetti Bingemer, "A mulher na Igreja hoje. A partir e além do Concílio Vaticano II," *Revista Eclesiástica Brasileira* 63, no. 249 (2003): 23–46; Maria Clara Lucchetti Bingemer, "Saborear a fé em meio à pluralidade. Os caminhos da teologia em meio ao diálogo inter-religioso," *Perspectiva Teológica* 36, no. 99 (2004): 221–39; Bernardino Leers, *A moral do burro* (São Paulo: Paulinas, 2004); João Batista Libânio, *Olhando para o futuro: Prospectivas teológicas e pastorais do Cristianismo na América Latina* (São Paulo: Loyola, 2003); Ivone Gebara, "A mulher, contribuição à teologia moral na América Latina," in *Temas Latino-Americanos de Ética*, ed. Márcio Fabri dos Anjos (Aparecida: Santuário, 1988), 195–209; Leonard M. Martin, "Exílio, Sodoma e o Deserto: uma ética teológica a partir das culturas dos submundos," in *Teologia Moral e cultura*, ed. Márcio Fabri dos Anjos (Aparecida: Santuário, 1992), 89–113; Ivone Gebara, *Teologia Ecofeminista: Ensaio para repensar o conhecimento e a religião* (São Paulo: Olho d'Água, 1997); Ivone Gebara, *Teologia em ritmo de mulher* (São Paulo: Paulinas, 1994); Ivone Gebara, *As incômodas filhas de Eva na Igreja da América Latina*, 2nd ed. (São Paulo: Paulinas, 1990); Ivone Gebara and Maria Clara Lucchetti Bingemer, *A mulher faz Teologia* (Petrópolis: Vozes, 1986); Ivone Gebara, *As águas do meu poço: Reflexões sobre experiências de liberdade* (São Paulo: Paulinas, 2005); José Antônio Trasferetti, *Entre e poética e a política: Teologia moral e espiritualidade* (Petrópolis: Vozes, 1998); Coleção Instituto Jacques Maritain, Maria Luiza Marcílio, and Ernesto Lopes Ramos, eds., *Ética na virada do século: Busca do sentido da vida* (São Paulo: LTr, 1997).

10. Bernardino Leers, *Jeito brasileiro e norma absoluta* (Petrópolis: Vozes, 1982); Lívia Barbosa, *O Jeitinho brasileiro: A arte de ser mais igual que os outros* (Rio de Janeiro: Campus, 1992); Bernardino Leers, "Ensinar Teologia Moral na América Latina," in *Temas Latino-Americanos de Ética*, ed. Márcio Fabri dos Anjos (Aparecida: Santuário, 1988), 279–310.

11. Luzenir Maria Caixeta, Juan Carlos Gutiérrez, and Pedro Lariço Fernandez,

"Ousando sonhar," in *Ética na relação entre Igreja e sociedade*, ed. Márcio Fabri dos Anjos (Aparecida: Santuário 1994), 194–95.

Sebastian Mier, S.J.

1. The respective literature is broad, and we have three collections of essays with magnificent syntheses by outstanding authors. The first was published in 1990, twenty-two years after CELAM in Medellín (1968), which symbolizes the birth of a specifically Latin American theology, a time when the Berlin wall was falling and a few months after the martyrdom of the Jesuits in San Salvador. Its first section presents the history and methodology, while the second gives the "systematic content," which covers practically all the fields of theology. The book is Ignacio Ellacuría and Jon Sobrino, eds., *Mysterium Liberationis: Conceptos Fundamentales de la Teología de Liberación*, 2 vols. (Madrid: Editorial Trotta, 1990).

The second presents a journey of thirty years with eight women and twenty-six men narrating their experience, influences, and works. This book clearly shows an evolution through the decades but retains their original fundamentals. The way they broaden their themes and diversify their social and ecclesial focus is especially relevant. The book is Juan Tamayo and Juan Bosch, eds., *Panorama de la Teología Latinoamericana* (Estella, Spain: Verbo Divino, 2001).

The third appeared this year, with twenty-five essays on theology and its socioeconomic context: Pablo Bonavía, ed., *Tejiendo Redes de Vida y Esperanza* (Bogotá: Indo-American Press Service, 2006).

2. The evolution of this situation is illustrated by the documents of the Latin American episcopal conferences of Medellín (1968), Puebla (1979), and Santo Domingo (1992). *Tejiendo Redes* offers a broad picture of the current reality.

3. See several articles in *Christus* 703 (November 1997) and 752 (January 2006). Also Rosita Milesi, "Peregrinos de la exclusión," in *Tejiendo Redes*.

4. I want to explain and reaffirm this expression, "relatively large." Considering the terribly adverse conditions in which we are surviving, these hundreds of thousands who represent millions of people are a source of admiration and hope. If we focus on their effective power to transform those conditions, we may fall into realism, indifference, skepticism—or a highly arduous hope. Theologically, they call to mind the biblical expressions "the remnant of Israel," "the poor of Yahweh," and "the servant of Yahweh." Several articles in *Christus* 747 (March 2005), and *Theologica Xaveriana* 154 (April 2005) deal with the theme of hope.

5. There are several articles on the World Social Forum in *Christus* 749 (July 2005); also see Chico Whitaker, "¿Qué es lo que el Foro Social Mundial aporta?" in *Tejiendo Redes*, 141–51.

6. On the methodology of theological ethics, in relation to other branches of theology and assorted sciences, see the several articles in *Theologica Xaveriana* 150 (April 2004), and 153 (June 2005).

7. See Jon Sobrino, "Centralidad del Reino de Dios," in *Mysterium Liberationis*, vol. 1, 467–510; and Leonardo Boff, "Trinidad," in *Mysterium Liberationis*, vol. 1, 513–30; see also Sobrino's development of the theme in *Tejiendo Redes*, 267–88.

8. The *Revista de Interpretación Bíblica Latinoamericana* in general is a good source of material on this theme.

9. See Javier Jiménez, "Sufrimiento, Muerte, Cruz y Martirio," in *Mysterium Liberationis*, vol. 2, 477–93; Jon Sobrino, "Espiritualidad y Seguimiento de Jesús," in *Mysterium Liberationis*, vol. 2, 449–75; and Alvaro Quiroz, "Eclesiología en la Teología de Liberación," in *Mysterium Liberationis*, vol. 1, 253–72.

10. On this dialogue, see José María Vigil, "Pluralismo Cultural y Religioso," in *Tejiendo Redes*, 229–40; and Camilo Maccise, "Espiritualidad Macroecuménica y Mística," in *Tejiendo Redes*, 373–86.

11. See Ricardo Falla, *Esa Muerte que nos Hace Vivir* (San Salvador: UCA editores, 1984); Diego Irrazával, "Religión Popular," in *Mysterium Liberationis*, vol. 2, 345–76; Sebastián Mier, *María en el Evangelio Liberador* (Mexico: Buena Prensa, 2006).

12. See Gustavo Gutiérrez, "La Opción Profética de una Iglesia," in *Tejiendo Redes*, 307–20; Marcelo Azevedo, "Comunidades eclesiales de base," in *Mysterium Liberationis*, vol. 2, 245–66; and my doctoral thesis, Sebastián Mier, "El Sujeto Social en Moral Fundamental. Una Verificación: las CEBs en México" (Ph.D., Mexico, Universidad Pontificia, 1996).

13. Eleazar López, "Mi Itinerario Teológico-Pastoral," in *Panorama*, 317–36; and several articles in *Christus* 756 (September 2006).

14. Carlos Novoa, "¿Favorece el TLC a las Mayorías Empobrecidas?" in *Theologica Xavieriana* 156 (October 2005), 643–66. See also several articles in *Tejiendo Redes*.

15. In addition to the citation in note 13, see Ricardo Robles, "Los Derechos Colectivos de los Pueblos Indios," in *Christus* 724 (May 2001): 46–51.

16. Marina Hilario, "Corrupción e Impunidad," in *Tejiendo Redes*.

17. Floriberto Díaz, "Principios Comunitarios," in *México Indígena, 34.*

18. The conference itself exemplified this point. In the plenary I was asked about the difference between women's and feminist theologies, and my opinion sparked some emotional comments. This suggests a need for dialogue at the highest possible level of respect and sincerity, since we are clearly dealing with painful living experiences. The articles by María Clara Luchetti Bingemer and Pilar Aquino in *Panorama* exemplify the positions of some Latin American women.

Tony Mifsud, S.J.

1. By the latest available figures (for 2003), 18.7 percent of the population lived in conditions of poverty; 4.7 percent in indigence or extreme poverty.

2. See United Nations Development Programme (UNDP), *Informe sobre el Desarrollo Humano: Nosotros los Chilenos, un Desafío Cultural* (Santiago, 2002); Jorge Larraín, *Identidad Chilena* (Santiago: LOM, 2001); Eugenio Tironi, *El Sueño Chileno* (Santiago: Taurus, 2005).

3. This is indicated by the following surveys conducted in Chile: Census 2002; Centro de Estudios Públicos, social surveys and public opinion polls, June 1998 and November 2001; Fundación Futuro, 2001; "Encuesta Nacional de la Iglesia Católica," conducted by the Dirección de Estudios Sociológicos of the Catholic

University, 2001; Centro de Etica, Alberto Hurtado University, 2001; poll conducted by *El Mercurio*-OPINA, March 2006.

4. The Interamerican Development Bank report, *América Latina Frente a la Desigualdad* (Washington, 1998, 28) shows the income distribution differential for Chile as 1.3 percent for the lowest tenth of the population, 45.8 percent for the highest tenth.

5. See Jorge Marshall, "La Política Monetaria y la Distribución del Ingreso," in *Economía Chilena* 2, no. 1 (April 1999): 5–22; Interamerican Development Bank, *América Latina Frente a la Desigualdad* (Washington, 1998): 1–26.

6. See Javier Nuñez and Roberto Gutiérrez, "Class Discrimination and Meritocracy in the Labor Market: Evidence from Chile," in *Estudios de Economía* 31, no. 2 (December 2004): 113–32.

7. See Centro de Investigaciones Socioculturales, *Jóvenes: Orientaciones Valóricas, Religión e Iglesia Católica* (Santiago: CISOC, 2005).

8. *Lumen Gentium*, no. 12.

9. John Paul II, *Veritatis Splendor*, no. 4

10. Immanuel Kant, *Crítica de la Razón Práctica* (Madrid: Espasa-Calpe, 1984), 181.

11. See Marciano Vidal, *Nueva Moral Fundamental: El hogar teológico de la Etica* (Bilbao: Desclée de Brouwer, 2000).

12. See St. John Chrysostom, *Homilies on Matthew* 1, no. 1; St. Thomas Aquinas, *Summa Theologica*, I-II, q. 106, art. 1.

13. Acts 2:22–36.

14. 1 John 4:20–21; James 2:17.

15. On the relationship between spirituality and morality, see Sergio Bastianel, *Prayer in the Christian Moral Life* (Mahwah, N.J.: Paulist Press, 1998); Mark O'Keefe, O.S.B., *Becoming Good, Becoming Holy: on the Relationship of Christian Ethics and Spirituality* (Mahway, N.J.: Paulist Press, 1997); Marciano Vidal, *Moral y Espiritualidad: de la Separación a la Convergencia* (Madrid: Editorial P.S., 1997); Tony Mifsud S.J., *Una Fe Comprometida con la Vida: Espiritualidad y Etica, Hoy* (Santiago: Ediciones San Pablo, 2002).

David Hollenbach, S.J.

1. The statement was prepared by Prof. Kenneth R. Himes, O.F.M., and myself, and was entitled: "Letter to the President and Board of Trustees of Boston College: Condoleezza Rice Does Not Deserve a Boston College Honorary Degree." Excerpts from the letter were published in *Origins* 36, no. 1 (May 18, 2006).

2. "Hiding Behind the Veil," *Pilot* (May 12, 2006): 12.

3. Cardinal Joseph Ratzinger, "Worthiness to Receive Holy Communion: General Principles," *Origins* 34, no. 9 (July 29, 2004): 133–34.

4. Bishop Michael J. Sheridan, "A Pastoral Letter to the Catholic Faithful of the Diocese of Colorado Springs on the Duties of Catholic Politicians and Voters," http://www.diocesecs.org/CPC/Corner/pastoralletters/2004/May.pdf (accessed December 31, 2004).

5. On sexual ethics, see especially Margaret A. Farley, *Just Love: A Framework for a Christian Sexual Ethics* (New York: Continuum, 2006).

6. Congregation for the Doctrine of the Faith, "Doctrinal Note on Some Questions Regarding the Participation of Catholics in Political Life," November 24, 2002, no. 4, http://www.vatican.va/roman_curia/congregations/cfaith/documents/rc_con_cfaith_doc_20021124_politica_en.html (accessed December 31, 2004).

7. For further discussion of the role of Catholicism and recent U.S. politics, see Thomas Massaro, S.J., "Catholic Bishops and Politicians: Concerns about Recent Developments," *Josephinum Journal of Theology* 12, no. 2 (2005); *Taking Faith Seriously*, ed. Mary Jo Bane, Brent Coffin, and Richard Higgins (Cambridge, Mass.: Harvard University Press, 2005); *The Catholic Church, Morality, and Politics*, ed. Charles E. Curran and Leslie Griffin (New York: Paulist Press, 2001); Kristin E. Heyer, *Prophetic and Public: The Social Witness of U.S. Catholicism* (Washington, D.C.: Georgetown University Press, 2006). The U.S. Catholic bishops have collected a number of recent official church statements on this topic in *Readings on Catholics in Political Life* (Washington, D.C.: United States Conference of Catholic Bishops, 2006).

8. See Joseph Cardinal Bernardin, *Consistent Ethic of Life*, ed. Thomas G. Fuechtmann (Kansas City, Mo.: Sheed & Ward, 1988); and idem, *A Moral Vision for America*, ed. John P. Langan (Washington, D.C.: Georgetown University Press, 1998).

9. For an example of this sort of argument in the secular literature, see R. J. Vincent, *Human Rights and International Relations* (Cambridge: Cambridge University Press, 1995), 143–51. Mary Ann Glendon, a scholar whose work bridges the secular and Catholic discussions, has made a similar argument in her study of the writing of the Universal Declaration of Human Rights: *A World Made New: Eleanor Roosevelt and the Universal Declaration of Human Rights* (New York: Random House: 2001), esp. 172–91, and 240, where she sees all human rights linked together in an "ecology of freedom." I have outlined such an approach to human rights in R. Bruce Douglass and David Hollenbach, eds., *Catholicism and Liberalism: Contributions to American Public Philosophy* (Cambridge/New York: Cambridge University Press, 1994), chap. 5 and afterword.

10. See Glen Harold Stassen, "Pro-life? Look at the Fruits," on the Web site of Sojourners, *Sojomail: A Weekly Email-zine of Spirituality, Politics, and Culture*, October 13, 2004, http://www.sojo.net/index.cfm?action=sojomail.display&issue=041013#5 (accessed May 19, 2006). This electronic site also contains links to subsequent debate about the empirical data and what they demonstrate.

11. I have discussed the possibilities for developing an ethic of the common good that respects freedom in a pluralistic society in my *The Common Good and Christian Ethics* (Cambridge: Cambridge University Press, 2002). Such an approach to relating Catholic thought to politics in the United States is being pursued by two advocacy groups: The Catholic Alliance for the Common Good and The Catholic Democracy Institute. See their Web sites http://www.thecatholicalliance.org (accessed May 24, 2006) and http://www. catholicdemocracy.org (accessed May 24, 2006).

12. I am grateful to James F. Keenan for drawing my attention to this point in personal conversation.

13. For recent discussions of the importance of casuistry, see Albert R. Jonsen and Stephen Toulmin, *The Abuse of Casuistry* (Berkeley, Calif.: University of California Press, 1988); James F. Keenan and Thomas A. Shannon, eds., *The Context of Casuistry* (Washington, D.C.: Georgetown University Press, 1995).

14. See Andrew Greeley, *The American Catholic: A Social Portrait* (New York: Basic Books, 1977), chap. 3.

15. Bruce Berkowitz, *The New Face of War: How War Will Be Fought in the 21st Century* (New York: Free Press, 2003), 4.

16. *National Security Strategy of the United States of America*, September, 2002, 30, http://www.whitehouse.gov/nsc/nss/2002/nss.pdf (accessed May 15, 2006).

17. Charles Krauthammer, "The Bush Doctrine," *Weekly Standard* 6, no. 36 (June 4, 2001): 21–25, at 24.

18. See H. W. Crocker III, "The Case for an American Empire," *Crisis*, October 2004, http://www.crisismagazine.com/october2004/crocker.htm (accessed May 24, 2006), and Daniel McCarthy, "Bush vs. Benedict," *The American Conservative*, August 29, 2005, http://www.amconmag.com/2005/2005_08_29/article.html (accessed May 24, 2006).

19. Andrew J. Bacevich, *The New American Militarism: How Americans Are Seduced by War* (New York: Oxford University Press, 2005), 225.

20. William T. Cavanaugh, *Torture and the Eucharist* (Oxford: Blackwell, 1998), 13–14, and chap. 6.

21. See John Milbank, Catherine Pickstock and Graham Ward, eds. *Radical Orthodoxy: A New Theology* (London: Routledge, 1999).

22. See Benedict XVI, *Deus Caritas Est*, encyclical issued on December 25, 2005, http://www.vatican.va/holy_father/benedict_xvi/encyclicals/index_en.htm (accessed May 24, 2006); J. Bryan Hehir, "The Just-War Ethic and Catholic Theology: Dynamics of Change and Continuity," in Thomas A. Shannon, ed., *War or Peace? The Search for New Answers* (Maryknoll, N.Y.: Orbis, 1980), 15–39; George Weigel, *Tranquillitas Ordinis: The Present Failure and Future Promise of American Catholic Thought on War and Peace* (New York: Oxford University Press, 1987). Other examples of the thinking of these authors could also be cited.

23. For the classic discussion in U.S. theological ethics of the possible distortions that can be introduced into moral judgment by the possession of significant power, see Reinhold Niebuhr, *The Nature and Destiny of Man*, vol. 1 (New York: Scribner's, 1941), chaps 7 and 8.

24. See my *The Global Face of Public Faith: Politics, Human Rights, and Christian Ethics* (Washington, D.C.: Georgetown University Press, 2003), esp. chaps. 1, 2, and 12. See also Lisa Sowle Cahill, *Between the Sexes: Foundations for a Christian Ethics of Sexuality* (Philadelphia: Fortress Press, 1985).

25. See Kwame Anthony Appiah, *The Ethics of Identity* (Princeton, N.J.: Princeton University Press, 2005), chap. 6; and idem, *Cosmopolitanism: Ethics in a World of Strangers* (New York: W. W. Norton, 2006), chapter 1 and passim.

Jean Porter

1. The developments summarized here have been widely documented and debated in the national and international press. For a good summary of the relevant legal claims and debates, see Bruce Ackerman, *Before the Next Attack: Preserving Civil Liberties in an Age of Terrorism* (New Haven: Yale University Press, 2006), 13–76.

2. William Cavanaugh and Jeremy Waldron provide two chilling and theologically sensitive accounts and assessments of the processes through which torture has become "normalized" within government practice and, increasingly, in social perception; see, respectively, "Making Enemies: The Imagination of Torture in Chile and the United States," and "What Can Christian Teaching Add to the Debate about Torture?" in *Theology Today* 63, no. 3 (October 2006): 307–23; 330–43. In addition, see Jane Mayer, "The Memo," *The New Yorker* (Feb. 27, 2006): 32–41, for further details on the defense of torture within the U.S. government.

3. Ackerman, *Before the Next Attack*, 20–21.

4. For an illuminating discussion of these issues, see Lawrence Rosen, *The Anthropology of Justice: Law as Culture in Islamic Society* (Cambridge: Cambridge University Press, 1989). Rosen's remarks are particularly timely in light of the fact that the supposedly repressive or backwards character of traditional Muslim societies is manifested, inter alia, by their disregard for the rule of law. I have no desire to lend credence to this kind of facile moralizing. My point, rather, is that for us, given our own history, context, and legal arrangements, procedures of due process represent one of the most important ways of expressing and safeguarding ideals of public reasonableness and equity; correlatively, we cannot undermine these procedures without compromising and ultimately undermining these ideals—to say nothing of the harms we inflict on individuals and communities along the way.

5. Even on this issue, Christian theologians and church leaders have not spoken out as forcefully as we might have hoped, as Waldron points out: "For most of this period [in which torture has been debated], the voices of Christian leaders—clergy and laypeople—have been silent" (Waldron, "What Can Christian Teaching Add," 331). The generally excellent essays collected in the volume of *Theology Today* cited above comprise one welcome example of this general observation.

6. Kenneth Pennington, *The Prince and the Law, 1200 -1600: Sovereignty and Rights in the Western Legal Tradition* (Berkeley, Calif.: University of California Press, 1993), 132–64.

7. Ibid., 143.

8. Ibid., 143– 44.

9. On the right to due process in canon law, see James F. Keenan, "Framing the Ethical Rights of Priests," *Review For Religious*, 64, no. 2 (2005), 135–51; Keenan, "Toward an Ecclesial Professional Ethics," in *Church Ethics and Its Organizational Context*, ed. Jean M. Bartunek, Mary Ann Hinsdale, and James F. Keenan (Lanham, Md.: Rowman & Littlefield, 2006); John Beal, "It Shall Not Be So Among You! Crisis in the Church, Crisis in Church Law," 88–102 in *Governance, Accountability, and the Future of the Catholic Church*, ed. Francis Oakley and Bruce Russett (New York: Continuum, 2004), 88–102.

10. Francis Oakley, *The Conciliarist Tradition: Constitutionalism in the Catholic Church 1300–1870* (Oxford: Oxford University Press, 2003), 14–15.

11. Oakley, "Constitutionalism in the Church?" in *Governance, Accountability, and the Future of the Catholic Church*, 76–87, at 81.

12. The essays collected in *Governance, Accountability*, together with Oakley's introductory remarks in *The Conciliarist Tradition*, 1–19, provide a fine entree into these discussions.

Kenneth R. Melchin

1. Don Butler, "Slum," *Ottawa Citizen*, sec. A1, A7–10, June 18, 2006.
2. See, e.g., Anthony Westell, "We Need Separation of Church and Politics," *CBC News*, June 15, 2005, http://www.cbc.ca/news/viewpoint/vp_westell/20050615.html (accessed July 3, 2006); Arthur Sheps, "Religion and Politics: The Religious Component of Public Life," *CBC News*, June 28, 2004, http://www.cbc.ca/canadavotes 2004/analysiscommentary/religionandpolitics.html (accessed July 3, 2006).
3. See, e.g., Leigh Eric Schmidt, "Spirit Wars: American Religion in Progressive Politics," *The Pew Forum on Religion & Public Life*, Dec. 6, 2005, http://pew forum.org/events/index.php? EventID=94 (accessed July 3, 2006).
4. Reginald Bibby, *Restless Churches: How Canada's Churches Can Contribute to the Emerging Religious Renaissance* (Toronto: Novalis, 2004), 170–72.
5. Gregory Baum, *The Priority of Labor: A Commentary on "Laborem exercens,"* Encyclical Letter of Pope John II (New York: Paulist Press, 1982); idem, *Karl Polanyi on Ethics and Economics* (Montreal: McGill-Queens University Press, 1996); Gregory Baum and Duncan Cameron, *Ethics and Economics: Canada's Catholic Bishops on the Economic Crisis* (Toronto: James Lorimer, 1984).
6. See http://www.cccb.ca/MediaReleases.htm (accessed July 3, 2006); and http://www.cccb.ca/ PublicStatements.htm (accessed July 3, 2006). I focus on June 2002 to May 2006.
7. David Hollenbach, *The Common Good and Christian Ethics* (Cambridge, Mass.: Cambridge University Press, 2002); Charles Curran, *Catholic Social Teaching, 1891–Present: A Historical, Theological and Ethical Analysis* (Washington, D.C.: Georgetown University Press, 2002); Donal Dorr, *Option for the Poor: A Hundred Years of Vatican Social Teaching* (Maryknoll, N.Y.: Orbis Books, 1983); Michael Schuck, *The Social Teachings of the Papal Encyclicals, 1740–1989* (Washington, D.C.: Georgetown University Press, 1991).
8. John T. Noonan, Jr., "Development in Moral Doctrine," *Theological Studies* 54, no. 4 (December 1993): 662–63; idem, "Experience and the Development of Moral Doctrine," *The Catholic Theological Society of America Proceedings* 54 (1999): 47–49; John E. Thiel, "Faithfulness to Tradition: A Roman Catholic Perspective," *The Cresset* (Easter 2006): 8, http://www.valpo.edu/cresset/2006_Easter_ Thiel.pdf (accessed July 3, 2006).
9. See John E. Thiel, "Perspectives on Tradition," *Catholic Theological Society of America Proceedings* 54 (1999): 1–18; "The Analogy of Tradition: Method and Theological Judgment," *Theological Studies* 66, no. 2 (June 2005): 358–80.
10. Noonan, "Experience," 43–56; Richard A. McCormick, "Moral Doctrine: Stability and Development," *Catholic Theological Society of America Proceedings* 54 (1999): 92–100.
11. M. Kathleen Kaveny, "A Response to John T. Noonan, Jr." *Catholic Theological Society of America Proceedings* 54 (1999): 57–64.
12. See Bernard Lonergan, *Method in Theology* (1972; repr., Toronto: University of Toronto Press, 1990), 125–45; 365–67. See also Charles Hefling, *Why Doctrines?* (Chestnut Hill, Mass.: Lonergan Institute at Boston College, 2000); and

Robert M. Doran, *What Is Systematic Theology?* (Toronto: University of Toronto Press, 2005).

13. See Noonan, "Development," 672–77; idem, "Experience," 54–56.

14. On doctrinal development, see Lonergan, *Method*, 319–30; "Doctrinal Pluralism," in *Philosophical and Theological Papers 1965–1980*, ed. Robert Croken and Robert Doran (Toronto: University of Toronto Press, 2004), 70–104; "Theology as Christian Phenomenon," in *Philosophical and Theological Papers 1958–1964*, ed. Robert Croken, Frederick Crowe, and Robert Doran (Toronto: University of Toronto Press, 1996), 244–72.

15. Noonan, "Development," 662–63; idem, "Experience," 47–49; Thiel, "Faithfulness," 8.

16. John T. Noonan, Jr., "A Backward Look," in "John T. Noonan, Jr.: Retrospective," *Religious Studies Review* 18, no. 2 (April 1992): 111–12.

17. Ibid., 111. See also John T. Noonan, Jr., *The Scholastic Analysis of Usury* (Cambridge, Mass.: Harvard University Press, 1957), 407–8.

18. Noonan, *Scholastic*, 14, 17, 45–47, 49–50, 72.

19. Ibid., 15–17, 33–35, 42, 45–46, 48–50, 74, 401.

20. Ibid., 34–35.

21. Ibid., 19–20.

22. See Jean Porter's discussion of the natural law tradition in *Natural and Divine Law: Reclaiming the Tradition for Christian Ethics* (Grand Rapids, Mich.: Eerdmans; Ottawa: Novalis, 1999).

23. Noonan, *Scholastic*, 38–39, 41–42, 46–47, 51–57, 80–81.

24. Ibid., 51–57, 80–81, 193–95, 358–62, 395–96.

25. See, e.g., Jean-Yves Calvez and Michael Naughton, "Catholic Social Teaching and the Purpose of the Business Organization: A Developing Tradition," in *Rethinking the Purpose of Business: Interdisciplinary Essays from the Catholic Social Tradition*, ed. S. A. Cortright and Michael Naughton (Notre Dame, Ind.: University of Notre Dame Press, 2002), 3–19.

26. Bernard J. Lonergan, *Macroeconomic Dynamics: An Essay in Circulation Analysis*, ed. Frederick Lawrence, Patrick Byrne, and Charles Hefling (Toronto: University of Toronto Press, 1999).

27. Noonan, *Scholastic*, 358–62, 377–78.

28. See Doran, *What Is Systematic Theology?* 40–41.

29. Dorr, *Option*; Stephen J. Pope, "Proper and Improper Partiality and the Preferential Option for the Poor," *Theological Studies* 54, no. 2 (June 1993): 242–71; Patrick H. Byrne, "*Ressentiment* and the Preferential Option for the Poor," *Theological Studies* 54, no. 2 (June 1993): 213–41.

30. See Hollenbach, *Common Good*. See also Lisa Sowle Cahill, "Globalization and the Common Good," in *Globalization and Catholic Social Thought: Present Crisis, Future Hope*, ed. John Coleman and William F. Ryan (Ottawa: Novalis; Maryknoll, N.Y.: Orbis Books, 2005), 42–54.

31. Hollenbach, *Common Good*, 65–86.

32. Ibid., 173–200.

33. Porter, *Natural and Divine*, 310.

34. See, e.g., Eric Shragge and Jean-Marc Fontan, *Social Economy: International Debates and Perspectives* (Montréal: Black Rose Books, 2000); Chantier de

l'Économie Sociale, *Social Economy and Community Economic Development in Canada: Next Steps for Public Policy* (Montréal: Chantier de l'Économie Sociale, 2005), http://www.ccednet-rdec.c/en/docs/pubs/Issues%20Paper_Sept_2005.pdf (accessed Sept 12, 2006).

35. Gregory Baum, *Karl Polanyi*; see also "Religion and Globalization," in *Globalization and Catholic Social Thought*, 141–56. See also David Cayley's five-part series, "Markets and Society," broadcast in CBC/Radio Canada's "Ideas" series, July 4– Aug 1, 2005, http://www.cbc.ca/ideas/calendar/2005/07_july.html (accessed Sept 12, 2006).

36. Christopher Lind, *Something's Wrong Somewhere: Globalization, Community and the Moral Economy of the Farm Crisis* (Halifax: Fernwood Publishing, 1995).

37. See http://www.grameen-info.org/ (accessed Sept 12, 2006); http://www.unesco.org/education/poverty/grameen.shtml (accessed Sept 12, 2006); and http://www.justpeace.org/ mondragon.htm (accessed Sept 12, 2006).

38. Jim Lotz, *The Humble Giant: Moses Coady, Canada's Rural Revolutionary* (Ottawa: Novalis, 2005).

39. See Kenneth R. Melchin, "What Is 'the Good' of Business? Insights from the Work of Bernard Lonergan," *Anglican Theological Review* 87, no. 1 (Winter 2005): 43–62.

40. Cortright and Naughton, eds., *Rethinking the Purpose of Business*; Helen Alford, Charles Clark, S.A. Cortright, and Michael Naughton, eds., *Rediscovering Abundance: Interdisciplinary Essays on Wealth, Income and Their Distribution in the Catholic Social Tradition* (Notre Dame, Ind.: University of Notre Dame Press, 2005); Helen Alford and Michael Naughton, *Managing As If Faith Mattered: Christian Social Principles in the Modern Organization* (Notre Dame, Ind.: University of Notre Dame Press, 2001).

41. Daniel K. Finn, *The Moral Ecology of Markets: Assessing Claims about Markets and Justice* (Cambridge, U.K.: Cambridge University Press, 2006).

Robert Gascoigne

1. Claus Westermann emphasizes that this verse "is emphatic that the Servant's suffering isolated him in the community—this is also the case in the psalms of lamentation—and that he was despised and held in loathing." See his *Isaiah 40–66* (London: SCM, 1969), 262. In her "The New Anthropological Subject at the Heart of the Mystical Body of Christ," M. Shawn Copeland recounts and reflects on the story of Fatima Yusif, reported in the London *Times* (February 12, 1992): "The plight of a Somali woman who gave birth unassisted beside a road in Southern Italy as a crowd stood by and jeered prompted telephone calls yesterday of solidarity and job offers. . . . I will remember those faces as long as I live," Ms. Yusif, who was born in Mogadishu, told *Corriere della Sera* as she recovered in hospital. "They were passing by, they would stop and linger as if they were at the cinema careful not to miss any of the show. There was a boy who, sniggering, said, 'Look what the negress is doing.'" See *Proceedings of the Fifty-Third Annual Convention of the Catholic Theological Society of America* 53 (June 11–14, Ottawa, 1998), 37. In his *When Bad*

Things Happen to Other People (New York: Routledge 2000), John Portman notes that "unlike pain, suffering always entails a psychological and/or social component. . . . Whereas pain calls out for medication or bandages, suffering waits for sympathy. The experience of suffering marginalizes us all by isolating us from other people" (52).

2. "In the middle of the last century, when ten-year-old children were suffering agonies in the factories of France and thirty-year-olds were being dismissed as old men, a bishop wrote to his diocese, in which the poor made up forty percent of the population: 'Comfort yourselves with the thought that the divine Saviour wanted to put you in the most happy situation of working for your salvation by giving you a share in his cup of need and deprivation . . . and if you share in these you will share in the crown of glory. . . . That he chastizes (even the good) in this world according to his mercy so as not to punish them according to his righteousness in the other.'" See Norbert Greinacher, "The Ambivalence of Failure and Human Ambivalence," in *Coping with Failure*, ed. Norbert Greinacher and Norbert Mette (*Concilium*, 1990/5), 4, citing M. Legree, "Die Sprache der Ordnung" (*Concilium* 12, 1976), 555. In his *Social Catholicism in Europe: From the Onset of Industrialization to the First World War* (New York: Crossroad, 1991), Paul Misner notes that even for the prominent nineteenth-century French liberal Catholics Lacordaire and Montalembert (in contrast to Frederic Ozanam) "the commitment to freedom in society went along with a lack of sensitivity toward the problem of social and economic inequality" (85).

3. In his commentary on Article 21 of *Gaudium et Spes*, Joseph Ratzinger argued that the document's affirmation of the harmony between eschatological hope and concern for this world failed to include a recognition of the church's failures in the social field in the nineteenth century: "Here, too, a deeper examination of conscience was needed, and it should have been admitted that at bottom, after all, we owe it to the atheists' attack that we have become properly aware once more of our own duties." See *Commentary on the Documents of Vatican II*, vol. 5: *Pastoral Constitution on the Church in the Modern World*, ed. H. Vorgrimler (New York/London: Herder & Herder/Burns & Oates, 1969), 156.

4. For comprehensive studies of this development, see, e.g., Charles Curran, *Catholic Social Teaching 1891—Present: A Historical, Theological and Ethical Analysis* (Washington, D.C.: Georgetown University Press, 2002), and Kenneth R. Himes, ed., *Modern Catholic Social Teaching: Commentaries and Interpretations* (Washington, D.C.: Georgetown University Press, 2004).

5. As, for example, in the palpable urgency resonating in these words of Paul VI in *Populorum Progressio*, 53: "Countless millions are starving, countless families are destitute, countless men are steeped in ignorance; countless people need schools, hospitals, and homes worthy of the name. In such circumstances, we cannot tolerate public and private expenditures of a wasteful nature; we cannot but condemn lavish displays of wealth by nations or individuals; we cannot approve a debilitating arms race. It is Our solemn duty to speak out against them. If only world leaders would listen to Us, before it is too late!"

6. In their editors' introduction to *The Spectre of Mass Death* (Concilium; London/Maryknoll, N.Y.: SCM/Orbis Books, 1993) David Power and Kabasele Lumbala speak of the wars and massacres of the twentieth century as an age of "absurd death": in this age, not only is death "without reason, but too often it is brought on

by the meaningless, vicious or more prosaically callous behaviour of human societies. And it always opens up in the heart the question of the absence of God" (viii).

7. In his *The Gospel According to Luke X-XXIV* (Anchor Bible; New York: Doubleday, 1985), Joseph Fitzmyer notes that this verse is the first mention of the "specifically Lucan Christologoumenon that the Messiah must suffer," something unknown in the Old Testament or pre-Christian Judaism (1565).

8. See, for example, the discussion of von Balthasar's theology of Holy Saturday in Anne Hunt, *The Trinity and the Paschal Mystery: A Development in Recent Catholic Theology* (Collegeville, Minn.: Michael Glazier, 1997), "The descent into hell," 68–76: "Descending into hell, Jesus is dead with the dead: he is in solidarity with humanity in the experience of death" (69); and in Michel Deneken's "God at the Heart of Hell: From Theodicy to the Word of the Cross," in *The Spectre of Mass Death*: "So God is in solidarity to the point of the Son's being among the dead. Eastern theology has always attributed soteriological value to this descent into hell. God is dead there, but in the dynamism of the resurrection he also draws humanity from eternal death by giving his hand to Adam" (61).

9. For Paul, in Romans 5:3–4, we can "boast in our sufferings, knowing that suffering produces endurance, and endurance produces character, and character produces hope." In the exegesis of this verse in his *Romans* (Sacra Pagina; Collegeville, Minn.: Michael Glazier/Liturgical Press, 1996), Brendan Byrne notes that Paul presupposes both Jewish and Stoic conceptions of "disciplinary" suffering, whereas, for moderns, suffering may lead to bitterness and despair, and hope seen to be illusory. For Paul, "what excludes this is the sense of God's love made palpable in the experience of the Spirit" (Rom 5:5) who is "the eschatological gift par excellence" (167). In his *Suffering and Hope: The Biblical Vision and the Human Predicament* (Grand Rapids, Mich.: Eerdmans, 1987), J. Christiaan Beker argues that the power of Paul's response to suffering stems from his combination of two distinct theological responses: a vigorously prophetic stance against suffering caused by human injustice and idolatry together with an apocalyptic hope in the face of suffering caused by the power of death (103). If suffering and hope are separated—in contrast to Paul's vision—suffering leads to despair and hope becomes merely wishful thinking (115).

10. For Oliver Davies, in his *A Theology of Compassion: Metaphysics of Difference and the Renewal of Tradition* (Grand Rapids, Mich.: Eerdmans, 2001), "in compassion we can say that the self re-enacts the alienation and dispossession of the one who suffers through a voluntary act of displacement and dispossession." Drawing on the thought of Edith Stein, Davies argues that in compassion we experience the other as an "epiphany," displacing our own world-centeredness, and "the opening of a new horizon as enhanced or enriched existence, which we have called being." In this sense, compassion has an ontological dimension: self-emptying can lead to experiencing the other "not as an object of knowledge but primordially, as the mutuality or sociality of consciousness itself" (232–33). Davies introduces his reflections with three narratives of the "compassionate self," drawn from the diaries and letters of Edith Stein, Etty Hillesum, and Ivica Jurilj (a woman caught up in the war in Bosnia-Hercegovina in the 1990s). Dorothee Sölle's *Suffering* (Philadelphia: Fortress Press, 1975) also offers a Christian reflection on suffering based on a number of narrative accounts.

11. For a discussion of the ways in which the encounter with the "other" in historical experience can develop Christian tradition, see my "Revelation and a Theol-

ogy of Mediation," *The Public Forum and Christian Ethics* (Cambridge: Cambridge University Press, 2001), 127–36.

12. As Charles Curran notes in his *The Moral Theology of John Paul II* (Washington, D.C.: Georgetown University Press, 2005), John Paul "distinguishes between the divine dimension in the mystery of redemption and the human dimension" (70). Clearly, his reflection on the meaning of suffering in *Salvifici Doloris* includes the possibility that human suffering can be part of this "human dimension" of redemption, even to the extent that, although "Christ achieved the redemption completely and to the very limits . . . it seems to be part of the very essence of Christ's redemptive suffering that this suffering requires to be unceasingly completed" (24). In their commentary on *Colossians* (Anchor Bible; New York: Doubleday, 1994), Markus Barth and Helmut Blanke note the interpretation of Col 1:24 by Ernst Percy, who argued that "Paul is said to be suffering now for the same purpose as Christ . . . namely in the execution of his commission and thus for the external and internal growth of the community" (294). In their own judgment, however, the verse refers to Paul's need to undergo a predetermined measure of suffering as part of his own commission as an apostle, rather than as any completion of Christ's suffering. Part of their justification for this exegesis is the need to avoid any implication that Christ's suffering is incomplete. Yet, John Paul's interpretation of the passage seeks rather to hold together the divine and human dimensions of redemption, acknowledging that human suffering can be a way in which Christ's redemption is realized in human history.

Maureen Junker-Kenny

1. See Lisa Sowle Cahill, *Between the Sexes* (Philadelphia: Fortress Press, 1985), 4–8, 12–13, with reference to the Methodist "quadrilateral" test inspired by John Wesley, to Robert J. Daly and to James M. Gustafson.

2. See Robert Gascoigne, "Suffering and Theological Ethics: Intimidation and Hope," pp. 163–66 in this volume.

3. See Dionisio Miranda, "What Will You Have Me Do for You? The Theological Ethics Agenda from an Asian Perspective," pp. 176–84 in this volume.

4. Paul Ricoeur, *Oneself as Another*, trans. K. Blamey (Chicago: University of Chicago Press, 1992), 289.

5. This passage summarizes Thomas Pröpper's exposition of the problem in his "Exkurs 2: Ist das Identische der Tradition identifizierbar? Zur Aufgabe und Hauptschwierigkeit einer historischen Rekonstruktion der Überlieferungsgeschichte des christlichen Glaubens," in *Erlösungsglaube und Freiheitsgeschichte*, 3rd ed. (Munich: Kösel, 1991), 230–35.

6. Robert Schreiter, *Constructing Local Theologies* (Maryknoll, N.Y.: Orbis Books, 1985), 75–94.

7. See Miranda, "What Will You Have Me Do for You?"

8. I have treated the Irish exegete Sean Freyne's debates of these questions in his *Jesus, a Jewish Galilean* (London: T & T Clark, 2004) in my article "Virtues and the God Who Makes Everything New," in *Recognising the Margins: Essays in Honour of Sean Freyne*, ed. Andrew Mayes and Werner Jeanrond (Dublin: Columba Press, 2006), 298–320.

9. Jürgen Habermas, "Vorpolitische Grundlagen des demokratischen Rechtsstaates?" in *Zwischen Naturalismus und Religion: Philosophische Aufsätze* (Frankfurt: Suhrkamp, 2005), 106–18, 118.

10. See Rainer Forst, *Contexts of Justice: Political Philosophy between Liberalism and Communitarianism,* trans. J. M. M. Farrell (Berkeley: University of California Press, 2002), 142, 188.

11. John Rawls, *A Theory of Justice* (Cambridge, Mass.: Harvard University Press, 1971), 92.

12. Friedrich Schweitzer, "Practical Theology, Contemporary Culture, and the Social Sciences—Interdisciplinary Relationships and the Unity of Practical Theology as a Discipline," in *Practical Theology—International Debates,* ed. Friedrich Schweitzer and Johannes Van der Ven (Frankfurt: P. Lang, 1999), 307–21, 317.

13. Paul Ricoeur, *Parcours de la Reconnaissance* (Paris: Ed. Stock, 2004), 226, translated into English as *The Course of Recognition,* trans. D. Pellauer (Cambridge, Mass.: Harvard University Press, 2005), 152.

14. Jürgen Habermas, "Philosophy as Stand-In and Interpreter," in *Moral Consciousness and Communicative Action,* trans. C. Lenhardt and S. W. Nicholson (Cambridge, Mass.: MIT Press, 1991), 1–20.

15. See Oskar Negt, "The Unrepeatable: Changes in the Cultural Concept of Dignity," in *The Discourse of Human Dignity, Concilium* 2003/2, ed. Regina Ammicht-Quinn, Maureen Junker-Kenny, and Elsa Tamez (London: SCM Press, 2003), 25–34, 26, 28–29.

16. See Miranda, "What Will You Have Me Do for You?"

17. Onora O'Neill, *Towards Justice and Virtue: A Constructive Account of Practical Reasoning* (Cambridge: Cambridge University Press, 1996), 52.

18. Ricoeur, *Oneself as Another,* Seventh to Ninth Study, 169–296, 172.

19. The challenge that the Kantian concept of legality poses to neo-Aristotelian ethics has been pointed out by Herbert Schnädelbach in "Was ist Neoaristotelismus?" in *Zur Rehabilitierung des animal rationale* (Frankfurt: Suhrkamp, 1992), 205–30, esp. 227–28.

20. Lewis Mudge, *The Sense of a People: Toward a Church for the Human Future* (Philadelphia: Trinity Press, 1992), 88.

21. See, e.g., Margit Eckholt, *Poetik der Kultur: Bausteine einer interkulturellen dogmatischen Methodenlehre* (Freiburg: Herder, 2002).

22. Hans Joas, *The Genesis of Values,* trans. G. Moore (Chicago: University of Chicago Press, 2000), 174.

23. John May and Linda Hogan, "Constructing the Human: Dignity in Interreligious Dialogue," in *Discourse of Human Dignity,* 78–89.

24. M. Eckholt, "Kultur—Zwischen Universalität und Partikularität. Annäherung an eine kulturphilosophische Interpretation Paul Ricoeurs," in *Das herausgeforderte Selbst: Perspektiven auf Paul Ricoeurs Ethik,* ed. Andris Breitling, Stefan Orth, and Birgit Schaaff (Würzburg: Königshausen und Neumann, 1999), 95–115, 98–100.

Dionisio M. Miranda, S.V.D.

1. Stephen Bevans, *Models of Contextual Theology* (Maryknoll, N.Y.: Orbis Books, 2002); Adolfo Nicolas, "Christianity in Crisis: Asia. Which Asia? Which

Christianity? Which Crisis?" in *Concilium 2005/3: Christianity in Crisis?* ed. Jon Sobrino and Felix Wilfred (London: SCM Press, 2005): 64–70.

2. Felix Wilfred, "Christianity between Decline and Resurgence," in *Concilium 2005/3*, 27–37.

3. Stephen Bevans and Roger Schroeder, *Constants in Context: A Theology of Mission for Today* (Maryknoll, N.Y.: Orbis Books, 2004).

4. The FABC papers are available at http://www.fabc.org (accessed Jan. 15, 2007) or http://www.ucanews.com (accessed Jan. 15, 2007).

5. James Bretzke, "Moral Theology Out of East Asia," *Theological Studies* 61 (2000): 106–21; George Evers, *The Churches in Asia* (Delhi: ISPCK, 2005).

6. Jaime Belita, *From Logos to Diwa: A Synthesis of Theological Research in Catholic Graduate Schools in the Philippines (1965–1985)* (Manila: De la Salle University Press, 1986).

7. Karl-Heinz Pesche, *Christian Ethics*, 2 vols. (Alcester and Dublin: C. Goodliffe Neale, 1997).

8. Evelyn Monteiro and Antoinette Gutzler, eds., *Ecclesia of Women in Asia* (Delhi: ISPCK, 2005); Virginia Fabella and Sun Ai Lee Park, eds., *We Dare to Dream: Doing Theology as Asian Women* (Manila: EATWOT Women's Commission in Asia, 1989); Victoria Tauli-Corpuz, Chair—UN Permanent Forum on Indigenous Issues (UNPFII), Tebtebba Foundation (Indigenous Peoples' International Centre for Policy Research and Education) at www.tebtebba.org (accessed Jan. 15, 2007).

9. Ladislav Nemet, *Inculturation in the Philippines: A Theological Study of the Question of Inculturation in the Documents of CBCP and Selected Filipino Theologians in the Light of Vatican II and the Documents of FABC* (Rome: Gregorian University, 1994).

10. Brian Johnstone, "Can Tradition Be a Source of Moral Truth?" *Studia Moralia* 37, no. 2 (1999): 431–51.

11. Dionisio Miranda, *Kaloob ni Kristo: A Filipino Christian Account of Conscience* (Manila: Logos Publications, 2003); Osamu Takeuchi, *Conscience and Personality: A New Understanding of Conscience and Its Inculturation in Japanese Moral Theology* (Chiba: Kyoyusha, 2003).

12. Tonia Bock, "A Consideration of Culture in Moral Theme Comprehension: Comparing Native and European American Students," *Journal of Moral Education* 35, no. 1 (March 2006): 71–87.

13. Walbert Bühlmann, *The Search for God: An Encounter with the Peoples and Religions of Asia* (Maryknoll, N.Y.: Orbis Books, 1980); K. C. Abraham, *Third World Theologies: Commonalities and Divergence* (Maryknoll, N.Y.: Orbis Books, 1990); William Burrows, *Redemption and Dialogue: Reading Redemptoris Missio and Dialogue and Proclamation* (Maryknoll, N.Y.: Orbis Books, 1994).

14. John Paul II, *Ecclesia in Asia: Apostolic Exhortation on Jesus Christ the Savior and his Mission of Love and Service in Asia* (Manila: Paulines, 1999).

15. Servais Pinckaers, *The Sources of Christian Ethics* (Washington, D.C.: Catholic University of America Press, 1995); *Morality: The Catholic View* (Notre Dame, Ind.: St. Augustine's Press, 2000); Vicente Gómez Mier, *La Refundacion de la Moral Catolica: El cambio de matriz disciplinar después del Concilio Vaticano II* (Estella: Verbo Divino, 1995); Terence Kennedy, "Paths of Reception: How *Gaudium et Spes* Shaped Fundamental Moral Theology," *Studia Moralia* 42/2 (2004): 115–45.

16. James Gustafson, *Ethics from a Theocentric Perspective*, vol. 1: *Theology and Ethics* (Chicago: University of Chicago Press, 1983); *Ethics from a Theocentric Perspective*, vol. 2: *Ethics and Theology* (Chicago: University of Chicago Press, 1992); Harlan Beckley and Charles Swezey, eds., *Ethics from a Theocentric Perspective: Interpretations and Assessments* (Macon, Ga.: Mercer University Press, 1988).

17. Marciano Vidal García, *Nueva Moral Fundamental: El Hogar Teológico de la Etica* (Bilbao: Desclée de Brouwer, 2000).

18. Hans Küng, *A Global Ethic for Global Politics and Economics* (New York: Oxford University Press, 1998); Jean Porter, "The Search for a Global Ethic," *Theological Studies* 62 (2001): 105–21; Lisa Sowle Cahill, "Toward Global Ethics," *Theological Studies* 63 (2002): 324–44; William Schweiker, *Theological Ethics and Global Dynamics* (Oxford: Blackwell, 2004); Arthur Dyck, "Taking Responsibility for our Common Morality," *Harvard Theological Review* 98:4 (2005): 391–417.

19. Dionisio Miranda, *Pagkamakabuhay: On the Side of Life, Prolegomena for Bioethics from a Filipino-Christian Perspective* (Manila: Logos Publications, 1994); Hyun Kyung Chung, "Opium or the Seed of Revolution? Shamanism: Women-centred Popular Religiosity in Korea," *Concilium 1988/5: Theologies of the Third World, Convergences and Differences*, ed. Virgil Elizondo and Leonardo Boff (London: SCM): 96–104.

20. Catholic Bishops Conference of the Philippines (CBCP), *Acts and Decrees of the Second Plenary Council of the Philippines, 20 Jan—17 Feb 1991* (Manila, 1992).

21. Peter Black and James Keenan, "The Evolving Self-Understanding of the Moral Theologian, 1900–2000," *Studia Moralia* 39 (2001): 291–327.

22. Karen Lebacqz, "The Ethics of Ethical Advising: Confessions of an Ethical Advisor" (May 14, 2003), in Markkula Center for Applied Ethics, Spring 2003 Ethics Events at www.scu.edu/ethics/publications (accessed Jan. 15, 2007).

23. Sabatino Majorano, "Il Teologo Moralista Oggi," *Studia Moralia* 33, no. 1 (1995): 21–44; Basilio Petrà, "Le Sfide del Teologo Moralista Oggi" *Studia Moralia* 33, no. 1 (1995): 5–20.

24. Catholic Bishops Conference of the Philippines (CBCP), *Pastoral Exhortation on the Church and Politics* (Manila: Paulines, 1997); CBCP, *Pastoral Exhortation on Economy* (1998); CBCP, *Pastoral Exhortation on Philippine Culture* (CBCP-ECC, 2000).

25. Ecumenical Association of Third World Theologians, webmaster@eatwot.org (accessed Jan. 15, 2007).

Paul Valadier, S.J.

1. Especially in an article published in the *Rambler* in 1859, "On Consulting the Faithful on Matters of Doctrine." This position is maintained throughout Newman's entire oeuvre. See *Essays Critical and Historical*, 2 vols. (London: Pickering, 1881). Other works on the subject include: Yves Cardinal Congar, "Les laïcs et la fonction prophétique dans l'Église," in *Jalons pour une théologie du laïcat* (Paris: Cerf, 1959), chap. 6; idem, *Église et papauté: Regards historiques* (Paris: Cerf, 1964), chap. 11; Jan Kerkhofs, "Le peuple de Dieu est-il infaillible? L'importance du 'sensus fidelium' dans l'Église postconciliaire," *Freiburger Zeitschrift für Philosophie und Theologie*

35 (1988): 3–19; Leo Cardinal Scheffczyk, "Le *'sensus fidelium,'* la force de la communauté," *Revue internationale catholique/Communio* 13 (1988): 84–100; Bernard Sesboüé, "Le *'sensus fidelium'* en morale à la lumière de Vatican II," *Le Supplément* 181 (July 1992): 153–56; Francis Sullivan, *Magisterium: Teaching Authority in the Catholic Church* (New York: Gill & MacMillan, 1983); idem, *Creating Fidelity: Weighing and Interpreting Documents of the Magisterium* (Dublin: Gill & MacMillan, 1986); Jean-Marie Tillard, "Magistère, théologie et *sensus fidelium*," *Introduction à la pratique de la théologie*, vol. 1 (Paris: Cerf, 1982), chap. 3, 163–82.

2. Accordingly, we must not replace the traditional expression *sensus fidelium* by *sensus fidei*—or else we must explain such a substitution. The former phrase takes account of the life and the faith of the ecclesial community; the latter risks a restriction to dogmas that are proposed in abstract terms, independently of their profession of faith by believing persons. These dogmas would then float in some way above the church, or else they would be regulated by "experts" who were exempt from control by the conscience and the judgment of believers.

3. Original title: "*Sensus fidelium*, un concept en désuétude?"

Nathanaël Yaovi Soédé

1. Leonard K. Santedi, *Dogme et inculturation en Afrique* (Paris: Karthala, 2003).

2. Meinrad P. Hebga, *Emancipation d'Eglise sous tutelle* (Paris: Présence Africaine, 1976), 166–67.

3. Bernard Lauret and François Refoulé, eds., *Initiation à la pratique de la théologie: Introduction* (Paris: Cerf), 161–82; Bernard Sesboüe, *Le magistère à l'épreuve* (Paris: DDB, 2001), 100–108; Paul Valadier, *La condition chrétienne* (Paris: Seuil, 2003), 218–41.

4. Nathanaël Yaovi Catholic Social Thought, *Sens et enjeu de l'éthique: Inculturation de l'éthique chrétienne* (Abidjan: UCAO, 2005), 94–129; idem, "Anthropologie et éthique de l'être-vie. Approche afrique chrétienne," in Claudius Luterbacher-Maineri and Stephanie Lehr-Rosenberg, eds., *Weisheit in Vielfalt: Afrikanisches und westliches Denken im Dialog. Sagesse dans la pluralité. L'Afrique et l'Occident en dialogue* (Fribourg: Academic Press Fribourg, 2006), 111–23; Engelbert Mveng, *L'Afrique dans l'Église: Parole d'un croyant* (Paris: L'Harmattan, 1985), 7–18.

5. John Paul II, *Ecclesia in Africa*, no. 63ff.

6. Bénézet Bujo, *The Ethical Dimension of Community: The African Model and the Dialogue between North and South* (Nairobi: Pauline Publications Africa, 1997), 58–87; idem, *Foundations of an African Ethic: Beyond the Universal Claims of Western Morality* (Nairobi: Pauline Publications Africa, 2001), 68–97.

7. François Varillon, *L'humilité de Dieu* (Paris: Le Centurion, 1974).

8. Paulin Poucouta, *Lettres aux Eglises d'Afrique: Apocalypse 1–3* (Paris and Yaounde: Karthala and Presses de l'UCAC, 1997).

9. *Gaudium et spes*, no. 93.

10. Catholic Social Thought, *Sens et enjeux*, 49–130; Marcel Dumais, *Le sermon sur la montagne: Etat de la recherche, interprétation, bibliographie* (Paris: Letouzey & Ane, 1995).

11. *Gaudium et Spes*, no. 93.
12. Original title: "*Sensus fidelium* et discernement moral: Le principe de l'inculturation et de l'amour."

Giuseppe Angelini

1. On the genesis of moral theology, the study by Johann Theiner, *Die Entwicklung der Moraltheologie als eigenständiger Disziplin* (Regensburg: Pustet, 1970), remains fundamental.

2. I refer the reader to analytical reconstructions of the theological literature on the topic of the *sensus fidelium*, with particular reference to the period after the Second Vatican Council. For a general history of this subject, see Dario Vitali, "*Sensus fidelium.*" *Una funzione ecclesiale di intelligenza della fede* (Brescia: Morcelliana, 1993); for the subsequent debates, see especially the two bulletins by John Burkhard, "Sensus fidei: Theological Reflection since Vatican II (1965–1989)," *Heythrop Journal* 34 (1993): 41–59, 123–36; "Sensus fidei: Recent Theological Reflection (1990–2001), Part I," *Heythrop Journal* 46 (2005): 450–75; Vitali, "'Universitas fidelium in credendo falli nequit' (LG 12). Il sensus fidelium al concilio Vaticano II," *Gregorianum* 82 (2005/3): 607–28; Cardinal L. Scheffczyk, "Sensus fidelium: testimonianza della comunità," *Communio* 2 (1988): 110–25.

3. One of the most influential organs of theological dissent was the periodical *Concilium*, which dedicated a fascicle exclusively to this topic: *Autorità dottrinale dei fedeli* (1985, no. 4). The scheme of thought adopted in some of the essays (Elisabeth Schüssler Fiorenza, 66–79; Jon Sobrino, 79–89) posits an antithesis between the many (i.e., the faithful) and the few (i.e., the bishops, indeed pastors in general). Herbert Vorgrimler presents this question in a more subtle manner ("Dal 'sensus fidelium' al 'consensus fidelium,' 15–26); see also Edward Schillebeeckx, "Autorità dottrinale di tutti. Riflessioni sulla struttura del Nuovo Testamento," 27–39. In these essays, however, there is no consideration of the practical forms by means of which one moves from the *sensus fidei* to the *consensus fidelium*. With regard to the authority of the magisterium, we should note the justified criticism of a purely statistical interpretation of the *sensus fidelium* which is expressed by the Congregation for the Doctrine of the Faith in its instruction *Donum veritatis*, no. 35, "On the ecclesial vocation of the theologian" (official English text, May 24, 1990): "Dissent sometimes also appeals to a kind of sociological argumentation which holds that the opinion of a large number of Christians would be a direct and adequate expression of the 'supernatural sense of the faith.' Actually, the opinions of the faithful cannot be simply identified with the 'sensus fidei.' The sense of the faith is a property of theological faith; and, as God's gift which enables one to adhere personally to the Truth, it cannot err. This personal faith is also the faith of the Church since God has given guardianship of the Word to the Church. Consequently, what the believer believes is what the Church believes. The 'sensus fidei' implies then by its nature a profound agreement of spirit and heart with the Church, 'sentire cum Ecclesia.'"

4. The conflict that followed the publication of the encyclical *Humanae vitae* has a decisive importance here. As is well known, the reception of this document was prejudiced from the outset by the contrary view expressed by the majority of the theological commission which Paul VI himself had appointed.

5. For brief but precise information about the use and abuse of this category in the postconciliar period, see Vitali, "Universitas fidelium"; he cites all the major theologians who have made theoretical contributions to this subject. See also the earlier and more analytical account by Daniel J. Finucane, *Sensus fidelium: The Use of a Concept in the Post-Vatican II Era* (San Francisco: International Scholars Publications, 1996); and more recently, John Burkhard, "Sensus fidei."

6. Interest in the participation of all the faithful in the definition of the truth of the faith begins with the celebrated essay by John Henry Newman, *On Consulting the Faithful in Matters of Doctrine* (1859/1871). On the difficulties of understanding aright the proposals of this essay in the present day, see Gerald O'Collins, "Note a proposito della consultazione dei fedeli," *La Civiltà Cattolica* 138/4 (1988): 40–45.

7. Vitali offers a useful account of the problems posed by the relationship between the *sensus fidelium* and public opinion: "Sensus fidelium e opinione pubblica nella Chiesa," *Gregorianum* 82 (2001): 689–717. He underlines the gulf that separates the encouraging assessment of an opinion in the church expressed by Pius XII many years ago, in 1950, and the forms that the alleged ecclesial public opinion assumed de facto in the years of dissent. He then discusses the distinction, which must be drawn in every case, between the concepts of the *sensus fidelium* and of public opinion. Under certain conditions, the promotion of a public opinion in the church is an appropriate instrument for the elaboration of the *sensus fidelium*, but it is certainly not possible simply to equate public opinion and *sensus fidelium*.

8. I use the term "conscience" here in the sense of the German noun *Gewissen*. As Hegel's reflections suggest, the *Gewissen* is something very different from the *moralisches Bewusstsein* (moral consciousness). He deals with this subject above all in two passages: at greater length and with greater descriptive attention in the *Phänomenologie des Geistes* (chap. 6, "Der Geist," third part: "The spirit aware of itself") and more briefly but with a more precise theoretical concern in the *Grundlinien des philosophischen Rechts* (appendix to §136, "The exalted rank of the point of view of the conscience"). The inability of any awareness that can be put into words to grasp the full meaning of the *Gewissen* has been well described in the famous analysis by Martin Heidegger in §§57–60 of his *Sein und Zeit*. These paragraphs close with the theorem of the substantial ineffability of the *Gewissen*. From the perspective of action in the world, the recalling of the subject to that possibility which is most fully his own does not recall him to anything determinate.

9. This accusation is leveled in a book that made a tremendous impact: Alasdair C. MacIntyre, *Dopo la virtù: Saggio di teoria morale* (Milan: Feltrinelli, 1988). After morality was separated from customs, from tradition, and from religion, the project of understanding takes the form of its alleged *rational* foundation, emancipated from any obligation vis-à-vis those authorities which even the direct and naïve conscience of the human person recognizes: "It is impossible to give an adequate account of the history of moral discourse without a description of the attempts to supply a rational justification of morality in that period (roughly from 1630 to 1850) in which it acquired a general and specific global meaning. In that period, morality became the name for that particular sphere in which an autonomous cultural space is granted to rules of conduct which are neither theological, juridical, nor aesthetic. It is only at the end of the seventeenth century and in the course of the eighteenth century, when this distinction of the moral sphere with regard to the theological, juridical, and aesthetic

spheres has become a generally accepted doctrine, that the project of an independent rational justification of morality is no longer simply the concern of individual thinkers, but becomes a central question of European culture. One of the central theses of this book is that the failure of this project provides the historical background against which we can understand the difficulties which torment our culture today" (55). The accusation that moral philosophy had come to an end had been made earlier by Giulio Preti, *Alle origini dell'etica contemporanea: Adamo Smith* (1957; repr., Florence: La Nuova Italia, 1977) in his introduction, which is devoted to "the moral problem of contemporary philosophy." Here he proposes a distinction between *moral philosophy* and the *philosophy of morality.* "The latter differs from the former primarily because the practical, i.e. normative task of moral philosophy yields place to a task which we may (at least provisionally) call epistemological. It is no longer a question of harmonizing the world of moral experiences, of customs, feelings and values, in keeping with the perspective offered by an ideal, but rather of discovering the structures and laws of the development of moral experience itself. It is no longer the specific task of thought to generate this moral experience, nor even simply to harmonize and regulate. Rather, moral experience is a presupposition, a *de facto* given which must be analyzed in its conditions, its structures, and its connections" (17–18).

10. As is well known, the radical difficulty of the human person with regard to the will is at the heart of Nietzsche's reflections. It is in the light (or shadow) of this difficulty that we must understand the concept of the "will to power." The idea of the *Übermensch* ("superman") resolves this difficulty in a way that is too banal and irrelevant.

11. See Giuseppe Angelini, "Etica pubblica e morale cristiana," *La rivista del clero italiano* 71 (1980): 567–80; idem, "Ritorno all'etica? Tendenze e ambiguità di un fenomeno recente," *Il Regno* 35 (1990): 438–49.

12. This thesis is set out here with telegraphic brevity. I have attempted to explain it in detail in the lengthy section about the biblical message in my manual: Giuseppe Angelini, *Teologia morale fondamentale: Tradizione, Scrittura e teoria* (Milan: Glossa, 1999), 239–51.

13. Original title: "*Sensus fidelium* e discernimento morale."

Eberhard Schockenhoff

1. See Karl Rahner, "Über den Dialog in der pluralistischen Gesellschaft," in idem, *Sämtliche Werke*, vol. 15: *Verantwortung der Theologie* (Freiburg i. Br: Herder, 2001), 354–63.

2. See John Kekes, *The Morality of Pluralism*, (Princeton, N.J.: Princeton University, 1993).

3. Otfried Höffe, "Pluralismus/Toleranz," in Peter Eicher, ed., *Neues Handbuch theologischer Grundbegriffe*, vol. 3 (Munich: Kösel, 2005), 363–78, at 369.

4. See no. 70–71.

5. See Klaus Demmer, *Fundamentale Theologie des Ethischen* (Freiburg i. Ue: Herder, 1999), 22–24.

6. See Nicolas Rescher, *Pluralism: Against the Demand for Consensus* (Oxford: Oxford University Press, 1993).

7. See F. Wagner, "Theologie zwischen normativem Einheitsanspruch und faktischem wissenschaftlich-kulturellem Pluralismus," in Joachim Mehlhausen, ed., *Pluralismus und Identität* (Gütersloh: Gütersloher Verlagshaus, 1995), 153–67, esp. 165.

8. Original title: "Die Herausforderung des Pluralismus."

Lisa Sowle Cahill

1. "The practical reason . . . is busied with contingent matters, about which human actions are concerned: and consequently, although there is necessity in the general principles, the more we descend to matters of detail, the more frequently we encounter defects," Thomas Aquinas, *Summa Theologiae* I-II., q. 94, art. 4, "Whether the Natural Law Is the Same in All Men," trans. Fathers of the English Dominican Province (New York: Benziger Brothers, 1948).

2. See Charles E. Curran and Richard A. McCormick, eds., *Readings in Moral Theology No. 1: Moral Norms and Catholic Tradition* (New York/Ramsey/Toronto: Paulist Press, 1979).

3. See Bernard Hoose, *Proportionalism: The American Debate and Its European Roots* (Washington, D.C.: Georgetown University Press, 1987).

4. See Richard A. McCormick, *The Critical Calling: Reflections on Moral Dilemmas since Vatican II* (Washington, D.C.: Georgetown University Press, 2006) (originally published 1989).

5. See Charles E. Curran, Margaret A. Farley, and Richard A. McCormick, eds., *Feminist Ethics and the Catholic Moral Tradition* (New York/Mahwah, N.J.: Paulist Press, 1996).

6. Among many possible examples are Virginia Fabella and Mercy Amba Oduyoye, eds., *With Passion and Compassion: Third World Women Doing Theology* (Maryknoll, N.Y.: Orbis Books, 1989); Robert J. Schreiter, ed., *Faces of Jesus in Africa* (Maryknoll, N.Y.: Orbis Books, 1991); and R. S. Sugirtharaja, ed., *Asian Faces of Jesus* (Maryknoll, N.Y.: Orbis Books, 1993). On constructive engagement with non-Christian traditions, see Anozie Onyema, *The Moral Significance of African Traditional Religion for Christian Conscience* (Port Harcourt, Nigeria: Lynno Nigeria Coy, 2004); and Francis X. Clooney, *Theology after Vedanta: An Experiment in Comparative Theology* (Albany, N.Y.: State University of New York Press, 1993).

7. Hillary Charlesworth, "Martha Nussbaum's Feminist Internationalism," *Ethics* 111 (2000): 76–77, available online at www.jstor.org (accessed Jan. 15, 2007).

8. Sharon D. Welch, *A Feminist Ethic of Risk*, rev. ed. (Minneapolis, Minn.: Augsburg Fortress, 2000), 104.

9. Elias Omondo Opongo, *Making Choices for Peace: Aid Agencies in Field Diplomacy* (Nairobi: Paulines Publications Africa, 2006), 176.

10. Ibid., 177.

11. Ethics may be understood as "aiming at the good life with and for others, in just institutions," a life which is true, good, virtuous and happy. See Paul Ricoeur, *Oneself As Another*, trans. Kathleen Blamey (Chicago: University of Chicago Press, 1992), 172.

Márcio Fabri dos Anjos

1. Second Vatican Council, *Optatum Totius: Decreto sobre a Formação Sacerdotal* (Vatican: Libreria Ediditrice, 1965), n. 16.

2. Marciano Vidal, *Nueva Moral Fundamental: El Hogar Teológico de la Etica* (Bilbao: Desclée de Brouwer, 2000), 258.

3. Charles Taylor, *Sources of the Self: The Making of the Modern Identity* (Cambridge, Mass.: Harvard University Press, 1989), 1.3.

4. CELAM (General Conference of Latin American Bishops), *Conclusões da Conferencia de Medellín—1968* (São Paulo: Paulinas Editorial, 1998).

5. CELAM (General Conference of Latin American Bishops), *Evangelização no Presente e no Futuro da América Latina: Conclusões da Conferência de Puebla* (São Paulo: Paulinas Editorial, 1979).

6. CELAM (General Conference of Latin American Bishops), *Rio, Medellín, Puebla e Santo Domingo* (São Paulo: Paulus, 2004).

7. Julio Lois, *Teología de la Liberación: Opçión por los Pobres* (San José, Costa Rica: DEI, 1988); Jorge Pixley and Clodovis Boff, *Opcão pelos Pobres: Experiência de Deus e Justiça* (Petrópolis, Brazil: Editora Vozes, 1987).

8. José Vico Peinado, *Eticas Teológicas de Ayer y Hoy* (Madrid: San Pablo, 1993).

9. On the Ecclesial base communities (CEBs), see *O Povo Descobre a Sociedade: Capitalismo x Socialismo, Subsidio para Reflexões de CEBs* (São Paulo: Paulinas Editorial, 1984); Sebastián G. Mier, *El Sujeto Social en Moral Fundamental: Una Verificación: Las CEBs en México* (Mexico: Universidad Pontificia de México, 1996); Faustino L. C. Teixeira, Rogério Valle, Clodovis Boff, and Regina Novaes, *CEBs, Cidadania e Modernidade: Uma Análise Crítica* (São Paulo: Paulinas Editorial, 1993); Faustino L. C. Teixeira, *Os Encontros Intereclesiais de CEBs no Brasil* (São Paulo: Paulinas Editorial, 1996); CEBs and 10° Encontro Intereclesial, *CEBs, Cidadania e Modernidade: Uma Análise Crítica* (Paulo Afonso, Brazil: Fonte Nova, 1999); Conferência Nacional dos Bispos do Brasil, *CEBs: Espiritualidade Libertadora: Secretariado Nacional do 11 Intereclesial das CEBs. Seguir Jesus no Compromisso com os Excluídos, texto base* (Belo Horizonte, Brazil: O Lutador, 2004).

10. Bernardino Leers, *Jeito Brasileiro e Norma Absoluta* (Petropolis: Vozes, 1982); Livia Barbosa, *O Jeitinho Brasileiro: A Arte de Ser Mais Igual do que os Outros* (São Paulo: Editora Campus, 2006).

11. David Harvey, *The Condition of Postmodernity: An Inquiry into the Origin of Cultural Change* (Oxford/Malden, Mass.: Blackwell Publishers, 2000).

12. Manfredo Araujo de Oliveira, *Desafios Eticos da Globalização* (São Paulo: Paulinas Editorial, 2001), 91–99.

13. Manfredo Araujo de Oliveira, *Desafios*, 113–15; 118.

14. Luiz Roberto Benedetti, "A Experiência no Lugar da Crença," in *Experiência Religiosa, Risco ou Aventura?*, ed. Márcio Fabri dos Anjos (São Paulo: Paulinas Editorial, 1998).

15. José Comblin, *Cristãos rumo ao Século XXI: Nova Caminhada de Libertação* (São Paulo: Paulus, 1996), 154.

16. José Comblin, *O Povo de Deus* (São Paulo: Paulus, 2002), 93–95.

17. José Comblin, *O Povo de Deus*, 99–202.

18. Hans Hinkelammert, *El Grito del Sujeto* (San José, Costa Rica: DEI, 1998).

19. Manfredo Araújo de Oliveira, *Desafíos*, 111; see also Enrique Dussel, *Ética de la liberación en la edad de la globalización y de la exclusión* (Madrid: Editorial Trotta, 1998), 167–233; Jung Mo Sung, "The Human Being as Subject: Defending the Victims," in *Latin American Liberation Theology: The Next Generation*, ed. Ivan Petrella (Maryknoll, N.Y.: Orbis Books, 2005), 1–19.

20. Axel Kahn and Dominique Lecourt, *Bioéthique et Liberté* (Paris: Presses Universitaires de France, 2004), 38.

21. Paulo Freire, *Educação como Prática da Liberdade* (Rio de Janeiro: Paz e Terra, 1980); idem, *Conscientização: Teoria e Prática da Libertação* (São Paulo: Moraes Ed., 1980); idem, *Pedagogia do Oprimido* (Rio de Janeiro: Paz e Terra, 1978); idem, *Pedagogía de la Esperanza* (Mexico: Siglo XXI, 1993).

22. Dietmar Mieth, *Diktatur der Gene: Biotechnik zwischen Machbarkeit und Menschenwürde* (Freiburg im Breisgau, 2003).

23. Axel Kahn and Dominique Lecourt, *Bioéthique*, 40.

24. Manfredo Araujo de Oliveira, *Desafíos*, 120.

25. Márcio Fabri dos Anjos, "Power and Vulnerability: A Contribution of Developing Countries to the Ethical Debate on Genetics," in *Genetics, Theology and Ethics: An Interdisciplinary Conversation*, ed. Lisa S. Cahill (New York: Crossroad, 2005), 144–48; Márcio Fabri dos Anjos, "Rumos da Liberdade em Bioética: Uma Leitura Teológica," in *Bioética e Longevidade Humana*, ed. Leo Pessini and Christian P. Barchifontaine (São Paulo: Loyola, 2006), 129–40.

26. Jon Sobrino, *El Principio-Misericordia: Bajar de la Cruz a los Pueblos Crucificados* (Santander: Sal Térrea, 1992).

27. Gustavo Gutiérrez, *A Força Histórica dos Pobres* (Petrópolis/ Rio de Janeiro: Vozes, 1981).

28. José Comblin, *O Povo de Deus*, 275–77.

29. Gustavo Gutiérrez, *Onde dormirão os pobres?* (São Paulo: Paulus, 1998).

30. Enrique Dussel, *Etica de Liberación en la Edad de la Globalización y de la Exclusión* (Madrid: Editorial Trotta, 1998), 452.

31. J. B. Metz, "Proposta de Programa Universal do Cristianismo na Idade da Globalizacão," in *Prospectivas Teológicas para o Século XXI*, ed. Rosino Gibellini (Aparecida: Santuário, 2005), 355.

Enrico Chiavacci

1. St. Thomas Aquinas, *Summa Theologica*, II-II, q.29, a.3, ad.2; *ibid.*, q.58, a.5, ad.3.

2. Charter, Preamble: "faith in fundamental human rights, in the dignity and worth of the human person, in the equal rights of men and women. . . . " Universal Declaration of Human Rights, Preamble: "Recognition of the inherent dignity of all members of the human family." See Ian Brownlie, *Basic Documents in International Law* (Oxford: Clarendon Press, 2002).

3. Bénézet Bujo, *Wider den Universalanspruch westlicher Moral: Grundlage afrikanischer Ethik* (Quaestiones disputatae 182) (Basel: Herder, 2000). English translation by Brian McNeil: *Foundations of an African Ethic: Beyond the Claims of Western Morality* (New York: Crossroad, 2001). For Latin American culture, see Enrique

Dussel, *Ética de la liberación en la edad de la globalización y de la exclusión* (Madrid: Trotta, 1998).

4. *Gaudium et Spes*, no. 37, 55.

5. For extensive quotations and comments, see Luciano Orabona, *Cristianesimo e proprietà* (Rome: Studium, 1964); Maria Grazia Mara, *Ricchezza e povertà nel cristianesimo primitivo* (Rome: Città Nuova, 1980).

6. Aquinas, *Summa Theologica*, II-II, q.66.

7. Ferdinand Braudel, *Civilisation matérielle, économie et capitalisme (XV-XVIIIe siècle)* (Paris: Librairie Arnaud Colin, 1979).

8. John Locke, *The Second Treatise of Government* (Oxford: Blackwell, 1956).

9. This doctrine was still proposed by Leo XIII in the encyclical *Rerum Novarum*.

10. See *Merriam-Webster Collegiate Dictionary*, 10th ed., (1993). This is President G. W. Bush's theme of the "compassionate state." In Europe, however, we have the great tradition of the "social state," linked to two centuries of the elaboration of socialist, communist, Catholic, and liberal doctrine. The 1948 constitution of the Italian Republic is perhaps the best work of juridical synthesis of the various schools of thought. Johann B. Metz, "Vorschlag für ein Weltprogramm des Christentums im Zeitalter der Globalisierung," in Gunther Virt, ed., *Der Globalisierungsprozess: Facetten einer Dynamik aus ethischer und theologischer Perspektive* (Basel: Herder Verlag, 2002), 130–41, interprets "compassion" differently: it means feeling the sufferings of all the poor as one's own sufferings (*com-passio*). He proposes "compassion as the world program of Christianity" (135). In a private conversation, he told me, "Only the poor are our masters. They are the only persons before whom we should bow down, the only ones we should serve."

11. For an excellent discussion of the problem, see William K. Frankena, *Ethics*, 2nd ed. (London: Prentice-Hall International, 1973).

12. A. Sen, *Development as Freedom* (New York: A. Knopf, 1999). On the same lines, see the reports of the United Nations Development Program, with the contribution of Sen, especially 1997 and 2000.

13. *Gaudium et Spes*, no. 16, 92.

14. *Optatam Totius*, no. 16.

15. T. Hoppe, "Gibt es ein kulturübergreifendes Ethos?" in G. Virt, ed., *Globalisierungsprozess*, 179–86, with the response by H. Haker, 187–91; see also G. Luf, "Globalisierung und Menschenrechte," in G. Virt, ed., *Globalisierungsprozess*, 102–13.

16. E. Chiavacci, *Morale Generale*, rev. ed. (Assisi: Citadella Editrice, forthcoming).

17. Original title: "Globalizzazione e giustizia."

Vimal Tirimanna, C.Ss.R

1. See Sergio Bernal Restrepo, "An Ethical Assessment of Globalization," in *Globalization: Ethical and Institutional Concerns*, Proceedings: Seventh Pontifical Plenary Session, April 25–28, 2001, Acta 7 (Vatican City: Pontifical Academy of Social Sciences, 2001), 75.

2. Tissa Balasuriya, "Challenge of Globalization to the Universal Church," *Logos* 41, nos. 2–3 (2003): 19.

3. The United Nations' *Human Development Report* 1999, 34. Hereafter referred to as HDR, followed by the page number.

4. Joseph Stiglitz, *Globalization and Its Discontents* (New Delhi: Penguin Books, 2002), x.

5. See Paul Valley, "Will the Rich Nations Deliver?" *Tablet*, 24 (September 2005): 14–15.

6. HDR 2005, 10.

7. HDR 2000, 6.

8. HDR 2005, 3–4.

9. June O'Connor, "Making a Case for the Common Good in a Global Economy: United Nations *Human Development Reports* [1990–2001]," *Journal of Religious Ethics* 30, no.1 (Spring 2002): 158.

10. O'Connor, "Making a Case," 159.

11. See Pope Paul VI, *Populorum Progressio*.

12. See Amartya Sen, "Development Thinking at the Beginning of the 21st Century," in *Economic and Social Development into the XXI Century*, ed. Louis Emmerji (Washington D.C.: Inter-American Development Bank, 1997).

13. See HDR 2003.

14. See Vimal Tirimanna, "Moral Theological Implications of Globalization from a Third World Perspective," *Vidyajyoti Journal of Theological Reflection* 65, no. 4 (April 2001): 296–98.

15. June O'Connor, "Making a Case," 160.

16. June O'Connor, "Making a Case," 159–60.

17. See John Rawls, *A Theory of Justice* (Cambridge, Mass.: Harvard University Press, 1971).

18. Thomas W. Ogletree, "Corporation Capitalism and the Common Good: A Framework for Addressing the Challenges of Global Economy," *Journal of Religious Ethics* 30, no. 1 (Spring 2002): 79–106.

19. David A. Crocker, "Globalization and Human Development: Ethical Approaches," in *Globalization: Ethical and Institutional Concerns*, 49.

20. Stiglitz, *Globalization and Its Discontents*, xv.

21. Balasuriya, "Challenge of Globalization to the Universal Church," 23–24.

22. S. Arokiasamy, "Relationality and Inculturation in Morals," in *Encounters with the Word: Essays to Honour Aloysius Pieris S.J.*, ed. Robert Crusz et al. (Colombo: Ecumenical Institute for Study and Dialogue, 2004), 462.

23. Archbishop Justin Rigali, "What Church Social Teaching Is: An Overview," *Origins* 26, no. 14 (September 19, 1996): 216.

24. Stiglitz, *Globalization and Its Discontents*, xv.

25. HDR 2005, 11.

26. Stephen Rehrauer, "Globalazión como Corresponsabilidad o como Irresponsibilidad Social," *Universitas Alphonsiana*, no. 9 (July 2006): 33.

27. Ian Linden, "Can We have Faith in the Global Economy?" *Doctrine and Life* 49, no. 5 (1999): 292–93.

28. Stiglitz, *Globalization and Its Discontents*, ix–x.

29. Ibid., 22.

John Mary Waliggo

1. Cecil McGarry, 'The Impact of Globalization on African Culture and Society: Dangers and Opportunities," in *The New Strategies for a New Evangelization in Africa*, ed. Patrick Ryan (Nairobi: Paulines Publication Africa, 2002), 13–22.

2. John M. Waliggo, "The Role of the Christian Churches in the Democratization of Africa," in *Missionary Ministry and Missiology in Africa Today*, Tangaza Occasional Papers, no. 1 (Nairobi: Paulines Publications Africa, 1994), 61.

3. Bénézet Bujo, *African Christian Morality* (Nairobi: Paulines Publications Africa, 1990); Michael Kirwen, ed., *African Cultural Knowledge: Themes and Embedded Beliefs* (Nairobi: MIAS Books, 2005).

4. D. Nkurunziza and L. Mugunya, eds., *Developing a Culture of Peace and Human Rights in Africa*: African Peace Series, vol. 1–2 (Kampala: Konrad Adenauer Stiftung, 2004); Desmond Tutu, *No Future without Forgiveness* (Johannesburg: Rider Publishers, 1999).

5. On August, 10, 2006, theologian Peter Kanyandago of Uganda Martyrs University led a peaceful demonstration against the use of DDT and made a prophetic presentation to the environmental activists in Kampala.

6. Peter Kanyandago, "Is God African? Theological Reflections on the AIDS Scourge," in *Challenges and Prospects of the Church in Africa*, ed. N. W. Ndung'u and P. N. Mwaura (Nairobi: Paulines Publications Africa, 2005), 145–59.

7. G. S. N. Wanene, "Response: The Good Samaritan and HIV/AIDS Victims in Africa," in *Challenges to Theology in Africa Today*, ed. Patrick Ryan (Nairobi: CUEA Publications, 2002), 23–26.

8. Larry Elliot and Victoria Brittain, "The Rich and the Poor are Growing Further Apart," *Guardian Weekly* 20 (September 1998): 19; J. M. Waliggo, "The Historical Roots of Unethical Economic Practices in Africa," in *Fraud and the African Renaissance*, ed. G. J. Rossouw and D. Carabine (Nkozi University Press, 1999).

9. Emmanuel Katongole, "Globalization and Economic Fundamentalism in Africa: On Politics That Intensify the Cries of the Poor," in *The Cries of the Poor: Questions and Responses for African Christianity*, ed. Peter Kanyandago (Kisubi: Marianum Press, 2002), 57–78; Aquiline Tarimo, *Applied Ethics and Africa's Social Reconstruction*, (Nairobi: Acton Publishers, 2005).

10. David Kyeyune, *Liturgical/Animation Programme for the 15th AMECEA Plenary, 2005* (Uganda Catholic Secretariat, 2004). One of the central themes was promotion of natural African foods as opposed to the GMFs.

11. J. M. Waliggo, "Corruption and Bribery: An African Problem?" in *Business Ethics in the African Context Today*, ed. Michael Lejeune and Phillip Roseman (Nkozi: Uganda Martyrs' University Press, 1996), 115–39.

12. Laurenti Magesa and Zablon Nthamburi, eds., *Democracy and Reconciliation: A Challenge for African Christianity* (Nairobi: ESEAT, Acton Publishers, 1999).

13. National Council for Higher Education (Uganda), "Statistical Data on Brain-Drainage of Professionals from Africa, Kampala," 2004.

14. N.W. Ndung'u, "Environmental Management: Constraints and Prospects in Africa in the 21st Century," in *Challenges and Prospects of the Church in Africa*, 61–62; J. M. Waliggo "Analysis of the Church in Africa," in *Cast Away Fear: A Contribution to the African Synod* (Nairobi: New People Media Centre, 1994), 2–8.

15. We shall continue to be haunted by the Parable of the Rich Man and Lazarus (Luke 16:19–31).

16. J. M. Waliggo, "Inculturation in the Age of Globalization," in *Challenges to Theology in Africa Today*, 95–113.

17. Cecil McGarry, "The Impact of Globalization," 13–22.

18. J. M. Waliggo, "The External Debt in the Continual Marginalization of Africa: What Action by Christian Theologians," in *Marginalized Africa: An International Perspective,* ed. Peter Kanyandago (Nairobi: Paulines Publications Africa, 2002), 52–61.

19. Equality of rights without any discrimination and equality before the law are among the two principal pillars of all UN human rights instruments since the Universal Declaration on Human Rights of 1948.

20. The journal *AFER (African Ecclesial Review)*, the monograph series *Spearhead* (Eldoret, Kenya: Gaba Publications), the journal *The African Christian Studies* (Nairobi: CUEA), and the current twelve volumes by the Ecumenical Symposium of Eastern African Theologians (ESEAT), since 1988 published by Acton and lately by Paulines Publications in Nairobi and Uganda Martyrs' University Press Publications, form the main channels on the discussion on the missing link.

Authors and Participants

Antonio Papisca
Director, Interdepartmental Center on Human Rights and the Rights of Peoples and UNESCO Professor of Human Rights, University of Padua.
Latest Publication: Papisca, Antonio. *Le relazioni internazionali nell'era dell'interdipendenza e dei diritti umani.* 3rd ed. Padua: CEDAM, 2004.

Adela Cortina
Chair of Ethics and Political Philosophy, University of Valencia and Director of Fundación ETNOR, Valencia.
Latest Publication: Cortina, Adela. *Covenant and Contract: Politics, Ethics and Religion.* Leuven: Peeters, 2003.

Henk ten Have
Director of the Division of Ethics of Science and Technology, UNESCO, Paris, France.
Latest Publication: Ten Have, Henk, ed. *Environmental Ethics and International Policy.* Paris: UNESCO Publishing, 2006.

Mawuto R. Afan, O.P.
Professeur d'Ethique et de Théologie morale, Université Catholique de l'Afrique de l'Ouest (UCAO/UUA).
Latest Publication: Afan, Mawuto R. *La participation démocratique en Afrique: Ethique politique et engagement chrétien.* Paris/Fribourg: Cerf/Editions Universitaires, 2001.

Laurenti Magesa
Chaplain, Baraki Postulancy, Musoma, Tanzania and visiting lecturer at the Maryknoll Institute of African Studies in Nairobi, Kenya.
Latest Publication: Magesa, Laurenti. *Anatomy of Inculturation: Transforming the Church in Africa.* Maryknoll, N.Y.: Orbis Books, 2004.

Sébastien Muyengo Mulombe
Recteur du Grand Séminaire Jean XXIII et Professeur de Morale Fondamentale et de la Bioéthique aux Facultés Catholiques de Kinshasa-RD, Congo.

Latest Publication: Mulombe, Sébastien Muyengo. *Ethique et Génie Génétique*. Kinshasa: Presses Universitaires du Sud, 2004.

Thomas Hong-Soon Han
Professor, Hankuk University of Foreign Studies.
Latest Publication: Hong-Soon Han, Thomas. "The Promotion of Human Rights in Korea." In *Human Rights in the Pacific Rim*. Edited by Edmund Ryden, S.J., and Barbara K. Bundy. Taipei: Fu Jen Catholic University Press, 2006.

Agnes M. Brazal
Associate Professor, Maryhill School of Theology, Manila, Philippines.
Latest Publication: Brazal, Agnes M., and Andrea Lizares Si, eds. *Body and Sexuality: Theological-Pastoral Perspectives of Women in Asia*. Quezon City, Philippines: Ateneo de Manila University Press, 2007.

Clement Campos, C.Ss.R.
Professor of Moral Theology and Rector, St. Alphonsus College, Bangalore, India.
Latest Publication: Campos, Clement, C.Ss.R. "The Challenge of Euthanasia: To Kill or to Care." In *Health in Abundance (A Journal of the Commission for Healthcare of the Catholic Bishops' Conference of India)* 4 no. 3 (July–September 2006).

Marciano Vidal, C.Ss.R.
Profesor Ordinario del Instituto Superior de Ciencias Morales (Madrid), agregado a la Universidad Pontificia Comillas.
Latest Publication: Vidal, Marciano, C.Ss.R. *Orientaciones para tiempos inciertos: Entre la Escila del relativismo y la Caribdis del fundamentalismo*. Bilbao: Editorial Desclée, 2007.

Marianne Heimbach-Steins
Professor of Christian Social Ethics, Faculty of Catholic Theology, University of Bamberg, Germany.
Latest Publication: Heimbach-Steins, Marianne. *Christliche Sozialethik: Ein Lehrbuch*. 2 vols. Regensburg, Germany: Pustet-Verlag, 2005.

Piotr Mazurkiewicz
Professor, Cardinal Stefan Wyszyński University in Warsaw, Poland; Director of the Institute of Political Science, Chair of Social and Political Ethic Violence in politics, Ossolineum, Warszawa-Wrocław 2006; Profesor Ordinario del Instituto Superior de Ciencias Morales, Madrid, agregado a la Universidad Pontificia Comillas.

Latest Publication: Mazurkiewicz, Piotr. *Orientaciones para tiempos inciertos: Entre la Escila del relativismo y la Caribdis del fundamentalismo.* Bilbao, Spain: Editorial Desclée, 2007.

Ronaldo Zacharias, S.D.B.
Director, Pio XI School of Theology, São Paulo, Brazil; Coordinator, Post Graduate Course in Sexual Education and Committee of Ethical Research, Salesian University Center, São Paulo, Brazil; Secretary, Brazilian Society of Moral Theology.
Latest Publication: Zacharias, Ronaldo. "Abuso sexual: aspectos ético-morais." *Revista de Catequese* 29, no. 113 (2006): 6–14.

Sebastian Mier, S.J.
Professor of Moral Theology, Universidad Iberoamericana and Universidad Pontificia de Mexico.
Latest Publication: Mier, Sebastian, S.J. *El Sujeto Social en Moral Fundamental: Una verificación las CEBs en México.* 2nd ed. Mexico: Universidad Pontificia de México, 2002.

Tony Mifsud, S.J.
Researcher, Center for Ethics, Alberto Hurtado University, Santiago, Chile, and Professor of Moral Theology, Pontifical Catholic University of Chile.
Latest publication: Mifsud, Tony. *Ethos cotidiano: un proceso de discernimiento.* Santiago: Revista Mensaje, 2006.

David Hollenbach, S.J.
Director, Center for Human Rights and International Justice and Margaret O'Brien Flatley Professor of Theology, Boston College.
Latest Publication: Hollenbach, David, S.J. *The Global Face of Public Faith: Politics, Human Rights, and Christian Ethics.* Washington, D.C.: Georgetown University Press, 2003.

Jean Porter
John A. O'Brien Professor of Theological Ethics, University of Notre Dame.
Latest Publication: Porter, Jean. *Nature as Reason: A Thomistic Theory of the Natural Law.* Grand Rapids, Mich.: Eerdmans, 2005.

Kenneth R. Melchin
Vice-Dean, Faculty of Theology, Saint Paul University, Ottawa, Canada.
Latest Publication: Melchin, Kenneth R. *Living with Other People: An Introduction to Christian Ethics Based on Bernard Lonergan.* Ottawa/Collegeville, Minn.: Novalis/Liturgical Press, 1998.

Robert Gascoigne
Professor, School of Theology, Australian Catholic University.
Latest Publication: Gascoigne, Robert. *Freedom and Purpose: An Introduction to Christian Ethics.* Mahwah, N.J.: Paulist Press, 2004.

Maureen Junker-Kenny
Associate Professor of Theology, University of Dublin, Trinity College, School of Religions and Theology.
Latest Publication: Junker-Kenny, Maureen, and Peter Kenny, eds. *Memory, Narrativity, Self, and the Challenge to Think God: The Reception within Theology of the Recent Work of Paul Ricoeur.* Münster: LIT-Verlag, 2004.

Dionisio Marcelo Miranda, S.V.D.
Provincialate Office Consultant, Society of the Divine Word.
Latest Publication: Miranda, Dionisio Marcelo, s.v.d. *Kaloob ni Kristo: A Filipino Christian Account of Conscience.* Manila, Philippines: Logos Publications, 2003.

Paul Valadier, S.J.
Professeur émérite et directeur des Archives de Philosophie, Facultés jésuites de Paris (Centre Sèvres).
Latest Publication: Valadier, Paul, S.J. *La condition chrétienne: Du monde sans en être.* Paris: Editions du Seuil, 2003.

Nathanaël Yaovi Soédé
Professeur à l'Université Catholique de l'Afrique de l'Ouest/Unité Universitaire d'Abidjan.
Latest Publication: Soédé, Nathanaël. *Sens et enjeux de l'éthique. Inculturation de l'éthique chrétienne.* Abidjan: ICAO, 2005

Giuseppe Angelini
Professore Ordinario di Teologia Morale, Facoltà Teologica dell'Italia Settentrionale, Milan, Italy.
Latest Publication: Angelini, Giuseppe. *Eros e agape: Oltre l'alternativa.* Milan, Italy: Editrice Glossa, 2006.

Eberhard Schockenhoff
Lehrstuhl für Moraltheologie, Albert-Ludwigs-Universität, Freiburg im Bresgau.
Latest Publication: Schockenhoff, Eberhard. *Grundlegung der Ethik: Ein theologischer Entwurf.* Freiburg im Bresgau, forthcoming.

Lisa Sowle Cahill
Monan Professor of Theology, Boston College.
Latest Publication: Cahill, Lisa Sowle. *Theological Bioethics: Participation, Justice and Change.* Washington, D.C.: Georgetown University Press, 2005.

Márcio Fabri dos Anjos
Professor of Centro Universitário Sao Camilo (Sao Paulo, Brazil) and of Pontificia Faculdade de Teologia N.S. Assunçao (S.Paulo, Brazil).
Lastest Publication: Anjos, M. F., ed. *Vida Religiosa: memória, poder e utopia.* Aparecida: Editora Santuário, 2007.

Enrico Chiavacci
Professor Emeritus, Moral Theology, Theological Faculty of Central Italy (Italia Centrale), Florence.
Latest Publication: Chiavacci, Enrico. *Morale Generale.* Assisi: Cittadella Editrice, 2007.

Vimal Tirimanna, C.Ss.R.
Professor, Systematic Moral Theology, Alphonsianum, Rome; Lecturer, National Seminary, Kandy, Sri Lanka; Executive Secretary, Office of Theological Concerns (OTC), Federation of the Asian Bishops' Conferences (FABC).
Latest Publication: Tirimanna, Vimal, C.Ss.R. *Catholic Teaching on Violence, War and Peace in Our Contemporary World: A Collection of Essays.* Bangalore, India: Asian Trading Corporation, 2006.

John Mary Waliggo
Commissioner, Uganda Human Rights Commission and Uganda Martyrs University.
Latest Publication: Waliggo, John Mary. *Struggle for Equality: Women and Empowerment in Uganda.* Eldoret, Kenya: AMECEA Gaba Spearhead Publicatons, 2002.

Acknowledgments

There are so many people to thank for these papers and the conference, and the danger of naming some leads, of course, to the possibility of overlooking others. But let me try.

First and foremost, the planning committee was the heart and soul of the conference: Soosai Arokiasamy, Bénézet Bujo, Margaret Farley, Linda Hogan, José Roque Junges, José Rojas, and Paul Schotsman. Renzo Pegoraro as the site coordinator was an inspiration to everyone and a dream-maker in the actual execution of the conference. Hans Wennink and Peter Merkx provided wisdom and support every step of the way, and still do. Toni Ross and Lúcás Chan Yiu Sing were my wonderful assistants and constant companions both here at Boston College and there in Padua.

Support from the Italian theological ethicists in *ATISM* (*Associazione Teologica Italiana per lo Studio della Morale*) was before, during, and after the conference expressed in so many ways. Several others provided invaluable advice in terms of fund-raising, recruiting participants, or assisting on the program, in particular, Aloys Buch, Karl Golser, Tony Mifsud, Marie-Jo Thiel, Antonio Autiero, Kevin O'Neil, Kerry Robinson, Barbara Andolsen, and Frank Bultler.

Our benefactors were many. Their generosity made this an international event. Among the foundations: Stichting Porticus, Missio Aachen, Renovabis Adveniat, Mary Ann Donnelly Foundation, McCarthy Foundation, Weiss Family Foundation, and the Raskob Foundation for Catholic Activities, Inc. Religious orders also supported us: New York Province Franciscans, The Redemptorists of the Baltimore Province, The Redemptorists of Canada, The Redemptorists of Florida, California Province of the Society of Jesus, Chicago Province of the Society of Jesus, Detroit Province of the Society of Jesus, Great Britain Province of Society of Jesus, Irish Province of the Society of Jesus, Maryland Province of the Society of Jesus, New England Province of the Society of Jesus, New Orleans Province of the Society of Jesus, New York Province of the Society of Jesus, Oregon Province of the Society of Jesus, and Wisconsin Province of the Society of Jesus. One private individual was very generous to us, Enrico Dolazza. My own university, Boston College, was extraordinarily supportive, with gifts from John Paris, S.J., the Office of Academic Affairs (and here especially Pat De Leeuw), the

Jesuit Community, Lisa Sowle Cahill, David Hollenbach, S.J., and T. Frank Kennedy, S.J., and the Jesuit Institute. Finally, Renzo's organization, Fondazione Lanza, provided a variety of assistance.

From the city of Padua, first we thank Archbishop Antonio Mattiazzo, who wrote to foundations for us, welcomed us to the conference, presided over the Eucharist for us, and led us in prayer at our closing banquet. He remains, in many ways, our organization's archbishop. From the University Rector Professor Vincenzo Milanesi and Padua's Mayor Flavio Zanonato, we received extraordinary support, particularly on opening night where in the Great Hall of the University of Padua and afterwards on the Loggia of Padua's City Hall all four hundred conference participants were received and feted. We also thank the major seminary that hosted our closing banquet as well as a variety of other institutions in Padua that were especially hospitable: the abbey of Santa Giustina, the diocese of Padua, Veneto Banca, Casa dell Pellegrino and the Hotel Donatello. At the Antonianum, besides the Jesuit community and its rector, Roberto Boroni, we want to thank Mario Picech, S.J., the director of the youth center for his sensitive work and oversight that made the conference site itself so memorable. Our last word of thanks to Paduans extends to Paolo Pegoraro and all those at Zip Viaggi, particularly Alessandra and Laura, but most especially Elena, who made sure our participants got to Padua.

Finally as these papers go to press, I want to thank our presenters. These were originally fifteen-minute presentations during the plenaries; and in light of their actual presentations and subsequent discussions, the presenters developed and expanded their positions. Each of these thirty scholars submitted essays that make this volume as successful as the conference. All along the way, Linda Hogan, who is editing the thirty applied ethics papers to be published by Orbis Press later this year, has been an invaluable consultant. Brian McNeil translated from the French the essays by Mawuto R. Afan, Sébastien Muyengo Mulombe, Paul Valadier, and Nathanaël Yaovi Soédé; from Italian those by Antonio Papisca, Giuseppe Angelini, and Enrico Chiavacci; and from the German, Eberhard Schockenhoff. Margaret Wilde translated from the Spanish the essays by Adela Cortina, Marciano Vidal, Sebastian Mier, Tony Mifsud, and Márcio Fabri dos Anjos. Christian Cintron provided fine research assistance, and Kevin Vander Schel made the editing of this volume a remarkably less onerous affair. Finally, to my friend and editor at Continuum International, Frank Oveis, thank you.

Index

wealth, American: and Christian iden-
tity, 144, 145, 146
Weber, Max, 9, 23
Weigel, George, 145
Weiler, Joseph, 113
Welch, Sharon, 226
Wennink, Hans, 1
West, influence of, 237
Wilfred, Felix, 87
wisdom, African, 46, 47, 48
women
in Africa, 52
and Jesus, 226
in Mexican society, 129

and moral theology, 222
violence against, 75, 76
world, dangers facing, 11
World Commission on the Ethics of
Scientific Knowledge and Technology, 29
world poverty, 152-57
World Social Forum, 125

Yunus, Muhammad, 20, 21

Zacharias, Ronaldo, 114, 116
Zapatista Army of National Liberation
(Mexico), 125